EXPLORATIONS IN
CRIMINAL PSYCHOPATHOLOGY

ABOUT THE EDITOR

Louis B. Schlesinger, Ph.D. is Professor of Forensic Psychology at John Jay College of Criminal Justice, City University of New York, and a Diplomate in Forensic Psychology of the American Board of Professional Psychology. He is also a Distinguished Practitioner in the National Academies of Practice. Dr. Schlesinger served as President of the New Jersey Psychological Association in 1989 and as a Member of the Council of Representatives of the American Psychological Association from 1991 to 1994. He was the 1990 recipient of the New Jersey Psychological Association's "Psychologist of the Year" Award, as well as a recipient of the American Psychological Association's Karl F. Heiser Presidential Award (1993). Dr. Schlesinger was appointed by the Governor of New Jersey and the Commissioner of Corrections to be a member (and later chair) of the Special Classification Review Board at the Adult Diagnostic and Treatment Center (1980–1987), the State's forensic facility; he was also appointed (2001) by the President of the New Jersey State Senate and Acting Governor to serve as a member of a Senate Task Force that re-wrote Megan's Law. Dr. Schlesinger is co-principal investigator of a joint research project between John Jay College and the FBI Behavioral Science Unit studying various types of violent crimes including sexual and serial murder, rape, bias homicide, suicide-by-cop, and other extraordinary criminal behaviors. He has testified in numerous forensic cases and has published many articles, chapters, and nine other books on the topics of homicide, sexual homicide, and criminal psychopathology.

Second Edition

EXPLORATIONS IN CRIMINAL PSYCHOPATHOLOGY

Clinical Syndromes With Forensic Implications

Edited by

LOUIS B. SCHLESINGER, Ph.D.

CHARLES C THOMAS • PUBLISHER, LTD.
Springfield • Illinois • U.S.A.

Published and Distributed Throughout the World by

CHARLES C THOMAS • PUBLISHER, LTD.
2600 South First Street
Springfield, Illinois 62704

ISBN 13 978-0-398-07687-0 (hard)   ISBN 10 0-398-07687-1 (hard)
ISBN 13 978-0-398-07688-7 (paper) ISBN 10 0-398-07688-X (paper)

Library of Congress Catalog Card Number: 2006045507

Printed in the United States of America
SM-R-3

Library of Congress Cataloging-in-Publication Data

Explorations in criminal psychopathology : clinical syndromes with forensic
 implications / edited by Louis B. Schlesinger. -- 2nd ed.
     p. cm.
  Includes bibliographical references and indexes.
  ISBN 0-398-07687-1 (hc) -- ISBN 0-398-07688-X (pbk.)
  1. Criminal psychology. 2. Psychology, Pathological. 3. Forensic
psychology. I. Schlesinger, Louis B.

HV6080.E885 2006
364.3--dc22
                                                                    2006045507

This book is dedicated to my son Gene.

CONTRIBUTORS

JAMES A. COCORES, M.D.
Independent Practice
Boca Raton, Florida

STEVEN HERRON, M.D.
Assistant Professor of Clinical Psychiatry
University of Arizona

SHEILAGH HODGINS, Ph.D.
Institute of Psychiatry
Kings College, University of London

GREGORY B. LEONG, M.D.
Clinical Professor of Psychiatry, School of Medicine
University of Washington, Seattle

HENRY R. LESIEUR, Ph.D.
Rhode Island Hospital

DANIEL A. MARTELL, Ph.D.
Neuropsychiatric Institute
University of California at Los Angeles School of Medicine

J. REID MELOY, Ph.D.
Department of Psychiatry
University of California, San Diego

V. BLAIR MESA
John Jay College of Criminal Justice
City University of New York

ROBERT D. MILLER, M.D., Ph.D.
Professor of Psychiatry
Colorado Health Sciences Center

vii

BARRY MORENZ, M.D.
Associate Professor of Clinical Psychiatry
University of Arizona

NATHANIEL J. PALLONE, Ph.D.
University Distinguished Professor of Psychology & Criminal Justice
Rutgers University

ROBERT J. PANDINA, Ph.D.
Professor of Psychology
Center for Alcohol Studies
Rutgers University

RICHARD ROGERS, Ph.D.
Professor of Psychology
University of North Texas

RICHARD J. ROSENTHAL, M.D.
University of California, Los Angeles

DEBORAH ROSS, Ph.D.
Riverview Hospital
British Columbia, Canada

KAREN L. SALEKIN, Ph.D.
Assistant Professor of Psychology
University of Alabama

GEORGE SERBAN, M.D.
Department of Psychiatry
New York University Medical Center

J. ARTURO SILVA, M.D.
Independent Practice of Forensic Psychiatry
San Jose, California

LANDY F. SPARR, M.D.
Associate Professor of Psychiatry &
Director, Forensic Psychiatry Training Program
School of Medicine
Oregon Health & Science University

JARI TIIHONEN, Ph.D.
Kuoplio University, Finland

ROBERT WEINSTOCK, M.D.
Clinical Professor of Psychiatry, School of Medicine
University of California, Los Angeles

W. A. WESTON, M.B.
University of Calgary
Calgary General Hospital

FOREWORD

For over two decades, I have examined cases involving some of the cruelest and most inhumane actions perpetrated upon human beings. These cases have included adolescents as actors, as well as victims; women who kill, as well as women killed in apparently senseless ways; individuals diagnosed as suffering from mental illness, as well as those with no history of mental illness; law enforcement officers as victims and officers using their positions to target objects of their pathology. In each of these cases, I was presented with the same question: "Why did they do it?"

Many cases of violence fall neatly into various categories such as instrumental and expressive violence. Some cases of violence appear very well organized . . . and others less organized. In examining many of these cases, strange and complex as they are, our explanations are satisfying, even if only intuitively so.

But there are other cases that defy explanation or easy categorization. Cases of anthropophagy and vampirism; situations where mere children brutally murder playmates or other young children; sexual behaviors inextricably bound with aggression. These cases, gratefully infrequent, challenge most categories of criminal behavior and human development. They stretch even our categories of psychopathology and abnormality. Cases which appear very similar on the surface turn out to have quite different explanations as to why the perpetrators behaved as they did.

Psychoanalytic theory, once the staple of psychiatry and psychology, maintains a relatively small following today. Biological explanations, psychological theories, and environment are currently all offered as internal and external causes of crime. But to those of us who maintain a psychoanalytic perspective, biology, the psyche, and one's environment have always played a significant role in explaining why one acts . . . normally or pathologically. As a neurologist, Dr. Freud himself long understood the influence of biology on behavior. He clearly saw the relationship between environment, particularly that of early environment, and one's behavior. And it is precisely how a particular individual processes these experiences within a specific environment that results in action or lack of action. Current understanding and explanation of human behavior cannot ignore any of these factors: biology, psychology, and environment. All three play a vital and interactive role in human behavior.

Dr. Schlesinger's compilation of chapters addresses this complex approach to understanding a very specific and important aspect of human behavior: criminal psychopathology. Updated and expanded articles in this second edition approach these complexities largely from a psychodynamic perspective that also addresses biological, psychological and environmental aspects of behavior. Sections on Disorders of Behavior, Disorders of Thought and Borderline and Psychotic Disorders bring together chapters written by experienced practitioners and scientists that examine the dark and macabre expressions of human conduct in ways that give meaning and understanding to these behaviors.

Although these kinds of criminal activities do not occur with great frequency in our society, when they do, they create loathing and fear. Explanations for these actions that speak to motivation of an individual can assist in the investigation, the interviewing of subjects, and, importantly, in society's sense of well-being by beginning to understand why people behave this way. As with each of us individually, the more a society can understand WHY someone acts, however bizarrely, the easier it becomes to deal with these experiences.

We will never have a full or comprehensive understanding of why some people commit the acts they do. However, with the continued work and assistance of authors such as these, we come closer each day.

ANTHONY J. PINIZZOTTO, Ph.D.
Senior Scientist
Forensic Psychologist
FBI Behavioral Science Unit
Quantico, Virginia

INTRODUCTION

When *Explorations in Criminal Psychopathology: Clinical Syndromes with Forensic Implications* was first published in 1996, the purpose was, in part, to correct an imbalance in the field, specifically with regard to the coverage of the important topic of psychopathology and its relationship to crime. The emphasis of forensic practitioners was–and to a large extent continues to be–on various legal tests and legal standards. And when criminal psychopathology was mentioned, the reference, typically, was to traditional mental disorders and how each of these conditions relates to various legal issues such as criminal responsibility and competency. Although knowledge of legal standards and traditional mental disorders is obviously necessary in conducting forensic assessments and engaging in forensic practice, it is not sufficient. Practitioners also need to have expertise in a wide range of clinical conditions–beyond those covered in the *Diagnostic and Statistical Manual of Mental Disorders (DSM)*–that relate to various forms of criminal conduct.

The *DSM–IV–TR* (2000) does a very good job delineating criteria for various mental disorders common in clinical settings (hospitals, out-patient clinics, private practice), but it does not do a satisfactory job with clinical disorders that have forensic implications. For example, under the general diagnostic category of impulse-control disorders, the *DSM–IV–TR* lists–in addition to intermittent explosive disorder–kleptomania, pyromania, pathological gambling, trichotillomania, and impulse-control disorder, *nos* (not otherwise specified). However, kleptomania is not an impulse-control disorder; rather, it is a result of an internal drive with a compulsion to steal objects not needed for personal use or monetary gain. Pyromania (repetitive fire-setting) is often engaged in for psychosexual gratification and is also a result of an internal drive to act rather than of an external event or circumstance. Pathological gambling is generally thought of as an addiction rather than as an impulse-control disorder; in fact, the treatment of choice for pathological gambling is an addiction model. Trichotillomania (repetitive hair pulling) is considered a symptom of an obsessive-compulsive disorder rather than of an impulse-control disorder. And finally the *DSM–IV–TR* diagnosis of impulse-control disorder, *nos*, with skin picking provided as an example, also seems incorrectly categorized; rather than being an impulse-control disorder, repetitive skin picking is connected to trichotillomania and obsessive-compulsive symptoms. Accordingly, the *DSM–IV–TR's* placement of these disorders under impulse-control disorders is unhelpful, confusing, and incorrect.

Although the field of forensic psychology and psychiatry has come a long way since the 1970s, its lack of emphasis on the connection between criminal behavior and psychopathology is noteworthy. In the second edition of *Explorations in Criminal Psychopathology*, chapters covering a number of psychopathological conditions that have direct forensic implications have been updated. A conscious attempt has been made to exclude psychopathy and antisocial personality disorder because this topic has been covered adequately elsewhere.

The current book is divided into three sections primarily for organizational purposes. Part I includes five different types of psychopathology that lead to distinct overt types of behavior. Part II provides discussions of various disorders of thought resulting in criminal conduct, but not disordered thinking indicative of a formal thought disorder per se. And the last section concerns borderline and psychotic-like conditions as well as malingering and deception, important topics in forensic practice. All the authors, experts in their respective areas, have spent considerable time thinking about, researching, and studying their topics, and their updated chapters present the most current information available.

The need for forensic practitioners to understand psychopathology and the psychodynamics of crime cannot be overemphasized. I hope that this book will continue to inform forensic clinicians concerned not only with the practicalities of forensic work—such as techniques in testifying or recent court rulings regarding various mental health laws—but also with gaining a deeper understanding of the psychopathology and psychodynamics of the criminal defendants upon whom their ultimate opinions are based.

LOUIS B. SCHLESINGER
Maplewood, New Jersey
April 2006

ACKNOWLEDGMENTS

This is the tenth book that I have published, including second editions. The same people who have been helpful previously–colleagues, students, family, and friends–have been helpful once again. So without listing a series of names and running the risk of leaving somebody out, my sincere thanks, appreciation and respect, once again, to you all.

CONTENTS

SECTION III: BORDERLINE AND PSYCHOTIC DISORDERS

EXPLORATIONS IN
CRIMINAL PSYCHOPATHOLOGY

SECTION I
DISORDERS OF BEHAVIOR

INTRODUCTION TO SECTION I

Section One is comprised of five chapters that present different clinical syndromes, with distinct behavioral manifestations, all of which have important forensic implications. In Chapter 1, Louis B. Schlesinger describes the catathymic process, a disorder that has a long history in forensic practice. Catathymic process is an extreme violent reaction triggered when an underlying emotionally charged conflict erupts and overwhelms psychic integration. Both the acute and chronic forms of the syndrome are presented along with specific symptoms and characteristics that differentiate each. Dr. Schlesinger reviews the development and various uses of the term *catathymic* since the beginning of the century and illustrates the various forms of catathymic process with rich clinical material. Issues of differential diagnosis are dealt with in-depth, as well as a discussion of some forensic issues associated with catathymic process and its relationship with extreme interpersonal violence.

In Chapter 2, Richard J. Rosenthal and Henry R. Lesieur explore the problem of pathological gambling and its relationship to criminal behavior. The authors discuss the history of gambling, the nature and course of pathological gambling, the various clinical phases of the disorder, and the relationship between gamblers and various forms of criminal activity. Issues including the investigation of the finances of gamblers, the use of pathological gambling as a defense in criminal cases, prison and pathological gamblers, as well as diagnostic screening instruments and treatment approaches are all discussed in this very important chapter. The authors discuss the need to reach out to problem gamblers and intervene prior to the development of severe difficulties.

Robert Pandina explores the problem of pathological intoxication in Chapter 3. Pathological intoxication, an idiosyncratic reaction to small amounts of alcohol, is often manifested by extreme violent behavior. The disorder has been recognized for almost a hundred years, but recently its existence as a true independent entity has been questioned. The author provides an in-depth review of the literature on pathological intoxication including the major issues that have emerged in the past fifteen years. Dr. Pandina concludes that pathological intoxication, possibly present in some very unusual cases, does not seem to have the general acceptance among most senior scientists at this point in our stage of understanding. Notwithstanding, pathological intoxication has been used as a criminal defense and continues to be used in some forensic cases.

Organic brain dysfunctions and criminality are reviewed and examined by Daniel A. Martell in Chapter 4. The author considers the neurobehavioral components of violent criminality which are important to the forensic practitioner. Dr. Martell reports clinical experience and clinical opinion on one end, and contrasts this with solid empirical evidence, specifically the relationships between brain dysfunction, violence, crime, and the criminal law. The author reviews and discusses the research evidence on brain-behavior relationships in forensic populations, as well as specific neurological problems. Dr. Martell describes a model for clinical forensic evaluation and research regarding the role of brain impairment and violent criminal behavior.

In the last chapter of Section I, Nathaniel J. Pallone discusses sadistic criminal aggression from the perspectives of psychology, criminology, and neuroscience. Dr. Pallone begins with the varying definitions of sadism, changes in the psychiatric perception of sadism, the incidence of sadistic criminal aggression, as well as psychometric markers for this type of behavior and conduct. The relationship between sadism and psychopathy, the etiology of sadism, and theoretical models that help to explain such behavior are all reviewed within the context of relevant research. The author, throughout the chapter, highlights the role of psychological evaluation, criminological findings, and brain-behavior relationships.

Chapter 1

THE CATATHYMIC PROCESS: PSYCHOPATHOLOGY AND PSYCHODYNAMICS OF EXTREME INTERPERSONAL VIOLENCE

LOUIS B. SCHLESINGER

Hans W. Maier, a well-known Swiss psychiatrist who succeeded Eugen Blueler as director of the Zurich Psychiatric Hospital Burghölzli, introduced the concept of catathymia in 1912. The term is derived from the Greek *kata* and *thymos*, best defined as "in accordance with emotions." Maier conceived of catathymia (*Katathyme*) as a psychological process that is activated by a strong and tenacious emotion attached to underlying complexes of ideas. The emotion, when stimulated, overwhelms the individual's psychological stability and disrupts thinking. Paranoid delusions, according to Maier, would be catathymic in origin because they are rooted in an underlying complex, but delusions and hallucinations resulting from intoxication would not be considered catathymic, because they stem from a change in brain functioning rather than from psychogenesis.

Since Maier introduced catathymia, this broadly defined concept has been adapted by many different writers to explain various forms of violence. For example, Wertham (1937) used it to explain certain otherwise inexplicable acts of violence perpetrated by an individual who has had a long-term relationship with the victim. Gayral, Millet, Moron, and Turnin (1956) spoke of *crises catathymiques*–nonepileptic emotional paroxysms with secondary neurovegetative reactions lasting from minutes to days and then suddenly stopping. Revitch (1964), in his study of a female prison population, borrowed this term to describe a similar condition: nonepileptic, seemingly unprovoked violent explosions, with partial amnesia. Revitch referred to such explosions as "catathymic attacks."

Cases described by Satten, Menninger, and Mayman (1960) illustrate a kind of catathymic violence that differs from the form discussed by Wertham in that the Satten et al. cases of murder were sudden, without logical motivation, and were activated by an individual whom the perpetrator had just met: "The murderous potential can become activated, especially if some disequilibrium is already present, when the victim-to-be is unconsciously perceived as a key figure in some past traumatic configuration. The behavior, or even the mere presence of this figure adds a stress to the unstable balance of forces which results in a sudden extreme discharge of violence, similar to the explosion that takes place when a percussion cap ignites a charge of dynamite" (p. 52). In reviewing their cases, these authors elucidated single or multiple unconscious meanings the victim may have triggered in the perpetrator; for instance, ambivalent feelings, incestuous feelings, self-hatred, or even deflected suicide. The offenders were "predisposed to gross lapses in reality contact and extreme weakness in impulse control during periods of heightened tension and disorganization. Thus, the victim seems to have had symbolic significance to the offender. At such times, a chance acquaintance or even a stranger was easily able to lose his real meaning and assume an identity in the unconscious traumatic configuration. The old conflict was reactivated and the aggression swiftly mounted to murderous proportions" (p. 52). According to Satten and his associates, this form of catathymic violence is a category of episodic dyscontrol, previously described by Menninger and Mayman (1956).

Revitch (1975, 1977), Revitch and Schlesinger (1978, 1981, 1989), and Schlesinger (2004) were influenced not only by Wertham's conception of catathymic crisis–involving a long-term relationship with the future victim–but also by Satten and his associates' conception of sudden violence triggered interpersonally by an individual whom the perpetrator has met for the first time. In the next two sections, catathymic crisis as viewed by Wertham and by Revitch and Schlesinger is discussed in detail.

WERTHAM'S CATATHYMIC CRISIS

Fredric Wertham first presented his concept of catathymic crisis at a lecture given at the Johns Hopkins Medical School on the occasion of the twenty-fifth anniversary of the Phipps Psychiatric Clinic and the celebration of psychiatrist Adolf Meyer's seventieth birthday. Wertham's lecture was published in 1937. Influenced greatly by Maier's (1912) concept of catathymia–used as an explanation for the formation of the content of delusions–Wertham defined the concept in this way: [Catathymic crisis is] "the transformation of the stream of thought as the result of certain complexes of ideas that are charged with a strong affect–usually a wish, a fear, or an ambivalent striving. . . . The [future offender] acquires the idea that he must carry out a violent act against others or against himself . . . [the idea] appears as a definite plan [and is] accompanied by a tremendous urge to carry it out. The plan itself meets such resistance in the mind of the [subject] that he is likely to hesitate and delay. The violent act usually has some symbolic significance over and above its obvious meaning. There are no definite projections, although the thinking of the [individual] may have an almost delusional character in its rigidity and inaccessibility to logical reasoning" (p. 974).

Wertham went on to describe the clinical development of catathymic crisis: "A traumatic experience creates an unresolvable inner conflict that, in turn, produces extreme emotional tension. The individual believes that an external situation is responsible for his inner tension, and his thinking becomes more and more egocentric and disturbed. Eventually and suddenly, he decides that a violent act against another or against himself is the only way out" (p. 974). The idea to carry out a violent act–as a solution to an internal conflict–becomes fixed and quasi-delusional. For awhile the individual struggles against and resists the urge to commit violence, but ultimately the act is carried out or attempted. Afterward, the subject experiences a feeling of relief from the emotional tension; and this tension release is followed by a period of superficial normalcy, during which the offender momentarily achieves insight and recovers psychic homeostasis.

The various stages and sequences of events of Wertham's catathymic crisis constitute a clinical entity, diagnosable only by exclusion of all other mental conditions that could be considered. Sometimes catathymic crisis may occur as a syndrome in association with another mental disorder. Wertham did not limit catathymic crisis to interpersonal violence; he stated that it could also involve such acts as firesetting, self-castration, self-blinding, and suicide. Wertham was struck by a period of superficial normalcy and calm that follows unsuccessful suicides or acts of violence. During this time, an inner adjustment shifts the person's attitude and results in insight and a reestablishment of psychic stability. Wertham believed that the explosion of aggression represents an attempt to safeguard one's personality from a more serious disruption, such as psychosis.

Five stages of the catathymic crisis were outlined by Wertham (1978): (1) initial thinking disorder; (2) crystallization of a plan and increase of emotional tension; (3) emotional tension culminating in violence; (4) superficial calmness and normalcy; and (5) reestablishment of an inner equilibrium. In two of his books, *Dark Legend* (1941) and *The Show of Violence* (1949), Wertham described catathymic crisis and provided rich clinical examples of its characteristics.

REVITCH AND SCHLESINGER'S CATATHYMIC PROCESS

Revitch and Schlesinger conceived of catathymia not as a clinical entity as such, but rather as a psychological, psychodynamic—or what Meloy (1992) has referred to as a motivational—process with an acute and a chronic form. Similarities between acute and chronic catathymic homicides are the following (Schlesinger, 2004, p. 138):

- Cases primarily involve men killing women.
- Victim is viewed in symbolic terms.
- Victim triggers underlying emotionally charged conflicts.
- Conflicts center on strong feelings of inadequacy, extending to the sexual area.
- Homicide releases emotional tension.
- Following homicide, psychic homeostasis is quickly reestablished.
- Feeling of relief or flattening of emotions (or both) is common after the act.
- Offenders typically do not attempt to elude authorities for long and often tell a friend about the homicide or call the police themselves.
- Mental health professionals do not recognize the ominous significance of the offender's conflicts prior to the act.
- Investigators sometimes miss the underlying sexual motivation because overt manifestations of genitality are often absent.

Acute Catathymic Process

In contrast to situational acts of violence or impulsive assaults committed explosively out of anger, fear, or jealousy—or under the influence of alcohol, drugs, or paranoid states—the acute catathymic process taps deeper levels of emotional tension and is triggered by an overwhelming emotion attached to an underlying conflict. Sometimes the perpetrator can give an explanation for the act, but many times the event is only partially recalled. The acute catathymic process is consistent with several cases described by Satten et al. (1960).

Many other writers have described and discussed sudden explosive murders without apparent motive (e.g., Blackman, Weiss, & Lambert, 1963; Dicke, 1994; Kirschner & Nagel, 1996; Lambert, Blackman, & Weiss, 1958; Weiss, Lambert, & Blackman, 1960). Ruotolo (1968) described five cases of sudden murder triggered by an injury to the pride system, basing his dynamic explanation on the work of Karen Horney. As the relationship to the victim becomes closer, an "insult" leads to aggressive feelings, which culminate in murder. Karpman (1935) believed that unresolved oedipal problems generate such outbursts. And, in most cases, the victim has some symbolic relationship to the underlying conflicts (Schlesinger, 2004). The following cases illustrate acute catathymic violence resulting in murder.

Case 1:

An 18-year-old part-time gas station attendant (S. T.) strangled a 22-year-old female nightclub entertainer with a rubber hose after she entered the station to make a phone call. S. T. was completing his senior year of high school and planning to go to a junior college in the fall. One evening, while he was working at the station, a nightclub entertainer approached him and asked whether she could make a telephone call. Following the brief call, the woman pulled up her dress and invited S. T. to have sexual relations with her. He stated that "she grabbed me by the waist and pulled me toward her. I pulled my hand away. She continued, saying, 'Come on, I won't hurt you.' Then I went to the panel room to check the switches. I came out of the panel room, and she was still saying it. Then I went to the time clock, and as I grabbed the handle to pull it down, she came behind and started kissing my neck. She unbuttoned my pants; I turned around and looked at her. I started having sex standing up."

Apparently S. T. had a premature ejaculation, which prompted the victim to taunt, "Go back to your mother." At this, S. T. grabbed some rubber tubing, approached the victim from behind, put the tube around her neck, and strangled her: "She scratched my nose and said that her husband was coming back to pick her up. Then I think she stopped moving. I guess I imagined she was dead. I pulled my car up to the front door, opened the trunk, and put her in. I drove to a dirt road where people dump things; I took her out of the trunk and her hand grabbed my pants; it scared me." S. T. then covered her body with some leaves and left.

S. T. went home that evening, slept adequately, and woke up thinking "I dreamed it." But while he was at school, fragments of memories of the event began to seep into his consciousness. After midday, he became anxious and checked his trunk because he had a feeling that the event might not have been a dream. When he found the woman's eyeglasses in the car trunk, he realized that the murder had actually occurred. He drove to the field where he had dumped the body; at that point, the police were there, and he turned himself in.

S. T. was very cooperative during the entire evaluation. He described his family background as working class, and he had not had any prior difficulties with the authorities. He sometimes drank alcohol and occasionally smoked pot. He was able to describe the homicide in a clear manner with great detail. His emotions during the description of the event were flat–a typical defense mechanism used by offenders as a way of separating the intensity of the emotion from the event in order to protect psychological homeostasis.

Comment:

This is a typical case of an acute catathymic homicide. The violent explosion was triggered by the victim's comment "Go back to your mother," which tapped a deep underlying sexual conflict that was emotionally charged and, once activated, overwhelmed S. T.'s controls. The incubation phase lasted several seconds, and after the event he displayed emotional flatness, detachment, and initial amnesia. Once the homicide was no longer suppressed, his memory of it was excellent, and he reported it in detail. He described the event as having an unreal, dreamlike quality. Not only did the victim trigger underlying conflicts when she told him to "Go back to your mother," but the fact that she approached him in an aggressive way was ego-threatening and rendered him confused, helpless, and unable to effect a complete erection. This homicide was a primitive reaction to a noxious stimulus that had symbolic significance; the perpetrator's controls were overwhelmed by a strong emotion attached to an underlying complex.

Case 2:

A 44-year-old male (C. W.) shot, but did not kill, a store owner. C. W. entered a pawnshop to make a purchase. The owner "showed pornography to me, with women with dogs and horses. I told him it was trash." C. W. and the victim then talked for approximately an hour about various topics of the day. The next day he again went to the shop. On this second visit, he had coffee with the store owner and also spoke with a customer. He had to go to the restroom "a few times because I drank a lot of coffee; I went to the bathroom a number of times on both days." After one of his trips to the restroom I was "fixing my fly, and the owner asked me if I was interested in selling pornographic pictures. He grabbed me by the arm; I told him it was trash. He hung on and I shoved him; he wanted me to deal in pornographic merchandise and drugs." C. W. stated further that he did not know "one drug from another; I am totally against drugs." At that point, he and the owner got into a shoving match. "I wore a gun because it [the pawnshop] didn't have security."

C. W. continued: "My shirt opened up and he reached for my gun. When I felt him on my pants, I grabbed his hands. . . . I took my hands and hit him on the head. His hands and my hands were on the gun; I split his head open. He kept coming after me; we were wrestling on the floor; I had blood all over me, head to foot. One of the last things I remember was he went like this [as if he were pointing a gun]. I could have sworn he had a gun. I had a gun shoved in my face many times. I lost it when I saw the gun pushed in my face. . . . I was told that I ran right through the window." The offender indicated, however, that he had no memory of running through the plate glass. C. W. shot the victim as he ran after him down the street. He did not regard the owner's touching as a sexual advance, but rather as an effort to get his attention: "He held me to tell me what he wanted."

Comment:

The extent of violence used against the store owner and the fact that C. W. ran through a plate glass window indicate that he was reacting to a much deeper source of conflict than just being asked to sell drugs. The incident occurred against the background of a conversation about pornography, while C. W. was pulling up his zipper and the owner's hand was placed on his trousers. The sexual advance agitated C.W., loosening underlying, longstanding sexual conflicts that he rigidly defended. His logical reasoning broke down to such an extent that he continued to shoot at the victim in front of numerous witnesses, including the police. He displayed evidence of compulsive and paranoid personality traits, and his lifestyle and attitudes were ultraconservative. In this acute catathymic reaction, the offender did not have a relationship with the victim, but the trigger was obviously sexual and the extent of the violence was greatly out of proportion to the event.

Chronic Catathymic Process

Wertham's conception of catathymic crisis basically applies to Revitch and Schlesinger's chronic form. To simplify Wertham's various stages of development of his clinical entity, Revitch and Schlesinger (1981, 1989) divided the process into three stages: incubation, violent act, and relief. The incubation stage may last for several days to even a year or somewhat longer. During this period, the future offender becomes obsessively preoccupied with the prospective victim and develops the idea that violence is the solution to a conflict or problem that has created a tremendous amount of inner tension. Depression, as well as loose schizophrenic-like thinking, often develops. Frequently, suicidal thoughts intermingle with homicidal thoughts, and suicide may follow the murder if the catathymic tension is not discharged after the violent event.

The offender often views the violent act, as well as the obsessive preoccupation with the future victim, as ego-alien and unreal. He may struggle against the impulse to commit violence, and he may even inform friends, therapists, or clergy of his plans. But the offender's warning (which is a plea for help) often is ignored or misunderstood. The most common type of catathymic murder occurs within some type of male/female relationship that brings out deep inner conflict. As the conflict comes to the surface and disrupts logical thinking, the future victim often pulls back from the relationship with the offender, thereby creating more anger, tension, and disorganization. It is the relationship itself–and the conflicts it triggers–that disrupts the offender's psychological integration. The authorities frequently try to supply a logical motive for the violent act, stating, for example, that the offender reacted in violence because the victim pulled away and tried to cool down or leave the relationship. Table 1–1 lists differentiating characteristics of the acute and chronic catathymic processes.

Several novels graphically describe the chronic form of the catathymic process. In Dostoevsky's *Crime and Punishment*, the main character, Raskolnikov, kills a woman who practices usury. There are several levels of motivation for this crime. Dostoevsky supplies a superficial motivation involving the idea of great men daring to cross ethical barriers. Raskolnikov, however, becomes obsessively preoccupied with the lender, considering her to be socially useless. After deciding to kill her, he develops a strong urge to carry out the act and feels some degree of relief following the murder. All these elements– obsessive preoccupation, urge to commit violence, relief after commission of the act–are illustrative of a chronic catathymic process.

Yukio Mishima's *Temple of the Golden Pavilion* (1971) is another deep psychological penetration into the mind of an individual who, in this case, is preoccupied with the beauty of a golden temple in Japan. This individual, Mizoguchi, feels inadequate, ugly, and unable to establish relationships with females. He also develops an obsession with the beauty of the golden temple and contrasts such beauty with his own ugliness. He decides to burn down the temple and feels greatly relieved while watching the fire. Arlow (1978) concluded that Mizoguchi's motivation was primarily sexual and involved witnessing the primal scene, with fire-setting as some type of retaliatory act. Whether or not this level of explanation is accurate does not at all detract from the phenomenological account of Mizoguchi and the chronic catathymic process.

The following case is a typical chronic catathymic homicide.

Case 3:

A 29-year-old male (G. W.) stood charged with murdering his wife. G. W. was employed as a salesman and had a good work record and

Table 1–1.
Differentiating Characteristics of Acute and Chronic Catathymic Processes.

Characteristic	Acute	Chronic
Activation of process	Triggered by a sudden overwhelming emotion attached to underlying sexual conflicts of symbolic significance	Triggered by a buildup of tension, a feeling of frustration, helplessness, and inadequacy sometimes extending into the sexual area
Relationship to the victim	Usually a stranger	Usually a close relation such as an intimate or former intimate partner
Victim symbolization	Often a displaced matricide	Rarely a displaced matricide, but victim may have symbolic significance
Incubation period	Several seconds	One day to a year; or more; may involve stalking
Level of planning	Unplanned	Planned, frequently in the form of an obsessive rumination
Method of attack	Sudden, violent; often overkill	Violent but not sudden
Crime scene	Very disorganized, reflecting complete lack of planning	Less disorganized
Sexual activity	Occasional sexual activity just before attack; impotency common	Sexual activity rare at time of homicide
Postmortem behavior	Sometimes necrophilia and occasionally dismemberment	Rarely necrophilia or dismemberment
Feeling following the attack	Usually a flattening of emotions	Usually a feeling of relief
Memory of event	Usually poor	Usually preserved

Source: L. B. Schlesinger (2004). *Sexual murder: Catathymic and Compulsive Homicides.* Boca Raton, FL: CRC Press, p. 162.

no prior involvement with the authorities. His first marriage, to his childhood sweetheart, had ended in divorce after one year. He met his second wife shortly after his divorce and indicated that he always felt somewhat uncomfortable with her "because she was overly protected as a child; she was weak-minded. Her parents were very dominant; she always went back to her parents when we had an argument or a problem." About nine months prior to the homicide–after going home to her parents many times and threatening G. W. with divorce–his wife decided to live with her parents permanently and to end the marriage.

After his wife's departure, G. W. became deeply depressed and had suicidal thoughts. He received treatment at a local mental health clinic, but the depression did not abate despite psychotherapy and medication. Eventually, he bought a gun and went to his wife's workplace: "I thought of suicide. I talked to her for a final time with the gun in my car; then I put the gun to my head and told her 'I am going to kill myself.' She then promised she'd come back to me." His wife brought charges against G. W. for this incident, and he spent a brief time in jail "with animals." When released on bail, he bought another gun and also thought of suicide, but he still maintained some hope that his wife would come back to him.

The approaching Christmas season apparently made G. W. feel worse. He saw others being happy and with their families while he was all alone. He stated, "I cried and I could feel that something was happening." He felt an enormous state of tension and developed a plan to kill his wife, thinking that this act would resolve his dilemma.

On Christmas Eve, he decided to go to the church that he knew his wife and her family would attend. While driving there, he felt depersonalized, "as if things were not real." He followed his wife and her family from the church to their home. When they pulled into the garage, he took out his gun: "I put numerous shots into my wife. I wanted them to know I meant business. The parents were all scattered. I stepped into the driver's seat and shot her in the head again and again. She fell out the passenger's side. I saw no blood on her. I said to her that I loved her and kissed her on the lips. Then I shot her again from close range directly in the head. I think I fired two more shots. I walked away and felt I would throw up. I pulled the hammer back again and pointed it to my head. My hands shook so bad I couldn't pull the trigger. I looked at her eyes; I really felt ill. I saw the police coming, so I dropped the gun. I was afraid that my father-in-law would go for it and start shooting me. I yelled at the cops to pick up the gun that I dropped." G. W. explained the event in detail and with accompanying emotion. He expressed great remorse over the murder as well as a need to commit suicide and "join her."

Comment:

In this case, the incubation phase of the catathymic process was approximately nine months. G. W. had a tremendous feeling of tension, depression, and helplessness, and the homicide itself was followed by a feeling of relief. The relationship with the victim was long and filled with conflict and anger. His difficulties emanated from this conflictual relationship with his wife, graphically illustrated by his expressions of love while killing her. Their marriage created a state of confusion and helplessness so that the only way the catathymic tension could be released was through eliminating the source of the tension (his wife) or removing himself by suicide. G. W.'s psychiatrist paid little attention to G. W.'s violent thoughts. Because G. W. "expressed" these thoughts instead of keeping them private, the psychiatrist incorrectly believed that he would not resort to any aggressive acts.

DIFFERENTIAL DIAGNOSIS

Not all explosions of interpersonal violence are necessarily catathymic reactions. Many primary psychiatric conditions may also result in explosive/homicidal behavior. Violence is often a direct outgrowth of a psychosis or the result of some organic states (such as temporal-lobe epilepsy or postictal confusion) or perhaps toxic conditions (such as those brought on by alcohol or drug abuse). Borderline personality disorder often results in explosive acts, and borderline individuals involved in longstanding conflictual relationships frequently manifest repetitive episodes of violence. Manic individuals also exhibit aggressive behavior in states of both mania and depression.

At the same time, individuals with some type of diagnoseable psychiatric condition can experience a catathymic reaction; but here the catathymic process is paramount in understanding the violence, and the psychiatric condition plays only a secondary role. A chronic schizophrenic for example, may experience either an acute or a chronic catathymic process. Diagnosticians often mistakenly conclude, however, that extreme violence is always an outgrowth of a condition specified in the American Psychiatric Association's *Diagnostic and Statistical Manual of Mental Disorders* (2000). The *DSM–IV–TR*, although helpful in categorizing mental and behavioral disorders, accounts for only a small percentage of all human behavior. All too often, a forensic expert simply diagnoses a psychiatric condition and assumes that the violent behavior is a result of this condition, but in many cases the condition may produce a general weakening of controls but otherwise has virtually no relationship to the violent conduct.

Violent behavior, as well as crime in general, is not a unitary event that lends itself to a rigid system of classification. Such complex human behavior is always a result of a combination of biological, psychological, and social factors, with one factor perhaps playing a dominant role. Thus, many individuals with underlying and deeply rooted conflicts do not explode with catathymic violence even when irritated, but some do.

Monroe (1970, 1974) described a condition that he referred to as "episodic behavioral disorder," which is characterized by outbursts of violence precipitated by a trivial irritation. Monroe attributed such violence to a combination of "faulty equipment" (the neurophysiological substrate) and "faulty learning" (life experience, family surroundings). Such a disorder comes close to catathymic process, and those who diagnose the condition as a catathymic process detect an underlying emotional conflict that is triggered by the minor irritation.

Catathymic process should be differentiated not only from episodic dyscontrol and traditional psychiatric disorders but also from violence caused by plain anger. Some cases of homicide are not at all a direct result of episodic dyscontrol, a primary psychiatric disorder, or catathymic process, but are simply a result of anger with clear, situationally derived motives. The following case is illustrative.

Case 4:

A 22-year-old male (L. P.) murdered his uncle and aunt and attempted to murder his nephew. L. P. had been a high school football star, captain of the team, and student-body president. His life, however, fell apart after he was in a serious auto accident in which three of his friends, also football stars, were killed.

L. P. and his 20-year-old female cousin planned to kill the cousin's parents for motives that were never very clear. Initially, they attempted to poison the victims, but they were unsuccessful. They then decided to take more directly aggressive action. L. P. went to the victims' home, took an iron pipe from his car, and hit his uncle in the head from the back. He then went to his aunt's bedroom and "took care of her." He struck each of the adults several times with the iron pipe and then realized that his 9-year-old nephew was in an adjoining room and apparently had witnessed the murder. He hit the youngster once in the head with the same iron pipe.

Comment:

This is a complicated case from a psychodynamic perspective. The offender felt depressed, misunderstood by his parents, angry, and unable to adjust to life after his friends had died and many of the other students in his high school blamed him in some way for the accident. Whatever the exact psychodynamics, careful analysis clearly indicates that this was not a case of catathymic process, despite the explosion and the excessive amount of force used. L. P. had been diagnosed as depressed and as having a personality disorder, but these conditions also did not cause his violent acts.

In the following case an individual killed as a result of anger and not, again, as a result of a catathymic process, although perhaps some catathymic elements were involved.

Case 5:

A 37-year-old male (H. C.) killed his wife in a fit of rage following an escalating argument that had begun several hours earlier during marital therapy. The defendant was employed as an engineer and had never been in any legal difficulty before. From the day they were married, he and his wife experienced a great deal of conflict and turmoil. His wife had attempted suicide after she became pregnant. H. C. believed he was not the father and suspected her of having relations with one of the dentists she worked with. She became pregnant again three years later, but H. C. did not want to have the child because "I wanted [to buy] a house before a child." He also suspected his wife of having been unfaithful with a carpenter several years earlier. In fact, he thought that his wife had been involved sexually with others throughout their marriage.

H. C. had two master's degrees (one in computer science and one in finance), and he had held many important jobs throughout his marriage. His wife was often unhappy about his long work hours, and he felt pressured to be home more. After he was terminated from a job several years prior to the offense, he began working for the state government. His wife then ridiculed him for making half his salary: "She said I was making peanuts; she said I was a spineless jellyfish." H. C. also described a number of other events that created a great deal of distress, including the death of his father and the "interference" of his wife's family.

The marital and family problems continued. On one occasion H. C. "found divorce papers," but when he confronted Mrs. C., she indicated that she did not want a divorce. H. C. was opposed to divorce (despite the severe marital problems) because he felt it would "hurt the children." H. C. admitted that he had had a "bad temper for his entire life," and several years prior to the offense, he attended a domestic-violence program. The offender stated that he became increasingly violent after his father died, and after he lost his job, his wife became afraid of him.

After one fight, Mrs. C. "threatened" H. C. The police were called by a tenant, and H. C. was arrested. At the request of Mrs. C., the court issued a restraining order, which H. C. eventually violated. In another episode H. C. barricaded the door because "I was scared of the police." He was subsequently arrested, and the police confiscated several of his guns. At this point, a new restraining order, taking into account a number of legal technicalities, was drawn up. This restraining order allowed H. C. to live in the house, but in a separate room from Mrs. C., and he was not to "harass her" in any way. He apparently had lived this way for several months prior to the offense: "During this period of time, life was hell. I catered to her every need." He indicated that he had done a great deal of the housework, apparently in an attempt to "win her back." Family therapy began one month prior to the homicide. During this time, Mrs. C. attended a domestic-violence program for victims.

H. C. described the homicide as follows. During a counseling session with the marital therapist, Mrs. C. finally admitted that she did in fact want a divorce. H. C. then realized that "it was over" and that "there would be no family anymore." He planned to go to another state to live with his brother and to take their young son with him. After the visit to the therapist, the family went to Burger King® to have dinner. The couple began arguing about divorce again. The family eventually returned home, with H. C. and his wife traveling separately, and they continued arguing about their son's going with him to Oregon. H. C. then said to his wife, "You've been lying to me all along; you had an attorney all along; you kept stringing me along. If I didn't get out of there, I'd be arrested."

They continued to argue about Mrs. C.'s having an attorney. H. C. stated: "I realized she was lying to me, and things started to flash. I felt blood rushing to my head. I had rubbery legs like I was floating. I don't remember picking up the bat. Dominic came to my mind [referring to the carpenter whom H. C. believed Mrs. C. had a relationship with]. Everything was fuzzy, like a dream. I heard my son saying, 'No, Daddy, no', and I remember hitting her. She was on the floor, and I hit her again. After the second or third blow, I heard two screams. Someone called the police. When I heard the word 'police,' I dropped the bat. I jumped in the car. I was frightened of the police beating the hell out of me." After he passed a state trooper, he parked his car and took a train because he was afraid the trooper would arrest him. The offender then went to Canada "because I figured no one would find me in Canada."

Comment:

Prior to the homicide H. C. was depressed, felt a great deal of anxiety, and had suicidal thoughts. As a result of the stress and marital discord, his depression intensified, and his overall level of control weakened. For whatever reason (or reasons), H. C. did not want a divorce; and even though the marital problems were severe, at least one part of him believed that the marriage could be saved. When he learned in a direct and unambiguous way (at the marital therapist's office) that Mrs. C., in fact, wanted a divorce, H. C. became more and more angry. He lost control of his emotions, and the subsequent violent explosion resulted in homicide. H. C. had a fairly good memory for the event, although he did report feeling in a dreamlike state, which indicates that he may have been, at least partially, in some type of mild dissociative state. His behavior immediately following the homicide reveals that H. C. knew that what he had done was wrong and he ran away so that he would not be apprehended.

This case contains some catathymic elements, to the extent that there was a conflictual relationship with Mrs. C., but there was no deep underlying conflict. Therefore, this case should not be categorized as the result of a catathymic process but, rather, as a homicide prompted by anger, within the context of severe marital discord and some weakening of defenses because of depression.

The following case is another example of explosive violence directed against the offender's wife, also within the context of depression and mild marital discord, with anger generated by a feeling of weakness. Once again, some catathymic elements are present (the conflictual relationship with the victim), but there was no deeper symbolism nor were there any deeper psychodynamic conflicts.

Case 6:

A 66-year-old wealthy businessman (M. C.) and his wife had owned and operated a company together for approximately 25 years. Mrs. C. ran the business, while M. C. was the salesman. Because of his easy-going nature, he got along well with all the employees. Mrs. C. wanted to retire and explained that she would leave the company within the next year. Her decision created a feeling of weakness and tremendous self-doubt in M. C., who had never run the business himself. Angry that his wife would leave him in this manner, he felt "tension, stress, and depression for about three to four weeks" before the homicide. "I was off my pace. I didn't remember things." He had many disagreements with his wife. "Trying to find someone to replace her overpowered me. I magnified things that weren't there. We weren't as close as before. I was afraid she'd leave without a replacement. The rifts became more frequent."

M. C. described a number of business problems that he believed he did not handle correctly. He had a billing problem and was being investigated by the state, although Mrs. C. apparently met with the authorities and resolved it. But M. C. did not believe the case was settled: "I felt the man told her what she wanted to hear, but the problem wasn't resolved." They were arguing almost daily at this point.

On the night of the homicide, "We went to bed around 11 or 12 o'clock, but I kept dwelling [on the problem]. I felt a state of rejection from her. I paced back and forth. I went to bed, but I didn't sleep." He got up and was feeling angry. "She heard me get up. I sat on the edge of the bed. I asked her if she meant what she [had] said [about his being a wimp]. I tied a shirt around her neck. I was in a rage. I really lost it when she said she meant what she said. This was in my mind. I had the shirt over my shoulder. If I let go, maybe I'd do damage that would be irreparable, so I held on. I wasn't thinking. She said, 'Mike, what are you doing?' I sat there. I couldn't believe it. I didn't know what to do." He then put on his trousers and "rode to my office at 7:30 A.M. I put her on the floor to make her comfortable. I went back home after I walked in and out of my office to say farewell. I sat in the bedroom thinking what to do next." M. C. called the police, told them what had happened, and was arrested.

Comment:

Depression played a major part in this homicide. The obsessive worry and the egocentric (somewhat paranoid) nature of M. C.'s thinking typify the way that severely depressed individuals experience the world. In all likelihood, M. C. was suffering from an agitated form of depression on the evening of the offense; he became obsessively preoccupied with the state's investigation of the company and was unable to put it out of his mind despite reassurance. He had angry and irritable outbursts, was unable to sleep, and paced the floor. The homicide was explosive and unplanned, but it was not a catathymic murder. There are catathymic elements (the suddenness of the act and M. C.'s feeling of abandonment), but this case is more parsimoniously explained as an explosion of anger within the context of depression and irritability. If M. C. had not been suffering from depression, he likely would not have behaved in such an uncontrolled way. In true catathymic violence, depression–if it is present at all–plays only a secondary role in triggering the explosion.

Sometimes a compulsive, sexually motivated homicide (i.e., one in which where the offender has an inner drive to kill and the murder itself is sexually arousing) is mistaken for a catathymic offense. Table 1–2 lists the differentiating characteristics of acute catathymic processes and unplanned compulsive homicides, and Table 1–3 presents the characteristics that differentiate chronic catathymic processes and planned compulsive homicides. The following case of a serial, sexually motivated compulsive offender who acted with explosive violence– but not catathymic violence–is illustrative.

Table 1–2.
**Differentiating Characteristics of Acute Catathymic
and Unplanned Compulsive Homicides.**

Characteristic	Acute Catathymic	Unplanned Compulsive
Compulsion to kill	Not present	Present for years
Sadistic fantasy	Not present	Present in simple, undifferentiated form
Motive	Sexual, stemming from feelings of inadequacy extending into the sexual area	Sexual, involving a fusion of sex and aggression
Relationship to Victim	Often a stranger who triggers underlying conflict	Often known; does not trigger conflicts, but vulnerability provides an opportunity for offender to kill
Warning signs	Sometimes makes threats to explode, which is often ignored	Makes no threats but has many ominous signs in background
Sexual activity at time of crime	Necrophilia or dismemberment common	Insertion of objects into orifices; sometimes sexual assault
Postcrime behavior	Does not try to elude authorities for long	Attempts to elude authorities but typically is unsuccessful

Source: L. B. Schlesinger (2004). *Sexual Murder: Catathymic and Compulsive Homicides.* Boca Raton, FL: CRC Press, p. 294.

Case 7:

A 30-year-old male (E. P.) was evaluated to help determine his state of mind at the time he committed a number of homicides. The exact details and psychodynamics were difficult to ascertain in this case because the defendant gave many different versions of the events, all of which were inconsistent with the crime scene information. The defendant had read a number of criminology books and, according to the authorities, was influenced greatly by the movie *Presumed Innocent.*

The first woman E. P. killed was a girlfriend of one of his friends. E. P. shaved his entire body and entered the victim's home wearing only socks so that he would not leave any evidence, such as footprints, body hair, or fibers. He smudged his fingerprints as well. After raping the victim, he hogtied, tortured, and eventually killed her. He also killed her children (8 and 6 years old) to avoid detection. "I strangled

Table 1–3.
**Differentiating Characteristics of Chronic Catathymic
and Planned Compulsive Homicides.**

Characteristic	Chronic Catathymic	Planned Compulsive
Compulsion to kill	Not present	Present and building for years
Sadistic fantasy	Not present; instead, has obsessive thoughts to kill a particular victim; sees murder as a solution to a problem	Present in elaborate form; not in reference to a particular victim–almost any victim (with certain characteristics) will do
Motive	Buildup of tension and feelings of helplessness and inadequacy extending to the sexual area	Fusion of sex and aggression
Relationship to victim	Intimate or former intimate partner or stranger with whom the offender becomes obsessed	Often a stranger; sometimes an acquaintance, but almost never an intimate or former intimate partner
Warning signs	Tells confidant of ego-dystonic ideas that are developing	Rarely warns others, but many ominous behavioral signs in background
Sexual activity at time of crime	Rare	Common
Postcrime behavior	Does not try to elude authorities; sometimes makes a suicide attempt following murder	Tries hard to elude authorities and, because of the planning, is often successful; as a result there are multiple victims

Source: L. B. Schlesinger (2004). *Sexual murder: Catathymic and Compulsive Homicides.* Boca Raton, FL: CRC Press, p. 297.

them. The little girl was sleeping, the boy was up." After killing the children, E. P. hit them both in the head with a hammer, crushing their skulls. The defendant poured alcohol into the victim's vagina in an attempt to remove any trace of semen so that he could not be detected. Following the rape and three murders, he went to a local restaurant and ate hamburgers and french fries. He then bought beer and went home to sleep. He did not know, however, that alcohol preserves sperm, and a perfect DNA match was eventually accomplished.

Several months later, when he was in a different state, E. P. murdered another woman who was an acquaintance of his. He entered the home undressed, brutally attacked, raped, tortured, and killed her. He went home and slept well that evening. When he awoke the next morning, he was aware that he had killed the woman but was unwilling to provide a clear motive: "I didn't intend to kill her; I just lost control. It was probably alcohol and drugs. I don't know why I killed her."

When asked whether he obtained any type of powerful or sexually arousing feeling from the killings, the defendant stated: "No, I am powerful in any way I need to be powerful. I get respect from everyone. I can conquer whatever I have to conquer. It is something I was born with. I do whatever it takes to overcome whoever it may be. People are scared of me. I am a martial-arts expert. I let you know I am not to be bothered. If I tell you something, it's not intimidation or fear. Either you do it or deal with me." In response to a suggestion that these statements and behaviors might reflect an attempt to compensate for inadequacy, he stated, "I have no worries. People try to overcompensate when they fear something. I have no fear, none whatsoever."

Comment:

E. P. was a sexually motivated compulsive murderer who killed because of an inner need to kill (Revitch & Schlesinger, 1981; Schlesinger, 2004) and not because the killing served any logical purpose. These homicides are not chronic catathymic events despite the presence of explosive violence. The relationships were not of a protracted nature, and the killings were not triggered by some type of inferred slur that unleashed repressed emotions attached to underlying conflicts. By constantly stressing that he was strong, adequate, and fearsome, this man was attempting to compensate for underlying weakness and inadequacy, as well as displaying a sexual-arousal pattern that involved a fusion of sex and aggression so that the aggressive act was eroticized. From a diagnostic perspective, he displayed evidence of a severe personality disorder with antisocial and narcissistic traits.

His Thematic Apperception Test (TAT) stories contained repetitive themes revealing anger and aggression toward women and a generalized negative view of females. The following excerpts are illustrative: "He is tired of arguing with her. She was probably messing around. She enjoyed it. It's what she wanted to do, and now he is outraged. He wants to leave her. He is mad and upset because she had an affair. It's her nature. She has been doing it all along, and he didn't know it. It makes him angry. She keeps the affair going. She dies of a disease, probably syphilis. She gets it from having so many affairs. She is a whore. She was born that way." "The guy killed his wife. She was sleeping around and was unfaithful and he couldn't take it anymore. He strangled her. She flaunted the affair. She didn't hide it, and he couldn't take it. She made him into an animal because of her actions. Once a woman finds out you love her, she changes and starts doing what she wants to do because she figures no matter what, you will be there. She figures she's got you. You are not going anywhere, so why not have an affair."

DISCUSSION

Professionals who are called as expert witnesses to assess a defendant's mental state in courtroom proceedings often can use catathymic process as a supplement to a traditional *DSM* diagnosis, particularly in cases where the motive is unclear. No *DSM* diagnosis, in and of itself, can establish a specific legal standard, and the same applies to the catathymic process, because the specific facts and circumstances of individual cases vary widely. The degree of control individuals have over their behavior is always of interest to the court and goes directly to assessments of legal responsibility. In Case 1, for example, the offender had a sudden loss of control, but he did attempt to cover up his crime. Prosecutors argue that defendants who admit to a crime are conscious of their guilt and had more control than their description of the event itself might indicate. In Case 2, the defendant's crashing through a plate glass window and shooting at the victim in front of the police were evidence of an extreme loss of control. In both cases, a type of diminished-capacity defense (which reduced the degree of intent and level of the crime) was successful; however, neither case rose to the level where a complete exculpatory defense was appropriate.

Cases of chronic catathymic homicide present the greatest challenge in a forensic setting. The jury almost always rejects an insanity plea in these cases for the following reasons: (1) there is no clear-cut psychosis; (2) the jury does not understand or appreciate the dissociative state; and (3), most important, the jury often considers obsessive rumination to be premeditation. Moreover, the press reports of such cases, as well as the prosecutions' theories, tend to be superficial and incorrect. In Case 3, for example, the press reported that G. W. killed his wife because she wanted to break up with him, as if this simple motive explained everything. Such superficial explanations are sometimes offered to impose logic on an act that—because it dramatically reveals a lack of control over one's own inner conflicts—appears bizarre and frightening to the general public.

Catathymic process has been recognized as a clinical entity for almost a century, although its usefulness has been undervalued. Increased understanding of both the acute and the chronic catathymic process, particularly in cases of extreme violence, but also in cases of suicide and even self-mutilation (Simpson, 1973; Greilsheimer & Groves, 1979), will be of great help to the practicing clinician. A clear explanation of the catathymic process to jury members can enable them to gain some understanding of the complexity and depth of many cases of aggression that have catastrophic consequences. Further clinical research into the catathymic process will undoubtedly provide increased understanding not only of its phenomenology, psychopathology, and psychodynamics, but of its true incidence as well.

REFERENCES

American Psychiatric Association (2000). *Diagnostic and statistical manual of mental disorders* (4th Ed., text rev.). Washington, DC: Author.

Arlow, J. A. (1978). Pyromania and the primal scene. *Psychiatric Quarterly*, *417*, 24.

Blackman, N., Weiss, J. M. A., & Lambert, J. W. (1963). The sudden murderer. *Archives of General Psychiatry*, *8*, 289.

Dicke, J. (1994). Catathymic violence and mental status defenses. *Colorado Criminal Defense Bar Rapsheet*, Winter, 10.

Gayral, L., Millet, G., Moron, P., & Turnin, J. (1956). Crises et paroxysmes catathymiques [catathymic rages and paroxysms]. *Annales médico-psychologiques*, *114*, 25.

Greilsheimer, H., & Groves, J. E. (1979). Male genital selfmutilation. *Archives of General Psychiatry*, *36*, 441.

Karpman, B. (1935). *The individual criminal*. Washington, DC: Nervous and Mental Disease Publishing Co.

Kirschner, D., & Nagel, L. (1996). Catathymic violence, dissociative state and adoption pathology: Implications for the mental status defense. *International Journal of Offender Therapy and Comparative Criminology*, *40*, 204.

Lambert, J. W., Blackman, N., & Weiss, J. (1958). The sudden murderer: A preliminary report. *Journal of Social Therapy*, *1*, 2.

Maier, H. W. (1912). Katathyme Wahnbildung und Paranoia [Catathymic delusions and paranoia]. *Zeitschrift für die gesamte Neurologie und Psychiatrie*, *13*, 545.

Meloy, J. R. (1992). *Violent attachments*. Northvale, NJ: Aronson.

Menninger, K., & Mayman, M. (1956). Episodic dyscontrol: A third order of stress adaptation. *Bulletin of the Menninger Clinic, 20*, 153.

Mishima, Y. (1971). *The temple of the golden pavilion.* New York: Berkley.

Monroe, R. R. (1970). *Episodic behavioral disorder.* Cambridge, MA: Harvard University Press.

Monroe, R. R. (1974). Episodic behavioral disorder: An unclassified syndrome. In S. Arieti (Ed.), *American handbook of psychiatry* (2nd Ed., Vol. 2, pp. 67–81). New York: Basic Books.

Revitch, E. (1964). Paroxysmal manifestations of non-epileptic origin: Catathymic attacks. *Diseases of the Nervous System, 25*, 662.

Revitch, E. (1975). Psychiatric evaluation and classification of antisocial activities. *Diseases of the Nervous System, 36*, 419.

Revitch, E. (1977). Classification of offenders for prognostic and dispositional evaluation. *Bulletin of the American Academy of Psychiatry and Law, 5*, 41.

Revitch, E., & Schlesinger, L. B. (1978). Murder: Evaluation, classification, and prediction. In I. L. Kutash, S. B. Kutash, & L. B. Schlesinger (Eds.), *Violence: Perspectives on murder and aggression* (pp. 138–164). San Francisco: Jossey-Bass.

Revitch, E., & Schlesinger, L. B. (1981). *Psychopathology of homicide.* Springfield, IL: Charles C Thomas.

Revitch, E., & Schlesinger, L. B. (1989). *Sex murder and sex aggression.* Springfield, IL: Charles C Thomas.

Ruotolo, A. (1968). Dynamics of sudden murder. *American Journal of Psychoanalysis, 26*, 162.

Satten, J., Menninger, K., & Mayman, M. (1960). Murder without apparent motive: A study in personality disintegration. *American Journal of Psychiatry, 117*, 48.

Schlesinger, L. B. (2004). *Sexual murder: Catathymic and compulsive homicides.* Boca Raton, FL: CRC Press.

Simpson, M. A. (1973). Female genital self-mutilation. *Archives of General Psychiatry, 29*, 808.

Weiss, J. M. A., Lambert, J. W., & Blackman, N. (1960). The sudden murderer. *Archives of General Psychiatry, 2*, 669.

Wertham, F. (1937). The catathymic crisis: A clinical entity. *Archives of Neurology and Psychiatry, 37*, 974.

Wertham, F. (1941). *Dark legend, a study in murder.* New York: Duell, Sloan & Pearce.

Wertham, F. (1949). *The show of violence.* New York: Doubleday.

Wertham, F. (1978). A catathymic crisis. In I. L. Kutash, S. B. Kutash, & L. B. Schlesinger (Eds.), *Violence: Perspectives on murder and aggression* (pp. 165–170). San Francisco: Jossey-Bass.

Chapter 2

PATHOLOGICAL GAMBLING AND CRIMINAL BEHAVIOR

RICHARD J. ROSENTHAL AND HENRY R. LESIEUR

Pathological gambling was first officially recognized as a valid medical disorder in 1980, when the American Psychiatric Association classified it as an impulse-control disorder. According to the latest edition of the diagnostic and statistical manual (American Psychiatric Association, 2000, page 663), other disorders of impulse-control include alcohol and chemical dependence, attention deficit hyperactivity disorder (ADHD), the paraphilias, the borderline and antisocial personality disorders, and several of the mood disorders (mania, cyclothymia) and eating disorders. While there is still some debate as to whether pathological gambling is a compulsive disorder, an addiction or learned defensive behavior, most clinicians and researchers view it as an addiction.

Rosenthal (1992) traces the derivation of the word (addiction means "to speak to someone," also "to be enslaved") and concludes that compulsive or pathological gambling may have been the earliest recognized addiction. He locates the origins of the term in early Roman law. The original *addictus* was someone who, because of unpaid debts, would be brought to court and sentenced into slavery (Glare, 1982; Wissowa, 1984). This did not only include gamblers, although it was a period when gambling was rampant. The judge would pronounce sentence, placing the addict in the possession of his creditor. Since most people were illiterate, the emphasis in the law was on what was spoken. The root of the word indicates how it was to be spoken; *deik* means "pronounce solemnly," and is common to both "addict" and "judge" (Watkins, 1985).

Support for this idea comes from legal history as well as the cross-cultural literature. Ancient Egypt was the first place with a recorded gambling law; the masses were forbidden to gamble under the penalty of slavery in the mines (Wykes, 1964). Vagrancy statutes, initiated in England in 1349, were modified in 1743 to include illegal betting, and offenders could be branded, enslaved, or executed for repeat offenses (Chambliss, 1964). Among Native Americans such as the Mandan Indians of the upper Missouri (Catlin, 1857), the Yurok (Erikson, 1943), and Bella Coola (Forsyth, 1948), individuals were known to gamble themselves into slavery. One could quite literally become a slave to the addiction.

The essential features of the disorder are a continuous or periodic loss of control over gambling; a progression in frequency and in amounts wagered and in the preoccupation with gambling and with obtaining monies with which to gamble; irrational thinking; and a continuation of the behavior despite adverse consequences. The irrationality includes the cognitive distortions, erroneous but fixed beliefs, superstitious thinking, denial, and omnipotence. The latter has been defined as an illusion of power and control that defends against helplessness and other intolerable feelings (Rosenthal, 1986).

While money is important, many gamblers say they are seeking "action," an aroused, euphoric state comparable to the "high" derived from cocaine or other drugs. Clinicians have noted the development of tolerance (increasingly larger bets or greater risks needed to produce the desired level of excitement [Lesieur, 1977]), and the experience of withdrawal symptoms (Wray & Dickerson, 1981; Meyer, 1989; Rosenthal & Lesieur, 1992). In addition to restlessness and irritability, pathological gamblers when they stop gambling commonly experience insomnia, headaches, gastrointestinal disturbances, loss of appetite, physical weakness, palpitations, muscle aches, sweating, chills, and fever (Rosenthal & Lesieur, 1992).

There is significant overlap between pathological gambling and chemical dependency. When chemically dependent patients were asked about gambling, 10-20 percent were found to be pathological gamblers (Lesieur, Blume & Zoppa, 1986; Lesieur & Heineman, 1988; Steinberg, Kosten & Rounsaville, 1992), while another 10-20 percent had gambling-related problems but fell short of the clinical diagnosis.

Conversely, when pathological gamblers were asked about substance use disorders, 50 percent had a positive history (Linden, Pope & Jonas, 1986; Ramirez, McCormick, Russo & Taber, 1983). For some patients there was a sequential pattern, with chemical dependency followed or preceded by pathological gambling, while for other patients, the two disorders occurred simultaneously.

The presence of more than one addiction may place pathological gamblers at greater risk of incarceration (Lesieur, 1987). In addition, substance dependent patients who are also pathological gamblers have higher rates of stress-related diseases and serious psychiatric problems including suicide attempts (Feigelman, Wallisch & Lesieur, 1998).

Genetic abnormalities in pathological gamblers offer evidence of a physiological predisposition for the disorder. Comings and his colleagues (1996) found abnormalities in the D2 dopamine receptor of pathological gamblers that could not be accounted for by a comorbid condition such as alcohol or substance abuse, ADHD or depression. When the pathological gamblers were divided into four groups according to severity of their gambling problem, there was a progressive increase in the number showing the abnormality, with 73 percent of those in the most severe group showing the genetic defect. Further research has found that different genes have an additive effect on the potential for addiction (Comings & Blum, 2000; Comings et al., 2001). Dopamine, serotonin, and norepinephrine genes contributed approximately equally to the risk for pathological gambling.

PATTERNS OF GAMBLING

Gambling includes a wide variety of activities: card games, dice, roulette, sports betting, parimutuel wagering, slot and video poker machines, keno, lottery, stocks and commodities, bingo, games of skill (such as pool, golf, and bowling), and myriad other pursuits. These games range in the degree to which they are potentially addictive with continuous games being more addictive than noncontinuous ones. Continuous games have little, if any, delay between events and the pace of play is rapid. Discontinuous games are slow and conducted on an intermittent basis. Using lottery games as an example, the lotto is discontinuous because it is played only once or twice a week, while instant scratch-off tickets or video lottery terminals (VLTs that are actually video slot or poker machines) can be played as fast as people can move their hands and put in the money. There is evidence that individuals who play continuous games get addicted within a shorter period of time than those who play discontinuous games (Breen & Zimmerman, 2002).

While wagering patterns can be complex, there are essentially two styles: rational and intuitive. Rational styles of gambling are those in which skill is a significant factor in determining the winner. Examples include percentage poker play, card counting at blackjack, and the handicapping of horse races and sporting events. Intuitive styles, in contrast, are not rational and involve no skill at all. Examples include selection of a specific "lucky" machine, the use of lucky charms, colors, birthdays or dream interpretation, or the playing of hunches in order to influence or predict the outcome of events.

There are four basic types of gamblers: social, professional, problem, and pathological. Approximately 95 percent of players are social gamblers, who wager for fun, often in the company of friends. They accept losing as part of the game and do not bet more than they can afford. Professional gamblers make a living at gambling, either by hustling (cheating), running games or gambling with measured control (Morehead, 1950; Hayano, 1982; Prus & Sharper, 1977). The critical factor is discipline. When playing they refrain from betting every race or hand, instead they wait until they have an advantage. Problem gamblers typically satisfy three or four of the diagnostic criteria for pathological gambling in *DSM-IV* (Lesieur & Rosenthal, 1998). They may have problems due to gambling, but do not show the long-term chasing, the compulsiveness or the progression of the pathological gambler. Some, however, will become pathological gamblers.

THE NATURE AND COURSE OF PATHOLOGICAL GAMBLING

Epidemiological studies reveal that about one-third of pathological gamblers are women (Gerstein et al., 1999; Welte et al., 2001). The natural history is somewhat different for the two sexes (Lesieur & Blume, 1991a). Women typically start gambling later in life, often after their adult roles are established. They are more apt to be depressed and to be gambling less for the action or excitement than for escape; specifically, escape into a state of emotional numbing or oblivion. They typically play less competitive forms of gambling in which luck is more valued than skill, and they are more likely to play alone than their male counterparts. Not all women follow this pattern. There are some who start earlier and are involved in more competitive games.

In states in which video poker machines have been legalized, the rates of female gamblers seeking treatment or attending Gamblers Anonymous (GA) has been rapidly rising and in some places exceeds the number of men. Video machine gamblers develop gambling problems more rapidly than do those engaged in more traditional forms of gambling. Two studies of pathological gamblers in treatment (Breen & Zimmerman, 2002; Breen, 2004) found that, after becoming regular gamblers, those who played more traditional games took longer to develop problems (3.89 years) than those who played video games (1.09 years). Breen (2004) found that the primary reason women have a quicker onset of pathological gambling problems is because they play video games.

Newer forms of gambling that are more accessible, faster, and more interactive pose a potentially greater threat. Many young people have been getting in trouble because of Internet gambling. Texas Hold'em and gambling on the Internet have both increased dramatically since 2000 (Messerlian, Byrne & Derevensky, 2004; Romer, 2005, September 28).

It is useful to distinguish between "action seekers" and "escape seekers." Action seekers look for big payoffs, play competitive, skill-oriented forms of gambling, and have a need to impress others. Escape seekers, on the other hand, speak of seeking out numbness or a sense of oblivion, and of blotting out pain. They are attracted to repetitive, even monotonous games, which they play by themselves.

The typical male gambler is an "action seeker," who characteristically began gambling in childhood or early adolescence. Although a few became "hooked" with their first bet, in most cases it was more insidious. There may be gradual dependence or years of social gambling followed by an abrupt change in their gambling behavior. The latter may be precipitated by greater accessibility or exposure to gambling or by some psychologically significant loss or life stressor.

Some of the factors extrinsic to the gambling situation which have hastened the progression or caused a social gambler to turn into a pathological gambler include: (1) the use of alcohol or drugs; (2) marital or other relationship difficulties; (3) the death of a parent or close relation; (4) the birth of a child; (5) a physical illness or threat to one's life; (6) a job or career disappointment; and (7) paradoxically a job or career success (Bolen & Boyd, 1968; Boyd & Bolen, 1970; Lesieur & Blume, 1991a; Rosenthal, 1987).

Early predisposing factors (Rosenthal, 1987, 1989) include a family history of alcoholism or pathological gambling; rejection, criticism, or neglect by an all-important parent; an emphasis within the family on status and material success; a history of attention deficit hyperactivity disorder; and early exposure to gambling under conditions in which it was valued. Many gamblers grew up believing that nothing they did was ever enough, and that they could never be good enough. Gambling offered them the opportunity for "spectacular success," which would bring them recognition and approval. At the same time it allowed them to express their resentment and rebellion.

It should be noted, however, that gambling has not only become more accessible, it has also become more acceptable. When behaviors once thought deviant are adopted into middle class culture, those who engage in them, even to excess, are a different population, and perhaps healthier, than those who first participated. Problem and pathological gamblers, however, are still stigmatized, and to a much greater extent than are those who abuse alcohol or drugs.

According to the literature on pathological gambling, the typical progression proceeds through four phases (Custer, 1982a; Custer & Milt, 1985; Lesieur & Mark, 1993; Rosenthal, 1989, November; Lesieur & Rosenthal, 1991).

1. The Winning Phase. "Action seekers" tend to get involved with gambling because they are good at it and get recognition for their early successes. Many describe themselves as highly competitive, and as being "good with numbers" and/or good at the strategy of games (Rosenthal, 1990, August; Rosenthal & Lorenz, 1992). As a larger portion of their self-esteem derives from gambling, they invest more time in it and wager larger stakes. There may be a "big win" (Custer, 1982b; Custer & Milt, 1985) early in the gambler's career. Believing then that they can do anything, they take even greater chances. But aside from actual winnings is the involvement with fantasies of winning and the need for spectacular success.

"Escape seekers" typically do not experience a big win early in their gambling careers. Instead, gambling is looked upon as a means of escape from overwhelming situations, including childhood problems, trauma, troubled relationships (for example, alcoholic, mentally ill or compulsive gambling spouses), or from loneliness and neglect. Gambling is viewed as a "time out" from worries. They refer to gambling as an "anesthetic" which "hypnotizes." Gamblers may experience dissociative states (Jacobs, 1986, 1988; Kuley & Jacobs, 1988; O'Donnell & Harvey, 1993; Brown, 1994, 1996; Lesieur & Rosenthal, 1995; O'Donnell, 1996; Kofoed et al., 1997; Diskin & Hodgins, 1999). They describe "memory blackouts," "trances," "out of body experiences," and the feeling of taking on another identity while gambling. Escape gamblers may value these experiences, particularly since they are combined with the euphoria of the action. Others want to numb out dysphoric feelings.

2. The Losing Phase. For the action seeker, there may be a string of bad luck or the gambler may discover that losing is intolerable. This is when chasing begins (Lesieur, 1977, 1979; Custer, 1982a; Rosenthal, 1989; Rosenthal & Rugle, 1994). Previous gambling strategies are abandoned as the gambler tries to win back everything all at once. Although there was previously a social context to gambling, he or she now gambles alone.

Escape seekers find that "time out" from problems is expensive. They borrow the household money and search out other sources of funds in order to keep gambling. When bills come due and they are unable to pay, they "chase" their losses in an attempt to get money.

For both types of gamblers, there is a sense of urgency; bets are made in larger amounts and with greater frequency. Only the most urgent debts are paid because money has to be used for gambling. Covering up and lying about gambling becomes the norm. When this is discovered, relationships with spouse, parents, and children deteriorate.

Jobs are exploited for all they can bring: time to gamble, money to pay for it. They use their own and their families' money, go through savings, take out loans, and exhaust all legitimate sources. Eventually there is a "crunch": they cannot borrow any more, and faced with physical threats from creditors or with the loss of their job or marriage, they go to their family and partially confess. The result is a "bailout." Debts are paid and, in return, the family extracts only a promise to cut down or stop gambling. This produces a massive upsurge of omnipotence; believing they can get away with anything, they now bet more heavily and lose control altogether.

3. The Desperation Phase. There is a "crossing the line," so that the gambler starts doing things that were previously unimaginable: writing bad checks, stealing from employers or other illegal activities. Where this "line" is differs from individual to individual, but once it is crossed it becomes easier to keep crossing it. The offense is rationalized initially as a short-term loan, and there is an intention to repay it just as soon as they win. The gambler still believes he or she is one winning streak away from solving all problems. There is a lack of concern for others as attention is taken up increasingly with these illegal "loans" and various schemes directed at getting money. The gambler becomes irritable and quick-tempered and sometimes abusive to family members. When others remind them of their responsibilities or put them in touch with guilt feelings, their response frequently is to get angry, and to blame the other for stimulating such feelings in them. They sleep and eat poorly and life holds little pleasure. A common fantasy during this period is of starting life over with a new name and identity.

4. The Hopeless Phase. Some gamblers progress to a fourth phase which begins with the realization that they cannot get even. They will never catch up, but they no longer care. They keep gambling, although they will say that they often know in advance they will lose. Their sloppy play, even when they have the right horse or the winning hand, serves to guarantee it. They insist that just playing is all that matters. They want the action or excitement for its own sake. Like the laboratory animal with electrodes implanted in its pleasure center, they gamble to the point of exhaustion.

In phases three and four, there is an increase in shame, guilt, and depression. Twelve to fourteen percent of all pathological gamblers will make gambling-related suicide attempts (Frank, Lester & Wexler, 1991; Petry & Kiluk, 2002). Stress-related physical illnesses are also common (Lorenz & Yaffee, 1988). There is a possibility the gambler will seek help, or that friends, family or employer will intervene. There is also the possibility they will get caught and face incarceration.

PATHOLOGICAL GAMBLERS AND CRIMINAL ACTIVITY

Studies have revealed a wide variety of illegal behaviors among pathological gamblers. Livingston (1974) found them involved in check forgery, embezzlement and employee theft, larceny, armed robbery, bookmaking, hustling, running con games, and fencing stolen goods. Lesieur (1977) uncovered these patterns as well, and also found gamblers engaged in systematic loan fraud, tax evasion, burglary, pimping, prostitution, drug dealing, and hustling at pool, golf, bowling, cards, and dice. He found that pathological gamblers first employ legal avenues for funding. As involvement in gambling intensifies, legal options dwindle, and gamblers seek money through increasingly serious illegal activity. For some, the amount of money runs into the millions of dollars. Larceny, embezzlement, forgery, and fraud are the most common offenses among pathological gamblers (Blaszczynski & McConaghy, 1992; Brown, 1987; Lesieur, 1977; Lesieur & Blume, 1991a). Pathological gambling-related crime has been uncovered in research done in Australia, Germany, and Scotland (Brown, 1987; Blaszczynski & McConaghy, 1992; Meyer & Fabian, 1992) as well as in the U.S. All of the studies report that pathological gambling is associated with income-generating crime and only rarely with violent crime.

Lorenz (1988) has observed that it is not only rare for the gambler to use a weapon in the commission of a crime, but that when he or she does so, it is likely to be a plastic or wooden gun, one that is unloaded, or without a firing pin or trigger. Regardless of the effectiveness of the weapon, the crime is usually punished as armed robbery. In addition to the bizarreness of some of these crimes (going to a bank in one's own neighborhood or writing the demand for money on a piece of paper with one's name and address on it), the gambler may be amnesic for what occurred, may describe confusion, altered perceptions or other features of dissociation.

A study of jailed arrestees found that 14.5 percent of Las Vegas and 9.2 percent of Des Moines arrestees were problem or pathological gamblers (McCorkle, 2002). Older and Caucasian arrestees had higher rates than younger (under 25) and nonwhite arrestees. Problem gamblers were more likely to have substance abuse and dependence problems than low-risk gamblers. Dual disordered arrestees were more likely to report having committed assaults, thefts, and drug sales in the past year.

Studies of prison populations in the United States, Great Britain, New Zealand, and Australia have found that 12 to 30 percent of the inmates are probable pathological gamblers (Abbott, 2002, June;

Jones, 1990; Kennedy & Grubin, 1990; Lesieur & Klein, 1985, April; Maden, Swinton & Gunn, 1992; Templer, Kaiser & Siscoe, 1993). Lesieur and Klein (1985, April), in a survey of 230 male and 118 female inmates, found that while 30 percent were probable pathological gamblers, 13 percent stated that gambling was either partially or totally related to why they were in prison.

Pathological gamblers in inpatient gambling treatment programs, in Gamblers Anonymous, and in prisons admit involvement in a wide range of illegal behaviors in order to finance their gambling activities or to pay gambling debts, but they vary in the types of crimes they commit (Lesieur, 1987). This difference appears to be based on socioeconomic variation among the samples. Whereas prisoners are more likely to have been unemployed, Gamblers Anonymous members and gamblers in inpatient programs are more likely to be involved in embezzlement, employee theft, tax evasion, and tax fraud—that is, in *white-collar crimes.* An exception to this pattern is the greater likelihood of forgery among female prisoners, with no significant difference among the other samples (Blaszczynski & McConaghy, 1992; Brown, 1987; Lesieur, 1987).

By contrast, prisoners are more likely to commit *commonplace crimes.* With the exception of larceny, all the financially motivated commonplace crimes—including burglary, robbery, pimping, selling drugs, and fencing stolen goods—are engaged in much more frequently by prisoners. In addition, female prisoners engage in prostitution at a greater rate than do female Gamblers Anonymous members. Selling drugs is more popular among the prisoners and hospital inpatients than among the GA members. Virtually all of the pathological gamblers who sell drugs to finance their gambling habit are either drug addicts or abusers (Lesieur & Klein, 1985, April).

A third cluster of crimes engaged in by pathological gamblers are *gambling-system-related crimes* such as bookmaking, writing numbers, and working in an illegal gambling setting. These are connected to pathological gambling in much the same way that selling drugs is related to drug addiction (Lesieur, 1977). Pathological gamblers are also heavily involved in gambling-related hustles and cons. Pool, bowling, and golf hustling, as well as card and dice cheating (also called hustling), are more likely to occur earlier in their careers. While engaging in these activities, pathological gamblers become embroiled in heavy wagering and losses at other forms of gambling. Pathological gambling hustlers move on to other crimes like bookmaking and con games due to increasing indebtedness.

For most gamblers, illegal acts are turned to out of desperation and occur late in the course of the disorder. In a detailed analysis of 50 cases, Lesieur (1977, 1979) described the sequence of events through which pathological gambling leads to criminal behavior. He outlined the "spiral of options and involvement" wherein legal avenues for funding are utilized until they are closed off. As the individual becomes more deeply involved in gambling, options are used up. The typical route into crime for the pathological gambler involves immense stress due to gambling losses, family pressures, and stresses at work. These combine to produce anxiety, depression, and cognitive distortions that impair judgment and decision-making. The gambler is so focused on the need for money in order to get out of trouble, that money is seen as the only possible solution to all of life's problems (Lesieur, 1977, 1979; Meyer & Fabian, 1992). At what point the gambler turns to illegal activities will depend on personal value systems, legitimate and illegitimate opportunities, perceptions of risk, the existence of threats (for example, loan sharks), and chance (Lesieur, 1977).

Meyer and Fabian (1992) found that pathological gamblers who committed crimes gambled more often, placed higher bets, and had greater debt. The delinquent group felt dependent upon gambling, suffered from sleep disorders, restlessness, irritability, sweating, nightmares, and headaches. The offenders displayed a high degree of psychosocial stress, and experienced more problems with partners, jobs, social contacts or leisure time possibilities.

Researchers found that of the pathological gamblers they studied, 14 percent met criteria for antisocial personality disorder (Blaszczynski & McConaghy, 1994; Blaszczynski, McConaghy & Frankova, 1989; Lesieur, 1987). However, the overwhelming majority of pathological gamblers who engage in illegal behavior do not exhibit this disorder. Crime for them is typically a response to the stresses produced by excessive gambling. Blaszczynski and McConaghy (1994) administered a structured interview to 109 pathological gamblers who were either seeking treatment or who were members of Gamblers Anonymous. They divided subjects into four groups: those who committed no offense (36.7%), those committing only gambling-related offenses (40.4%), those committing only nongambling offenses (9.2%), and those committing both gambling and nongambling offenses (13.7%).

The latter group was composed primarily of those of lower socioeconomic status and was most apt to be antisocial.

INVESTIGATING FINANCES

Because of the centrality of indebtedness, it is essential for the clinician or forensic expert to examine finances. The credit history and pattern of indebtedness need to be documented in as much detail as possible. This would include borrowing from friends, acquaintances, all possible relatives (including children); legitimate creditors (stores, banks, finance companies and credit unions, credit cards); borrowing at work (employer or employees, suppliers and wholesalers); gambling-setting borrowing (debts to casinos or card clubs, bookmakers, loan sharks, fellow gamblers); outstanding checks; borrowing under false pretenses; so-called "borrowing" from work. Forensic experts are advised to request physical evidence (bills, credit statements) whenever possible.

In asking one's questions it is imperative to be as concrete as possible. Most pathological gamblers will have a history of borrowing and repayment, in contrast with the antisocial pathological gambler who will have a repeated pattern of "borrowing" with little or no evidence of attempts to make repayment. Perhaps the greatest distinction is that the pathological gambler typically has a substantial credit history with an increasing degree of financial indebtedness over a period of time.

Illegal behavior patterns may be intermingled with borrowing and obtaining money legitimately. Regardless, it is not uncommon to see a pathological gambler borrow money from one source in order to pay another. For example, a credit card loan may be used to put back embezzled money or cover bad checks.

PATHOLOGICAL GAMBLING AS A DEFENSE

After the American Psychiatric Association (1980) recognized pathological gambling as a disorder of impulse control, there were numerous cases in which it was used as the basis for an insanity defense (McGarry, 1983). There were several acquittals and hung juries, but these went mostly unreported. Rose (1988) explained that:

Defense attorneys are often more flexible than their prosecutorial counterparts in creating new legal doctrines and in utilizing expert witnesses. Ultimately, the enormous resources of the prosecution will even out the fight, once the government bureaucracy has grasped the new rules of battle. It is thus not surprising that the first few cases led to victories by the defense . . . nor that the prosecutors have now learned how to refute this new defense strategy. (p. 243)

The issue of relevance then became the important question of law. An individual may or may not be able to control his or her impulse to gamble but that should have no bearing on an impulse to steal or commit other crimes. In a series of cases involving pathological gamblers, the doctrine was established for each crime and in each district (Burglass, 1989; Rose, 1988). The disorder could no longer serve as the basis of a defense to a nongambling offense.

Pathological gambling is now being raised as a mitigating circumstance in the argument for a less severe punishment. Particularly when the court believes in rehabilitation, some combination of treatment, restitution, community service, and probation offers an alternative to prison. This is consistent with the position of responsible therapists that restitution and assumption of responsibility by the gambler are integral aspects of recovery (Rosenthal & Lorenz, 1992). In our experience, once they stop gambling, pathological gamblers are often hardworking individuals who, because of their energy, competitiveness, need to excel, and compulsive work habits, are often capable of restitution and of making valuable contributions to their community.

In Amherst, New York, a new "gambling court" has been established (Farrell, 2005, May). Modeled on drug courts, the premise is that therapeutic justice can occur. The defendant is arraigned on formal charges. The judge requests an evaluation when there is an indication of problem gambling. An initial assessment is completed in two to seven days and a full assessment is completed within two weeks. Plea negotiations between defense and the prosecutor result in diversion to Gambling Court if appropriate. The defendant begins an individualized, contractual, judicially monitored, gambling recovery program. The defendant is regularly monitored and subjected to sanctions in the event of failure to comply with the contract.

With regard to the Federal Guidelines, courts have taken two conflicting approaches with regard to a downward departure for pathological gambling (Lorenz & Rose, 2003, May). Under the strict rule, only illegal gambling would be eligible for downward departure.

Alternatively, departure may be warranted if a defendant can show that there was a "significantly impaired ability to control behavior that the defendant knows is wrongful." The first interpretation comes from the failure of the Sentencing Commission to specifically mention pathological gambling in the guidelines. The second interpretation comes from an "Application Note" defining "significantly reduced mental capacity."

Because many judges are unfamiliar with pathological gambling, in making an argument for mitigation the expert's principal task is often to educate about the nature of the disorder. Several features need to be outlined: the prevalence of the problem in the general population; the addictive features of the disorder; the progression through the four phases; and the distinction between financial problems and gambling problems. The ego-syntonic (acceptable, compatible) nature of the disorder in its early phases needs to be contrasted with the ego-dystonic (alien, compulsive) features as it progresses.

PRISON AND THE PATHOLOGICAL GAMBLER

It has been our experience that many judges do not have an accurate perception of the vast amount of gambling that goes on in prisons. As one pathological gambler/offender (Jarvis, 1988) wrote from prison: "There is just as much gambling here as can be found in Las Vegas. Bookies here will let you bet on anything and poker games are plentiful. I myself ran a football parlay while at another prison, and I played poker every day. . . . Gambling is against the rules here and in other prisons, but it is not enforced." In fact, correctional officials sometimes participate in these enterprises, even acting as bookies. In prison, the medium of exchange is different. Instead of money, prisoners gamble for cigarettes, coffee, food, services, and sexual favors. They may also gamble for money, with visitors making exchanges among bank accounts on the outside.

Given the high rate of pathological gamblers among prison populations, one would expect to find Gamblers Anonymous meetings. There are very few (less than a dozen in the United States) and a dearth of professional help. Where professional help exists, it is sometimes part of a substance abuse program. Gambling-specific training among these professionals is rare.

DIAGNOSTIC AND SCREENING INSTRUMENTS

The only way to make a diagnosis of pathological gambling is with the *DSM–IV* criteria. Five or more of ten items need to be present; most gamblers who present for treatment will meet at least eight. The items include the preoccupation with gambling and with getting money with which to gamble; tolerance; loss of control; withdrawal; gambling to escape from problems and intolerable feelings; chasing behavior; lying to conceal the extent of the gambling; illegal activities due to gambling; having jeopardized or lost a significant relationship, school or vocational opportunity; and the presence of a bailout.

Unlike previous sets of criteria, the emphasis is not just on losing money; the criteria are multidimensional, and include loss of control, dependence, and disruption. The criteria were thoroughly tested beforehand, and should be easy to use. Difficulty will most likely be encountered when there is a lot of denial or when the individual is lying. In such cases, it is extremely useful to talk to family members or, if conducting a forensic evaluation, to speak with the attorney and review records prior to seeing the individual. Some clinicians particularly like having as much information beforehand, so that they will be asking questions to which they already know the answer, and can tell when the person is being less than truthful. Of course, as in all evaluations, the more cooperative the individual and the better the rapport, the more reliable the information one will be getting.

The South Oaks Gambling Screen, a 20-item test, is the most useful of the screening instruments. Its validity and reliability have been field tested (Lesieur & Blume, 1987, 1993) in a variety of clinical settings (therapeutic communities, psychiatric outpatient clinics, alcohol and drug rehabilitation programs), and it has been translated into 38 languages. It may be used either in an assessment interview or as a paper and pencil test. The SOGS has been used in a group setting following a gambling-related lecture or film, as well as on a "blind" basis. Given the ease of application, it is readily translatable to a wide variety of clinical and epidemiological settings, including telephone, interview, and questionnaire-type studies (see Lesieur & Blume, 1993).

TREATMENT

Most treatment professionals rely on Gamblers Anonymous as a resource, in addition to whatever form of treatment they provide. There are over 1,600 chapters of GA in this country.[1] Gam-Anon[2] meetings, which traditionally have been held at the same time as GA meetings and in a nearby room, are available for the spouse and family members. GA is based on the twelve steps and twelve traditions of Alcoholics Anonymous (AA). However, there are some changes in the wording of the GA steps that suggest a decreased emphasis on a higher power (Lesieur, 1990; Browne, 1994, June). Additionally, the fourth step includes a financial as well as a moral inventory, reflecting the gambler's need to cope with financial problems. GA also offers the opportunity for a "pressure relief" session, in which the newcomer and his or her spouse or sometimes their parents meet with several GA members who have been in the organization for a long time. The gambler is encouraged to uncover hidden financial indebtedness and to create a financial plan for the future. Typically scheduled a month after one starts in the program, the pressure relief session can be more beneficial than traditional debt counseling.

GA is not as available a resource as AA. In only a few cities can one find daily meetings, and it is not uncommon for someone to have to drive great distances to attend a meeting. There are also fewer types of meetings. One cannot count on there being meetings for young people, women, people from different ethnic backgrounds or who do not speak English. Sponsorship is also not as prevalent or as structured in most GA communities as it is in AA.

Not all problem gamblers need treatment. Some quit gambling without the aid of Gamblers Anonymous or professional treatment. Research by Hodgins and el-Guebaly (2000) has demonstrated that these individuals tend to have less serious problems than those who have gone through treatment programs.

Treatment providers favor stepped-up levels of care, depending upon the individual needs of the gambler based on presenting prob-

---

[1] Gamblers Anonymous, National Service Office, P.O. Box 17173, Los Angeles, CA 90017. Tel: (213) 386-8789. See their website at www.gamblersanonymous.org.
[2] Gam-Anon, International Service Office, P.O. Box 157, Whitestone, NY 11357. Tel: (718) 352-1671. See their website at www.gam-anon.org.

lems, gambling severity, environmental support, and personality characteristics. Therapy should be the least intensive that is likely to be effective in addressing the gambler's problems, with more intensive levels of care reserved for more severe problems. Thus, we find that some gamblers will benefit from brief interventions, self-help manuals or the use of Internet-based programs. Hodgins, Currie, and el-Guebaly (2001) compared a self-help manual with a brief motivational enhancement intervention. While the self-help manual worked better than no treatment, it was more effective if used in combination with the motivational enhancement. Online assistance (Cooper, 2003) has been found useful because it reduces the stigma attached to having a gambling problem.

Treatment programs are primarily psychodynamic, cognitive behavioral, pharmacological, addiction-based, or self-help (National Research Council, 1999). Often these methods are combined. For example, Rosenthal and Rugle (1994) integrate a traditional psychodynamic approach with an addictions model. Understanding the positive aspects of gambling for the individual, in other words what he or she gets out of it, helps to clarify its defensive and adaptive purpose. Gambling may be used to avoid or escape an intolerable feeling or situation, or to help medicate problems in self-regulation. An emphasis in therapy on the meaning and consequences of one's behavior is similarly applied to chasing, triggers for one's gambling urges, covert ways of staying in action (Rosenthal, 2005), and fluctuations in self-esteem. There are no randomized or controlled studies of the effectiveness of psychodynamic treatment for pathological gamblers, either in its pure form or when combined with other approaches, although a number of authors have noted the value of psychodynamic psychotherapy for addictive behaviors (Kaufman, 1994; Khantzian, 1981; Shaffer, 1995; Wurmser, 1978).

Clinicians and researchers have emphasized the cognitive distortions and irrational beliefs held by problem and pathological gamblers (Blaszczynski & Silove, 1995; Gaboury & Ladouceur, 1989; Walker, 1992). Cognitive behavior therapy aims to counteract these attitudes and beliefs by teaching concepts of probability and randomness, and by correcting superstitious thinking and the illusion of control held by the gambler. Gamblers are taught strategies for correcting their erroneous thinking (Ladouceur et al., 2002). Studies have demonstrated the effectiveness of individually conducted cognitive-behavioral therapy (Ladouceur et al., 2002; Sylvain, Ladouceur & Boisvert, 1997). Evidence suggests that combining cognitive behavior therapy with Gamblers Anonymous is more effective than either alone (Petry, 2005). The addition of a relapse prevention component adds to effectiveness (Echeburia, Fernandez-Montalvo & Baez, 2000).

Inpatient treatment is not available in most parts of the U.S. Where available, it should be considered when the individual is unable to stop gambling, lacks sufficient support from family and others, is multiply addicted or has significant comorbid pathology, is physically or emotionally exhausted, severely depressed, suicidal or contemplating some dangerous activity. The handful of programs that exist tend to be in private hospitals or run by the Veterans Administration. The oldest of these, at the Brecksville, Ohio Veterans Hospital, has been in continuous existence since 1972.

For the most part, inpatient gambling treatment programs follow an eclectic (Taber & McCormick, 1987) or disease model (Blume, 1986), with educational lectures and videos; the use of peer counselors; a combination of individual, group and family therapy; involvement in GA; relapse prevention; and aftercare planning. Relapse prevention includes knowledge of specific triggers, responsibility in avoiding slippery situations, tools and techniques for dealing with urges. Programs may also offer relaxation and assertiveness training, vocational counseling, and the teaching of social skills. Although there are many similarities with the treatment of alcohol and substance dependence, there are also important differences.

As we described earlier, multiple addictions may occur simultaneously or sequentially. When not addressed, they pose a risk for relapse just as the recovering alcoholic who starts to gamble is put at risk. Studies of Gamblers Anonymous members (Linden, Pope & Jonas, 1986), VA inpatients (Ramirez, McCormick, Russo & Taber, 1983), female gamblers (Lesieur & Blume, 1991a), and private outpatients (Rosenthal, 1989, November) reveal that approximately 50 percent of pathological gamblers have or have had problems with substance abuse or dependence. There is variability as to which is primary and the level of difficulty in obtaining and maintaining abstinence. One study of a combined pathological gambling-chemical dependency treatment program (Lesieur & Blume, 1991b) found that both disorders could be treated simultaneously with equal effectiveness. However, there appears to be no relationship between success in treatment for pathological gambling and the existence of prior substance abuse treatment (Stinchfield, Kushner & Winters, 2005).

Other comorbid disorders for which there is a high incidence in treatment seeking pathological gamblers are mood disorders (depression, bipolar disorder), attention deficit hyperactivity disorder, and personality disorders (narcissistic or antisocial in men, avoidant or dependent in women) (Rosenthal, 2004). These may be considered subtypes, especially with regard to treatment indications, but it is important not to diagnose too quickly. In the first weeks following cessation of gambling, one sees denial, detachment, depression, and emotional numbing, and conversely, emotional lability. Withdrawal symptoms have been described (see above) and there may be cognitive changes. There are no data on how long such changes might last. Gambling may exacerbate any of the above disorders, just as it may be secondary to one of them.

Pharmacotherapy research for pathological gambling is in its infancy. To date there have been about 18 clinical trials; these have involved serotonin reuptake inhibitors, mood stabilizers, and opioid antagonists (see review by Rosenthal, 2004). The clearest indication for using medication is for the treatment of comorbid disorders, primarily depression, bipolar disorder, and attention deficit hyperactivity disorder. Medication may also be used to treat specific symptoms, traits, or symptom clusters; to make negative affects more tolerable; and to reduce cravings. Future approaches will be directed at subgroups of gamblers.

Family therapy is often essential. As is common with addictive disorders, family members may resort to a host of inappropriate behaviors that interfere with, or even prevent, recovery (Grodsky & Kogan, 1985; Heineman, 1987, 1989; Lorenz, 1989). Family members have incurred their own illnesses and need treatment (Lorenz & Yaffee, 1988, 1989). Because a relapse is harder to recognize (no substance to be smelled on the gambler's breath, no slurred speech, or staggered gait) and because the potential for damage to family finances is great, the spouse and other family members tend to hold on to their anger and mistrust for a long time. Family sessions offer an opportunity to make amends, to learn communication skills, and to deal with preexisting intimacy problems.

OUTREACH TO THE PROBLEM GAMBLER

Presently, 23 of the 50 states provide some financial support for education, treatment or research into pathological gambling. The amount of money involved tends to be quite small, ranging from $20,000 (to fund a hotline in Maryland) to $5 million (in Iowa). In some states, the lottery partially funds advertisements, helplines, and other services. Some Indian tribes and casinos also provide support.

Currently there are toll-free helplines in 28 of the 50 states and a nationwide helpline run by the National Council on Problem Gambling. The National Council and its 34 state affiliates serve as referral and information sources on problem gambling.[3] They also conduct training programs, support a national certification program for gambling counselors, and put on an annual conference for treatment professionals.

REFERENCES

Abbott, M. (2002, June). Problem gambling in prisons: How common? What can be done to help? Paper presented at the 16th Annual Conference on Problem Gambling, sponsored by the National Council on Problem Gambling, Dallas, Texas.

American Psychiatric Association (1980). *Diagnostic and Statistical Manual of Mental Disorders, Third Edition.* Washington, D.C.: American Psychiatric Association.

American Psychiatric Association (2000). *Diagnostic and Statistical Manual of Mental Disorders, Fourth Edition, Text Revision.* Washington, D.C.: American Psychiatric Association.

Blaszczynski, A., & McConaghy, N. (1992). *Pathological Gambling and Criminal Behaviour.* Report to the Criminology Research Council, Canberra, Australia.

Blaszczynski, A. P. & McConaghy, N. (1994). Antisocial personality disorder and pathological gambling. *Journal of Gambling Studies, 10*(2), 129.

Blaszczynski, A., McConaghy, N., & Frankova, A. (1989). Crime, antisocial personality and pathological gambling. *Journal of Gambling Behavior, 5*(2), 137.

Blaszczynski, A., & Silove, D. (1995). Cognitive and behavioral therapies for pathological gambling. *Journal of Gambling Studies, 11*(2), 195.

Blume, S. B. (1986). Treatment for the addictions: Alcoholism, drug dependence and compulsive gambling in a psychiatric setting. *Journal of Substance Abuse Treatment, 3*, 131.

Bolen, D. W., & Boyd, W. (1968). Gambling and the gambler: A review and preliminary findings. *Archives of General Psychiatry, 18*, 617.

Boyd, W., & Bolen, D. W. (1970). The compulsive gambler and spouse in group psychotherapy. *International Journal of Group Psychotherapy, 20*, 77.

---

[3] National Council on Problem Gambling, 216 G Street, N.E., Suite 200, Washington, DC 20002. Tel: (800) 522-4700. See their website at www.ncpgambling.org.

Breen, R. B. (2004). Rapid onset of pathological gambling in machine gamblers: A replication. *eCommunity: International Journal of Mental Health and Addiction*, *2*(1), 44. Available at: http://www.pasinfo.net.

Breen, R. B., & Zimmerman, M. (2002). Rapid onset of pathological gambling in machine players. *Journal of Gambling Studies*, *18*(1), 31.

Brown, R. I. F. (1987). Pathological gambling and associated patterns of crime: Comparison with alcohol and other drug addictions. *Journal of Gambling Behavior*, *3*(2), 98.

Brown, R. I. F. (1994, June). Disassociation phenomena among addicted gamblers. Presented at the Ninth International Conference on Gambling and Risk Taking, Las Vegas, NV.

Brown, R. I. F. (1996, August). Dissociation phenomena among normal and addicted gamblers. Presented at the Second European Conference on Gambling and Policy Issues, Amsterdam, The Netherlands.

Browne, B. R. (1994). Really not God: Secularization and pragmatism in Gamblers Anonymous. *Journal of Gambling Studies*, *10*, 247.

Burglass, M. E. (1989). Compulsive gambling: Forensic update and commentary. In H. J. Shaffer, S. A. Stein, B. Gambino, & T. Cummings (Eds.) *Compulsive Gambling: Theory, Research, and Practice* (pp. 205–222). Lexington, MA: Lexington Books.

Catlin, G. (1857). *Illustrations of the Manners, Customs, and Conditions of the North American Indians*. Vol. 1. London: Henry G. Bohn.

Chambliss, W. J. (1964). A sociological analysis of the law of vagrancy. *Social Problems*, *12*, 67.

Comings, D. E., & Blum, K. (2000). Reward deficiency syndrome: Genetic aspects of behavioral disorders. *Progress in Brain Research*, *126*, 325.

Comings, D. E., Gade-Andavolu, R., Gonzalez, N., Wu, S., Muhleman, D., Chen, C., Koh, P., Farwell, K., Blake, H., Dietz, G., MacMurray, J. P., Lesieur, H. R., Rugle, L. J., & Rosenthal, R. J. (2001). The additive effect of neurotransmitter genes in pathological gambling. *Clinical Genetics*, *60*, 107.

Comings, D., Rosenthal, R. J., Lesieur, H. R., Rugle, L., Muhleman, D., Chiu, C., Dietz, G., & Gade, R. (1996). A study of the dopamine D2 receptor gene in pathological gambling. *Pharmacogenetics*, *6*, 223.

Cooper, G. (2003). Exploring and understanding online assistance for problem gamblers: The pathways disclosure model. *eCommunity: International Journal of Mental Health and Addiction*, 1, 2. Available: http://www.pasinfo.net/journal/v1i2a04article.html

Custer, R. L. (1982a). An overview of compulsive gambling. In P. A. Carone, S. F. Yoles, S. N. Kiefer, & L. Krinsky (Eds.) *Addictive Disorders Update: Alcoholism, Drug Abuse, Gambling*. New York: Human Sciences Press.

Custer, R. L. (1982b). Gambling and addiction. In R. J. Craig, & S. L. Baker (Eds.) *Drug Dependent Patients: Treatment and Research* (pp. 367–381). Springfield, IL: Charles C Thomas.

Custer, R. L., & Milt, H. (1985). *When luck runs out*. New York: Facts on File Publications.

Diskin, K. M., & Hodgins, D. C. (1999). Narrowing of attention and dissociation in pathological video lottery gamblers. *Journal of Gambling Studies*, *15*(1), 17.

Echeburia, E., Fernandez-Montalvo, J., & Baez, C. (2000). Relapse prevention in the treatment of slot-machine pathological gambling: Long-term outcome. *Behavior Therapy*, *31*, 351.

Erikson, E. H. (1943). *Observations on the Yurok: Childhood and world image*. Berkeley: University of California Press.

Farrell, M. G. (2005, May). The gambling treatment court experience. Presented to the Florida Think Tank on Problem Gambling and Crime: Impact and Solutions, Orlando, Florida.

Feigelman, W., Wallisch, L., & Lesieur, H. R. (1998). Problem gamblers, problem substance users, and dual-problem individuals: An epidemiological study. *American Journal of Public Health, 88,* 467.

Forsyth, T. (1948). *The Bella Coola Indians.* Vol. 1. Toronto: University of Toronto Press.

Frank, M. L., Lester, D., & Wexler, A. (1991). Suicidal behavior among members of Gamblers Anonymous. *Journal of Gambling Studies, 7*(3), 249.

Gaboury, A., & Ladouceur, R. (1989). Erroneous perceptions and gambling. *Journal of Social Behavior and Personality, 4,* 411.

Gerstein, D., Hoffman, J., Larison, C., Murphy, S., Palmer, A., Chuchro, L., Toce, M., Johnson, R., Buie, T., Hill, M. A., Volberg, R., Harwood, H., Tucker, A., Christiansen, E., Cummings, W., & Sinclair, S. (1999). *Gambling Impact and Behavior Study.* Report to the National Gambling Impact Study Commission.

Glare, P. G. W. (1982). *Oxford Latin Dictionary.* Oxford, England: Clarendon Press.

Grodsky, P. B., & Kogan, L. S. (1985). Does the client have a gambling problem? *Journal of Gambling Behavior, 1,* 51.

Hayano, D. M. (1982). *Poker faces: The life and work of professional card players.* Berkeley, CA: University of California Press.

Heineman, M. (1987). A comparison: The treatment of wives of alcoholics with the treatment of wives of pathological gamblers. *Journal of Gambling Behavior, 3*(1), 27–40.

Heineman, M. (1989). Parents of male compulsive gamblers: Clinical issues/treatment approaches. *Journal of Gambling Behavior, 5*(4), 321.

Hodgins, D. C., Currie, S. R., & el-Guebaly, N. (2001). Motivational enhancement and self-help treatments for problem gambling. *Journal of Consulting and Clinical Psychology, 69,* 50.

Hodgins, D. C., & el-Guebaly, N. (2000). Natural and treatment-assisted recovery from gambling problems: A comparison of resolved and active gamblers. *Addiction, 95*(5), 777.

Jacobs, D. F. (1986). A general theory of addictions: A new theoretical model. *Journal of Gambling Behavior, 2*(1), 15.

Jacobs, D. F. (1988). Evidence for a common dissociative-like reaction among addicts. *Journal of Gambling Behavior, 4*(1), 27.

Jarvis, J. (1988). From the view of a compulsive gambler/recidivist. *Journal of Gambling Behavior, 4*(4), 316.

Jones, G. (1990). Prison gambling. *The National Association for Gambling Studies* [Newsletter], *2,* 5.

Kaufman, E. (1994). *Psychotherapy of addicted persons.* New York: Guilford Press.

Kennedy, H. G., & Grubin, D. H. (1990). Hot-headed or impulsive? *British Journal of Addiction, 85,* 639.

Khantzian, E. J. (1981). Some treatment implications of the ego and self disturbances in alcoholism. In M. H. Bean, E. J. Khantzian, J. E. Mack, G. E. Vaillant, & N. E. Zinberg (Eds.) *Dynamic approaches to the understanding and treatment of alcoholism* (pp. 163–188). New York: Free Press.

Kofoed, L., Morgan, T. J., Buchkowski, J., & Carr, R. (1997). Dissociative experiences scale and MMPI-2 scores in video poker gamblers, other gamblers, and alcoholic controls. *Journal of Nervous and Mental Disease, 185*(1), 58.

Kuley, N. B., & Jacobs, D. F. (1988). The relationship between dissociative-like experiences and sensation seeking among social and problem gamblers. *Journal of Gambling Behavior, 4*(3), 197.

Ladouceur, R., Sylvain, C., Boutin, C., & Doucet, C. (2002). *Understanding and treating the pathological gambler.* New York: John Wiley.

Lesieur, H. R. (1977). *The chase: Career of the compulsive gambler.* Garden City, New York: Anchor Books. Rpt. by Schenkman Books: Rochester, VT, 1984.

Lesieur, H. R. (1979). The compulsive gambler's spiral of options and involvement. *Psychiatry*, *42*(1), 79.

Lesieur, H. R. (1987). Gambling, pathological gambling and crime. In T. Galski (Ed.). *The handbook of pathological gambling* (pp. 89–110). Springfield, IL: Charles C Thomas.

Lesieur, H. R. (1990). Working with and understanding Gamblers Anonymous. In T. J. Powell (Ed.) *Working with self-help* (pp. 237–253). Silver Spring, Maryland: NASW Press.

Lesieur, H. R., & Blume, S. B. (1987). The South Oaks Gambling Screen (The SOGS): A new instrument for the identification of pathological gamblers. *American Journal of Psychiatry*, *144*, 1184.

Lesieur, H. R., & Blume, S. B. (1991a). When Lady Luck loses: The female pathological gambler. In Nan van den Bergh (Ed.) *Feminist perspectives on addictions*. New York: Springer Publications.

Lesieur, H. R., & Blume, S. B. (1991b). Evaluation of patients treated for pathological gambling in a combined alcohol, substance abuse and pathological gambling treatment unit using the Addiction Severity Index. *British Journal of Addiction*, *86*, 1017.

Lesieur, H. R., & Blume, S. B. (1993). Revising the South Oaks Gambling Screen. *Journal of Gambling Studies*, *9*(3), 213.

Lesieur, H. R., Blume, S. B., & Zoppa, R. (1986). Alcoholism, drug abuse and gambling. *Alcoholism: Clinical and Experimental Research*, *10*, 33.

Lesieur, H. R., & Heineman, M. (1988). Pathological gambling among multiple substance abusers in a therapeutic community. *British Journal of Addiction*, *83*, 765.

Lesieur, H. R., & Klein, R. (1985, April). Prisoners, gambling and crime. Paper presented at Academy of Criminal Justice Sciences Annual Meetings, Las Vegas, Nevada.

Lesieur, H. R., & Mark, M. (1993). *Women Who Gamble Too Much* (pamphlet). New York: National Council on Problem Gambling.

Lesieur, H. R., & Rosenthal, R. J. (1995, August). Self-reported physiological and dissociative experiences among pathological gamblers. Presented at the First European Conference on Gambling and Policy Issues, Cambridge, England.

Lesieur, H. R., & Rosenthal, R. J. (1998). Analysis of pathological gambling for the Task Force on *DSM-IV*. In T. A. Widiger, A. Frances, H. Pincus,& R. Ross (Eds.) *Source Book for the Diagnostic and Statistical Manual, Fourth Edition*. Vol. 4 (pp. 393–401. Washington, D.C.: American Psychiatric Press.

Linden, R. D., Pope, H. G., & Jonas, J. M. (1986). Pathological gambling and major affective disorder: Preliminary findings. *Journal of Clinical Psychiatry*, *47*, 201.

Livingston, J. (1974). *Compulsive gamblers: Observations on action and abstinence*. New York: Harper Torchbooks.

Lorenz, V. C. (1988). On being an expert witness for the compulsive gambler facing legal charges. *Journal of Gambling Behavior*, *4*(4), 320.

Lorenz, V. C. (1989). Some treatment approaches for family members who jeopardize the compulsive gambler's recovery. *Journal of Gambling Behavior*, *5*(4), 303.

Lorenz, V. C., & Rose, I. N. (2003, May). Using the compulsive gambling ïactionï inventory: An argument for downward departure. Presented at the Twelfth International Conference on Gambling and Risk Taking, Vancouver, British Columbia.

Lorenz, V. C., & Yaffee, R. A. (1986). Pathological gambling: Psychosomatic, emotional and marital difficulties as reported by the gambler. *Journal of Gambling Behavior*, *2*(1), 40.

Lorenz, V. C., & Yaffee, R. A. (1988). Pathological gambling: Psychosomatic, emotional and marital difficulties as reported by the spouse. *Journal of Gambling Behavior*, *4*(1), 13.

Lorenz, V. C., & Yaffee, R. A. (1989). Pathological gamblers and their spouses: Problems in interaction. *Journal of Gambling Behavior*, *5*(2), 113.

Maden, T., Swinton, M., & Gunn, J. (1992). Gambling in young offenders. *Criminal Behaviour and Mental Health, 2*, 300.

McCorkle, R. C. (2002). *Pathological Gambling in Arrested Populations.* Final report prepared for the National Institute of Justice. U.S. Department of Justice Grant #1999 IJ-CX-K011.

McGarry, A. L. (1983). Pathological gambling: A new insanity defense. *Bulletin of the American Academy of Psychiatry and the Law, 11*, 301.

Messerlian, C., Byrne, A. M., & Derevensky, J. L. (2004). Gambling, youth and the Internet: Should we be concerned? *Canadian Child and Adolescent Psychiatric Review, 13*(1), 3.

Meyer, G. (1989). *Glucksspieler in Selbsthilfegruppen: Erste Ergebnisse einer empirischen Untersuchung.* Hamburg: Neuland.

Meyer, G., & Fabian, T. (1992). Delinquency among pathological gamblers: A causal approach. *Journal of Gambling Studies, 8*(1), 61.

Morehead, A. H. (1950). The professional gambler. *The Annals of the American Academy of Political and Social Sciences, 269*, 81.

National Research Council (1999). *Pathological gambling: A critical review.* Washington, DC: National Academy Press.

O'Donnell, R. (1996). Gambling severity and dissociation in a group of inpatient gamblers. Presented at the Tenth National Conference on Gambling Behavior, Chicago, IL.

O'Donnell, R. & Harvey, F. (1993, July). Dissociation in a group of inpatient pathological gamblers. Presented at the Seventh National Conference on Gambling Behavior, New London, Connecticut.

Petry, N. (2005). Gamblers Anonymous and cognitive behavioral therapies for pathological gamblers. *Journal of Gambling Studies, 21*(1), 27. Available: www.springeronline.com/sgw/cda/frontpage/0,11855,4-40109-70-35680327-0,00.html

Petry, N. M., & Kiluk, B. D. (2002). Suicidal ideation and suicide attempts in treatment-seeking pathological gamblers. *Journal of Nervous and Mental Disease, 190*(7), 462.

Prus, R. C., & Sharper, C. R. D. (1977). *Road hustler: The career contingencies of professional card and dice hustlers.* Lexington, MA.: Lexington Books.

Ramirez, L. F., McCormick, R. A., Russo, A. M., & Taber, J. I. (1984). Patterns of substance abuse in pathological gamblers undergoing treatment. *Addictive Behaviors, 8*, 425.

Romer, D. (2005, September 28). Card playing trend in young people continues. Annenberg Public Policy Center of the University of Pennsylvania. *2005 National Annenberg Risk Survey of Youth (NARSY).* Available: www.annenbergpublicpolicycenter.org

Rose, I. N. (1988). Compulsive gambling and the law: From sin to vice to disease. *Journal of Gambling Behavior, 4*(4), 240.

Rosenthal, R. J. (1986). The pathological gambler's system of self-deception. *Journal of Gambling Behavior, 2*(2), 108.

Rosenthal, R. J. (1987). The psychodynamics of pathological gambling: A review of the literature. In T. Galski (Ed.) *The handbook of pathological gambling* (pp. 41–70). Springfield, IL: Charles C Thomas. Rpt. in D. L. Yalisove (Ed.) *Essential papers on addiction* (pp. 184–212). New York and London: New York University Press, 1997.

Rosenthal, R .J. (1989). Pathological gambling and problem gambling: Problems in definition and diagnosis. In H. Shaffer, S. A. Stein, B. Gambino, & T. N. Cummings (Eds.) *Compulsive gambling: Theory, research and practice* (pp. 101–125). Lexington, MA: Lexington Books.

Rosenthal, R. J. (1989, November). Compulsive gambling. Presented to the California Society for the Treatment of Alcoholism and Other Drug Dependencies, San Diego.

Rosenthal, R. J. (1990, August). The psychological basis for chasing. Presented at the Eighth International Conference on Risk and Gambling, London.

Rosenthal, R. J. (1992). Pathological gambling. *Psychiatric Annals, 22*, 72.

Rosenthal, R. J. (2004). The role of medication in the treatment of pathological gambling: Bridging the gap between research and practice. *eGambling: The Electronic Journal of Gambling Issues*, 10(February), [Online]. Available: http://www.camh.net/egambling/issue 10/ejgi_10_rosenthal/html

Rosenthal, R. J. (2005). Staying in action: The pathological gambler's equivalent of the dry drunk. *Journal of Gambling Issues: eGambling*, 13 March [Online]. Available: http://www.camh.net/egambling/issue13jgi_13_rosenthal.html

Rosenthal, R. J., & Lesieur, H. R. (1992). Self-reported withdrawal symptoms and pathological gambling. *American Journal on Addictions*, 1, 150.

Rosenthal, R. J., & Lorenz, V. C. (1992). The pathological gambler as criminal offender. *Psychiatric Clinics of North America*, 15, 647.

Rosenthal, R. J., & Rugle, L. J. (1994). A psychodynamic approach to the treatment of pathological gambling: Part I. Achieving abstinence. *Journal of Gambling Studies*, 10(1), 21.

Shaffer, H. J. (1995). Denial, ambivalence and countertransference hate. In J. D. Levin, & R. Weiss (Eds.) *Alcoholism: Dynamics and treatment*. Northdale, NJ: Jason Aronson.

Steinberg, M. A., Kosten, T. A., & Rounsaville, B. J. (1992). Cocaine abuse and pathological gambling. *American Journal on Addictions*, 1, 121.

Stinchfield, R., Kushner, M. G., & Winters, K. (2005). Alcohol use and prior substance abuse treatment in relation to gambling problem severity and gambling treatment outcomes. *Journal of Gambling Studies*, 21, 273.

Sylvain, C., Ladouceur, R., & Boisvert, J. M. (1997). Cognitive and behavioral treatment of pathological gambling: A controlled study. *Journal of Consulting and Clinical Psychology*, 65, 727.

Taber, J. I., & McCormick, R. A. (1987). The pathological gambler in treatment. In T. Galski (Ed.) *The handbook of pathological gambling* (pp. 137–168). Springfield, IL: Charles C Thomas.

Templer, D., Kaiser, G., & Siscoe, K. (1993). Correlates of pathological gambling propensity in prison inmates. *Comprehensive Psychiatry*, 34(5), 347.

Walker, M. B. (1992). *The psychology of gambling*. Oxford: Pergamon Press.

Watkins, C. (1985). *American Heritage Dictionary of Indo-European Roots*. Boston: Houghton Mifflin.

Welte, J., Barnes, G., Wieczorek, W., Tidwell, M. C., & Parker, J. (2001). Alcohol and gambling pathology among U.S. adults: Prevalence, demographic patterns and comorbidity. *Journal of Studies on Alcohol*, 62(5), 706.

Wissowa, G. (1984). *Paulys Real-Encyclopadie der Classischen Altertumswissenschaft*. Stuttgart, Germany: Metzler.

Wray I., & Dickerson, M. (1981). Cessation of high frequency gambling and 'withdrawal' symptoms. *British Journal of Addiction*, 76, 401.

Wurmser, L. (1978). *The hidden dimension: Psychodynamics of compulsive drug use*. New York: Jason Aronson.

Wykes, A. (1964). *The complete illustrated guide to gambling*. Garden City, NY: Doubleday.

Chapter 3

IDIOSYNCRATIC ALCOHOL INTOXICATION (Revisited): A CONSTRUCT THAT HAS LOST ITS VALIDITY (Still)?

Robert J. Pandina

When the original chapter that is reprinted here was published in 1996, there was some remaining controversy in the scientific literature, in general, and in clinical and forensic arenas, in particular, regarding the validity of the diagnosis of "alcohol idiosyncratic intoxication" also characterized in the literature as pathological alcohol intoxication. Of particular significance were the uses of this diagnosis in the forensic arena to either negate guilt resulting from a criminal act (i.e., an affirmative intoxication defense, relieving total responsibility for the act) or to diminish the actor's responsibility in the commission of the act (i.e., diminished capacity, often used to inform sentencing parameters). An essential feature of the full-blown alcohol idiosyncratic intoxication or pathological intoxication defense is that the actor can be said to be incapacitated to the extent the he or she would be unable to act with knowledge and purpose in performing the criminal act or unable to form the request intent to perform the act. Interestingly, there are instances when the behavior of a victim is attributed to idiosyncratic alcohol intoxication (e.g., a women who has consumed relatively small amount of alcohol and who claims prostration of faculties, blackout or other extreme alcohol-related consequences during a sexual encounter and where the level of alcohol and her past use pattern have not produced such extreme outcomes in the past).

A second essential feature of such defenses, requires that the amount of alcohol consumed be considerable less than might otherwise be expected to result in even "mild intoxication" or otherwise impair the functioning of the actor. This latter essential provision is central for a number of reasons. Most importantly it is an attempt to overcome important legal and logical hurdles. Specifically, so-called "voluntary intoxication" cannot be used as an affirmative defense in most jurisdictions unless the level of intoxication is so severe as to result in a "prostration of faculties," thusly rendering an individual unable to act with knowledge and purpose in performing the criminal act or unable to form the request intent to perform the act. This is a high standard indeed. The precise language of the laws governing such defenses varies to some extent among jurisdictions. However, the basic tenets that underlie such defenses are fairly consistent across jurisdictions. In many respects, such defenses paralleled so-called "insanity" defenses and related pleas.

There is, of course, a practical and social hurdle to overcome. The question is one of permitting the invocation of intoxication, particularly, levels induced by minimal use levels to serve as a "threshold condition" to excuse or dismiss responsibility for behaviors that would not be tolerated in or by the average citizen. A related concern is the degree to which such low threshold conditions would be in the least bit convincing to the general public, including the segments of social spectrum most likely to be selected to serve in judgment of their peers (i.e., jurors).

In 1994, the revised *Diagnostic and Statistical Manual of Mental Disorders (DSM–IV)* published by the American Psychiatric Association announced the elimination of "alcohol idiosyncratic intoxication" as a diagnostic entity citing lack of empirical support for the condition that had been included in *DSM–III* (1980). The original chapter reproduced in full in this volume examined the issue in greater detail than was presented in the *DSM–IV* (1994) analysis. The conclusions rendered provided detail support for the position adopted by the authors of the *DSM–IV*. The chapter did leave open the possibility that the door was not yet closed on the concept and suggested that new information could come forward that might revitalize the construct.

In 2000, the American Psychiatric Association issued an updated version of the manual, *DSM–IV–TR* (2000). That version made no adjustments to alcohol-related diagnoses and continued to indicate that there was not sufficient scientific support to justify a diagnosis of "alcohol idiosyncratic intoxication." This version of the *DSM* indicated that the diagnosis should be replaced by "alcohol intoxication" or "alcohol-related disorder not other wise specified."

When I was asked to revisit the construct of alcohol idiosyncratic intoxication and the related construct of pathological alcohol intoxication, it seemed like an important inclusion for this scholarly volume. Revisiting these concepts was particularly relevant inasmuch as the quasi-diagnoses of alcohol idiosyncratic and intoxication pathological alcohol intoxication appear with some regularity in the forensic arena. Remarkably, a search of the literature revealed not a single empirical article providing support for the validity and reliability of either alcohol idiosyncratic intoxication or pathological alcohol intoxication.

Hence, the question remains why do the constructs appear to hold on to life particularly in the clinical and forensic arenas? I believe the answers lies, in part, to account for extreme behavior on the part of individuals who have a minimal history of such behavior (e.g., social drinkers with no history of violent behavior). In such case, it may also be coupled with circumstances that do not appear, at least superficially, to warrant such extreme behavior (e.g., situations where there is no apparent provocation for an assault). Forensic applications appear to be the last stronghold for evoking such concepts. Unfortunately, for those who would seek to employ these constructs as either exculpatory or to diminish an actor's responsibility for extreme behavior are on no firmer ground in 2006 than in 1994, 1996 or 2000. In fact the paucity of empirical support for these concepts over such a long interval suggests that the search for support has been abandoned, or at least has been suspended. It appears that the very high standards related to alcohol intoxication as exculpatory or, as evidence of diminished capacity will still be pinned to the standards of "prostration of faculties," rendering an individual unable to act with knowledge and purpose in performing the extreme act or resulting in the actor being unable to form the request intent to perform the act.

Nevertheless, it is likely that clinicians and those who work in forensic venues will continue to encounter such explanations. Part of the reason may be the result of statues in many jurisdictions that leave open at least a small crack in the door permitting such explanation for extreme behavior that appear to have no other obvious causes. Thus, in consideration of the fact that many of you will, no doubt, be confronted with these terms and be asked to make determinations using these constructs, it seems advisable to reprint the article originally penned for the inaugural volume of this series.

Krafft-Ebing is generally credited with introducing and characterizing the notion of an atypical and pathologic reaction to alcohol to the medical and scientific communities (Banay, 1944). The basic parameters of this syndrome are explicated in his two seminal articles published in 1869 and 1897.

Since its introduction as a construct, it has proven to be controversial in medical, scientific, and forensic circles and related applications. Most recently, the validity and utility of the construct has been seriously challenged in the medical and scientific literature (Urschel & Woody, 1994). In fact, during the past decade fewer than a dozen citations can be culled from scientific and medical literature which can be considered as lending empirical support for the validity of the construct.

Nevertheless, the concept of an atypical reaction to alcohol remains of interest, especially in the legal arena, and therefore remains of import to scientists, physicians, and other experts who are called upon to render opinions on the subject in a variety of venues. Tiffany and Tiffany (1990a, 1990b) present a comprehensive analysis of the construct's history which clearly demonstrates the continuing relevance and importance in the context of its forensic applications. Even though more recent and arguably authoritative writings on the subject of psychological status and criminal responsibility (e.g., Slovenko, 1995) fail to even reference the construct of pathological intoxication, the volume of cases in which atypical reaction to alcohol (and by extension similar reaction to other substances including psychotropic medication) is offered as exculpatory or, at least, mitigating factors continues to be sufficiently high enough to warrant careful consideration of its validity.

In their classic and comprehensive taxonomy of alcohol-related terminology, Keller, McCormick, and Efron (1982) provide a concise yet comprehensive summary characterization of the historic predecessor of the construct of "alcohol idiosyncratic intoxication" (APA, 1980) which captures the essence of Krafft-Ebing's syndrome. Pathological alcohol reaction is characterized as: "An extraordinarily severe response to alcohol, especially to small amounts, marked by apparently senseless violent behavior, usually followed by exhaustion, sleep, and amnesia for the episode. Intoxication is apparently not always involved, and for this reason *pathological alcohol reaction* is the preferred term. The reaction is thought to be associated with exhaustion, great strain, or hypoglycemia, and to occur especially in people poorly defended against their own violent impulses" (Keller et al., 1982, p. 189).

In defining this construct, Keller et al. (1982) cite the earlier work of Haggard and Jellinek (1942) who were careful to point out that this extreme reaction to alcohol was viewed as being unrelated to the processes associated with alcohol intoxication and hence should not be viewed as: " . . . ordinary intoxication occurring in an individual with extremely low tolerance to alcohol. There are none of the common symptoms of drunkenness: there is no flushing of the face, no staggering, and no slurring of speech. This peculiar reaction, which usually takes the form of furor, occurs mainly in individuals of psychopathic personality who, even when they do not drink, have unprovoked fits of rage and great changes in mood. It is significant that these individuals do not always react violently to alcohol. Sometimes they may be able to consume considerable quantities without showing any consequences except ordinary intoxication. Aside from these psychopathic individuals, pathological intoxication may occur in normal persons under exceptional conditions" (Haggard & Jellinek, 1942, p. 228).

Haggard and Jellinek (1942) also commented that what they viewed as a "violent reaction to alcohol" did not appear to share a common etiology with alcohol intoxication.

Keller et al. (1982) also document the evolution of the construct in the authoritative classification schema of the American Psychiatric Association (APA). The third revision of the APA's authoritative *Diagnostic and Statistical Manual of Mental Disorders* (*DSM–III*, APA, 1980) recasts pathological intoxication as "alcohol idiosyncratic intoxication"* and provided a separate classification subcategory (291.40) for the entity in the general domain of alcohol-related conditions and disorders.

DSM–III (APA, 1980) provides a comprehensive characterization of the syndrome which retains much of the character of the Krafft-

---

* Interestingly, Keller and his colleagues, always sticklers for accurate nomenclature, referenced the construct as "idiosyncratic alcohol reaction."

Ebing's initial delineation and reflects the admonitions of Haggard and Jellinek who argue that the syndrome be viewed as differentiated from simple alcohol intoxication and other forms of alcohol-related pathologies (e.g., alcoholism, alcohol dementias). The segment is presented in its entirety not only as a convenience to readers but also because it forms the basis of the brief but critical review of the construct presented in this chapter.

The *DSM–III* (APA, 1980) revised substantially the format in which all diagnostic entities were delineated. Alcohol Idiosyncratic Intoxication was catalogued under the general heading of alcohol-related disorders and given its own subclassification, 291.40. The entity was characterized under eight separate headings as were most other disorders and their subschema: essential features, age at onset, course, prevalence, complications, predisposing factors, differential diagnosis, diagnostic criteria. The following text is drawn from the *Diagnostic and Statistical Manual of Mental Disorders, Third Edition* (APA, 1980, p. 132): "The essential feature is a marked behavioral change–usually to aggressiveness–that is due to the recent ingestion of an amount of alcohol insufficient to induce intoxication in most people. There is usually subsequent amnesia for the period of intoxication. The behavior is atypical of the person when not drinking–for example, a shy, retiring, mild-mannered person may, after one weak drink, become belligerent and assaultive. During the episode the individual seems out of contact with others.

This disorder has also been called "Pathological Intoxication."

Age at onset. No information.

Course. The change in behavior begins either while the individual is drinking or shortly thereafter. The duration is quite brief, and the condition ceases within a few hours. The individual returns to his or her normal state as the blood alcohol level falls.

Prevalence. Apparently extremely rare.

Complications. The individual may do harm to himself or herself or to others.

Predisposing factors. A small percentage of individuals with this disorder have been reported to have temporal lobe spikes on an electroencephalogram after receiving small amounts of alcohol. Although the reports are still anecdotal, it is thought that people with brain damage lose "tolerance" for alcohol and behave abnormally after drinking small amounts. The types of brain injury most often associated with this syndrome are from trauma and encephalitis. The loss of tolerance may be temporary or permanent. It is also reported that individuals who are unusually fatigued or have a debilitating physical illness may have a low tolerance for alcohol and respond inappropriately to small amounts.

Differential diagnosis. Other exogenous agents, especially **barbiturates and similarly acting substances**, may occasionally cause abrupt changes in behavior. **Temporal lobe epilepsy**, during the interictal period, may be associated with fits of destructive rage. In **Malingering**, the individual may wish to avoid responsibility for aggressive behavior, claiming that it occurred while he or she was intoxicated from a small amount of alcohol.

Diagnostic criteria for Alcohol Idiosyncratic Intoxication

A. Marked behavioral change, e.g., aggressive or assaultive behavior that is due to the recent ingestion of an amount of alcohol insufficient to induce intoxication in most people.

B. The behavior is atypical of the person when not drinking.

C. Not due to any other physical or mental disorder.

The *DSM–III* delineation, presented above, demonstrates high fidelity with the initial characterization of the Krafft-Ebing syndrome and takes into consideration the concerns and admonitions of the pioneer alcohol investigators such as Jellinek. However, the careful and systematic delineation of the syndrome exposed in detail a number of serious problems for scientific investigators and clinicians of the next decade to consider. Recall that the decade of the 80s was marked by significant advances in biological sciences in general and the "brain" and "addiction" sciences in specific.

A central problem was the detailing of a potential mechanism to account for the onset of the response. Note that the construct was constrained in several essential ways. The amount of alcohol consumed could not be enough to induce "intoxication." Hence, in most individuals this translated into consumption of amounts insufficient to raise blood alcohol levels much beyond .04 percent. In a male weighing 160 lbs., about 1.5 twelve-ounce portions of standard (about 4.5% alcohol content) beer consumed in an hour would result in a BAC of .04 percent. In a female weighing 130 lbs., less than one twelve-ounce portion would be required.

The evoked response (i.e., marked aggressiveness or assaultive behavior) needed to be quite specific; almost stereotypic. Yet, such behavior would have to be atypical of the affected individual (i.e., virtually absent from the behavioral repertoire) even though the behavior would likely appear to be quite organized. Further, the baseline repertoire of the affected individual would be characterized by a general tendency opposite to that which characterized the evoked, rather specific target response.

The target response would need to occur proximal to drinking while alcohol level was rising (within 30 to 60 minutes of drinking), last for a relatively short period, and dissipate as BAC returned to zero. Any reasonable calculation would result in an extremely narrow window for the occurrence of such a behavior. Finally, the individual would need to be amnesic for the window in which the evoked behavior occurred. Of course, other physical or mental disorders (for example, temporal lobe epilepsy in which a putative mechanism could be identified) capable of evoking the response needed to be ruled out.

These well-specified guidelines posed a serious if not insurmountable challenge for theoreticians and model builders. Some explanatory models could be evoked for one or more of the necessary conditions. For example, state dependent learning could account for the cue value of a small dose of alcohol. However, the evoked response would have had to be reasonably well learned in order for it to be evoked. Hence, reasonable explanations for one or more aspects of the syndrome negated or were negated by other constraints.

Needless to say, in the decade of the eighties few cases could be reliably documented using the well-specified guidelines outlined by the more explicit *DSM–III* criteria. Thus, a second and equally difficult problem for proponents of the validity of the alcohol idiosyncratic intoxication syndrome was the lack of credible "clinical" data. Further, few convincing demonstrations of the phenomena could be mustered in the laboratory. (However, see Maletzky, 1976, as a partial laboratory confirmation of a limited aspect of the syndrome).

The lack of the identification of a mechanism or complex of mechanisms to account for the extreme behavior represented by an idiosyncratic response to alcohol coupled by the lack of clinical case material or convincing empirical demonstrations placed the validity of the "Krafft-Ebing syndrome" in serious question as it entered the decade of the nineties.

In 1994, the APA published its revised *Diagnostic and Statistical Manual of Mental Disorders (DSM–IV)*. In this edition the APA addressed the lack of evidence regarding the validity of the alcohol idiosyncratic intoxication diagnosis. The following passages excised from that document summarize the psychiatric communities' views on Krafft-Ebing's observations.

"Alcohol idiosyncratic intoxication," defined as marked behavioral change, usually aggressiveness, following the ingestion of a relatively small amount of alcohol, was included in *DSM–III–R* (APA, 1981). Because of limited support in the literature for the validity of this condition, it is no longer included as a separate diagnosis in *DSM–IV*. Such presentations would most likely be diagnosed as Alcohol Intoxication or Alcohol-Related Disorder Not Otherwise Specified.

Alcohol-Related Disorder Not Otherwise Specified. The Alcohol-Related Disorder Not Otherwise Specified category is for disorders associated with the use of alcohol that are not classifiable as Alcohol Dependence, Alcohol Abuse, Alcohol Intoxication, Alcohol Withdrawal, Alcohol Intoxication Delirium, Alcohol Withdrawal Delirium, Alcohol-Induced Persisting Dementia, Alcohol-Induced Persisting Amnestic Disorder, Alcohol-Induced Psychotic Disorder, Alcohol-Induced Mood Disorder, Alcohol-Induced Anxiety Disorder, Alcohol-Induced Sexual Dysfunction, or Alcohol-Induced Sleep Disorder" (*DSM–IV*, APA, 1994, p. 204).

Does this signal the end of pathologic intoxication as envisioned by Krafft-Ebing in 1867? Or, as defined by the APA in its *DSM–III* published in 1980? Not necessarily! The *DSM–IV* seems to leave open the possibility that new evidence may be presented to account for the seemingly unusual behavior associated with what appears on the surface to be rather trivial ingestion of alcohol. Further, the suggestion is made that individuals who could be seen as classified formerly under this diagnosis might be classified as alcohol intoxicated and that related behavior (unusual aggression or violent behavior) may be attributed to the direct action of alcohol in inducing intoxication even though the BAC of such affected individuals are relatively low. Note that although the *DSM–IV* does not include a separate classification for the disorder, the classification scheme suggests that patterns of behavior presumably involving at least some of the elements described in *DSM–III* could be classified **by exclusion** as an alcohol-related disorder

In spite of the rather sparse evidence developed by scientists and clinicians during the decade of the eighties which supported the validity of the syndrome, interest in the use of alcohol idiosyncratic intoxication as an explanation for violent and aggressive behavior remains. Some of the interest is no doubt driven by what appears to be a lack of alternative explanations for bizarre behavior exhibited by individuals whose violent and aggressive behavior appears to meet some if not all conditions delineated by Krafft-Ebing in his original formulation or the more recent amalgams represented in authoritative documents such as the *DSM-III.* Certainly interest remains high in the legal community which must continue to cope with a wide range of behaviors and which has established a long history through legislation and case law with regard to what constitutes culpability.

REFERENCES

American Psychiatric Association. (1980). *Diagnostic and Statistical Manual of Mental Disorders, Third Edition. (DSM-III).* Washington, D.C.: American Psychiatric Association.

American Psychiatric Association. (1987). *Diagnostic and Statistical Manual of Mental Disorders, Third Edition, Revised. (DSM-III-R).* Washington, D.C.: American Psychiatric Association.

American Psychiatric Association. (1994). *Diagnostic and Statistical Manual of Mental Disorders, Fourth Edition. (DSM-IV).* Washington, D.C.: American Psychiatric Association.

American Psychiatric Association. (2000). *Diagnostic and Statistical Manual of Mental Disorders, Fourth Edition. (DSM-IV-TR).* Washington, D.C.: American Psychiatric Association.

Banay, R. S. (1944). Pathologic reaction to alcohol. *Quarterly Journal of Studies on Alcohol, 4,* 580.

Haggard, H. W., & Jellinek, E. M. (1942). *Alcohol explored.* New York: Doubleday & Company, Inc.

Keller, M., McCormick, M., & Efron, V. (1982). *A Dictionary of Words about Alcohol.* New Brunswick, NJ: Rutgers Center of Alcohol Studies.

Maletzky, B. M. (1976). The diagnosis of pathological intoxication. *Journal of Studies on Alcohol, 37*(9), 1215.

Slovenko, R. (1995). *Psychiatry and criminal culpability.* New York, NY: John Wiley & Sons.

Tiffany, L. P., & Tiffany, M. (1990a). *The legal defense of pathological intoxication. With related issues of temporary and self-inflicted insanity.* Westport, CT: Quorum Books.

Tiffany, L. P., & Tiffany, M. (1990b). Nosologic objections to the criminal defense of pathological intoxication: What do the doubters doubt? *International Journal of Law and Psychiatry, 13*(1-2), 49.

Urschel, H. C. III, & Woody, G. E. (1994). Alcohol idiosyncratic intoxication. A review of the data supporting its existence. In Widiger et al. (Eds.), *DSM-IV Sourcebook, Volume 1.* Washington, DC: American Psychiatric Association, 117–128.

Chapter 4

ORGANIC BRAIN DYSFUNCTIONS AND CRIMINALITY

Daniel A. Martell

The neurobehavioral components of violence and criminality have become increasingly important to forensic behavioral science. While brain damage can impact the entire range of human behavior, its relationship to criminal behavior often springs from some combination of disinhibition, impaired social judgement, hypersexuality, aggression, and/or violence. Of these, research linking brain dysfunction to aggression and violence is perhaps the most developed relative to criminal-legal standards of behavior (Volavka, Martell, & Convit, 1992).

However, this is an area in which there is a marked divergence between clinical experience and opinion on the one hand, and solid empirical evidence on the other. Clinically, it seems very clear that brain damage and dysfunction can play a significant contributory role in violent behavior, and hence are of direct relevance to the criminal law. Unfortunately, while supportive of a link between brain and violence, much of the large and diverse research literature in this area is inconclusive due methodological confounds and inconsistent findings among the extant studies. This chapter explores these issues and offers a theoretical model that may be useful for conceptualizing both clinical forensic assessments and research efforts.

RESEARCH EVIDENCE

A comprehensive review of the research in this area is beyond the scope of this chapter, because the sheer volume of relevant studies is enough to fill books on its own. The interested reader may wish to pursue several recent volumes that attempt to tackle this literature (cf. Hillbrand & Pallone, 1994; Milner, 1991; Volavka, 1995). This section will provide an overview that addresses strengths and weakness of the literature and highlights major findings.

Most of the research on the brain and violence or criminality can be organized under four broad headings: (1) studies documenting the prevalence of brain abnormalities in various criminal and forensic populations; (2) correlational and group-difference studies associating brain impairment with violent behavior in criminal and forensic populations; (3) studies showing the incidence of violent and/or criminal behavior in populations of individuals with specific neurobehavioral disorders; and (4) localization studies that attempt to isolate specific brain sites in which lesions may produce violent behavior.

Prevalence Studies

Only a few studies have set out to determine the prevalence of organic brain dysfunction in populations of violent offenders, despite growing assertions by defense attorneys and forensic clinicians that mentally disordered offenders have significant rates of organic brain disorder (Dupree, 1990; Hamstra, 1986). If impaired brain functioning plays an important role in the etiology of violent behavior, one would expect the prevalence of organic brain impairment in violent criminal populations to be high. This kind of information has important implications for forensic assessment and evaluation, as well as expert testimony.

Mentally disordered offenders. Currently, the best estimates of the prevalence of brain dysfunctions in a violent criminal cohort come from studies of mentally disordered offenders. To date, these clues come from three diagnostic census studies, two of which were conducted outside the United States. Odejide (1981) studied the population of "criminal lunatics" at the Lantoro Psychiatric Institution in Nigeria. Using a structured questionnaire to assess psychopathology and determine diagnoses, his data indicate that 24.6 percent of the

subjects were either epileptic (18.9%) or suffered from organic psychoses (5.7%). Häfner and Böker (1982), working in the Federal
Republic of Germany, conducted an extensive epidemiological diagnostic study of a cohort of 533 mentally disordered offenders entering
the forensic mental health system over a 10-year period. Their data
suggest that 33.6 percent of these patients had a diagnosis reflecting
organic cerebral impairment. These included Mental Retardation
(12.7%), Late-Acquired Brain Damage (8%), Cerebral Atrophy (7.5%),
and Epilepsy (5.4%).

Martell (1992b) presents data from 50 randomly selected
American forensic psychiatric patients retained in a maximum-security state hospital in New York City. Multiple indicators of potential
brain dysfunction were present in 66 percent of these cases, with at
least one indicator present in 84 percent of the subjects. Specific findings included a history of severe head injury with loss of consciousness
(22%), seizure activity (8%), evidence of cognitive impairment (18%),
abnormal neurological findings (75%), and abnormal neuropsychological or neurodiagnostic findings (32%). Subjects with a diagnosis or history suggesting organic brain impairment were significantly more likely to have been indicated for violent criminal charges.

Incarcerated criminal offenders. There are fewer studies that
have examined brain disorders in jail or prison populations.
Neighbors (1987) conducted a psychiatric epidemiologic study of
1,000 prisoners randomly selected from the total prison population in
Michigan. Both the Diagnostic Interview Schedule (DIS) and the
Structured Clinical Interview for *DSM–III–R* (SCID) were used to
establish lifetime prevalence (DIS) and current primary diagnosis
(SCID). His data suggest that 8.2 percent of the prison population
meet diagnostic criteria for organic brain disorders (0.3% with Organic
Brain Syndrome/Cognitive Impairment, and 2.9% with Organic Personality Disorder–Explosive type). However, structured diagnostic
interviews are not adequately sensitive for the detection or diagnosis
of abnormal brain functioning. Hence, these findings undoubtedly
underestimate the extent of brain dysfunction in the population.

Studies using neuropsychological test batteries suggest much higher levels of brain impairment. Yeudall and Fromm-Auch (1979) document varying patterns of abnormal Halstead-Reitan Neuropsychological Battery (HRNB) findings in programmatic studies of numerous
forensic populations, including adolescent delinquents, forensic psy-

chiatric patients, aggressive psychopaths, sex offenders, and violent criminals. Among adult criminals, Yeudall (1977) reports abnormal HRNB findings in 90 percent of his sample, including 100 percent of rapists, 94 percent of homicide offenders, and 87 percent of assaultists. Studies of other violent populations have documented even higher levels of brain impairment. Elliott (1982) studied 286 nonpsychotic subjects with a history of recurrent uncontrollable rage attacks, and found evidence of developmental or acquired brain defects in 94 percent.

Lewis and her colleagues conducted uncontrolled, descriptive studies of both juvenile and adult prisoners on death row (Lewis, Pincus, Bard et al., 1988; Lewis, Pincus, Feldman et al., 1986). These studies reported significant brain dysfunction in the majority of these subjects, including neuropsychological impairment on the HRNB, histories of head injury, neurological impairment, and cognitive deficits.

Correlational and Group-Difference Studies in Forensic Populations

Studying the association between brain impairment and violent criminal behavior is another major area of interest, with research dating back over 30 years (cf. Monroe, 1978, 1981; Williams, 1969). Neuropsychological studies of brain function in violent groups have yielded support for theories that associate violent behavior with brain dysfunction (Pontius & Yudowitz, 1980; Spellacy, 1977, 1978; West, 1981). For example, Bryant, Scott, Golden, and Tori (1984) found a significant relationship between learning disability, neuropsychological deficits, and violent criminal behavior. Impaired scores on subscales of the Wechsler Adult Intelligence Scale have also been associated with violent behavior (Dicker, 1973; Kunce, Ryan, & Eckelman, 1976). Programmatic studies by Yeudall and his colleagues (Yeudall & Fromm-Auch, 1979) have documented significant neuropsychological deficits in both violent prisoners and forensic psychiatric patients.

Other neuropsychologists have also demonstrated the ability of neuropsychological findings to discriminate between violent and nonviolent offenders (Spellacy, 1978; West, 1981). Patterns of impairment on the HRNB consistently discriminate juvenile delinquents from matched controls (Berman & Siegal, 1976; Spellacy, 1977; Yeudall, Fromm-Auch, & Davies, 1982). Studies using the HRNB have also reported significant differences in the neuropsychological performance of psychopathic and nonpsychopathic criminals (Fedora & Fedora, 1983), suggesting greater impairment of dominant (left) hemisphere function among criminal psychopaths (see also Hare & McPherson, 1984; Jutai & Hare, 1983). Langevin et al. (1987) used both the LNNB and the HRNB in a study comparing murderers, other violent offenders, and nonviolent controls. They found that while the LNNB did not discriminate among these groups, the HRNB did detect significant differences, with killers and assaulters showing greater levels of impairment than controls on several of the subtests. Taken together, this literature suggests that neuropsychological impairment may play a significant role in the criminal behavior of certain offenders. However, the nature and extent of this role, and its interaction with other personal environmental and situational risk factors remains to be determined.

Violence and Specific Brain Disorders

Violent behavior is also known to occur in association with certain specific brain disorders. Researchers have begun to document the importance of several specific types of brain impairment in violent behavior, including head injury, seizure disorder, cognitive impairment, and neurological abnormalities (cf. Langevin, Ben-Aron, Wortzman et al., 1987; Nachshon & Denno, 1987; Silver & Yudofsky, 1987).

Head injury. Head injury is a major cause of acquired brain damage (Alexander, 1982; Reitan & Wolfson, 1986) often resulting in focal damage to the frontal and/or temporal lobes. Several studies have correlated damage to these specific brain regions with violent behavior (Heinrichs, 1989; Kling, 1976; Volkow & Tancredi, 1987; Will, 1986). For example, one study specifically associates temporal lobe lesions secondary to head injury with violence (Wood, 1984). Another study (McKinlay, Brooks, Bond et al., 1987) suggests that as many as 70 percent of those suffering a severe head injury experience significant levels of aggressive and irritable behavior. Severe head injuries have been reported in a significant proportion of murderers in Iceland (Petursson & Gudjonsson, 1981), and 100 percent of death-row inmates in the United States (Lewis, Pincus, Feldman et al., 1986).

Seizure disorder. Seizure disorder is another important area in which brain dysfunction appears to be associated with violent behavior (Devinsky & Bear, 1984; Lewis & Pincus, 1989; Stevens & Hermann, 1981). However, the precise nature of the relationship between epilepsy and violent behavior remains a controversial issue (Stone, 1984). Most studies associate "irritative" lesions arising within the temporal lobes with violence, as illustrated by the literature on temporal lobe epilepsy (Furguson, Rayport, & Corrie, 1986; Gunn & Bonn, 1971; Monroe, 1981; Stone, 1984), and the "episodic dyscontrol syndrome" (Monroe, 1986; Rickler, 1982). It is informative to note that current opinion (Devinsky & Bear, 1984; Stone, 1984; Bear, Freeman, & Greenberg, 1984) associates the increased risk of violence with behavior occurring during interictal periods, rather than with ictal or preictal behavior per se.

Cognitive impairment. Violent behavior is also prevalent in populations exhibiting various forms of cognitive impairment. Intellectual and neuropsychological deficits, mental retardation, Alzheimer's disease and other forms of dementia all have known associations with violent behavior (Silver & Yudofsky, 1987). Behavioral studies of mentally retarded adults have documented violent behavior in 30–40 percent of cases (Day, 1985; Reid, Ballinger, Heather et al., 1984). Bryant, Scott, Golden, and Tori (1984) found a significant relationship between learning disability, neuropsychological deficits and violent criminal behavior. Impaired scores on subscales of the Wechsler Adult Intelligence Scale have also been associated with violent behavior (Kunce, Ryan, & Eckelman, 1976). Programmatic studies by Yeudall and his colleagues (Yeudall, 1987; Yeudall & Fromm-Auch, 1979; Yeudall & Wardell, 1978) have documented significant neuropsychological deficits in both violent prisoners and forensic psychiatric patients. Other neuropsychologists have also demonstrated the ability of neuropsychological findings to discriminate between violent and non-violent offenders (Spellacy, 1978; West, 1981).

Neurological impairment. Neurological abnormalities also appear to play a role in violent behavior. Monroe, Hulfish, Balis, Lion, Rubin, McDonald, & Barcik (1977) were among the first to document abnormal neurological findings in recidivistically violent prisoners. More recently, programmatic studies by the violence research group at NYU Medical Center and Manhattan Psychiatric Center (Convit, Jaeger, Lin et al., 1988; Krakowski, Convit, Jaeger et al., 1989; Krakowski, Convit, & Volavka, 1988; Krakowski & Czbor, 1994) have repeatedly implicated neurological impairment in the behavior of violent psychiatric inpatients.

Localization Studies

Localization studies provide what is potentially the most intriguing branch of research into violent criminality and the brain, the search for the "seat of criminal violence." This has immediate intuitive value, and gives rise to the popular criminal defense strategy that "the lesion made me do it." Yet despite its apparent common-sense appeal as evidence for jurors, this is the one branch of research that is the most problematic and inconclusive.

Many brain areas have emerged as candidates, ranging from entire brain hemispheres, to studies that purport to relate particular brain sites with specific criminal behaviors (Hall & McNinch, 1988). For example, Corley, Corley, Walker, & Walker (1994) attempt to relate a very specific type of criminal behavior (i.e., sexual offending) with a very specific region of the brain (the left posterior hemisphere). This section will examine research findings in three areas: (1) hemispheric specialization; (2) frontal lobe dysfunction; and (3) temporal lobe dysfunction.

Hemispheric specialization. The problems with localization studies can be illustrated by looking at one such area: the research literature exploring the potential neurobehavioral role of hemispheric specialization in the production of violent behavior. Here, we are dealing with perhaps the largest subdivision of brain areas. However, the literature on hemispheric specialization and violence has produced apparently mixed and contradictory results, with methodological confounds encumbering much of what we know.

Table 4–1 summarizes much of the literature in this area, illustrating the variation in findings. Most of this variation is probably attributable to methodological issues in the studies themselves, and *not* to any enduring characteristic of brain function. First, the **populations** selected for study (i.e., juvenile delinquents, mentally disordered offenders, prisoners, and "psychopaths") vary widely and may not be comparable, either in terms of the nature or the quality of the violent behavior they express. Second, the **lateralization issues** examined (e.g., lateral preference, cerebral dominance, test evidence of lateralized structural or functional brain abnormalities) provide differing and

Table 4–1. Studies of brain lateralization and violence.

Authors	Sample Size	Lateralization Issue	Violence Measure	Findings
1) Mentally abnormal adult offenders				
Tancredi & Volkow (1987; 1988)	N = 4	Structural and Functional Abnormality (CT, PET, & EEG)	Criminal Violence	Mixed; bilateral frontal & temporal temporal
Howard (1984)	N = 265	EEG abnormalities	Criminal Violence	bilateral temporal and posterior slowing
Convit, Czbor, & Volavka (in press)	N = 21	EEG abnormalities	Inpatient Violence	bilateral temporal & parietal; left frontal
2) Juvenile Delinquents				
Yeudall, Fromm-Auch, Davies (1979; 1982)	n = 99 delnqnts n = 47 controls	Neuropsych tests EEG abnormalities	Group Membership (Delinquency)	Right hemisphere anterior abnormality
Wechsler(1958)	n = 500 delnqnts n = 5()0 controls	WAIS PIQ-VIQ	Adolescent Male Psychopaths	P > VIQ scores suggesting right hemisphere
Tarter, Hegedus, Winsten, & Alterman (1985)	N = 101	WISC-R PIQ-VIQ difference	Rated Aggression	No lateralized findings
Nachshon & Denno (1987)	N = 1066 Black adol.	Lateral Preference	Delinquency Measures	Offenders had greater right preference; and greater mixed hand foot-eye preferences
Andrew (1980)	N = 116	Lateral Preference	Seriousness of Violence Scale	Left-handed Ss had lower violence scores
Andrew (1981)	N = 33	Parietal Lobe Function (Weights Test)	Criminal Violence	Poorer right hemisphere functioning
3) Adult Criminals				
Nachshon (1988)	N = 127 inmates	Dichotic Listening	Criminal Violence	Abnormal Left Hemisphere Procesing of Auditory Stimuli
Barnett, Zimmer, & McCormack (1989)	N = 1792 inmates	PIQ-VIQ Differences	Group Comparison: Split/No Split	No personality differences between groups on MMPI or MCMI

Continued on next page

Table 4–1. Studies of brain lateralization and violence. *(continued)*

Authors	Sample Size	Lateralization Issue	Violence Measure	Findings
4) Adult Criminal Psychopaths				
Hare & Forth (1985)	N = 258 inmates	Lateral Preference	Psychopathy Scores, Criminal Violence	No differences, no association with violence
Hare & McPherson (1984)	n = 146 inmates, n = 159 controls	Dichotic Listening	Psychopathy Scores	Smaller Right Ear Ear Advantage implicating left hemisphere

generally incomparable data about brain status or function. Finally, the **measures of violence** employed are extremely diverse, and do not lend themselves easily to comparison. For example, some studies examined actual violent behaviors occurring in differing environmental contexts (e.g., institutional violence vs. violent criminal behavior in the community). Other studies contrast presumably "violent" and "nonviolent" groups–defining violence not according to any specific behavior but rather via membership in a presumably "violent" population (i.e., psychopaths, criminal offenders, juvenile delinquents).

Research on violence and the frontal lobes. Frontal lobe functioning (cf. Brown, 1987; Goldberg, 1987; Perecman, 1987; Stuss & Benson, 1986) has been related to violent behavior in several previous articles and studies (Heinrichs, 1989; Hall & McNinch, 1988; Yeudall, 1987; Pontius, 1984; Kling, 1976). However, the current state of knowledge on the role of frontal cortex in violent and especially criminal behavior is limited (Raine & Scerbo, 1991). There are several authors who have offered theoretical perspectives on the role of the frontal lobes in the control regulation, inhibition, or suppression of violent impulses (cf., Hall and McNinch, 1988; Tancredi & Volkow, 1988; Yeudall, 1980, 1987; Valzelli, 1981); however, there is little scientific evidence to support or refute their formulations.

At least five research articles have been published which in some way address the issue of violence and frontal lobe function. Two are case study reports. Volkow & Tancredi (1987) employed positron emission tomography (PET) to examine the brain function of four violent psychiatric inpatients. Dysfunction of frontal cortex was observed in two of the four patients, and temporal lobe dysfunction was present in all of them. Pontius (1984) studied eight white males who had committed violent acts (murder, attempted murder, or rape) allegedly evoked by specific stimuli which she postulated to be the result of a "seizure-like imbalance between frontal lobe and limbic systems," although no empirical measures of frontal lobe function were employed.

In an earlier, more systematic study Pontius (1980) employed a clinical narrative technique and a neuropsychological test (Trail Making, Part B) to study frontal lobe dysfunction in 30 young adult criminals. Her results suggested that a subgroup (33%) of these men demonstrated "specifically immature action behavior indicative of [frontal lobe system] dysfunctioning." Yeudall (1977) studied 25 aggressive psychopaths and 25 depressed forensic patients to examine the lateralization of neuropsychological impairments in psychiatric and forensic disorders. His findings suggested that the neuropsychological impairments of both groups were localized in the anterior regions of the brain, with dysfunction in the aggressive psychopaths more frequently lateralized to the dominant hemisphere, while nondominant lateralization was more common among the subjects with affective disorders. Finally, Heinrichs (1989) demonstrated that frontal cerebral lesions in particular (as opposed to general cerebral damage) was predictive of violent incidents during hospitalization among 45 chronic neuropsychiatric inpatients.

Taken together these studies suggest that frontal lobe dysfunction may play a role in violent behavior, however only Heinrich's (1989) study provides firm evidence to support that conclusion. Small sample sizes, lack of reliable and valid measures of frontal lobe functions, absent control or comparison groups, confounded research designs, and/or a combination of these methodological weaknesses in some way compromise the interpretation of results from the other studies.

Research on violence and the temporal lobes. Similarly there is a growing literature relating temporal lobe functioning and violence, including controversial studies of temporal lobe epilepsy (Devinsky & Bear, 1984; Furguson, Rayport, & Corrie, 1986; Gunn & Bonn, 1971; Gunn & Fenton, 1971; Delgado-Escueta et al., 1981; Monroe, 1986; Stone, 1984; Kligman & Goldberg, 1975), episodic dyscontrol (Mark & Ervin, 1970; Rickler, 1982), and temporal lobe lesions secondary to head injury (Wood, 1984). Here again, methodological limitations limit the conclusions that can be drawn.

THEORETICAL MODELS

A major problem with the literature on brain impairment and violence has been the reductionistic emphasis on localization at the expense of a more comprehensive understanding of the diversity of violent behaviors arising from interactions between lesions at various brain sites and larger psychological, situational, and environmental determinants. One compelling interpretation for the divergence in localization found in these studies is that damage or dysfunction in many brain areas can contribute to violent, antisocial, or criminal behavior. It is becoming increasingly clear that violent and aggressive behavior is regulated and controlled by several anatomical regions within the brain. Rather than rendering issues of cerebral localization and violence moot however, this interpretation suggests a new direction for research and forensic practice in this area.

Theories are beginning to emerge that abandon the reductionistic emphasis on localizing violence to one hemisphere or brain region, in favor of a more systemic understanding of violence and the brain. Theoretical models emerging from neuropsychology (cf. Gorenstein & Newman, 1980; Yeudall, Fedora, & Fromm, 1987) and neurology (cf. Tancredi & Volkow, 1988; Weiger & Bear, 1988) suggest that damage almost anywhere in the brain may increase the risk of violent behavior. Abnormal brain functioning may impair inhibition of violent impulses, and/or stimulate excesses in impulsivity and behavioral dyscontrol. Either mechanism may increase an individual's propensity to aggressive or violent behavior, particularly in combination with other characterological, environmental, or situational risk factors.

These theories seek to explain the unique forms and qualities of violent behavior arising from interactions between lesions at various brain sites and larger social-ecological determinants. They suggest new models to address the qualitative differentiation of violent behavior associated with brain lesions at various neuroanatomical sites. Describing the differential nature and quality of violent behavior associated with localized brain lesions is the goal of these theoretical formulations

Yeudall, Fedora, and Fromm (1987) have proposed one such theory to address the neurobehavioral concomitants of violent behavior and persistent criminality. Their work represents one of the first efforts to conceptualize an integrated theoretical model of violence and brain dysfunction. Their theory relates functional brain anatomy to violent behavior across three neuroanatomical dimensions: (1) **dominant versus nondominant** hemispheric functions; (2) **anterior versus posterior** brain functions; and (3) **cortical versus subcortical** brain systems.

On the dominant versus nondominant dimension, it is proposed that a certain reciprocal inhibition is maintained (via the corpus callosum) between the two hemispheres, with the dominant hemisphere serving an inhibitory function and the nondominant hemisphere serving an excitatory function in the regulation of mood, erotic states, and aggressive behavior. This equipoise may be intimately linked to the balance of neurotransmitters in the two hemispheres. Violent behavior may result from hyperfunctioning of the nondominant hemisphere and/or hypofunctioning in the dominant hemisphere. Contemporaneously, Nachshon (1988) and Nachshon and Denno (1987) have suggested a complementary hypothesis, centered on the *quality* of violence associated with unilateral right or left hemisphere dysfunction. Drawing on the work of Myslobodsky and Rattok (1977), they suggest that right hemisphere dysfunction may impair the emotional mediation of "fight or flight" behavior, resulting in violence characterized by impulsive emotional outbursts.

On the anterior-posterior dimension, Yeudall, Fedora and Fromm (1987) stress the integrative, executive and behavioral control functions of the frontal lobes in directing action based on the posterior brain areas' processing of incoming sensory stimuli. Two prefrontal syndromes (dysfunction of the neocortical dorsolateral convexity and the limbic basal-orbital regions) are postulated to play a key role in violent behavior, through increases in impulsivity and disinhibition. The cortical-subcortical dimension is viewed as a hierarchical system in which neocortex plays the greater regulatory role (both inhibitory and excitatory) over lower brain systems. Of special interest is the role of frontal cortex over limbic and brain stem regions, with frontal dysfunction being related to increased risk of impaired control, regulation, inhibition, or suppression of violent impulses. Providing some support for this formulation, the research literature has particularly linked lesions in the frontal and temporal brain regions with violent behavior (Kling, 1976).

A Model for Clinical Forensic Evaluation and Research Regarding the Role of Brain Impairment in Violent Criminal Behavior

Drawing on both the research literature and the extant theoretical models, it seems that a contextual approach that integrates brain status, psychological functioning, and environmental contingencies would provide the clearest understanding of the unique contributions of each domain to the production of a violent behavioral event. This section will suggest such a formulation that may prove useful as a model for conceptualizing both clinical forensic examinations and future research efforts aimed at explaining associations between brain impairment and violent crime.

Current theories are too structural and phylogenetic, prompting the need to look for a more psychological/neurobehavioral theory that *blends* brain, mind, and situation. This represents a move *away* from reductionistic emphasis on localization to encourage a more systemic and interactive understanding of brain and violent behavior.

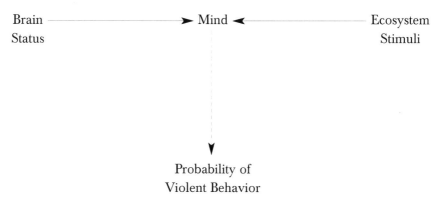

Figure 4–1. An interactive model of brain dysfunction and violent crime.

The proposed model (Figure 4–1) operates on two primary assumptions The first is that damage almost anywhere in the brain may increase the probability of violent behavior in combination with other personal, environmental, situational, and biochemical variables. However, with certain very limited exceptions, brain damage alone will almost never be sufficient to *cause* violent criminal behavior.

Rather, the second assumption is that the *nature, quality,* and *probability* of the violent behavior expressed will vary as a function of:

  a) **the condition of the brain itself,** as reflected in:
  1) the location of any lesion (e.g., right-left, anterior-posterior, cortical-subcortical, frontal, temporal, etc.),
  2) the nature of any lesion (i.e., structural vs. functional, progressive vs. static),
  3) the size or extent of any lesion (which may include adjacent brain areas, interfere with normal architectural pathways, or may exert remote effects via diaschisis).
  4) the acute impact of any psychoactive chemicals (including alcohol, street drugs, and/or psychotropic medications)
  and b) **the social-ecological context** defined to include:
  1) the *microsystem* or immediate behavioral context (situation)
  2) the *mesosystem* or larger social context (community)
  3) the *macrosystem* or sociopolitical context (society)
  and c) The **psychological context** as mediated by the "mind:"
  1) cognition (e.g., stress, appraisal, and coping)
  2) life experiences that lead to social learning (modeling, reinforcement)
  3) personality development/personality disorders
  4) abnormal mental states (intoxication, delirium, dementia, psychosis, and related major mental disorders)

Certainly the notion of mind, brain, and social context interacting to shape human behavior is not new to psychological science. However, this perspective has been largely underutilized in application to the problem of brain damage and violent crime. The adoption of such a model helps to clarify the multifactorial nature of the problem, and focuses attention in a more balanced way to the role of organic brain impairment in the etiology of violence and criminality.

The assessment of brain condition can be addressed using neuroimaging technologies, including both structural (e.g., CAT and MRI) and functional (e.g., PET, SPECT) brain scans. The impact of the brain's condition on behavior can then be assessed using both psychological and neuropsychological testing (Martell, 1992b). Both psychological and psychiatric assessments are clearly appropriate methods of assessing the presence and impact of mental disorders. However, assessing the larger social-ecological context in which criminal violence occurs is somewhat more difficult. At the individual level of analysis, this is obviously the primary role of forensic assessment. At the group level, research is beginning to examine the impact of the social ecological context in which violent behavior occurs, and its interaction with mental states (cf. Link & Stueve, 1994; Martell, Rosner, & Harmon, 1995; Swanson, Holzer, Ganju et al., 1990). Integrating data from each of these domains holds significant promise for informing both clinical forensic assessment and search regarding the role of brain dysfunction and violent criminal activity.

REFERENCES

Alexander, M. P. (1982). Traumatic brain injury. In D. F. Benson, & D. Blumer (Eds.), *Psychiatric aspects of neurologic disease, Vol. 2.* New York: Grune & Stratton, 219–249.

Bear, D., Freeman, R., & Greenberg, M. (1984). Interictal behavior in patients with temporal lobe epilepsy. In *Psychiatric aspects of temporal lobe epilepsy.* Washington, D.C.: American Psychiatric Association.

Borod, J., & Koff, E. (1989). The neuropsychology of emotion: Evidence from normal, neurological, and psychiatric populations. In E. Perecman (Ed.), *Integrating theory and practice in clinical neuropsychology.* Hillsdale, NJ: Lawrence Erlbaum and Associates, 175–215.

Bryant, E. T., Scott, M. L., Golden, C. J., & Tori, C. D. (1984). Neuropsychological deficits, learning disability, and violent behavior. *Journal of Consulting and Clinical Psychology, 52*(2), 323.

Convit, A., Jaeger, J., Lin, S., Meisner, M., & Volavka, J. (1988). Prediction of assaultiveness in psychiatric inpatients: A pilot study. *Hospital and Community Psychiatry, 39,* 429.

Corley, A. R., Corley, D., Walker, J., & Walker, S. (1994). The possibility of organic left posterior hemisphere dysfunction as a contributing factor in sex-offending behavior. *Sexual Addiction and Compulsivity, 1*(4), 337.

Day, K. (1985). Psychiatric disorder in middle aged and elderly mentally handicapped. *British Journal of Psychiatry, 147,* 660.

Devinsky, O., & Bear, D. (1984). Varieties of aggressive behavior in temporal lobe epilepsy. *American Journal of Psychiatry, 141*(5), 651.

Dupree, J. (1990). Organic brain disorders and violent behavior. *American Journal of Forensic Psychiatry, 11*(1), 71.

Elliott, F. A. (1982). Neurological findings in adult minimal brain dysfunction and the dyscontrol syndrome. *Journal of Nervous and Mental Disease, 170*(11), 680.

Furguson, S. M., Rayport, M., & Corrie, W. S. (1986). Brain correlates of aggressive behavior in temporal lobe epilepsy. In B. Doane, & K. Livingston (Eds.), *The limbic system: Functional organization and clinical disorders.* New York: Raven Press, 183–193.

Gorenstein, E. E., & Newman, J. P. (1980). Disinhibitory psychopathology: A new perspective and a model for research. *Psychological Review, 87*(3), 301.

Gunn, J., & Bonn, J. (1971). Criminality and violence in epileptic prisoners. *British Journal of Psychiatry, 118,* 337.

Häfner, H., & Böker, W. (1982). *Crimes of violence by mentally abnormal offenders: A psychiatric and epidemiological study in the Federal German Republic.* Cambridge: Cambridge University Press.

Hamstra, B. (1986). Neurobiological substrates of violence: An overview for forensic clinicians. *Journal of Psychiatry and Law*, Fall–Winter, 349.

Heinrichs, R. W. (1989). Frontal cerebral lesions and violent incidents in chronic neuropsychiatric patients. *Biological Psychiatry, Vol. 25*, 174.

Hillbrand, M., & Pallone, N. J. (1991). *The psychobiology of aggression: Engines, measurement, and control.* New York: The Haworth Press.

Kling, A. (1976). Frontal and temporal lobe lesions and aggressive behavior. In W. Smith, & A. Kling (Eds.), *Issues in brain/behavior control.* New York: Spectrum Publications.

Krakowski, M. I., Convit, A., Jaeger, J., Lin, S., & Volavka, J. (1989). Neurological impairment in violent schizophrenic inpatients. *American Journal of Psychiatry, 146*(7), 849.

Krakowski, M. I., Convit, A., & Volavka, J. (1988). Patterns of inpatient assaultiveness: Effect of neurological impairment and deviant family environment on response to treatment. *Neuropsychiatry, Neuropsychology, and Behavioral Neurology, 1*(1), 21.

Krakowski, M. I., & Czbor, P. (1994). Clinical symptoms, neurological impairment, and prediction of violence in psychiatric patients. *Hospital and Community Psychiatry, 45*(7), 700.

Kunce, J. T., Ryan, J. J., & Eckelman, C. C. (1976). Violent behavior and differential WAIS characteristics. *Journal of Consulting and Clinical Psychology, 44*(1), 42.

Lewis, D. O., & Pincus, J. H. (1989). Epilepsy and violence: Evidence for a neuropsychotic aggressive syndrome. *Journal of Neuropsychiatry, 1*(4), 413.

Lewis, D. O., Pincus, J. H., Bard, B., Richardson, E., Prichep, L. S., Feldman, M., & Yeager, C. (1988). Neuropsychiatric, psychoeducational, and family characteristics of 14 juveniles condemned to death in the United States. *American Journal of Psychiatry, 145*, 584.

Lewis, D. O., Pincus, J. H., Feldman, M., Jackson, L., & Bard, B. (1986). Psychiatric, neurological, and psychoeducational characteristics of 15 death row inmates in the United States. *American Journal of Psychiatry, 143*, 838.

Link, B., & Stueve, G. A. (1994). Psychotic symptoms and the violent illegal behavior of mental patients compared to community controls. In J. Monahan, & H. Steadman (Eds.), *Violence and mental disorder: Developments in risk assessment.* Chicago: University of Chicago Press.

Martell, D. A. (1992a). Estimating the prevalence of organic brain dysfunction in maximum-security forensic psychiatric patients. *Journal of Forensic Sciences, JFSCA, 37*(3), 878.

Martell, D. A. (1992b). Forensic neuropsychology and the criminal law. *Law and Human Behavior, 16*(3), 313.

Martell, D. A., Rosner, R., & Harmon, R. B. (1995). Base-rate estimates of criminal behavior by homeless mentally ill persons in New York City. *Psychiatric Services, 46*(6), 596.

McKinlay, W. W., Brooks, D. N., Bond, M. R., et al. (1981). The short-term outcome of severe blunt head injury as reported by the relatives of the injured person. *Journal of Neurology, Neurosurgery, and Psychiatry, 44*, 527.

Milner, J. S. (1991). *Neuropsychology of aggression.* Boston: Kluwer Academic Publishers.

Monroe, R. R. (1978). *Brain dysfunction in aggressive criminals.* Lexington, MA: D.C. Heath.

Monroe, R. R. (1981). Brain dysfunction in prisoners. In R. Hays, T. Roberts, & K. Solway (Eds.), *Violence and the violent individual.* New York: SP Medical and Scientific Books, 75–86.

Monroe, R. R. (1986). Episodic behavioral disorders and limbic ictus. In B. Doane, & K. Livingston (Eds.), *The limbic system: Functional organization and clinical disorders.* New York: Raven Press, 251–266.

Monroe, R. R., Hulfish, B., Balis, G., Lion, J., Rubin, J., McDonald, M., & Barcik, J. D. (1977). Neurological findings in recidivistic aggressors. In C. Sahass, S. Gershon, & A. J. Friedhoff (Eds.), *Psychopathology and brain dysfunction.* New York: Raven.

Nachshon, I. (1983). Hemisphere dysfunction in psychopathy and behavior disorders. In M. Myslobodsky (Ed.), *Hemisyndromes: Psychobiology, neurology, psychiatry*. New York: Academic Press, 389–414.

Nachshon, I. (1988). Hemisphere dysfunction in violent offenders. In T. E. Moffitt, & S. A. Mednick (Eds.), *Biological contributions to crime causation*. Dordrecht: Martinus Nijhoff, 55–67.

Nachshon, I., & Denno, D. (1987). Violent behavior and cerebral hemisphere function. In S. A. Mednick, T. E. Moffitt, & S. A. Stack (eds.), *The causes of crime: New biological approaches*. New York: Cambridge University Press, 185–217.

Odejide, A. O. (1981). Some clinical aspects of criminology: A study of criminal psychiatric patients at the Lantoro Psychiatric Institution. *Acta Psychiatrica Scandinavia, 3*(3), 208.

Petursson, H., & Gudjonsson, G. H. (1981). Psychiatric aspects of homicide. *Acta Psychiatrica Scandinavia, 64*, 363.

Raine, A., & Scerbo, A. (1991). Biological theories of violence. In Milner, J.S., (Ed.), *Neuropsychology of aggression*. Boston: Kluwer Academic Publishers.

Reid, A. H., Ballinger, B. R., Heather, B. B., et al. (1984). The natural history of behavioral symptoms among severely and profoundly mentally retarded patients. *British Journal of Psychiatry, 145*, 289.

Reitan, R. M., & Wolfson, D. (1986). *Traumatic brain injury. Volume 1. Pathophysiology and neuropsychological evaluation*. Tucson, AZ: Neuropsychology Press.

Rickler, K. C. (1982). Episodic dyscontrol. In D. F. Benson, & D. Blumer (Eds.), *Psychiatric aspects of neurologic disease, Vol. 2*. New York: Grune & Stratton, 49–73.

Spellacy, F. (1978). Neuropsychological discrimination between violent and nonviolent men. *Journal of Clinical Psychology, 34*(1), 49.

Stevens, J. R., & Hermann, B. P. (1981). Temporal lobe epilepsy, psychopathology, and violence: The state of the evidence. *Neurology, 31*, 1127.

Stone, A. (1984). Violence and temporal lobe epilepsy. *American Journal of Psychiatry, 141*(12), 1641.

Swanson, J. W., Holzer, C. E., Ganju, V. K., et al. (1990). Violence and mental disorder in the community: Evidence from the Epidemiologic Catchment Area surveys. *Hospital and Community Psychiatry, 41*, 761.

Tancredi, L. R., & Volkow, N. (1988). Neural substrates of violent behavior: Implications for law and public policy. *International Journal of Law and Psychiatry, 11*, 13.

Volavka, J. (1995). *Neurobiology of violence*. Washington, D.C.: American Psychiatric Press.

Volavka, J., Martell, D., & Convit, A. (1992). Psychobiology of the violent offender. *Journal of Forensic Sciences, JFSCA, 37*(1), 237.

Volkow, N. D., & Tancredi, L. (1987). Neural substrates of violent behavior: A preliminary study with positron emission tomography. *British Journal of Psychiatry, 151*, 668.

Weiger, W. A., & Bear, D. M. (1988). An approach to the neurology of aggression. *Journal of Psychiatric Research, 22*(2), 85.

West, L. Y. (1981). Discrimination of violent and non-violent inmates with the standardized Luria-Nebraska neuropsychological battery. *Dissertation Abstracts International, 42*(10), 4218.

Will, T. E. (1986). Temporal lobe neuropsychological dysfunction among violent psychiatric inpatients. *Dissertation Abstracts International, 49*(3), 923.

Williams, D. (1969). Neural factors related to habitual aggression: Consideration of differences between those habitual aggressives and others who have committed crimes of violence. *Brain, 92*, 503.

Wood, R. L. (1984). Behavior disorders following severe brain injury: Their presentation and psychological management. In N. Brooks (Ed.), *Closed head injury: Psychological, social, and family consequences*. New York: Oxford University Press.

Yeudall, L. T., Fedora, O., & Fromm, D. (1987). A neuropsychosocial theory of persistent criminality: Implications for assessment and treatment. In R. W. Rieber, (Ed.), *Advances in forensic psychology and psychiatry (Vol. 2)*. Norwood, N.J.: Ablex Publishing, 119–191.

Yeudall, L. T. (1977). Neuropsychological assessment of forensic disorders. *Canadian Mental Health, 25,* 7.

Yeudall, L. T., & Fromm-Auch, D. (1979). Neuropsychological impairment in various psychopathological populations. In J. Gruzelier, & P. Flor-Henry (Eds.), *Hemisphere asymmetries of function in psychopathology*. Amsterdam: Elsevier/North-Holland.

Yeudall, L. T., & Wardell, D. M. (1978). Neuropsychological correlates of criminal psychopathy. Part II: Discrimination and prediction of dangerous and recidivistic offenders. In L. Buliveau, C. Canepa, & D. Szabo (Eds.), *Human aggression and its dangerousness*. Montreal: Pinel Institute.

Chapter 5

SADISTIC CRIMINAL AGGRESSION: PERSPECTIVES FROM PSYCHOLOGY, CRIMINOLOGY, NEUROSCIENCE

Nathaniel J. Pallone

Wolves which batten upon lambs, lambs consumed by wolves, the strong who immolate the weak, the weak victims of the strong: there you have Nature, there you have her intentions, there you have her scheme: a perpetual action and reaction, a host of vices, a host of virtues, in one word, a perfect equilibrium resulting from the equality of good and evil on earth.

> −Donatien Alphonse Francois, le Comte de Sade, *Justine*, 1791

Cruelty, very far from being a vice, is the first sentiment Nature injects in us all. The infant breaks his toy, bites his nurse's breast, strangles his canary long before he is able to reason; cruelty is stamped in animals, in whom Nature's laws are more emphatically to be read than in ourselves; cruelty exists amongst savages, so much nearer to Nature than civilized men are; absurd then to maintain cruelty is a consequence of depravity. . . . Cruelty is simply the energy in a man civilization has not yet altogether corrupted: therefore it is a virtue, not a vice. . . . The debility to which Nature condemned women incontestably proves that her design is for man, who then more than ever enjoys his strength, to exercise it in all the violent forms that suit him best, by means of tortures, if he be so inclined, or worse.

> −Donatien Alphonse Francois, le Comte de Sade,
> *Philosophy in the Bedroom*, 1795

INTRODUCTION

In criminology and in the criminal justice processing of offenders, sadism carries very different connotations from those with which it is traditionally associated in the mental health sciences. In both the American Psychiatric Association's current nosological lexicon *(DSM–IV)* and in its international counterpart (ICD-10), sadism is identified as a sexual paraphilia, the defining characteristic of which is the derivation of pleasure from inflicting *either* physical *or* psychological pain *or* humiliation upon *either* a willing *or* an unwilling partner *during the course of sexual activity*. In the quaint prose of *DSM–IV*, redolent of the Marquis himself or even *The Story of O*, "Sadistic fantasies or acts may involve . . . forcing the victim to crawl or keeping the victim in a cage . . . restraint, blindfolding, paddling, spanking, whipping, pinching, beating, burning, electrical shocks [or] cutting, stabbing, strangulation, torture, mutilation. . . . " The key elements are that the inflictor requires that the "partner" undergo pain either to stimulate his/her own sexual arousal or that to intensify his/her own sexual gratification. Implicitly, the partner who is "willing" nominates himself/herself for diagnosis for the obverse companion disorder, sexual masochism.

In contrast, save when the clanking of chains or the lashing of whips disturbs the peace of the neighborhood, the criminal justice community (law enforcement officials, prosecutors, the courts, collectively the agents representing societal response to crime) takes little interest in *consensual* activity between adult parties, despite the pain or humiliation that may be inflicted on a "willing" partner through "bondage and discipline" practices. Similarly, "psychological" pain or humiliation that is not induced physically is not the business of law enforcement, whether the partner is "willing" or not. Such pain or humiliation may be adequate cause for dissolution of a marriage, or even for the assessment of liability in a civil court action (as in cases in which "psychological suffering" is alleged as a result of a pattern of harassment, not necessarily sexual), but it will not trigger criminal prosecution.

At base, the criminal justice community is concerned only with those situations in which one person victimizes another in an act that is specifically *not* consensual. Hence, the inflicting of *physical* pain, whether by the means litanized in *DSM–IV* or by any other means, or restraining the freedom of another (whether by "keeping the victim in a cage" or locked in an attic or cellar) upon an *unwilling* "partner" is the concern of the criminal law, whether during the course of sexual activity or not and whether or not the inflictor or restrainer is sexually motivated or derives sexual gratification therefrom.

Noun vs. Adjective

Whatever its origins, once a term has entered the general vocabulary, it becomes susceptible to competing interpretations, connotations, and denotations. In the mental health sciences, as exemplified by *DSM–IV* and ICD-10, "sadism" customarily appears as a noun, denoting a mental state liable to formal diagnosis as a mental disorder. But it is the corresponding adjective (or sometimes the adverbial form) that one encounters in the criminal justice community, where the goal is to describe behavior rather than to diagnose the mental condition which underlies that behavior.

In criminologic terms, the descriptor "sadistic" typically bears two connotations: (1) The use of physical force or aggression with disregard of the consequences, even in a situation in which deterrence may technically be justified, as in defense of the self or property, and (2) the use of physical force or aggression substantially beyond that which is required to effect a criminal act, whether that act is even remotely sexual in nature or not. In one prototypical scenario, the householder who riddles with buckshot the face, chest, and knees of an unarmed intruder, continuing to fire after the intruder has been incapacitated, will be said to have behaved sadistically, even though he/she may have been entitled to deter and to protect. In another, the armed robber who nonetheless pistol-whips a store clerk who has acceded, without resistance, to the demand that all the cash on hand be surrendered is said to have committed a "sadistic" robbery. In neither case will the criminal justice community be in the least concerned with whether the most modest level of covert, channelized, or symbolized sexual excitation or gratification is involved. Even in cases of sexual assault, law enforcement officials, prosecutors, and the courts readily distinguish the rapist who achieves his or her sexual goals by cajolery or even intimidation from his or her counterpart who is not satisfied unless the victim has been beaten, slashed, shot, or burned, before, during, or after the assault.

Psychological theorists and mental health professionals may

engage in acres of discussion about whether the humiliation of the victim *or* the gratification of sexual impulse has more potently motivated the "sadistic" rapist, but the law will be concerned only with the behavior, not its motivational genesis. Hence, in the criminological literature, one finds among the offenses discussed under the rubric "sadistic" such crimes as homicide with dismemberment and/or mutilation and robbery with atrocious assault and grievous bodily harm, especially when no resistance has been offered by the victim. Though alternate terminology (e.g., "wanton and reckless disregard," "inhumane treatment") may be used, sadistic elements in a crime of any sort constitute "aggravating factors" that, upon conviction of the perpetrator, may trigger either assignment of the maximum penalty permitted by law or, in some states, a specific "penalty enhancement" through selective incapacitation or other means.

Changing Fashions in Psychiatric Perceptions of Sadism

DSM–III (1980) tellingly and accurately observed that "it should not be assumed that all or even many rapists are motivated by Sexual Sadism. Often a rapist is not motivated by the prospect of inflicting suffering and may even lose sexual desire as a consequence" (275). Perhaps for reasons well articulated by Thomas Szasz (1987) in his incisive if cynical description of the sociopolitics that informed the construction of *DSM–III–R* (1987, 287–288), that statement had been considerably altered in the successor edition:

> Rape or other sexual assault may be committed by people with this disorder (i.e., Sexual Sadism). In such instances the suffering inflicted on the victim is far in excess of that necessary to gain compliance, and the visible pain of the victim is sexually arousing. In most cases of rape, however, the rapist is not motivated by the prospect of inflicting suffering. . . . Studies of rapists indicate that fewer than 10% have Sexual Sadism.

But *DSM–III–R* had included, in that catch-all grouping titled "proposed diagnostic categories needing further study," the description of sadistic personality disorder (369–370), in which "the essential feature . . . is a pervasive pattern of cruel, demeaning, and aggressive behavior directed toward other people, beginning by early adulthood," and it is observed that "Many people with this disorder use physical violence or cruelty to establish dominance in interpersonal relationships (not merely to achieve some noninterpersonal goal, such as striking someone in order to rob him or her). This violence is frequently resorted to or escalated when the person perceives that his or her victims are no longer willing to be intimidated or controlled."

That definition of sadistic behavior resonates well indeed with conceptualizations drawn from criminologic data. That the "proposed category" has utterly disappeared in *DSM–IV* is a cause of wonderment but not surprise to criminologists, who are often baffled by the "here today, gone tomorrow" fashions in mental health nosology under which, within a space of years, the same set of behaviors is at one point litanized as a mental disorder but at another totally invisible–with homosexuality's odyssey the prime exemplar. With such shifts within the mental health community, there is little mystery that there continues but indifferent intercourse with criminology.

RELATIVE INCIDENCE OF
SADISTIC CRIMINAL AGGRESSION

Neither *DSM–IV* nor ICD-10 estimates the relative prevalence of sexual sadism as a formal mental disorder. Although that massive compendium of criminologic data of all sorts, the *Sourcebook of Criminal Justice Statistics* (Maguire & Pastore, 1994, 288–291), enumerates the number of episodes of rape reported to law enforcement authorities annually, it does not report the proportion of rape victims who suffer injury (whether sadistically or not). But Quinsey and Upfold (1985) found that approximately half (49%) the rape victims they studied suffered injury of some sort (including 11% who were "seriously injured" and another 1.5% who were murdered) in addition to the degradation and humiliation of the sexual assault itself. *Sourcebook* data indicate that some 138,000 rapes (lone- and multiple-offender victimizations aggregated) were reported in the year under review; extrapolation of the Quinsey and Upfold rates suggests that injuries ensued in some 67,000 cases, with 15,000 of those injuries "serious." (If the sexual assault ended in the murder of the victim, owing to the peculiarities which guide the Federal data reporting mechanisms upon which the *Sourcebook* is based, the offense is enumerated only as "homicide.") If we assume that each episode of rape that results in injury of *any* sort to the victim reflects sexual sadism at some level on the part of the perpetrator (a somewhat questionable assumption, for there are many factors in addition to the perpetrator's motivation to which victim injury might be attributed, including the degree and means of victim resistance), there results a very rough gauge to which sexual sadism constitutes a *social* problem in *criminologic* terms. But there is simply no rational way on which to estimate the prevalence of sexual sadism among *consenting* parties (i.e. among those who are not *victimized* in a formal sense but instead voluntarily engage in "bondage and discipline" sexual practices or in particularly virulent forms of psychological denigration outside the sexual arena and perhaps with no physical contact).

To place the matter in context, however, it is worth noting that the *Sourcebook* estimates that nearly 410,000 victims of robbery were "seriously" injured during the same year. If the operational meaning of "serious injury generalizes between Quinsey and Upfold and the Federal crime reporting system (a questionable assumption), and again bracketing aside issues like victim resistance, it may be that more than 27 times as many robbery as rape victims suffered serious, perhaps sadistically-motivated, physical injuries. Moreover, there is some fragmentary evidence that deliberately-inflicted serious injuries are statistically more frequently associated with robbery, "bias" crimes, and gang-to-gang assaults than with other criminal offenses, including sexual offenses.

PSYCHOMETRIC MARKERS FOR
SADISTIC CRIMINAL AGGRESSION

A mere inventory of occurrence does not inform us about whether we can reasonably assume that each sadistically aggressive criminal offense represents a discrete event committed by a single offender or whether some, most, or all offenders repeatedly re-offend in the same or similar ways; and it clearly tells us little about the characteristics of those who are responsible for sadistically aggressive criminal offenses, nor about their motivations. On the basis of familiar concepts from the psychology of learning, we might readily expect that offenders who behave sadistically (whether in sexual or non-sexual offenses) because they experience an inner drive, compulsion, or urge to do so are likely to re-offend if their behavior produces tangible evidence of pain or suffering in the victim—that is to say, that reinforcement will follow precisely to the extent that the sadistic behavior produces the intended result. Both psychological and criminological research evidence lends some support to that inference.

The Megargee "Under-Controlled Hostility" Scale

Nearly 30 years ago, Megargee (1966) reasoned that persistent criminal aggression is prototypically committed by an actor who is "under-controlled" in his or her responses to even mildly provocative situations or stimuli; alternately, some acts, particularly acts of extreme aggression on the part of an actor whose responses to provocation have usually been well modulated, result from an "eruption" of "over-controlled" hostility. Megargee, Cook and Mendelsohn (1967) were able to identify 31 items on the MMPI to which differential responses had reliably been given by (1) offenders whose persistent offense history consisted of repeated convictions for brutally assaultive crimes, typically evincing "wanton disregard" and resulting in victim injury; (2) those convicted of moderately assaultive crimes; (3) those convicted of nonassaultive crimes; and (4) non-offenders. They extracted these items to constitute the Overcontrolled-Hostility (O–H) scale on the MMPI, on which low scores identify the "under-controlled" subject.

The scale has thus far proved valuable as a vehicle to differentiate what Volavka (1991) has termed "one-time aggressives," corresponding roughly to Megargee, Cook and Mendelsohn's overcontrolled group, from "habitual aggressives," corresponding to their under-controlled group. It has been utilized in a number of subsequent investigations, with results generally supportive of the conceptual model. Arnold, Quinsey and Velner (1977) cross-validated the O–H scale in a study of offenders committed to a forensic psychiatric hospital. In consonance with the conceptual model, the scale successfully differentiated persistently assaultive offenders from those who had been free of serious criminal behavior before the instant offense. Lane and Kling (1979) related both the severity of the instant offense and the chronicity of the prior offense pattern to over-controlled hostility both among prisoners and forensic psychiatric patients. Quinsey, Maguire and Varney (1983) used the O–H scale to effectively differentiate "murderers without previous criminal records from men who have committed less serious assaults and murderers with extensive histories of assault." In a partial replication in which the offense histories of prisoners were categorized by "expert" raters, DuToit and Duckitt (1990) found clear differences between the over- and the under-controlled. Race has emerged as a factor in overcontrolled hostility in some studies. Fisher (1970) reported consistently higher O–H scores among Blacks than among whites, a finding replicated among forensic psychiatric patients by Hutton, Miner, Blades and Langfeldt (1992), even when controlling for socioeconomic status and educational attainment. In an ambitious study of all offenders incarcerated in Iceland, Gudjonsson, Petursson, Sigurdardottir and Skulason (1991) investigated the relationship between O–H scores and measures of denial and deception. Results indicated significant relationships between O–H scores and both other- and self-deception.

Age-Related Decline in Persistent Sadistic Behavior with Parallels in MMPI Scores

Psychological research on persistent aggressive offending suggests a precipitate increase, particularly among males, in adolescence and early adulthood, with a rather sharp decline in the age range 35–40 and level rates of offending thereafter. Thus, Hare, McPherson and Forth (1988) analyzed the "criminal careers" over a 25-year period of Canadian offenders who had been identified psychometrically and by offense history in Hare's earlier studies as psychopaths or as nonpsychopaths, reporting that "the criminal activities of nonpsychopaths were relatively constant over the years, whereas those of psychopaths remained high until around age 40, after which they declined dramatically," adding that "The results are consistent with clinical impressions that some psychopaths tend to 'burn out' in middle age." After reviewing the relevant published research, Loeber (1990) concludes that "Patterns of antisocial behavior tend to change during preadolescence and adolescence: the number of youths who engage in overt antisocial acts declines." In Moffitt's (1993, 1994) interpretation, there is evidence of two distinct patterns of aggressive criminal behavior, with the first encompassing "a small group" of offenders (perhaps accounting for 15% of all offenders) who exhibit "life-course persistent antisocial behavior culminating in a pathologic personality" but who may be responsible for a major portion of all offenses, and a second group that exhibits "adolescence-limited antisocial behavior." It is not incidental that, in Moffitt's view, "children's neuropsychological problems interact cumulatively with their criminogenic environments" in the "adolescence-limited" group. Moffitt's "life-course persistent" offenders correspond to those identified as "under-controlled" in the experience and expression of hostility by means of Megargee's O–H scale.

Among the standard (i.e., the so-called "original 13") MMPI scales, those which have consistently differentiated aggressive from non-aggressive offenders are the scales which measure psychopathic deviation and mania, respectively (Pallone & Hennessy, 1992, 168–181). A decade ago, a major restandardization study of the MMPI was undertaken at the Mayo Clinic to provide contemporary norms inflected by age and sex (Colligan, Osborne, Swenson & Offord, 1989). It is germane to consider "incidental" findings reported by Colligan and his associates (44) that negative correlations were found between age and scores on the mania (Ma) and psychopathic deviation (Pd) scales, respectively, among both male and female subjects in their restandardization sample. These findings emerged from a restandardization study whose subject pool represented the general population, putatively free of criminal offenders. But they are remarkably congruent with the data on the epidemiology of aggressive criminal offending and with the general direction of research in "career criminality," so much so that one cannot help but wonder whether the same naturally-occurring psychological phenomenon is not also reflected in decreases in overt aggressive criminal behavior.

SADISTIC BEHAVIOR AND PSYCHOPATHY

From its probable origins in early Victorian notions of "moral insanity" to its present incarnation as "antisocial personality disorder" in *DSM–IV*, few constructs relevant to the mental health sciences have led so precarious an existence as has "psychopathic deviation" (Pichot, 1978). Lykken (1987) argues that the construct is readily divisible into "genus" and "species," identifying four "genera": the dissocial, the neurotic, the organically impulsive, and the sexually explosive. While one could wax eloquent for eons on the topic, suffice it to say that descriptions of the disorder tend toward tautology in the extreme–and insufficiently correlate psychopathy and sadistic behavior. Yet among the "diagnostic criteria" for antisocial personality disorder specified in *DSM–IV* (649–650) are included "a pervasive pattern of disregard for and violation of the rights of others," "repeatedly performing acts that are grounds for arrest," "reckless disregard for the safety of others," indifference or rationalization about "having hurt, mistreated, or stolen from, another." Except for its anchorage in sexual behavior, that litany sounds very like the *DSM–IV* description of sexual sadism—save also that there is no escape clause about "voluntariness" prompted by masochism in whomever is on the receiving end of mistreatment which pivots on "reckless disregard."

Criminologists with some frequency disdain the fine conceptual discriminations made by psychologists and psychiatrists, especially when such discriminations seem not congruent with real-time data on criminal offending. Thus, Rachlin, Halpern and Portnow (1984) have argued that psychopathic deviation should be regarded as socially deviant behavior rather than as mental illness: "There is a tremendous difference between . . . acts that are truly irresistible and those that are merely not resisted." And Wheeler (1976) has argued that the "so-called psychopathic deviate is an individual whose behavior conforms to the standards of his subculture but not to 'normal' social standards [who] often does not show any significant abnormality in behavior outside adherence to non-normative standards and values." In that view, *self-aggrandizement* rather than sexual stimulation or gratification becomes the driving force; pain is inflicted because to inflict pain is pleasurable.

Particularly since there is reason to believe that, in the real-time terms reflected in criminal justice data, criminally sadistic behavior directed at nonvoluntary victims is associated, more frequently than not, with situations that are not (or at least not overtly and explicitly) sexual in nature, it may be past time to decouple sadistic behavior from its anchorage in the arena of explicit sexuality. In such a reconceptualization, sexual sadism might be reconstrued as the manifestation of psychopathy in the sexual arena, in an overarching definition sufficiently encompassing to embrace both sadistic sexuality, whether "voluntary" or not, and nonsadistic sexual assault as manifestations of psychopathy.

THE ETIOLOGY OF SADISTIC BEHAVIOR

The Psychodynamic Interpretation

Though it is clear enough that the term derives either from the notoriety of the Marquis' actual practices or his writings (which resulted in his incarceration in prisons or asylums for more than one of every three days he lived on earth), the precise historico-etymological origins of the term "sadism" are lost. But there is little mystery as to how the term found its way into the lexicon of the mental health sciences; and its pathway perhaps dictated its virtually exclusively immersion in the arena of overt sexuality.

From his earliest works on psychosexual development (for him, equivalent to psychological development), and especially in the *General Introduction* published originally in 1920, Freud had distinguished an "oral erotic" and an "oral sadistic" stage in early infancy, with the first associated with the pleasurable (and vaguely erotic) experience of passive oral incorporation, typically associated with sucking, and the second with oral aggression, typically associated with biting. Traditional psychoanalytic views site the genesis for sadism in fixation at the oral-aggressive stage. Yet in his later work, Freud confessed dissatisfaction with that early formulation. In the *New Introductory Lectures* of 1932–33, published near the end of his life, for example, he observes (143) that "we have made no further progress along this path. Both sadism and masochism are very hard to account for by the theory of the libido."

It requires something akin to a dogmatic adherence to a very early paradigm to hold that whether an infant experienced too much or too little pain or pleasure while cutting the baby teeth or whether the pacifier Mother provided was too hard or too soft will determine whether he/she will, in adulthood, commit sadistic acts of brutality against another person—since alternative hypotheses are available and especially since, upon later reflection, the originator of that paradigm confessed himself less than satisfied with that explanation.

A Social Learning Interpretation

One attractive competing hypothesis derives from social learning theory as formulated by Albert Bandura (1962, 1969, 1973, 1979, 1986) and in particular from the well-known studies on the legitimization of aggression conducted during the 1960s by Stanley Milgram (1974). In brief, a model for sadistic behavior rooted in social learning theory holds that such behavior is learned through social imitation, sometimes via long-distance vicarious conditioning (through such agencies as films, television, and, in today's world, video games, gangster rap, and skinhead rap) that portray cruelty and/or brutality as normal and normative, with the effect particularly potent when third-parties are present in a behavioral interaction either to urge or to approbate (as in the Milgram studies) the actor to behave sadistically toward a victim.

Evidence to support that hypothesis is to be found both in social psychological and in criminological studies. A wide and impressive array of studies has confirmed exposure to violence and/or violent pornography (summarized by Pallone, 1990, 60–66), often in laboratory analogue situations, as a determinant of aggressive sexual violence. Indeed, that effect is now so well established that criminal sexual aggression is o*en held to result from the acceptability of violent male behavior toward women, supported by frequent depictions of their victimization in the mass and entertainment media (Briere, Malamuth & Check, 1985; Malamuth, 1986, 1988; Malamuth & Check, 1985; Marolla & Scully, 1986). A large number of investigations has rather convincingly demonstrated abnormal psychophysiological reactivity and sexual arousal, as measured by penile tumescence (and/or by such other indicators as electrodermal activity and vasoconstriction, generally accepted as manifestations of anxiety and tension respectively), among sex offenders when exposed *in vitro* to aberrant sexual stimuli of various sorts (Lalumiere & Quinsey, 1994). Indeed, Quinsey, Chaplin and Upfold (1984, 656), utilizing penile tumescence calibrated by means of the plethysmograph as the dependent measure, found strong evidence that rapists differ markedly from offenders convicted of nonsex crimes not only in their responses to sexual stimuli but also to stimuli which depict nonsexual violence, such that (with added emphases):

> [Stimuli] that involve vicious attacks and victim injury differentiate rapists from nonrapists. . . . Rapists [are] differentiable from nonrapists on the basis of their relative responsiveness to rape cues and consenting sex cues . . . rapists respond more to rape stimuli than to consenting sex stimuli . . . rapists respond to nonsexual violence involving female but not male victims . . . *non-sex-offenders' sexual arousal is inhibited by victim pain, whereas rapists' arousal is not . . . [the*

sexual responses of] non-sex-offenders are inhibited by descriptions of violence and victim injury, whereas [those of] rapists are not.

Congruent with Milgram's work, there is evidence that the interactive effect between intrapersonal susceptibility to social influence ("other-directedness") and direct social modeling is particularly potent. In a study in Canada in which subjects watched a videotape of a "fight-filled ice hockey" game in the presence of an experimental confederate who either "deplored, watched passively, or supported" violent behavior, Russell and Pigat (1991) concluded that "endorsement of violence is mediated by the social dependency needs" brought to the situation by subjects in conjunction with the extent to which "others" in a social interaction situation express approval or disapproval of the violence depicted. In this experimental situation (which, since it involved the use of deliberate deception, could not have been conducted in the U.S. because it counters Federal policy on research on human subjects legislated in some part as a consequence of negative public reactions to Milgram's studies on "mandates for evil"), direct and immediate (through the presence of the experimental confederate who conveyed to the subject a belief that violence is normal and normative) social reinforcement coalesced with more remote or long-distance (through the videotape depiction itself) social conditioning to deliver the same set of attitudes toward violence. That situation is surely replicated hundreds of thousands of times weekly and is clearly a key element in gang-perpetrated violence. Moreover, a number of criminologic studies (Felson, 1982; Steadman, 1982; Felson & Steadman, 1983; Henderson & Hewstone, 1984; Felson, Ribner & Siegel, 1984; Felson, 1993) analyzing the circumstances under which crimes of particularly brutal aggressive violence are actually committed confirm that the presence of third parties serves to potentiate both violence and brutality.

A Neuroscience Interpretation

Based on the explosion of knowledge about the brain and its effect on behavior derived from research in the neurosciences over the past quarter century utilizing advanced imaging techniques (e.g., CAT, PET, SPECT, BEAM, QEEG, and similar devices), the hypothesis perhaps best grounded in the data of "hard" science posits sadistic behavior as a direct consequence of naturally-occurring (e.g., congenital) or induced (more or less permanently as a result of injury or temporarily as the result of ingestion of mood-altering substances, particularly the psychotomimetics) disorder in the brain and/or central nervous system, whether morphological or neurochemical.

As a consequence of that knowledge explosion, there is now highly persuasive evidence that aggressive behavior in general is rooted in disordered brain morphology or brain biochemistry, with those conclusions resting on evidence from both human and animals studies (Pallone & Hennessy, 1992, 1993; Mills & Raine, 1994). Let us take as a case in point the evidence that links damage or dysfunction in the frontal lobes of the brain to impulsive violence both among humans and in laboratory animals. The frontal lobes are generally held to be the "seat" of such mental functions as cognition, memory, abstraction, concentration, and judgment. Both clinical (Cicerone & Wood, 1987; Joseph, 1990; Wood, 1987) and empirical evidence (Gorenstein, 1982) linking frontal lobe dysfunction among humans is sufficient to warrant the inclusion of *frontal lobe syndrome* as a distinct *organic mental disorder* in ICD-9 (U.S. Public Health Service, 1989). According to that source, at least when engendered by an identifiable injury to the brain (so that baseline data can be inspected for purposes of contrast), the "principal manifestations" of the disorder include "general diminution of self-control, foresight, creativity, and spontaneity . . . manifest[ed] as increased irritability, selfishness, restlessness, and lack of concern for others . . . [with] a change toward impulsiveness, boastfulness, temper outbursts . . . [although] measurable deterioration of intellect or memory is not necessarily present." That litany contains precisely those characteristics which have been held, at least from Cleckley (1941) onward, to be the distinguishing attributes of persons labeled psychopathically deviant and are clearly inferable from the behavior of persistently sadistic criminal aggressors.

Let us next consider some evidence from infra-human species. The naturally-occurring rate of generational maturation in such laboratory species as the white rat, coupled with the wide availability and relatively low cost of videotape equipment, enables animal experimenters to record every moment of the life of a laboratory animal, including the animal's learning history (or, if one insists on anthropomorphism, "pattern of socialization" to reinforcers and contingency conditions of various sorts) from birth onward (or at least until the point of an experimental intervention)—a set of conditions under which the usual academic debate about nature vs. nurture essentially evaporates. Rather, it is possible to specify with high precision those conditions under which a laboratory animal has been trained or "nurtured"–for example, to behave aggressively or peaceably to intrusion or attack by another animal. And the very character of the laboratory itself permits the induction of a "target" dysfunction in ways that are simply not possible in research on human subjects. Under these conditions, we can determine what happens when we deliberately damage the frontal lobes of the brain in laboratory rats who have been reared to respond peaceably or aggressively. According to distinguished neuropsychopharmacologists Robert Feldman and Linda Quenzer (1984, 248–252), the consequences are uniform, whether the animals had been "socialized" to respond aggressively or non-aggressively to intrusion. Not only did the deliberately brain-damaged animals respond with lethal aggression "intruded" into the cage, but with a particularly virulent form thereof:

> . . . the topography of the killing is different in that . . . [animals] with frontal lobe lesions are particularly vicious and ferocious, biting the [victim] again and again even though the victim is dead.

That is surely an operational definition of sadistic behavior– indeed, of oral sadism into the bargain. It is hardly surprising, then, that Feldman and Quenzer conclude that "each form of aggression has a *particular* anatomical and endocrine basis." Nor is there, in this experiment, much tolerance for the customary chicken-and-egg discussion about what preceded what or which is the causative and which the resultant variable. Such findings from animal studies are reflected in a variety of neurological and/or neuropsychological studies of persistent aggressive offenders, with remarkably similar findings. Thus:

• British neuropsychiatrist Denis Williams (1969) summarized data linking bioelectrical anomalies to aggressive crime in some 1250 prisoners he had examined over two decades. Among those whose criminal histories classified them as "habitual aggressives," he found that 65 percent displayed such anomalies, as measured by abnormal EEG readings; among those who had committed a "solitary major crime" of an aggressive nature, only 12 percent had abnormal EEG readings.

• Yeudall and Fromm-Auch (1979) found evidence of neuropathology through administration of a comprehensive neuropsychological battery in 94 percent of the homicide offenders, 96 percent of the sex offenders, 89 percent of the assaulters, and 86 percent of the juvenile offenders they examined, with these findings confirmed by subsequent EEG readings.

• DeWolfe and Ryan (1984) found left hemisphere dysfunction in 87 percent of the sexual assaulters (rapists) they examined. In a more extensive investigation that involved both administration of a comprehensive neuropsychological test battery, measures of penile tumescence in response to erotic stimuli of varying character (male/female, adult/child), and CT scans, Hucker, Langevin, Wortzman & Bain (1986) found a high incidence of neuropathology involving the left temporo-parietal region of the brain among subjects whose criminal histories classified them as focused pedophiles. In another investigation, Langevin and his colleagues (1988) reported a 30 percent incidence of neuropathology (primarily in temporal lobe disorders as measured by CT) among incest offenders.

• Yeudall, Fedora and Fromm (1987) reviewed data on the incidence of head injury prior to offending among alcoholic psychopaths (77%), homicide offenders (75%), rapists (21%), and offenders who had committed single episodes of physical assault (25%).

• Galski, Thornton and Shumsky (1990) found evidence of brain damage, or of significant neuropsychological dysfunction, in 77 percent of the incarcerated criminal sexual psychopaths they examined on the Luria Nebraska Neuropsychological Battery, discovering as well so strong an association between neuropsychological impairment and the degree of violence associated with the most recent sex offense that they were led to conclude that "the organic brain impairment discovered . . . in this sample through neuropsychological examination establishes the link between brain dysfunction and aberrant sexual behavior . . . violent sexual offenses seem to be linked with more severe neuropsychological dysfunction, specifically associated with left hemisphere functioning," a finding that parallels that of DeWolfe and Ryan (1984). At the University of Alberta Medical Center, Flor-Henry, Lang, Koles and Frenzel (1991) examined brain anomalies among pedophiles utilizing the QEEG and the plethysmograph among pedophiles, incest offenders, and control subjects. Among those classified as "true" pedophiles in consequence of penile tumescence responses to deviant sexual stimuli depicting children ranging in age from 6 to 11, the investigators observed distinct abnormalities in frontal lobe functioning and impairment in communication between the left and right hemispheres. Similar anomalies were not found among incest offenders or controls. These anomalies parallel those found earlier among exhibitionists by the Flor-Henry research group (1988).

• A small number of studies have presented longitudinal evidence linking brain dysfunction measured (or uncovered diagnostically) prior to offending to later criminal behavior. Virkkunen, Nuutila and Huusko (1976) followed a sample of brain-injured World War II veterans for nearly 30 years, concluding that the incidence of later criminality was associated with injury to the fronto-temporal region; importantly, they found that "the criminal acts very often happened only after several decades following the head injury." In a rare instance in which longitudinal data were available on a large birth cohort, Petersen, Matousek, Mednick et al. (1982) reported that "previous EEG abnormalities" detected in childhood or early adolescence were associated with later criminal behavior.

• Similarly, Volavka (1991) reported that early indices of "a light slowing of the EEG frequency predicts later development of crime" and further observed that "The incidence of EEG abnormality was particularly high among those offenders who murdered without apparent motive." In a sample of 333 offenders, Volavka found neuropathology in 64 percent of the "habitual aggressives" but in only 12 percent of the "one-time aggressives," proportions that almost precisely match those reported by Williams (1969) more than two decades earlier.

To the extent that direct comparisons are possible in light of variant measurement neurological and neuropsychological protocols, these data are displayed in Figure 5–1. When massed in this fashion and read in juxtaposition to laboratory evidence on the induction of sadistic-like behavior in infra-human species, the data require little further interpretation. But it is particularly noteworthy that these data from neurological and neuropsychological studies tend to parallel psychometric findings from studies which have utilized Megargee's over-controlled hostility scale. It may be that the O–H scale is a differential sensitive gross marker for neuropathology.

Though fragmentary, there is also evidence for the proposition that psychopathic deviation or "antisocial personality disorder" (the personality trait or characteristic most frequently regarded, even in psychoanalytic interpretations, as the substratum for all aggressive criminal offending, whether sadistic or not) itself arises from a neurogenic

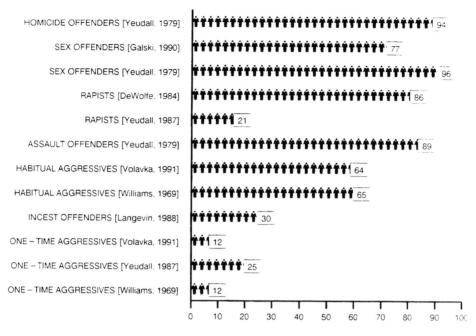

Figure 5–1. Relative incidence of neuropathology in sadistic offenders.

etiology. Robert Hare of the University of British Columbia, undoubtedly the leading authority worldwide on psychopathic deviation, has researched the relationship between psychopathy and cerebral function intensively (Hare, 1979, 1982), early (1970) distinguishing *hyper-arousability* as a characteristic of psychopaths. Support has been advanced in a number of studies:

• Blackburn (1975, 1979) found evidence of abnormally high cortical arousal, as measured through EEG readings, among prisoners diagnosed as psychopathic, findings that support Hare's view. Gorenstein (1982) reported evidence of dysfunction in the frontal lobe of the brain, held to govern such functions as foresight, planning, and the regulation of impulses among subjects otherwise diagnosed as psychopathic.

• Hare & McPherson (1984) administered a listening task that required activation of lateralized brain functions to inmates who had been classified as high or low in psychopathy and to control subjects, finding that "psychopaths are characterized by asymmetric low left-hemisphere arousal." Jutai, Hare and Connolly (1987) similarly found "asymmetric left-hemisphere arousal" patterns among subjects who had been identified through Hare's methodology as psychopathic. These results were replicated and amplified by Raine, O'Brien, Smiley and Scerbo (1990).

Neuropsychiatrists Siever, Steinberg, Trestman and Intrator (1994) evince no hesitance in grounding both psychopathy and impulsivity in disordered brain processes. Instead, reasoning that it is at least as likely that the so-called "underlying" patterns of behavior (technically, the Axis II disorders in the American Psychiatric Association's *DSM* nosologic system) as that specific symptom manifestations (the Axis I disorders) result from long-standing brain anomaly, they posit rather categorically a genesis for both impulsivity and psychopathy in impairment in brain biochemistry, specifically in the metabolism of the ubiquitous neurotransmitter serotonin:

> Impulsivity is a central feature of . . . antisocial personality disorder. A relative failure to suppress aggressive or otherwise risky behaviors with possible negative consequences may underlie the tendency toward fighting, irritability, drug abuse, promiscuity, and self-damaging acts characteristic of these disorders. Emerging evidence implicates biological abnormalities of behavior-inhibiting systems such as the 5-HT [i.e., serotonin-metabolizing] system in the expression of impulsivity. The individual with antisocial personality disorder displays characteristics of impulsivity. . . . "Psychopathy" is another basic characteristic and is defined by glibness and disregard of others' feelings associated with manipulative and exploitative behaviors . . . . A growing body of work suggests that psychophysiological correlates include inadequate detection of emotional cues and reduced cortical arousal [i.e., impaired capacity to inhibit behavior] compared with that observed in psychiatrically healthy individuals.

Such conclusions echo those of other investigators. Stein, Hollander and Liebowitz (1993) reviewed the accumulated research evidence on anomalies in serotonin metabolism in relation to impulsivity, concluding that "The concept that impulsivity is a failure in serotonergically mediated behavioral inhibition has proved remarkably fertile" and that "there has been notable convergence on the conclusion that impulsive aggression and auto-aggression correlate with serotonergic hypofunction and respond to treatment with serotonin reuptake blockers." Similarly, in their review of the accumulated research literature on both animal and human subjects, Albert Einstein College of Medicine neuropsychiatrists Brown, Botsis and Van Praag

(1994) concluded that "Decreased serotonin function has consistently been shown to be highly correlated with impulsive aggression across a number of different experimental paradigms," including the experimental manipulation of serotonin concentration and metabolism. They further note that "Such lowered serotonergic indices appear to correlate with the dimension of aggression dyscontrol and/or impulsivity rather than with psychiatric diagnostic categories per se." Brown and her colleagues also observe that "recent research has shown that a new class of drugs, the serenics, specifically cause the inhibition of antagonistic behavior, without causing sedation" in infra-human experiments and may be expected to produce similar effects in human subjects.

SUMMARY

This chapter has explored the disparate meanings attached to variants of the term "sadism" in the mental health sciences and in the criminal justice community. In the mental health sciences, sadism has traditionally been regarded as a mental disorder associated with aberrant sexual stimulation or gratification, but the adjectival (and/or adverbial) form has been used in the criminologic literature as a description of behavior rather than as an index to mental disorder. While the explicit criteria for the diagnosis of sexual sadism in *DSM–IV* and ICD-10 render it possible to apply the diagnostic label to consensual acts and to the inflicting of psychological rather than physical pain, the criminal justice community is concerned only with victimization in involuntary acts that involve either physical contact or restraint. Statistically, criminally sadistic behavior is more frequent as an aspect of nonsexual offenses than of sexual offenses. When sadistic behavior toward a victim is implicated in criminal offending, it constitutes an "aggravating factor" that triggers either the maximum or an "enhanced" penalty upon conviction. It is a matter of correlative interest that, in the American Psychiatric Association's (1984) policy statement on the insanity defense, psychopathic deviation and sexual sadism are excluded as the basis for a pleading of nonculpability for criminal behavior.

Psychometrically, sadistic criminal behavior has been associated with persistent under-controlled hostility. The over-controlled hostili-

ty scale on the MMPI developed by Megargee, Cook and Mendelsohn (1967) has proven a reliable index (at least "post-dictively") to
persistent, sadistic criminal offending, while the MMPI's psychopathic deviation and mania scales have proven robust indices to aggressive
criminal offending. Discerning reconsideration might address decou-
pling sadistic behavior from its ancient junction to sexual behavior. A
more contemporary perspective, consistent with the findings of the
neurosciences on the etiology of persistent brutal aggression, as
Lykken (1987) has intimated, might profitably link sadism to psychopathy as one of the principal avenues through which psychopathy
manifests itself.

Alternate explanations for the etiology of sadistic behavior, whether sexually oriented or not, have been explored briefly. The traditional psychoanalytic view holds that sadism has its origins in fixation
in the oral-aggressive stage in infantile psychosexual development.
Social learning theory proposes that sadism results from the influence
of negative models, aided and abetted by the acceptability of violence
as depicted in the entertainment media, with the effect enhanced
through direct social reinforcement. On the basis of both human and
animal studies, the contemporary neurosciences have linked persistent
sadistic behavior to dysfunction in the brain and/or the central nervous system, with an impressive array of investigations, many utilizing
advanced imaging techniques, to support that view.

It is a fair assessment to say that the most potent recent development in criminologic theory has been the "rational choice" model
(Clarke & Felson, 1993), which holds that criminal offending of any
sort is the result of rational decision on the part of the putative offender. That approach is congruent with a neuroscience interpretation of
the etiology of sadistic behavior, which sees a preference for the inflicting of pain upon a victim, whether in sexual circumstances or not, as
ego-syntonic rather than as ego-alien (Pallone & Hennessy, 1993). For
the rational choice theorist, the matter turns on *whether* the offender
perceives sadistic behavior as a rational response to stimuli; for the
psychologist informed by current neuroscience research, the matter
turns on *why* the putative offender perceives sadistic behavior as a
rational response. In a curious way, the construct *ego-syntonicity* returns
us to the view of the Marquis, as reflected in the headnotes to this
paper. Therapeutically and prophylactically, the task is to render
ego-syntonic sadistic drives, likely born of disordered neurology, into

resistible ego-alien impulses. Emerging neuroscience research on the pharmacological control of impulsivity and aggressivity may point the way.

REFERENCES

American Psychiatric Association. (1980). *Diagnostic and Statistical Manual of Mental and Emotional Disorders, Third edition.* Washington, DC: The Association.

American Psychiatric Association. (1984). *Issues in Forensic Psychiatry.* Washington, DC: The Association.

American Psychiatric Association. (1987). *Diagnostic and Statistical Manual of Mental and Emotional Disorders, Third edition, Revised.* Washington, DC: The Association.

American Psychiatric Association. (1994). *Diagnostic and Statistical Manual of Mental and Emotional Disorders, Fourth edition.* Washington, DC: The Association.

Arnold, L. S., Quinsey, V. L., & Velner, I. (1977). Overcontrolled hostility among men found not guilty by reason of insanity. *Canadian Journal of Behavioral Science, 9,* 333.

Bandura, A. (1962). Social learning through imitation. In M. R. Jones (ed.), *Nebraska Symposium on Motivation.* Lincoln: University of Nebraska Press.

Bandura, A. (1969). *Principles of behavior modification.* New York: Holt Rinehart Winston.

Bandura, A. (1973). *Aggression: A social learning analysis.* Englewood Cliffs, NJ: Prentice-Hall.

Bandura, A. (1979). Mechanisms of aggression from the social learning perspective. In H. Toch (ed.), *Psychology of crime and criminal justice.* New York: Holt, Rinehart, Winston.

Bandura, A. (1986). *Social foundations of thought and action: A social cognitive theory.* Englewood Cliffs, NJ: Prentice-Hall.

Blackburn, R. (1975). Aggression and the EEG: A quantitative analysis. *Journal of Abnormal Psychology, 84,* 359.

Blackburn, R. (1979). Cortical and autonomic arousal in primary and secondary psychopaths. *Psychophysiology, 16,* 143.

Briere, J., Malamuth, N., & Check, J. V. (1985). Sexuality & rape-supportive beliefs. *International Journal of Women's Studies, 8,* 398.

Brown, S. L., Botsis, A., & Van Praag, H. M. (1994). Serotonin and aggression. In M. Hillbrand, & N. J. Pallone (eds.), *The psychobiology of aggression.* New York: Haworth.

Cicerone, K. D., & Wood, J. C. (1987). Planning disorder after closed head injury: A case study. *Archives of Physical Medicine and Rehabilitation, 68,* 111.

Clarke, R. V., & Felson, M. Criminology, routine activity, and rational choice. In R. V. Clarke, & M. Felson (eds.), *Routine activity and rational choice: Advances in criminological theory.* New Brunswick: Transaction Publishers.

Cleckley, H. (1941). *The mask of sanity.* St. Louis: Mosby.

Colligan, R. C., Osborne, D., Swenson, W. M., & Offord, K. P. (1989). *The MMPI. A contemporary normative study,* 2nd ed. Odessa, FL: Psychological Assessment Resources.

DeWolfe, A. S., & Ryan, J. J. (1984). PIQ > VIQ index in a forensic sample: A reconsideration. *Journal of Clinical Psychology, 40,* 291.

DuToit, L., & Duckitt, J. (1990). Psychological characteristics of over- and under-controlled violent offenders. *Journal of Psychology, 124,* 125.

Feldman, R. S., & Quenzer, L. F. (1984). *Fundamentals of neuro-psychopharmacology.* Sunderland, MA: Sinauer.

Felson, R. B. (1982). Impression management and the escalation of aggression and violence. *Social Psychology Quarterly, 45*, 245.

Felson, R. B. (1993). Predatory and dispute-related violence: A social interactionist approach. In R. V. Clarke, & M. Felson (eds.), *Routine activity and rational choice: Advanced in criminological theory*. New Brunswick, NJ: Transaction Books.

Felson, R. B., & Steadman, H. J. (1983). Situational factors in disputes leading to criminal violence. *Criminology, 21*, 59.

Felson, R. B., Ribner, S. A., & Siegel, M. S. (1984). Age and the effect of third parties during criminal violence. *Sociology and Social Research, 68*, 452.

Fisher, G. (1970). Discriminating violence emanating from over-controlled versus under-controlled aggressivity. *British Journal of Social and Clinical Psychology, 9*, 54.

Flor-Henry, P., Lang, R. A., Koles, Z. J., & Frenzel, R. R. (1991). Quantitative EEG studies of pedophilia. *International Journal of Psychophysiology, 10*, 253.

Freud, S. (1920). *A general introduction to psychoanalysis*. New York: Liveright.

Freud, S. (1933). *New introductory lectures on psychoanalysis*. New York: W.W. Norton.

Galski, T., Thornton, K. E., & Shumsky, D. (1990). Brain dysfunction in sex offenders. *Journal of Offender Rehabilitation, 16*, 65.

Gorenstein, E. E. (1982). Frontal lobe functions in psychopaths. *Journal of Abnormal Psychology, 91*, 368.

Gudjonsson, G. H., Petursson, H., Sigurdardottir, H., & Skulason, S. (1991). Overcontrolled hostility among prisoners and its relationship with denial and personality scores. *Personality and Individual Differences, 12*, 17.

Hare, R. D. (1970). *Psychopathy: Theory and research*. New York: Wiley.

Hare, R. D. (1979). Psychopathy and laterality of cerebral function. *Journal of Abnormal Psychology, 88*, 605.

Hare, R. D. (1982). Psychopathy and physiological activity during anticipation of an aversive stimulus in a distraction paradigm. *Psychophysiology, 19*, 266.

Hare, R. D., & McPherson, L. M. (1984). Psychopathy and perceptual asymmetry during verbal dichotic listening. *Journal of Abnormal Psychology, 93*, 141.

Hare, R. D., McPherson, L. M., & Forth, A. E. (1988). Male psychopaths and their criminal careers. *Journal of Consulting and Clinical Psychology, 56*, 710.

Hare, R. D., Harpur, T., Hakstian, A. R., & Forth, A. E. (1990). The revised psychopathy checklist: Reliability and factor structure. *Journal of Personality Assessment, 2*, 338.

Henderson, M., & Hewstone, M. (1984). Prison inmates' explanations for interpersonal violence: Accounts and attributions. *Journal of Consulting and Clinical Psychology, 52*, 789.

Hucker, S., Langevin, R., Wortzman, G., & Bain, J. (1986). Neuropsychological impairment in pedophiles. *Canadian Journal of Behavioural Science, 18*, 440.

Hutton, H. E., Miner, M. H., Blades, J. R., & Langfeldt, V. C. (1992). Ethnic differences on the MMPI overcontrolled-hostility scale. *Journal of Personality Assessment, 58*, 260.

Joseph, R. (1990). *Neuropsychology, neuropsychiatry, and behavioral neurology*. New York: Plenum.

Jutai, J. W., Hare, R. D., & Connolly, J. F. (1987). Psychopathy and event-related brain potentials (ERPs) associated with attention to speech stimuli. *Personality and Individual Differences, 8*, 175.

Lalumiere, M. L., & Quinsey, V. L. (1994). The discrimination of rapists from non-sex offenders using phallometric measures: A meta-analysis. *Criminal Justice and Behavior, 21*, 150.

Lane, J., & Kling, J. S. (1979). Construct validation of the overcontrolled hostility scales of the MMPI. *Journal of Consulting and Clinical Psychology, 47*, 781.

Langevin, R., Wortzman, G., Dickey, R., Wright, P., & Hancy, L. (1988). Neuropsychological impairment in incest offenders. *Annals of Sex Research, 1*, 401.

Loeber, R. (1990). Families and crime. In L. J. Siegel (ed.), *American justice: Research of the national institute of justice*. St. Paul, MN: West.

Lykken, D. T. (1987). Psychopathic personality. In R. J. Corsini (ed.), *Concise Encyclopedia of Psychology*. New York: Wiley.

Maguire, K., & Pastore, A. L. (1994). *Sourcebook of Criminal Justice Statistics*. Washington, DC: Bureau of Justice Statistics, U.S. Department of Justice.

Malamuth, N. M. (1986). Predictors of naturalistic sexual aggression. *Journal of Personality and Social Psychology*, *50*, 953.

Malamuth, N. M., & Check, J. V. (1985). The effects of aggressive pornography on beliefs in rape myths: Individual differences. *Journal of Research in Personality*, *19*, 299.

Marolla, J. A., & Scully, D. (1986). Attitudes toward women, violence, and rape: A comparison of convicted rapists and other felons. *Deviant Behavior*, *7*, 337.

Megargee, E. I., Cook, J. C., & Mendelsohn, H. T. (1967). The development and validation of an MMPI scale of assaultiveness in overcontrolled individuals. *Journal of Abnormal Psychology*, *72*, 519.

Milgram, S. (1974). *Obedience to authority: An experimental view*. New York: Harper & Row.

Mills, S., & Raine, A. (1994). Neuroimaging and aggression. In M. Hillbrand, & N. J. Pallone (eds.), *The psychobiology of aggression*. New York: Haworth.

Moffitt, T. E. (1993). Adolescence-limited and life-course-persistent antisocial behavior: A developmental taxonomy. *Psychological Bulletin*, *100*, 674.

Moffitt, T. E. (1994). *Juvenile Delinquency: Seed Of A Career In Violent Crime, Just Sowing Wild Oats–Or Both?* Washington: Federation of Behavioral, Psychological & Cognitive Sciences.

Pallone, N. J. (1990). *Rehabilitating criminal sexual psychopaths: Legislative mandates, clinical quandaries*. New Brunswick, NJ: Transaction Books.

Pallone, N. J., & Hennessy, J. J. (1992). *Criminal behavior: A process psychology analysis*. New Brunswick: Transaction Publishers.

Pallone, N. J., & Hennessy, J. J. (1993). Tinderbox criminal violence: Neurogenic impulsivity, risk-taking, and the phenomenology of rational choice. In R. V. Clarke, & M. Felson (eds.), *Routine activity and rational choice: Advances in criminological theory*. New Brunswick: Transaction Publishers.

Petersen, K. G., Matousek, M., Mednick, S. A., Volavka, J., & Pollock, V. (1982). EEG antecedents of thievery. *Acta Psychiatrica Scandinavica*, *65*, 331.

Pichot, P. (1978). Psychopathic behaviour: A historical overview. In R. D. Hare, & D. Schalling (eds.), *Psychopathic behaviour: Approaches to research*. New York: Wiley.

Quinsey, V. L., & Upfold, D. (1985). Rape completion and victim injury as a function of female resistance strategy. *Canadian Journal of Behavioural Science*, *17*, 40.

Quinsey, V. L., Chaplin, T. C., & Upfold, D. (1984). Sexual arousal to non-sexual violence and sadomasochistic themes among rapists and non-sex offenders. *Journal of Consulting and Clinical Psychology*, *52*, 651.

Quinsey, V. L., Maguire, A., & Varney, G. W. (1983). Assertion and overcontrolled hostility among mentally disordered murderers. *Journal of Consulting and Clinical Psychology*, *51*, 550.

Rachlin, S., Halpern, A. L., & Portnow, S. L. (1984). The volitional rule, personality disorders and the insanity defense. *Psychiatric Annals*, *14*, 139.

Raine, A., O'Brien, M., Smiley, N., & Scerbo, A. (1990). Reduced lateralization in verbal dichotic listening in adolescent psychopaths. *Journal of Abnormal Psychology*, *99*, 272.

Russell, G. W., & Pigat, L. (1991). Effects of modeled censure/support of media violence and need for approval on aggression. *Current Psychology*, *10*, 121.

Siever, L. J., Steinberg, B. J., Trestman, R. L., & Intrator, J. (1994). Personality disorders. *Review of Psychiatry, Volume 13*. Washington, DC: American Psychiatric Press.

Steadman, H. J. (1982). A situational approach to violence. *International Journal of Law and Psychiatry, 5*, 171.

Stein, D. J., Hollander, E., & Liebowitz, M. R. (1993). Neurobiology of impulsivity and the impulse control disorders. *Journal of Neuropsychiatry and Clinical Neurosciences, 5*, 9.

Szasz, T. (1987). *Insanity: The idea and its consequences*. New York: Wiley.

U.S. Public Health Service. (1989). *International Classification of Diseases, 9th Revision, Clinical Modification: Third Edition*. Washington: U.S. Department of Health & Human Services. Publication No. (PHS) 89–1260.

Virkkunen, M., Nuutila, A., & Huusko, S. (1976). Effect of brain injury on social adaptability: Longitudinal study on frequency of criminality. *Acta Psychiatrica Scandinavica, 53*, 168.

Volavka, J. (1991). Aggression, electroencephalography, and evoked potentials: A critical review. *Neuropsychiatry, Neuropsychology and Behavioral Neurology, 3*, 249.

Wheeler, S. (1976). Trends and problems in the sociological study of crime. *Social Problems, 23*, 525.

Williams, D. (1969). Neural factors related to habitual aggression: Consideration of differences between those habitual aggressives and others who have committed crimes of violence. *Brain, 92*, 501.

Wood, R. L. (1987). *Brain injury rehabilitation: A neurobehavioral approach*. Rockville, MD: Aspen.

World Health Organization. (1992). *The ICD-10 Classification of Mental and Behavioural Disorders*. Geneva: The Organization.

Yeudall, L. T., & Fromm-Auch, D. (1979). Neuropsychological impairments in various psychopathological populations. In J. Gruzelier, & P. Flor-Henry (eds.) *Hemisphere asymmetries of function in psychopathology*. Amsterdam: Elsevier/North Holland Biomedical Press.

Yeudall, L. T., Fedora, O., & Fromm, D. (1987). A neuropsychological theory of persistent criminality: Implications for assessment and treatment. *Advances in Forensic Psychology and Psychiatry, 2*, 119.

SECTION II
DISORDERS OF THOUGHT

INTRODUCTION TO SECTION II

In Section Two, five topics have been selected that present various disorders of thought which lead to criminal conduct, and have significant forensic implications. In Chapter 6, J. Arturo Silva, Gregory B. Leong, and Robert Weinstock review forensic aspects of delusional misidentification associated with aggression and violence. Misidentification syndromes are a delusional belief that the self or another individual is no longer the same person, often thought to have been replaced by an imposter. The relationship between such a delusion and violent and aggressive behavior has obvious forensic implications. The whole concept of delusional misidentification is covered from a definitional perspective with a focus on how such disturbed thinking can result in violent acting out. The issue of dangerousness and delusional misidentification is reviewed, as well as the neuropsychiatric basis of delusional misidentification syndromes, along with other clinical considerations relevant to this unusual syndrome. The nature of individuals at risk of physical attack by persons with delusional misidentification is discussed along with diagnosis, treatment, and future directions for research and clinical practice. Biological factors, clinical and legal considerations are covered, along with some case descriptions to illustrate the authors' various points.

In Chapter 7, J. Reid Meloy presents a clinical investigation of the obsessional follower, commonly referred to as the stalker. Dr. Meloy eschews the term "stalking," as he believes obsessional follower is a more apt name for an individual who engages in a long-term pattern of threats and harassment towards another individual. The person's underlying obsessive thinking results in overt acts of pursuit that are unwanted by the victim, and are perceived as being threatening. The author reviews the research on obsessional followers and discusses demographic characteristics, psychiatric and psychological characteristics and patterns of pursuit, characteristics of the victim, as well as patterns of violence, threats, and several subtypes of the disorder. Dr. Meloy also examines the syndrome of erotomania as well as his concept of "borderline erotomania." The chapter concludes with the discussion of psychodynamics and some areas for future research, study, and practice.

In Chapter 8, Robert D. Miller discusses forensic aspects of factitious disorder (i.e., illnesses that are not real, not genuine or simulated, and thought to be motivated by an individual wanting to assume the patient role). The chapter begins with an in-depth consideration of diagnosis and diagnostic issues. Factitious disorder and its relationship to malingering, other disorders, clinical course, and etiology, are all noted. Dr. Miller also discusses the prevalence, treatment, and management of factitious disorders with physical symptoms. Other topics covered are factitious disorder with psychological symptoms, treatment within a forensic context, plus a very detailed and excellent review of the forensic issues (both criminal and civil) associated with factitious disorder. The author also deals with such important topics as Munchausen syndrome by proxy (i.e., an individual who presents unreal physical symptoms leading to hospitalizations in someone else, typically a child) and the forensic problems associated with this fascinating behavior. A number of important legal cases are reported and Dr. Miller advises how such matters should be handled in court by the forensic practitioner.

Barry Morenz and Steven Herron explore the relationship between morbid jealousy and criminal conduct in Chapter 9. The authors begin their chapter by defining morbid jealousy, and review the emotion of jealousy from sociological, psychological, and psychoanalytic perspective. They then describe clinical characteristics as well as the epidemiology of morbid jealousy, nosological considerations, phenomenology, treatment, and outcome of individuals with this condition. The potential for violence among persons afflicted with morbid jealousy is reviewed, as well as legal issues such as competency to stand trial, insanity, and considerations for sentencing. Issues involving a direction for future research and study of this interesting topic is also handled throughout.

The final chapter in Section Two, by W. A. Weston, is on the topic of pseudologia fantastica and pathological lying. So many types of criminal defendants manifest various forms of pathological lying, as well as nonpathological direct lying for obvious reasons. And the forensic implications of an individual who has a pathological need to lie and greatly exaggerate is obvious, since telling the truth is so important in legal matters. Pseudologia fantastica has not really achieved the type of recognition and the amount of research, study, and consideration that it clearly deserves. Much of the time, pseudologia fantastica is viewed as a manifestation of a more primary problem as opposed to being an independent entity. The syndrome is defined in a detailed way, and the literature (for the past 100 or so years) is reviewed. Dr. Weston discusses developmental factors associated with pathological lying, issues and differential diagnosis, social issues connected with lying, as well as biological and cognitive aspects. The author reviews classification systems, genetics, and some other related areas. This chapter makes an important contribution towards a better understanding of the entire phenomenon and syndrome.

Chapter 6

FORENSIC ASPECTS OF DELUSIONAL MISIDENTIFICATION ASSOCIATED WITH AGGRESSION AND VIOLENCE

J. Arturo Silva, Gregory B. Leong, and Robert Weinstock

DELUSIONS AND AGGRESSION

Psychosis has long been postulated as being associated with dangerous thoughts and actions (West & Walk, 1977). However, only recently have research findings given substantial credibility to this hypothesis (Swanson, 1994). About a decade ago, threat/control-override psychotic symptoms were found to be associated with increased violence risk (Link & Stueve, 1994). More recently, the MacArthur Violence Risk Assessment Study performed in the U.S. had added to the knowledge base on this topic, but has not significantly increased our ability to forecast violent behavior by delusional individuals on the basis of the delusion itself and questioned the utility of threat-control override delusions as a prognosticator of violence (Appelbaum et al., 2000). A recent review of the literature affirms the hypothesis of the complex relationship between mental disorder and violence (Nestor, 2002).

Nonetheless, a direct cause and effect relationship explicating the translation of the potential for physical harm to actualized harm remains elusive. This problem can be grossly dichotomized into clinical and forensic contexts. In the former, mental health providers implement clinical interventions when a patient presents as potential-

114

ly harmful (dangerous). In the latter, the legal system reacts when an actualized harm (crime or tort) has occurred. In this chapter, aggressive actions are examined from both the perspective of potential and of actualized harms as they relate to delusional misidentification.

Our limited understanding of the link between psychosis and resultant aggression is reflected in both the limited clinical approaches that have evolved in the treatment of dangerous psychotic individuals (Tardiff, 2003; Gerner, 2003) as well as in the resulting problematic legal issues (West & Walk, 1977; Miller, 2003a; Miller, 2003b).

Systematic research delving into the relationship between delusions and violence has been of recent origin. Some seminal work from a group of British psychiatrists has appeared only about a decade ago (Buchanan, 1993; Wessely et al., 1993; Buchanan et al., 1993). Researchers studied both patient and informant reports and found that actions associated with delusions were more common than previously suggested (Wessely et al., 1993). These clinical investigators found that reports by patients of their psychopathology indicated an association between action and delusional content, anxiety or dysphoria (Buchanan et al., 1993). However, these studies lacked in-depth analysis of the relationship of delusional thinking to aggression because the development of instruments to systematically measure the effect of delusions on behavior has only just begun (Taylor et al., 1994).

The relationship between aggression and delusional thinking has also been studied by focusing on the specific delusional content such as erotomania (Goldstein, 1987) or delusional jealousy (Leong et al., 1994) in which there are specific targets in association with violent behaviors. In this chapter, we adopt this approach and explore the potential relation between the delusional misidentification syndromes and violent behavior.

In this chapter, we define dangerous delusional misidentification as a delusional misidentification that appears to be an important, if not the main cause for verbal and/or physical aggression or violence resulting in the psychiatric hospitalization or incarceration of the delusional individual. We emphasize that the usual definition of dangerousness refers to the potential for harm (Leong et al., 2003). However, in this chapter we use the term in association with dangerous delusional misidentification to refer to both potential and actualized harms.

Lastly, in this chapter we use delusional misidentification syndromes interchangeably with delusional misidentification in deference to the historical perspective, which considered misidentification delusions to comprise specific syndromes. The names of these syndromes remain in the vernacular of the mental health professions, and in the literature. For example, Capgras syndrome (see next below) has also been described as the Capgras delusion or Capgras symptom in the psychiatric literature.

Definitions for Delusional Misidentification Syndromes

The main feature of a delusional misidentification syndrome is the presence of a delusion involving the personal identity of the self and/or others. A misidentification delusion may involve the physical and/or psychological identity of the self or of an object in the affected person's environment (Signer, 1987; Silva et al., 1990; Silva et al., 1992a). Furthermore, the physical misidentification of identity may refer to both the internal or external physical characteristics of the delusionally misidentified object. The three basic forms of delusional misidentification are known as Capgras syndrome (Capgras & Reboul-Lachaux, 1923), the Frégoli Syndrome (Courbon & Fail, 1927), and the syndrome of intermetamorphosis (Courbon & Tusques, 1932).

Capgras syndrome is the best known delusional misidentification syndrome. In this syndrome the affected individual delusionally believes that a person in his or her environment has experienced a radical change in psychological personal identity but the physical appearance remains unchanged (Capgras & Reboul-Lachaux, 1923; Kimura, 1986; Silva et al., 1990). Frequently, in Capgras syndrome the delusionally misidentified object is conceptualized by the affected person as a physical replica or impostor. The Frégoli syndrome presents with a delusion of radical change in physical but not psychological identity (Courbon & Fail, 1927; Silva et al., 1990). In this syndrome, the affected individual often views the misidentified object as an impersonator. In the syndrome of intermetamorphosis the affected person harbors the delusion that both the psychological and physical identities of another person are fundamentally changed (Courbon & Tusques, 1932; Silva et al., 1990; Silva et al., 1991a).

The aforementioned three forms of delusional misidentification may be directed at the affected person instead of persons in the environment. When this occurs, the delusional misidentification is termed delusional misidentification syndrome of the self (Silva et al., 1990) or a "reverse" delusional misidentification syndrome (Signer, 1987; Silva et al., 1990). There is a third type of delusional misidentification, known as the syndromes of "subjective" delusional misidentification (Christodoulou, 1978). The better known of these syndromes is the syndrome of subjective doubles (Christodoulou, 1978) or subjective Capgras (Silva et al., 1992a). It is characterized by the belief in the existence of physical replicas of the delusional person who are thought to harbor a different psychological makeup than that of the deluded person. A subjective Frégoli type of delusional misidentification in which the affected individual believes that his or her mind exists in the body of persons in the environment has also been reported (Vartzopoulos & Vartzopoulos, 1991; Silva & Leong, 1991). An exploration of the potential relation between delusional misidentification and violence is especially compelling, given the increased reporting of delusional misidentification associated with violence recently. A comprehensive understanding of a delusional misidentification may be of important psychiatric-legal value.

Delusional Misidentification Syndromes and Dangerousness

Many cases of individuals with delusional misidentification and violence have been reported in the psychiatric literature during approximately the past two decades. The psychiatric literature suggests that the most frequently associated mental disorders associated with delusional misidentification syndromes fall into the category of psychotic disorders irrespective of the etiology. In recent years, mental health professionals have also recognized that persons affected with a delusional misidentification syndrome arising out of dementia can act violently (Silva et al., 2001). Although individuals with all types of delusional misidentification have been found to harbor dangerous delusional misidentification, Capgras syndrome has been the most extensively studied type of delusional misidentification in reference to dangerousness (Silva et al., 1989; Silva et al., 1992a; Bourget & Whitehurst, 2004).

From a psychodynamic perspective, Capgras syndrome is thought to involve several psychological defense mechanisms (Silva et al., 1989). Some clinicians have been postulated that individuals with Capgras syndrome may have symptoms that originate with feelings of anger toward persons in their lives with whom they have an emotional connection, whether real or imagined. These persons may use the defense mechanism of denial as a way to cope with their anger. If this is insufficient, the delusional person may then use splitting as a defense mechanism. The affected individual accomplishes this usually by assigning positive attributes to the original identity and uniformly negative attributes to the delusionally altered identity. With the now delusionally misidentified object assuming a resulting "evil" or "malicious" character, the delusional individual can now righteously direct anger at the delusionally misidentified object without experiencing any conflicts. The defense mechanism of projection is also thought to operate in delusional misidentification because the affected individual is able to attribute his or her own hostile impulses as originating from the misidentified objects. Projective identification is thought to be utilized because the delusional individual projects his or her own dissociated thought or emotion onto another person while simultaneously continuing to experience these thoughts or feelings. The individual then misperceives these thoughts and feelings as emanating from the other person and thinks his or her own feelings are in response to those of the other person. Projective identification then causes the affected individual to fear others as being hostile, thereby mobilizing the person's attempts to combat others (Kernberg, 1985). Of course, psychodynamic explanations fail to explain the reason that not all those with delusional misidentification syndromes view their delusionally misidentified objects as malicious. Moreover, delusional misidentifications of the self involve different dynamics than those associated with delusional misidentification of others.

In addition to believing that the misidentified objects are malicious, the Capgras syndrome individual may take this one step further and come to believe the misidentified object endangers the delusional individual. In response to the perceived threat, the dangerous Capgras individual may physically attack the misidentified object either as an act of self-defense or in retribution for the alleged transgressions of the misidentified object (Silva et al., 1989; Silva et al., 1992a; Silva et al., 1995a; Silva et al., 1995b; Silva et al., 1995d). The following case is representative of a Capgras individual who became violent towards one of his misidentified objects.

> Mr. A. was a 20-year-old man who was arrested after he assaulted a policeman with a knife. Mr. A. believed that the policeman was an android who at the time of the attack, had intended to burn him with

a "high-tech" weapon and possibly kill him in the process. Mr. A. believed that the policeman was part of a large-scale conspiracy designed to rob the defendant of property rights for the construction of the starship Enterprise.

Mr. A. was referring to the spaceship featured in the television series *Star Trek*. He also claimed that his father, his sister, and various strangers had been reconfigured into robotic entities whose body surfaces were identical to the original persons. However, he believed that their internal bodily architectures were robotic in nature. Analyzing delusional experiences as complex multicomponent systems involving different thought contents may be advantageous in forensic-psychiatric settings. In Mr. A.'s case, he harbored a grandiose component because he thought that he was the rightful owner of the blueprints for constructing the starship Enterprise. He thought that the ownership of that information invested Mr. A. with power and wealth. He also harbored the intense paranoid component that was phenomenologically important in explaining the reason for Mr. A.'s attack on the police officer. Mr. A. reported a history of a head injury to the right frontal aspect of his head that required a brief hospitalization. He stated that a few months after this injury he began to experience psychotic symptoms associated with delusional misidentification. He added that the replicas had different personalities than his real parents and that the replicas were evil in nature. He also believed that his brothers and sisters were replicas of his original siblings who possessed different psychological make-ups than the originals. He said that the tone of voice of the impostors had convinced him of their inauthentic identity. In addition to these delusions, he experienced mood lability, markedly decreased need for sleep, pressured speech, and marked distractibility. Physical, including neurological, examination revealed no abnormalities. He had a scar at the right frontal aspect of his head. Complete blood count, serum chemistries, and urinalysis were within normal limits. On the Benton Facial Recognition Test (BFRT), a test designed to assess immediate unfamiliar face recognition, he scored 52 (i.e., within normal limits). The Warrington Recognition Memory Test (WRMT) was designed to explore potential indications for dominant versus nondominant cerebral damage associated with deficits in short-term memory. On the face subtest of the WRMT, he scored 31 (i.e., at the 1st percentile). This is consistent with a score associated with persons who suffer from nondominant brain abnormalities. He met *DSM–IV–TR* criteria for Psychotic Disorder Not Otherwise Specified (APA, 2000). Despite approximately two years of treatment with antipsychotic medication, his Capgras delusion persisted, though the negative affect associated with paranoia was substantially reduced.

Persons who suffer from Frégoli and intermetamorphosis syndromes may become dangerous for reasons similar to those of dangerous Capgras persons. Furthermore, the delusion of intermetamorphosis may also involve the experience of visual perceptual changes involving the physical makeup of the delusionally misidentified object. If these individuals perceive substantial distortions in the surface bodily structure of the misidentified object, an additional reason for acting aggressively arises.

In the syndrome of subjective Capgras, replicas of the delusional person are generally thought by the affected individual to be malicious in nature. Not infrequently, individuals who harbor dangerous subjective Capgras delusions believe that their replicas engage in antisocial activities for which the delusional person will be eventually blamed. Individuals who suffer from this syndrome can become dangerous because they may conclude that persons in their surroundings are accomplices or even creators of the affected person's replicas (Silva & Leong, 1993). The following is representative of a case of dangerous subjective Capgras:

> Mr. B. was a 30-year-old single man who was involuntarily hospitalized after threatening a bank teller. Mr. B. complained to the teller that several persons were passing "bad checks" in his name in order to ruin his reputation and to deplete his bank account. He believed that several people were impersonating him with face masks identical to his face in order to perpetrate misdeeds in his name. He appeared agitated and was threatening to attack his alleged impersonators when the police intervened. Mr. B. had a history of physically attacking others in the past but it was not clear if he had been suffering from misidentification delusions during these previous episodes of violence. Mr. B. also experienced auditory hallucinations and displayed loose associations. Mr. B. had a history of suffering from psychotic symptoms since age 24. Physical, including neurological, examination was unremarkable. His complete blood count, serum chemistries, and urinalysis were within normal limits. Mr. B. met *DSM–IV–TR* criteria for paranoid schizophrenia (APA, 2000).

Persons with delusional misidentifications of the self are dangerous for different reasons than those with delusional misidentification of objects in the environment. First, these individuals often present with a delusional component of grandiosity (Silva et al., 1995c) in that they frequently believe that they have become powerful and well-known figures who should be respected and revered. When others fail to participate in this adulation, these individuals may react with verbal threats and/or physical aggression toward others (Silva et al., 1992a). These individuals may also experience grandiose delusions of misidentification involving hyper-religiosity. For example, they may delusionally believe that they are Christ, a biblical archangel, or Buddha (Silva et al., 1995b; Silva et al., 1995d). The following case is illustrative of a man whose aggression was dominated by delusional misidentification of the self. Although he also presented with a delusional misidentification of others, there was no aggression associated with that delusion. The case also illustrates the common association of delusional misidentification of the self with religious and grandiose components to the delusional system as well as with Capgras delusions (Silva & Leong, 1994).

> Mr. C. was a 45-year-old man who had been imprisoned after he used a hammer to physically assault two former co-workers, who he misidentified as the devil. One of the victims sustained a serious head injury. For several weeks prior to his violent behavior, Mr. C. had delusionally misidentified his mother as the Virgin Mary, but did not attach any negative attributes to her. When he attended his mother's church, he introduced himself as Jesus Christ, and quickly identified several members of the congregation as various apostles, in part because those persons had the same first names as the biblical apostles. Mr. C. also thought that he had the ability to work miracles. Mr. C. described auditory hallucinations telling him he was the Messiah and warning him about potential aggressors. He exhibited pressured speech, decreased need for sleep, affective lability, and diminished attention span. He denied prior head injuries, epilepsy, or major medical illnesses. His family psychiatric history was negative. His complete blood count, serum chemistries, urinalysis, and head CT scan were normal. His physical, including neurological, examination revealed no abnormalities. Mr. C. met *DSM–IV–TR* diagnostic criteria for schizoaffective disorder (APA, 2000). Despite treatment with lithium carbonate and haloperidol, he continued to display delusional misidentification.

In 1993, Dinwiddie and Yutzy noted that little controlled research had been carried out in the area of dangerous delusional misidentification syndromes (Dinwiddie & Yutzy, 1993). Since then, Silva and colleagues published a study of a group of dangerous delusional misidentification syndrome persons involving 25 subjects. This group was compared to 25 dangerous individuals who harbored non-misidentification delusions (Silva et al., 1995b). The results of the Brief Psychiatric Rating Scale (BPRS) and other psychiatric-legal variables were studied. They found that the dangerous delusional misidentification syndrome group scored significantly higher than the dangerous nondelusional misidentification syndrome group in total BPRS score, indicating a higher level of psychopathology for the delusional misidentification syndrome group. The BPRS grandiosity item also was significantly higher for the delusional misidentification syndrome group than for the nondelusional misidentification syndrome group. This result is consistent with other studies which suggest that grandiosity may be an important factor in the genesis of dangerousness in at least some cases of delusional misidentification (Driscoll et al., 1991; Silva et al., 1992a; Silva et al., 1995b; Silva et al., 1995c; Silva et al., 1995d). The study also found that although the hostility subfactor of the BPRS was significantly higher for the delusional misidentification syndrome group than for the nondelusional misidentification syndrome group, it was the latter group that was significantly associated with attacks that used a weapon, i.e., suggesting that greater planning was involved. The authors concluded that although the individuals with delusional misidentification suffer from a greater degree of hostility than nondelusional misidentification individuals, the hostility may not result in physical aggression because the nondelusional misidentification group appeared to be better organized and as a result more capable of creating plans of attack and executing such plans" (Silva et al., 1995b).

Neuropsychiatric Bases of Delusional Misidentification

The study of delusional misidentification has led to useful models that have helped to clarify the neuropsychiatric basis of personal identity, face recognition, object familiarity and memory. The available information suggests that delusional misidentification is frequently associated with a variety of mild to severe biological abnormalities (Signer, 1987; Malloy et al., 1992). Other studies suggest that non-dominant cerebral deficits may be important in the genesis of delusional misidentification (Feinberg & Shapiro, 1984; Fleminger & Burns, 1993; Feinberg and Roane, 2005). However, in most cases, left brain abnormalities cannot be completely ruled out as important neuropsychiatric bases in the causation of delusional misidentification (Signer, 1987; Signer, 1994).

An association between delusional misidentification and face recognition processing has been postulated by several investigators (Ellis & Lewis, 2001). Two lines of evidence support this thesis. First, phenomenological study of cases of the intermetamorphosis syndrome, indicate that affected individuals may perceive substantially different facial structures in the resulting "personal identities" compared to the original facial structures of the misidentified objects (Silva et al., 1991a; Silva et al., 1993; Silva et al., 1994a). Even in cases of Capgras syndrome, in which the affected individual perceives the physical surface of the alleged replica as identical to that of the original identity of the misidentified object, the delusional individual may also report that the face of the misidentified object appears strange or changed in ways that are difficult or impossible for the delusional individual to describe. Second, several neuropsychological investigations have documented different types of face recognition deficits in individuals with delusional misidentification (Young et al., 1990; Silva et al., 1993; Ellis et al., 1993; Silva et al., 1994a; Ellis & Lewis, 2001). Some of the perceived changes in the faces of the misidentified objects have been described by dangerous delusional misidentification syndrome persons as having been altered with respect to texture, color, and shape. These alleged facial changes appear to predispose some delusional misidentification syndrome individuals to become more fearful of and/or hostile toward the misidentified object, resulting sometimes in physical attacks by the delusional person on misidentified object (Silva et al., 1993; Silva et al., 1994a).

The onset of dangerous delusional misidentification has also occurred in conjunction with psychoactive substance use. Alcohol has been implicated as a potentiating factor for aggression due to delusional misidentification in someone already suffering from a major mental disorder such as schizophrenia (Thompson & Swan, 1993). Of course, alcohol itself can be a significant factor in aggressive behavior, especially when an individual is intoxicated or otherwise under the influence. Amphetamine compounds, known for inducing psychotic states, can present with dangerous delusional misidentification syndrome of the self and/or others (Kimura et al., 1981). In addition, some drugs can worsen a preexisting delusional misidentification.

Phencyclidine can precipitate not only a psychotic state but also acts like an anesthetic that induces intense dissociative states involving depersonalization and delusional misidentification of the self. For example, a man under the influence of phencyclidine developed the delusion that he had transformed himself into the devil, and then proceeded to kill an unknown passer-by (Siegel, 1989).

Other Clinical Considerations Relevant to Delusional Misidentifications

An important factor that may help increase the potential for violence in delusional misidentification is the potential for the person with delusional misidentification to incorporate the mental health clinician as a misidentified object. In this situation the delusional misidentification patient may opt to avoid treatment, believing that the mental health clinician is a malicious impostor (Silva et al., 1995a). In the meantime, the untreated patient may act violently elsewhere.

By their very nature, misidentification delusions present with bizarre themes. For example, individuals may delusionally believe that the misidentified objects are robots, werewolves, full-fledged animals or extraterrestrial aliens. This is an important consideration in legal settings where the forensic psychiatric consultant may be more predisposed to think of the person with bizarre delusions as malingering a delusional state (Resnick, 1988). Likewise, a psychiatric expert witness who is well informed about delusional misidentification, may be better prepared when trying to explain to a judge or jury that the fantastic and bizarre content inherent in delusional misidentification represent real psychiatric entities rather than manufactured symptoms. With regard to dangerousness, the expert witness knowledgeable in the forensic aspects of delusional misidentification, may be in a better position to describe to the trier of fact, the growing psychiatric literature of serious acts of violence and aggression associated with delusional misidentification (Fishbain, 1987; DePauw & Szulecka, 1988; Silva et al., 1989; Silva et al., 1992a; Silva et al., 1994b; Silva et al., 1995a; Silva et al., 1995b; Silva et al., 1995c; Bourget & Whitehurst, 2004).

In psychiatric-legal settings, it may be argued that cases of delusional misidentification are rare, therefore casting doubt whether a psychotic person under legal scrutiny has such delusions. In this situation the forensic consultant may want to point out that although there has been some concern about the lack of reliable studies on the measurement and epidemiology of delusional misidentification (Fishbain, 1987; Dinwiddie & Yutzy, 1993), there is mounting evidence in the psychiatric literature that both violent and nonviolent cases of delusional misidentification, are clearly more frequent than previously thought (DePauw & Szulecka, 1988; Silva et al., 1992a; Joseph, 1994; Kirov et al., 1994; Silva et al., 1994b; Silva et al., 1995a; Silva et al., 1995b; Silva et al., 1995c; Silva et al., 1995d; Bourget & Whitehurst, 2004).

In our experience, a comprehensive understanding of dangerous delusional misidentification syndrome individuals may be effectively utilized by the psychiatric expert witness to provide well-reasoned psychiatric-legal opinions to the legal system. Some cases of delusional misidentification may be incompetent to stand trial due to their delusional misidentification (Silva & Miller, 2002). The trial court of Mr. A.'s found him incompetent to stand trial. Delusional misidentification may form the basis for an insanity defense as exemplified by the case of Mr. C. in which the court found him to be legally insane.

Nature of Persons at Risk of Physical Attack by Individuals with Delusional Misidentification

Most persons with DM are individuals who have emotional (affective) connections and ready geographical accessibility to the misidentified person. Those who appear to be at greatest risk of being physically attacked by delusional misidentification individuals are members of the affected person's family. In a study of 29 dangerous delusional misidentification syndrome individuals, the parents, siblings, and spouses were misidentified by 45, 14, and 21 percent of the sample, respectively (Silva et al., 1992a). A meta-analytic study encompassing 82 cases of dangerous delusional misidentification described in the anglophonic literature, revealed that parents and other relatives accounted for 27 and 29 percent, respectively, of all persons that had been dangerously, delusionally misidentified (Silva et al., 1994b). Health care workers, especially mental health care clinicians who work with psychotic patients, can be at increased risk of becoming delusionally misidentified objects. Given the frequent paranoid nature of delusional misidentification, some delusional misidentification patients direct their mistrust and hostility toward misidentified health care professionals. Therefore, these clinicians may be at risk of becoming the recipients of violence by persons with delusional misidentification. It is important to keep in mind that some misidentified health care providers have been harmed and even killed by delusional misidentification syndrome individuals (Silva et al., 1995a). High profile individuals, such as politicians and entertainment industry celebrities, are another group who may become targets of persons who harbor dangerous delusional misidentifications (Silva et al., 1991b; Silva & Leong, 1993).

Persons who suffer from delusional misidentification tend to misidentify those who are both emotionally and geographically close to the delusional person. However, sometimes an intense affective state can arise in the absence of any geographic proximity or prior contact or meeting between the delusional individual and the misidentified object. Delusionally misidentified objects of this type may be politicians or media celebrities. For example, an individual had come to believe that he himself was a well-known political figure while the actual incumbent was delusionally conceptualized as an impostor with the delusional misidentification syndrome individual threatening the politician (Silva et al., 1991b; Silva & Leong, 1993). Another case involves the first Presidential assassination attempt. A man who purportedly misidentified himself, as he believed that he was King Richard III of England and the United States, concluded that President Andrew Jackson was part of a conspiracy aimed at depriving him of his royal position. After an unsuccessful attempt to gain an audience with President Jackson, the man attempted to shoot the President. Fortunately, his guns misfired. Intimidating behaviors including stalking may occur in persons suffering from delusional misidentification (Silva & Leong, 1993).

Although most dangerous cases of delusional misidentification appear to have involved males, the frequency among females is not insignificant. Mothers who delusionally misidentify their relatively helpless children may be of particular concern (Silva et al., 1987). Several cases have been documented in which a mother delusionally misidentified her infant as a changeling (or similar transformant) with resultant serious injury to the child, including homicide (Silva et al., 1992b). Not all individuals who suffer from dangerous delusional misidentification may intend to harm their delusionally misidentified offspring. In one case, for example, a woman who delusionally misidentified a child as being her son attempted to abduct him in order to "protect" him. Fortunately, she was apprehended before she was able to relocate to another city with the child (Silva et al., 1992b).

Finally, it should be mentioned that not all objects who are victims of dangerous delusional misidentification of others, become targets because they are delusionally misidentified. It may be only necessary for someone to be thought of as an accomplice of a double to be endangered. For example, a 37-year-old man who not only killed his father and seriously injured a nephew believing them to be "clones" but also shot a nondelusionally misidentified stranger thought to be involved in a conspiracy with the man's delusionally misidentified relatives (Silva et al., 1989).

Diagnosis and Treatment

Psychiatric expert witnesses may be asked to recommend a plan of treatment for a person with a delusional misidentification. All cases of delusional misidentification form part of a diagnosable mental disorder. Commonly found co-occurring mental disorders include schizophrenia spectrum disorders, affective psychoses, psychoses secondary to drugs or medical problems, dementia with psychosis, and delusional disorders. delusional misidentification syndromes are treated according to the underlying mental or medical disorder. For example, identification and treatment of specific medical conditions such as diabetes mellitus and hypothyroidism can lead to resolution of the delusional misidentification (Khanna & Khanna, 1991; Madakasira & Hall, 1981). In cases of drug-induced delusional misidentification, the standard management for substance use disorders should be followed, including but not limited to abstinence from the inducing agent and treatment of the psychotic symptoms.

As psychosis of any type is the most frequent co-occurring disorder with a delusional misidentification syndrome, neuroleptic medication remains the mainstay of treatment for those with delusional misidentification (Christodoulou, 1977; Silva et al., 1996). Since many cases of delusional misidentification syndrome are associated with mood symptomatology (Signer, 1987) thymoleptics of the antidepressant or mood-stabilizing variety may be indicated (Christodoulou, 1976; Christodoulou, 1977; Wilcox & Waziri, 1983; Driscoll et al., 1991).

Electroconvulsive therapy has also been shown to be efficacious in the treatment of delusional misidentification associated with mood disturbances (Todd, 1957). Even when delusional misidentification fails to resolve with psychotropic medication(s), many patients experience clinical improvement based on a reduction in preoccupation with their misidentification delusions and/or a reduction in the paranoia (fear) experienced. The newer generation neuroleptic clozapine, although considered a treatment for refractory psychosis, may be particular effective when used, not only for treating the delusional thinking, but also in reducing the risk for acting aggressively (Silva et al., 1995d).

An previously mentioned, other symptoms may resolve before the misidentification delusion. Therefore, the clinician should not become complacent if symptoms such as hostility and grandiosity disappear. Furthermore, the clinician should be cautioned that dangerous misidentification delusions may be reluctant to openly express their misidentification delusions. Therefore, "silent" forms of DM may result in sudden unprovoked acts of violence that some psychotic patients experience. It is therefore helpful to query patients regarding delusional misidentification and dangerousness on a regular basis. We have found that group psychotherapy involving more than one person who suffers from delusional misidentification combined with pharmacotherapy may be helpful. This is especially the case when patients begin to develop insight into their problems with delusional misidentification and realize that other patients have experienced similar problems with interpersonal interactions because of their delusional misidentification. We recommend that delusional misidentification patients be considered for a trial in such group therapy even when the patient is frankly delusional. In our experience even patients who suffer from persistent delusional misidentification may benefit from group therapy to address the related issue of anger management in order to lessen the risk of aggressive actions aimed at delusionally misidentified objects. Since individuals with delusional misidentification appear to be more common than originally thought (Silva et al., 1992a; Silva et al., 1995a; Silva et al., 1995b; Silva et al., 1995c; Silva et al., 1995d; Edelstyn & Oyebode, 1999; Feinberg & Roane, 2005), group therapy of these patients may be a viable option.

Future Directions

Although the available information does not enable us to know the prevalence of dangerous delusional misidentification, the association of delusional misidentification with violence has been increasingly reported (Silva et al., 1992a; Silva et al., 1995a; Silva et al., 1995b; Silva et al., 1995c; Silva et al., 1995d; Bourget & Whitehurst, 2004). There is very little doubt that delusional misidentification may lead to aggressive behaviors. Future studies should be carried out in order to determine the incidence and prevalence of the problem, to improve the classification and measurement of delusional misidentification, and to refine treatment strategies. Newer technology including brain neuroimaging, computerized electroencephalography, and psychometric studies designed to measure the degree of delusional conviction, aggression, and other relevant psychopathology may offers a unique opportunity for greater understanding of dangerous delusional misidentification. Future investigations of persons with delusional misidentification will hopefully also lead to improved accuracy in assessing the dangerousness of the delusional misidentification individual, thereby potentially decreasing the likelihood of harm perpetrated by these individuals.

REFERENCES

American Psychiatric Association. (2000). *Diagnostic and Statistical Manual of Mental Disorders, Fourth Edition, Text Revision (DSM–IV–TR)*. Washington, D.C.: American Psychiatric Associations.

Appelbaum, P. S., Robbins, P. C., & Monahan, J. (2000). Violence and Delusions: Data from the MacArthur Violence Risk Assessment Study. *American Journal of Psychiatry, 157,* 566.

Bourget, D., & Whitehurst, L. (2004). Capgras syndrome: A review of the neurophysiological correlates and presenting clinical features in cases involving physical violence. *Canadian Journal of Psychiatry, 49,* 719.

Buchanan, A. (1993). Acting on delusions: A review. *Psychological Medicine, 23,* 123.

Buchanan, A., Reed, A., Wessely, S., Garety, P., Taylor, P., Grobin, D., & Dunn, G. (1993). Acting on delusions: II. The phenomenological correlates of acting on delusions. *British Journal of Psychiatry, 163,* 77.

Capgras, J., & Reboul-Lachaux, J. (1923). L'Illusions des 'Sosies' dans un Délire Systématisé Chronique. *Bulletin de la Société Clinique de Médecine Mentale, 11,* 6.

Christodoulou, G. N. (1976). Delusional hyper-identifications of the Frégoli Type: Organic pathogenic contributors. *Acta Psychiatrica Scandinavica, 54,* 305.

Christodoulou, G. N. (1977). Treatment of the syndrome of doubles. *Acta Psychiatnca Belgica, 77,* 254.

Christodoulou, G. N. (1978). Syndrome of subjective doubles. *American Journal of Psychiatry, 135,* 249.

Courbon, P., & Fail, G. (1927). Syndrome d'Illusion de Frégoli et Schizophrenie. *Bulletin de la Société Clinique de Médicine Mentale, 15,* 121.

Courbon, P., & Tusques, J. (1932). Illusions d'Intermétamorphose et de Charme. *Annales de Médico-Psychologiques, 90,* 401.

DePauw, K. W., & Szulecka, T. K. (1988). Dangerous delusions: Violence and the misidentification syndromes. *British Journal of Psychiatry, 152,* 91.

Dinwiddie, S. H., & Yutzy, S. (1993). Dangerous delusions? Misidentification syndromes and professional negligence. *Bulletin of the American Academy of Psychiatry and the Law, 212,* 513.

Driscoll, R., Chithiramohan, R., & Brockman, B. (1991). Capgras Syndrome, mania, and delusionally motivated assaults. *Journal of Forensic Psychiatry, 2,* 49.

Edelstyn, N. M., & Oyebode, F. G. (1999). A review of the phenomenology and cognitive neuropsychological origins of the Capgras syndrome. *International Journal of Geriatric Psychiatry, 14,* 48.

Ellis, H. D., DePauw, K. W., Christodoulou, G. N., Papageorgiou, L., Milne, A. B., & Joseph, A. B. (1993). Responses to facial and non-facial stimuli presented tachistoscopically in either or both visual fields by patients with the Capgras Delusion and paranoid schizophrenia. *Journal of Neurology, Neurosurgery, and Psychiatry, 152,* 91.

Ellis, H. D., & Lewis, M. B. (2001). Capgras delusion: A window on face recognition. *Trends in the Cognititive Neurosciences, 5,* 149.

Feinberg, T. E., & Roane, D. M. (2005). Delusional misidentification. *Psychiatric Clinics of North America, 28,* 665.

Feinberg, T. E., & Shapiro, R. M. (1989). Misidentification-reduplication and the right hemisphere. *Neuropsychiatry, Neuropsychology and Behavioral Neurology, 2,* 39.

Fishbain, D. A. (1987). The frequency of Capgras Delusion in a psychiatric emergency service. *Psychopathology, 20,* 42.

Fleminger, S., & Burns, A. (1993). The delusional misidentification syndromes in patients with and without evidence of organic cerebral disorder. A structured review of case reports. *Biological Psychiatry, 33,* 22.

Gerner, R. H. (2003). Pharmacological treatment of violent behaviors. In R. Rosner (Ed.), *Principles and Practice of Forensic Psychiatry, Second Edition.* London: Arnold.

Goldstein, R. L. (1987). More forensic romances: de Clérambault's Syndrome in men. *Bulletin of the American Academy of Psychiatry and the Law, 15,* 267.

Joseph, A. B. (1994). Observations on the Epidemiology of the Delusional Misidentification Syndromes in the Boston Metropolitan Area: April 1983-June 1984. *Psychopathology, 27,* 150.

Kernberg, O. F. (1985). Neurosis, psychosis and the borderline states. In H. Kaplan, and B. J. Sadock (Eds.), *Comprehensive Textbook of Psychiatry/IV, Fourth Edition.* Baltimore: Williams and Wilkins.

Khanna, R., & Khanna, N. (1991). Delusions of substitution and diabetes mellitus. *International Journal of Psychiatry in Medicine, 21,* 104.

Kimura, S. (1986). Review of 106 cases with the syndrome of Capgras. In G. N. Christodoulou (Ed.), *The Delusional Misidentification Syndromes.* Basel, Switzerland: Karger.

Kimura, S., Inamoto, Y., & Katsurada, T. (1981). A rare case of Capgras syndrome observed in wake-amine induced psychosis. *Folia Psychiatrica et Neurologica Japonica, 35,* 43.

Kirov, G., Jones, P., & Lewis, S. W. (1994). Prevalence of delusional misidentification syndromes. *Psychopathology, 27,* 148.

Leong, G. B., Silva, J. A., Garza-Treviño, E. S., Oliva, D., Ferrari, M. M., Komanduri, R. V., & Caldwell, J. C. B. (1994). The dangerousness of persons with the Othello Syndrome. *Journal of Forensic Sciences, 39,* 1445.

Leong, G. B., Silva, J. A., & Weinstock, R. (2003). Dangerousness. In R. Rosner (Ed.), *Principles and practice of forensic psychiatry, Second Edition.* London: Arnold.

Link, B. G., & Stueve, A. (1994). Psychotic symptoms and the violent/illegal behavior of mental patients compared to community controls. In J. Monahan, and H. J. Steadman (Eds.), *Violence and mental disorder: Developments in risk assessment.* Chicago: University of Chicago Press.

Madakasira, S., & Hall, T. B. (1981). Capgras Syndrome in a patient with myxedema. *American Journal of Psychiatry, 138,* 1506.

Malloy, P., Cimino, C., & Westlake, R. (1992). Differential diagnosis of primary and secondary Capgras delusions. *Neuropsychiatry, Neuropsychology and Behavioral Neurology, 5,* 83.

Miller, R. D. (2003a). Criminal competence. In R. Rosner (Ed.), *Principles and practice of forensic psychiatry, Second Edition.* London: Arnold.

Miller, R. D. (2003b). Criminal responsibility. In R. Rosner (Ed.), *Principles and practice of forensic psychiatry, Second Edition.* London: Arnold.

Nestor, P. G. (2002). Mental disorder and violence: Personality dimensions and clinical features. *American Journal of Psychiatry, 159,* 1973.

Resnick, P. J. (1988). Malingered Psychosis. In R. Rogers (Ed.), *Clinical assessment of malingering and deception.* New York: Guilford Press.

Siegel, R. K. (1989). *Intoxication: Life in Pursuit of Artificial Paradise.* New York: Pocket Books.

Signer, S. F. (1987). Capgras Syndrome: The delusion of substitution. *Journal of Clinical Psychiatry, 48,* 147.

Signer, S. F. (1994). Localization and lateralization in the delusion of substitution: Capgras Symptom and its variants. *Psychopathology, 27,* 168.

Silva, J. A., Jalali, B., & Leong, G. B. (1987). Delusion of exchanged doubles in an immigrant: A new Capgras variant? *International Journal of Social Psychiatry, 33,* 299.

Silva, J. A., & Leong, G. B. (1991). A case of Subjective Frégoli Syndrome. *Journal of Psychiatry and Neurosciences, 16,* 103.

Silva, J. A., & Leong, G. B. (1993). Delusional misidentification syndromes and prominent figures. *American Journal of Forensic Psychiatry, 14,* 39.

Silva, J. A., & Leong, G. B. (1994). Delusions of psychological change of the self. *Psychopathology, 27,* 285.

Silva, J. A., & Leong, G. B. (1995). Visual-perceptual abnormalities in delusional misidentification. *Canadian Journal of Psychiatry, 40,* 6.

Silva, J. A., Leong, G. B., & Ferrari, M. M. (1995a). Delusional misidentification of health care professionals. *Psychiatric Quarterly, 66,* 51.

Silva, J. A., Leong, G. B., Garza-Treviño, E. S., Le Grand, J., Oliva, D., Weinstock, R., & Bowden, C. L. (1994a). A cognitive model of dangerous delusional misidentification syndromes. *Journal of Forensic Sciences, 39,* 1451.

Silva, J. A., Leong, G. B., & Miller, A. L. (1996). Delusional misidentification syndromes: Drug treatment options. *CNS Drugs, 5,* 89.

Silva, J. A., Leong, G. B., & Shaner, A. L. (1990). A classification system for misidentification syndromes. *Psychopathology, 23,* 27.

Silva, J. A., Leong, G. B., & Shaner, A. L. (1991a). The syndrome of intermetamorphosis. *Psychopathology, 24,* 258.

Silva, J. A., Leong, G. B., & Weinstock, R. (1992a). The dangerousness of persons with misidentification syndromes. *Bulletin of the American Academy of Psychiatry and the Law, 20,* 77.

Silva, J. A., Leong, G. B., Weinstock, R., & Boyer, C. L. (1989). Capgras Syndrome and dangerousness. *Bulletin of the American Academy of Psychiatry and the Law, 17,* 5.

Silva, J. A., Leong, G. B., Weinstock, R., & Ferrari, M. M. (1991b). Misidentified political figures: An underappreciated danger. *Journal of Forensic Sciences, 36,* 1170.

Silva, J. A., Leong, G. B., Weinstock, R., & Klein, R. L. (1995b). Psychiatric factors associated with dangerous misidentification syndromes. *Bulletin of the American Academy of Psychiatry and the Law, 23,* 53.

Silva, J. A., Leong, G. B., Weinstock, R., & Penny, G. (1995c). Dangerous delusions of misidentification of the self. *Journal of Forensic Sciences, 40,* 570.

Silva, J. A., Leong, G. B., Weinstock, R., & Ruiz-Sweeney, M. (2001). Delusional misidentification and aggression in Alzheimer's disease. *Journal of Forensic Sciences, 46,* 581.

Silva, J. A., Leong, G. B., Weinstock, R., Sharma, K. K., & Klein, R. L. (1994b). Delusional misidentification syndromes and dangerousness. *Psychopathology, 27,* 215.

Silva, J. A., Leong, G. B., Weinstock, R., & Wine, D. B. (1993). Delusional misidentification and dangerousness: A neurobiologic hypothesis. *Journal of Forensic Sciences, 38,* 904.

Silva, J. A., & Miller, M. A. (2002). Competency to stand trial in a case of delusional misidentification of the self and delusional therioanthropy. *American Journal of Forensic Psychiatry, 23,* 21.

Silva, J. A., Sharma, K. K., Leong, G. B., & Weinstock, R. (1992b). Dangerousness of the delusional misidentification of children. *Journal of Forensic Sciences, 37,* 830.

Silva, J. A., Tekell, J. L., Leong, G. B., & Bowden, C. L. (1995d). Delusional misidentification of the self associated with nondominant cerebral pathology. *Journal of Clinical Psychiatry, 56,* 171.

Swanson, J. W. (1994). Mental disorder, substance abuse, and community violence: An epidemiological approach. In J. Monahan, and H. J. Steadman (Eds.), *Violence and Mental Disorder: Developments in Risk Assessment.* Chicago: University of Chicago Press.

Tardiff, K. (2003). Violence: Causes and non-psychopharmacological treatment. In R. Rosner (Ed.), *Principles and practice of forensic psychiatry, Second Edition.* London: Arnold.

Taylor, P. J., Garety, P., Buchanan, A., Reed, A., Wessely, S., Ray, K., Dunn, G., & Grubin, D. (1994). Delusions and violence. In J. Monahan, and H. J. Steadman (Eds.), *Violence and Mental Disorder: Developments in Risk Assessment.* Chicago: University of Chicago Press.

Thompson, A. E., & Swan, M. (1993). Capgras' Syndrome presenting with violence following heavy drinking. *British Journal of Psychiatry, 102,* 692.

Todd, J. (1957). The syndrome of Capgras. *Psychiatric Quarterly, 31,* 250.

Vartzopoulos, D., & Vartzopoulos, I. (1991). A variant of the syndrome of subjective doubles. *American Journal of Psychiatry, 148,* 394.

Wessely, S., Buchanan, A., Reed, A., Cutting, J., Everitt, B., Garety, P., & Taylor, P. J. (1993). Acting on delusions: I. Prevalence. *British Journal of Psychiatry, 163,* 69.

West, D. J., & Walk, A. (1977). *Daniel McNaughton—His trial and the aftermath.* Ashford, England: Gaskell Books.

Wilcox, J., & Waziri, R. (1983). The Capgras Syndrome and nondominant cerebral dysfunction. *Journal of Clinical Psychiatry, 44,* 70.

Young, A. W., Willis, H. D., Szulecka, T. K., & DePauw, K. W. (1990). Face processing impairments and delusional misidentification. *Behavioral Neurology, 3,* 153.

Chapter 7

A CLINICAL INVESTIGATION
OF THE OBSESSIONAL FOLLOWER:*

"she loves me, she loves me not . . ."

J. Reid Meloy

Ms. Lou Salomé abandoned Friedrich Nietzsche in October, 1882, ending a brief and humiliating sexual affair that marked his life's singular sojourn into matters of the heart. He subsequently penned in *Thus Spoke Zarathustra*, "There is always a certain madness in love. But also there is always a certain method in madness" (Nietzsche, 1883–92/1969, p. 68). The literary sublimation of his feelings surrounding his unrequited love gives us pause, particularly at the end of the twentieth century when we find the behavior of stalking, or what I refer to as "obsessional following," so ubiquitous and troubling.

My purpose in this chapter is to review the relevant clinical research on obsessional following published in scientific journals in the past twenty years. Although the studies are few in number, I hope to illuminate this psychopathology of thought that occasionally leads to criminal behavior. I will then discuss, in turn, the expectable demographic characteristics, psychiatric diagnoses, pursuit characteristics, victim characteristics, violence risk (including threats), subtyping, and psychodynamics of the obsessional follower.

* This is a revised and expanded version of a scientific paper that first appeared in *Aggression and Violent Behavior: A Review Journal,* *1*(2):1–16, 1996.

METHODOLOGY

Defining a clinical population on the basis of one pattern of behavior is quite problematic, and obsessional following is no exception. I have eschewed the term "stalking" for several reasons: most importantly, to avoid mimicking its sensationalistic use by the popular media, and to reserve its proper use for the description of a statutorily defined criminal act, now codified in similar ways in all fifty United States. The legal definition of stalking is typically "the willful, malicious, and repeated following and harassing of another person that threatens his or her safety" (Meloy & Gothard, 1995, p. 258).

The term *obsessional follower*, and its use in this chapter, is drawn from two clinical studies of this population conducted by Zona et al. (1993) and Meloy & Gothard (1995). It describes a person who engages in an abnormal or long-term pattern of threat or harassment directed toward a specific individual. An abnormal or long-term pattern of threat or harassment is defined as more than one overt act of unwanted pursuit of the victim that is perceived by the victim as being harassing. Although tautology is hardly avoided, and often embraced, by the law, I offer the following definition of harassing:

> A knowing and willful course of conduct directed at a specific person that seriously alarms, annoys, torments, or terrorizes the person, and that serves no legitimate purpose. (California Penal Code 646.9, 1995)

The term *obsession* is likewise difficult. Psychoanalytic theory has traditionally used it to refer to an unwelcome, or ego dystonic thought that repetitively forces itself into consciousness (Hinsie & Campbell, 1974). The *DSM–IV* essentially retained this definition, but added, "even in adults there is a broad range of insight into the reasonableness of the obsessions . . . any given individual's insight may vary across times and situations" (American Psychiatric Association, 1994, p. 418). Zona et al. (1993) equated obsession with persistent ideas, thoughts, impulses, or images that are clearly ego *syntonic*, and disavowed its unwanted or alien quality. My emphasis on the term obsession is the repetitive and persistent nature of the idea, thought, impulse or image, in contrast to its relationship to the ego. The latter characteristic may, in fact, be more temporally unstable than its quality of *preoccupation*, and may vary according to both the personality and mood of the individual. The use of the term obsessional follower, moreover, is not meant to infer that a diagnosis of obsessive-compulsive disorder or obsessive-compulsive personality disorder *(DSM-IV)* is warranted.

The use of the term *violence* in this review refers to an intentional act of aggression that results in, or is likely to result in, physical injury to another person. When data are available on other kinds of violence, such as sexual or property, the differentiation will be made. The term *erotomania* refers to the delusional disorder, erotomanic subtype, in which the individual falsely believes he or she is loved by another. Although the *DSM-IV* (APA, 1994) precludes a diagnosis of delusional disorder, erotomanic subtype, in the presence of schizophrenia or a mood disorder, I will refer to erotomania even if it is secondary to one of these diagnoses.

My review of the research focuses upon the identification of all cases, or studies, within which the subjects meet two criteria: first, they are clearly defined as obsessional followers (Meloy & Gothard, 1995; Zona et al., 1993); and second, all of the subjects had criminal charges arising from their obsessional following. Several subjects from various studies were eliminated since they were exclusively treatment cases, the obsessional following was ambiguous, or the evaluation was prompted by a civil issue, such as commitment, and never resulted in contact with law enforcement.[1]

RESULTS

The review of the research yielded ten studies published between 1978 and 1995. The studies are listed in Table 7–1.

The ten studies were conducted by nineteen different researchers in eight research groups. When specific subjects subsequently appeared in another publication, or samples were duplicated in different publications, they were not counted and the other publication is referred to in parentheses. All the studies involved nonrandom samples of convenience, which limits their generalizability. On the other hand, the cohorts were gathered from three large urban areas in the United States (New York, Los Angeles, and San Diego) and across

---

[1] On January 1, 1994 stalking became a tort in California. Another example of bad law when one considers the psychodynamics of this behavior, the tort of stalking may gratify both the retaliatory impulse of the victim and the voyeuristic impulse of the perpetrator.

Table 7–1.
Research studies of obsessional followers
charged with or convicted of criminal behavior.

Study	Population	Selection Criteria	N	Violence Freq.
Goldstein, 1978	New York forensic pract.	erotomania	1	–
Taylor et al., 1983	112 psychotic men in British prison charged with violence	erotomania	3	–
Goldstein, 1987 (Goldstein, 1986)	unknown	erotomania	7	–
Noone & Cockhill, 1987	unknown	erotomania	3	–
Meloy, 1992 (Meyers & Meloy, 1994)	Southern California forensic practice	violent erotomanic or borderline erotomanic	6	–
Zona et al., 1993	first Los Angeles PD Threat Management Unit cases	obsessional/erotomanic	74	2.7% (8% property)
Leong, 1994 (Leong & Silva, 1992)	Los Angeles court ref.	erotomania	4	–
Mullen & Pathé 1994a, 1994b	Australian forensic pract.	"pathology of love" and "stalking"	14	36%
Meloy & Gothard, 1995	300 referrals to a court clinic in San Diego	obsessional follower	20	25%
Harmon et al., 1995	337 referrals charged with harassment or menacing to a court clinic in New York	repetitive"stalking"	48	21%
Total Studies = 10	Total N = 180			

three continents (Europe, Australia and the United States) which lends a certain amount of external validity to the replicated findings of any one study. The studies depended upon retrospective data, which in some cases were only archival (Zone et al., 1993), and in other cases were a combination of archival and clinical data (Meloy & Gothard, 1995; Harmon et al., 1995). All the studies were noncomparative, except for within group comparisons in the Zona et al. (1993) and Harmon et al. (1995) studies, and between group comparisons in Meloy & Gothard (1995). Typically in behavioral science the investigation of an arguably new or novel observation begins with single or multiple case studies, proceeds to noncomparative and larger samples, and matures with comparative studies of larger samples. Obsessional following is no exception: eighty-seven percent of the aggregate sample was gathered in four studies published between 1993 and 1995 (Zona et al., 1993; Mullen & Pathé, 1994a, 1994b; Meloy & Gothard, 1995; Harmon et al., 1995).

The total sample size (N = 180), although too small for a meta-analysis, is large enough to draw some preliminary conclusions concerning obsessional following, with some limitations. The incidence of this behavior in the general population, or even in a criminal population, cannot be determined since the population characteristics from which these subjects were drawn are rarely described. Likewise, the frequency of violence in these subjects cannot be expressed as a base rate since the time frame within which the violence occurred was often unspecified. I have not given a violence frequency for the small sample studies since it would be statistically misleading.

Whether or not the frequency of obsessional following is increasing in the population also remains unanswered since none of the studies, with one exception, address this issue. Harmon et al. (1995) found a nearly threefold increase in stalkers as a percent of referrals to the Forensic Psychiatry Clinic (0.6% to 1.7%) in New York City between 1987–1993. Although this finding is only suggestive,[2] it is consistent with the sea change in legislation concerning stalking in the United States, of which the first law was signed in California in 1990.

The measurable psychological characteristics of obsessional followers also remain unknown, since there are virtually no published studies which have utilized any psychological tests. The one exception is Meloy's (1992) sample of six violent erotomanic or borderline erotomanic individuals, four of whom were tested using standardized psychological instruments, including the Rorschach and Minnesota Multiphasic Personality Inventory.

Perhaps the most important caveat in the application of this review to clinical work and further research is the likely underrepresentation of spouses or ax-spouses in these studies. This is probably a result of the exclusive focus upon erotomanic disorder in the early, small sample studies, and a selection bias on the part of law enforcement to

[2] New York State modified and strengthened its laws on menacing (120.13) and harassment (240.25) in 1992, which may partially account for this increase in referrals.

arrest and prosecute the more "high profile" or "stranger" obsessional followers during the periods of data gathering for the more recent and larger sample studies. This selection bias should correct with time as psychiatric diagnoses, motivational patterns, and criminal behavior are delineated and defined.[3]

DEMOGRAPHIC CHARACTERISTICS

Seventy-two percent (N = 130) of the sample are men. Twenty-eight percent (N = 49) are women. The gender of one subject was unknown (Zone et al., 1993). The gender ratio is slightly less than one would expect given the predominance of males among violent offenders, a ratio that usually averages ten to one (Wilson & Herrnstein, 1985). This difference is not attributable to the predominance of females among those with erotomania, since most of the individuals with erotomania in this research review were males. The data suggest that three out of four obsessional followers who engage in criminal conduct will be males.

Racial characteristics were unreported for 57 percent (N = 102) of the subjects, therefore no conclusions can be drawn. Twelve of the subjects were foreign born, excluding subjects from the Mullen & Pathé (1994a) study and the Harmon et al. (1995) study which did not report such data. The finding that 10 percent of the obsessional followers *where data were available* were immigrants highlights the importance of considering variable as a possible contributory factor in the genesis of this behavior, particularly in those with a diagnosis of erotomania. Meyers and Meloy (1994) emphasized this in a case study concerning a traditional Islamic male who grossly misconstrued the social behavior of a woman whom he subsequently pursued. Zona et al. (1993) found significantly more foreign born subjects in their erotomanic subgroup. Immigration clearly does not predict such behavior, however, and most obsessional followers are not immigrants to the country in which they offend.

Obsessional followers are generally older than other criminal

---

[3] Lt. John Lane noted that about 65% of the cases handled to date (N = 410) at the Los Angeles Police Department Threat Management Unit are "simple obsessional" types: individuals that did have a prior actual relationship with the victim, including customer, acquaintance, neighbor, professional relationship, dating, or sexual intimate (personal communication, April, 1995).

offenders. Meloy and Gothard (1995) found an average age of 35, which was significantly older than a random group of mentally disordered offenders. Their finding replicated exactly the mean age in the Zona et al. (1993) study. Mullen and Pathé (1994a) found the average age of their subjects to be 40 years, with a range of 28–50. Harmon et al. (1995) also found an average age of 40, with a range of 20–66. This consistent finding across the research suggests that chronic failures in social or sexual relationships through young adulthood may be a necessary predisposing experience for obsessional followers. In fact, failed relationships are the rule among these individuals. Meloy and Gothard (1995) found that half of their subjects had never married or were divorced, and three-quarters were without an intimate partner at the time of their evaluation. Zona et al. (1993) reported that only one out of seven subjects were married at the time of pursuit, and 72 percent of their erotomanic subgroup had never married. Likewise only 14 percent of the Mullen and Pathé (1994a) sample were married at the time of offense; only 6 percent of the Harmon et al. (1995) sample were married, and 63 percent had never been married. Raskin and Sullivan (1974) and Segal (1989) noted the isolated and lonesome existence of the erotomanic individual, and the adaptive nature of these symptoms to ward off feelings of depression and loss. Obsessional following may truly be a courtship disorder for some individuals as the normative behavior of seeking a partner in a socially acceptable manner is subsumed by an abnormal, voyeuristic, and unwanted pursuit (Freund et al., 1983).

Although there are little data on intelligence and educational characteristics in this population, Meloy and Gothard (1995) did find their sample to be significantly more intelligent (although IQ data were missing for 45% of their subjects) and better educated than a random group of mentally disordered offenders. Most had a high school education. They used these findings to explain the resourcefulness and manipulativeness of many of their subjects. Harmon et al. (1995) replicated this finding, and reported that 40 percent of their sample were college graduates.

Obsessional followers are also likely to have prior criminal and psychiatric histories. Meloy and Gothard (1995, p. 261) wrote, "(these) findings do not support the notion that stalking, or a similar pattern of unwanted following, is an aberrant behavior committed by an otherwise law-abiding and mentally healthy individual." Harmon et al.

(1995) found that 46 percent of their subjects had a history of prior similar offending, while 64 percent of the Mullen and Pathé (1994) sample had a history of unrelated offending. Almost two-thirds of the Meloy and Gothard (1995) sample had prior inpatient or outpatient treatment; the majority had a prior criminal history. Zona et al. (1993) noted, however, that the majority of their "simple obsessional" (prior relationship) subgroup appeared to be first time offenders.

There are also suggestive data from two studies that obsessional followers are usually unemployed or underemployed. Meloy and Gothard (1995) noted that the majority of their sample had "very unstable work histories" (p. 259) at the time of their offense, although they did not quantify this information. Forty-three percent of the Mullen and Pathé (1994b) sample were unemployed. Harmon et al. (1995) and Zona et al. (1993) did not report employment data, but given the average length of pursuits, variety of contacts, and preoccupation with the victim (see below), it is reasonable to assume that employment will be significantly impaired or nonexistent. More data, however, are needed to draw further conclusions about work history.

PSYCHIATRIC CHARACTERISTICS

The single and multiple case studies (Goldstein, 1978, 1987; Taylor et al., 1983; Noone & Cockhill, 1987; Meloy, 1992; Leong, 1994) in this review used selection criteria that focused on a diagnosis of de Clérambault syndrome or erotomania: what we would now refer to as delusional disorder, erotomanic subtype (American Psychiatric Association, 1994). The only exception to this pattern is the small group study of Meloy (1992) which used the term *borderline erotomania* (Meloy, 1989) to describe a sample of individuals who stalked their objects, sometimes violently, but did not evidence clear cut erotomanic delusions. His label has been more positively received by legal scholars (McAnaney et al., 1993) than by clinicians (Segal, 1990; Zona et al., 1993). The Zona et al. (1993) group were the first to use "major mental illness" as a dependent variable, with more refined diagnostic workups in the subsequent studies of Meloy & Gothard (1995), Mullen & Pathé (1994), and Harmon et al. (1995).

Zona et al. (1993) found in their file review that major mental illness was present in 63 percent of the subjects in which it could be ruled in or out. In their "simple obsessional" subgroup, they found an equal likelihood of presence or absence of mental disorder, and had the impression of a predominance of personality disorder. Their"erotomanic" subgroup was, of course, 100 percent mentally ill, but one half of their"love obsessional" subgroup had missing data concerning presence or absence of mental illness.

These suggestive findings prompted Meloy and Gothard (1995) to clinically investigate the psychiatric diagnoses of a sample of obsessional followers, and compare them to a random sample of mentally disordered offenders. Eighty-five percent of the obsessional followers had both an Axis I and an Axis II diagnosis at the time of evaluation for the study. The most likely Axis I disorder was substance abuse or dependence (35%) with a mood disorder in one out of four subjects (25%). Axis I diagnoses were not significantly different from the random comparison group. The most likely Axis II diagnosis was a cluster B personality disorder that was not antisocial personality disorder (ASPD). The random comparison group of offenders with mental disorders were significantly more likely to have ASPD, and significantly less likely to have another personality disorder. Meloy and Gothard (1995) interpreted this from an attachment theory perspective, asserting that less antisocial personality disorder in obsessional followers made sense since it was a disorder of chronic emotional detachment. An obsessional follower would be more likely to have an intense and pathological attachment to his object of pursuit, particularly in the face of continuous rejection. These findings parallel nicely the research of Dutton (1995) linking borderline psychopathology, attachment theory, and domestic violence.

Erotomania was present in 10 percent of the Meloy and Gothard (1995) sample, an exact replication of the proportion of erotomanics in the Zona et al. (1993) sample. Delusional disorder, erotomanic subtype, however, usually does not present in a pure, or primary form in any clinical sample. Rudden et al. (1990) found an additional mood disorder in one out of three erotomanic subjects, and schizophrenia in almost half their hospitalized clinical sample. The pure or primary form of erotomania (de Clérambault, 1942) seems to appear in only one out of four cases when erotomanic delusions are present. Taylor et al. (1983) found that depression coexisted with erotomania in their three cases; Leong (1994) noted the primary diagnosis of paranoid schizophrenia in his four cases of erotomanics; and Meloy (1992) found additional diagnoses of substance abuse, schizophrenia, mood disorder, and personality disorder in his six cases of erotomanics or borderline erotomanics who were violent.

Mullen and Pathé (1994) reported a diagnosis of schizophrenia in half their sample of "stalkers" and pure erotomania in almost one third, a small group finding consistent with Rudden et al's (1990) sample of nonforensic erotomanic patients. A mood or anxiety disorder was present in four of fourteen subjects as a primary or secondary diagnosis. They also looked carefully at Axis II. Seventy-nine percent had a personality disorder diagnosis, quite similar to the Meloy and Gothard finding (1995). Almost half were cluster B personality disorders, and 29 percent were antisocial personality disorder. Half of the entire sample was diagnosed with narcissistic personality disorder or "marked narcissistic traits." Paranoid, schizoid, and avoidant personality disorders were also diagnosed. A majority of the sample also exhibited "grandiosity" and "social incompetence."

Harmon et al. (1995) found that 29 percent of their sample met criteria for delusional (paranoid) disorder *(DSM–III–R)*, most likely the erotomanic and persecutory subtypes. One third of the female subjects were diagnosed with erotomania (N = 6), and five of these women knew or had prior relationships (usually employment) with their objects of pursuit. One of their two cases of homosexual obsession in their sample involved an erotomanic female. The next most common Axis I disorder was schizophrenia (21%). Twelve of their subjects had a primary or secondary Axis II diagnosis (25%), but none met criteria for antisocial personality disorder. A mood disorder was only diagnosed in one case.

The psychodiagnostic picture of the obsessional follower that emerges across these studies is complex and varied, as I would expect when a population is defined by one pattern of behavior. Axis I disorders are common, including schizophrenia, mood disorders, and substance abuse, similar to other offenders with mental disorders. Erotomania is unlikely to appear in a pure or primary form, but will clearly be represented in a minority of obsessional followers, usually in a secondary form (symptomatic of another mental disorder). Axis II personality disorder is likewise expected, both as a primary and secondary diagnosis; but it is unlikely to be antisocial personality disorder. The identification of Axis I psychopathology in an obsessional follower should not preclude the further investigation of Axis II personality disorder or traits, often appearing as a mixture of dramatic, acting out, narcissistically tinged cluster B character pathology.

PATTERNS OF PURSUIT

De Clérambault (1942) described five patients in his *Qeuvres Psychiatriques.* One 34-year-old man,

> had a morbid passion towards his ex-wife. Although she maintained she did not love him, he claimed her attitude always belied her words. After her re-marriage, he said she would once again become his mistress and that when he had satisfied his pride he would again reject her. He was constantly writing, ambushing her, and striking her in public. He carried a razor, threatening "if you remarry, I'll get you both." He alleged that her divorce from him was null and void. (pp. 315–22)

This first published case of de Clérambault syndrome in a man is curiously prescient of the patterns of pursuit that emerge in this research review. The three cases of Taylor et al. (1983) document multiple and various contacts, including aggressive letters, unwanted following, property damage, annoying phone calls, and assaults. Leong (1994) also noted multiple and various contacts, including letters, telephoning, following, and various approach attempts. Goldstein's (1978) first published case, a 39-year-old paranoid schizophrenic woman, included approach behavior, talking, and assault. His later cases (Goldstein, 1987) included stalking, telephoning, letter writing, gift giving, and various approaches to the object of pursuit. Noone and Cockhill (1987) documented letter writing, telephoning, various approach behaviors, and stalking of the victims.

The first systematic investigation of letter writing and approach behaviors, although not among a sample of obsessional followers per se, was conducted by Dietz et al. (1991a, 1991b), and focused on the characteristics of threatening and otherwise inappropriate letters sent to Hollywood celebrities and United States Congressmen. Letter characteristics were identified that were associated with an increased or decreased risk of an "approach" to the recipients of the letters from this large sample of subjects (N = 300).[4] Implicit in the design of the Dietz studies was the assumption that various kinds of contacts would

---

[4] For instance, approach positive characteristics of letters to Hollywood celebrities included (1) subject sends 10-14 letters; (2) duration of correspondence > 1 year; (3) subject desires face-to-face contact with the celebrity; (4) a specific time is announced when something would happen; (5) a specific location was announced where something would happen; (6) there was repeated mention of the celebrity's entertainment products; (7) the subject both telephoned and wrote letters; and (8) the letters were sent from two or more geographically different postmarks.

be initiated by a proportion of the letter writers, which proved to be true.

Zona et al. (1993) systematically investigated the patterns of pursuit of their 74 subjects divided into three subgroups: erotomanics, love obsessionals, and simple obsessionals. The erotomanic subgroup favored letter writing, phoning, and visiting the home of the love object. This subgroup was also twice as likely to stalk their victims than the other two subgroups. The only type of contact that the erotomanics pursued less vigorously than the love obsessionals or the simple obsessionals was face-to-face, most likely to prevent a loss of idealization of the victim.

The love obsessional subgroup, characterized by a primary psychiatric diagnosis or a fanatical love in which the object of pursuit was a stranger, also favored letter writing, but established phone contact at half the frequency of the erotomanics. One in five stalked their victims and attempted to visit their homes. The simple obsessional group, characterized by an actual, prior relationship with the victim that had turned "sour" or within which there was the perception of mistreatment, preferred phone contact, but were more likely than the other two subgroups to achieve face-to-face contact, an important violence risk factor that I will address later.

Zona et al. (1993) confirmed an anecdotal finding from the earlier research: obsessional followers will pursue a variety of means to achieve contact with their victims, including letter writing, phoning, visiting a particular location (e.g., worksite), stalking, visiting their home, and achieving a face-to-face meeting.

Meloy and Gothard (1995) documented a pattern of pursuit which was quite consistent with Zona et al. (1993). Two-thirds of their subjects went to the victim's home at least once, and almost half stalked their victims. Forty percent made contact by telephone, and 25 percent wrote letters. One in ten visited the victim's employment or sent gifts Meloy and Gothard's sample (N = 20) was too small to subgroup according to the Zona typology.

Mullen and Pathé (1994) also found similar varieties of pursuit. Ninety-five percent approached their victims, 80 percent followed their victims, and 40 percent telephoned or sent letters. Harmon et al. (1995) likewise found that their subjects (N = 48) had multiple avenues of pursuit: 41 percent telephoned, 27 percent accosted, and 33 percent sent letters or gifts. The consistent finding across the studies reviewed is a pattern of multiple and various contacts with the victims, with letter writing and telephoning often accompanying a physical approach.

The duration of the obsessional follower's pursuit of his victim is much longer than one would expect. It should be measured in months or years, rather than weeks. The earlier studies suggested this, and Meloy (1992) found that the length of time between the onset of the obsession and the violence among his six subjects ranged from 1 week to 8 years, with a mean length of five years. This surprisingly long, but only suggestive, finding concerning the duration of pursuit was consistent with the Dietz et al. (1991a) study showing a positive association between duration of letter writing and approach behavior toward Hollywood celebrities. In contrast, the number of letters, not the duration of communication, was associated with approach behavior to United States Congressmen (Dietz et al., 1991b).

Zona et al. (1993) found the duration of both the obsession and the pursuit to vary across his three subgroups. The duration of the erotomanic obsessions averaged 10 years; the duration of the love obsessions averaged 12 years. There was no information available for the simple obsessions. Active pursuit varied. The erotomanics attempted contact for an average of 19 months; the love obsessionals, 9.7 months; and the simple obsessionals, 5.1 months. The striking differential here is between the length of the obsession and the pursuit for the erotomanics and the love obsessionals. Zona et al. (1993) noted that some of the pursuit behavior in the love obsessional subgroup began when psychotropic medications ceased. Noone and Cockhill (1987) speculated that the erotomanic may seek contact with the victim when the delusion is dissipating or a more paranoid disorder is emergent. Taylor et al. (1983) inferentially offered the most cogent reason for the disinhibition of the obsession in Zona's first two subgroups when they discussed their own small sample: "all the men, even when depressed, had an air of grandiosity about them . . . these men were generally confident about being loved despite all the evidence to the contrary. It was only at moments when their belief was transiently threatened that they perpetrated physical assault on others" (p. 649).

The pursuit by the simple obsessionals, although much briefer, is usually precipitated by a single event, described by Zona et al. (1993) as "a sustainable rage in response to a perceived narcissistic injury." (p. 901). It is likely the reality testing of the simple obsessional is better than the other two groups since a mutual relationship actually exists, but the common psychodynamic across all three groups which may trigger a pursuit is a threat to the narcissistic equilibrium of the obsessional follower.

The number of contacts in the Meloy and Gothard (1995) sample was greater than 10 for almost half the subjects, but there were missing data for a third of the sample. Duration of pursuit in this study was likely shortened by the arrest of the perpetrator, but was typically at least a year. Mullen and Pathé found an average duration of 25 months, with a range of 1–96 months. Harmon et al. (1995) did not compute these data for their sample, but did note that almost half of their subjects had a history of prior offenses for the same charge, sometimes toward the same person, and sometimes toward others, with an average of four prior arrests.

Although the impact of restraining orders on the pursuit of the obsessional follower is a critical question, minimal data are proffered in these studies to suggest an answer. Harmon et al. (1995) found that almost half of their subjects ignored temporary restraining orders, and were more likely to do so if their pursuit was fueled by amorous or affectionate feelings rather than anger or the perception of persecution. Mullen and Pathé (1994) noted the presence of restraining orders in 43 percent (N = 6) of their cases, most of whom were subsequently violent. They wrote, "when restraining or intervention orders were obtained they were seldom heeded, and in some cases paradoxically served to strengthen the resolve of the erotomanic" (p. 476).

VICTIM CHARACTERISTICS

The potential victim pool of the obsessional follower is a predictive question that has important implications for both clinicians who work with traumatized individuals and law enforcement agencies. Early studies (de Clérambault, 1942) surmised that most erotomanic individuals were women who pursued men, but Taylor et al. (1983) asserted that erotomanic individuals in a forensic setting were likely to be men pursuing women. Their hypothesis has usually been confirmed when broadened to include obsessional followers in general.

There are two exceptions to this finding. First, among those individuals with erotomanic disorder there may be a predominance of women pursuing men, even in a forensic setting. Although the single and multiple case studies of erotomanic obsessional followers were usually men pursuing women (Goldstein, 1978, 1987; Taylor et al., 1983; Noone & Cockhill, 1987; Meloy, 1992; Leong, 1994), the larger studies found a significant number of erotomanic women pursuing men. Zona et al. (1993) found six out of seven erotomanics to be females. Mullen and Pathé (1994) found that two of their five pure or primary erotomanic cases were females. Harmon et al. (1995) reported that all six of their erotomanic cases were women. Meloy and Gothard (1995), however, found that their two erotomanic cases were both men. These data suggest that the victims of erotomanic obsessional followers *are more likely* to be men than victims of obsessional followers with other disorders and motivations. It is also apparent that the proportion of erotomanics who are females is likely to be greater in nonforensic than in forensic samples (Rudden et al., 1990).

Second, in most cases of obsessional following, the victim is likely to be the opposite sex of the perpetrator. There are, however, reported cases of homosexual obsessional following (Meloy, 1992; Zona et al., 1993; Harmon et al., 1995), but these appear to be quite infrequent, probably less than 1 percent.

Various attempts to classify the victims of obsessional followers have been made. Zona et al. (1993) divided them into two groups: no prior relationship and prior relationship. The latter group included customer, acquaintance, neighbor, professional relationship, dating, or sexual intimate. They currently report that 65 percent of their victims had a prior actual relationship with the obsessional follower, a proportional figure that has increased since their first published study (see footnote 3 above). Mullen and Pathé (1994) wrote that, "the majority of objects of affection had had some actual contact with the patient, albeit fleeting" (p. 471). Three of their victims were entertainers and were first seen in public. One had a brief sexual relationship with the perpetrator. Three were health care professionals who originally treated the pursuers. And most disconcertingly, four victims were initially just "seen in the street."

Meloy and Gothard (1995) divided the victims into "stranger" and "former intimate," the latter referring to any sexual intimacy prior to the obsessional following. They reported that 45 percent of the victims were strangers, but did not define their use of this term. Harmon et al. (1995) provided the most detailed breakdown of victim relationship prior to the obsessional following, which formed one axis of their classification system: personal, professional, employment, media, acquaintance, none, and unknown. Half of their victims had a professional or employment relationship with the obsessional follower prior to the pursuit. Thirteen percent had a personal relationship, and thirteen percent were initially seen in the media. Eight percent were superficial acquaintances, and 8 percent had no discernable prior contact with the obsessional follower.

These various classification systems lend confusion to the relationship question in this review, and future studies could simplify this task by dividing victims into three groups: (a) those who were prior acquaintances; (b) those who were prior sexual intimates; and (c) those who were strangers. If the Harmon et al. (1995) data are regrouped according to this classification, the patterns become clearer: 58 percent were prior acquaintances; 21 percent were strangers; and 13 percent were prior intimates (8% were unknown). My groupings do appear to be mutually exclusive, and demonstrate some utility by showing consistency between the Zona et al. (1993), Meloy and Gothard (1995), and Harmon et al. (1995) studies. It appears that a majority of obsessional followers will pursue prior acquaintances, and the rest will be divided, at some unpredictable proportion, between prior sexual intimates and complete strangers.

In most of the studies reviewed, the obsessional follower had one victim. Harmon et al. (1995) reported multiple victims for one-third of their sample, and Mullen and Pathé (1994) found that 22 percent of their perpetrators had multiple victims. This finding, however, is not conclusory since the natural course of the obsessional following was usually interrupted with arrest and prosecution, and prior victims may not have been known to the researchers. There are also case studies that report sequential victims (Taylor et al., 1983) and sound a cautionary note in assuming a one victim pattern. Further research will have to clarify this question, most likely a longitudinal study of a sample of obsessional followers, carefully tracked as they enter and exit the criminal system.

The most reliable data concerning the age of victims of obsessional following is found in the Zona et al. (1993) study. The erotomanic subgroup victims averaged 41.7 years; the love obsessionals, 34.1 years; and the simple obsessionals, 41.4 years. Data from other studies were not precise enough to draw conclusions, other than that the age range of the victims is extensive. For instance, Mullen and Pathé

(1994) noted a 14-year-old victim and one that was over 50 years of age. Victims do appear, on average, to be older than one would expect in a general crime victim population.

There are virtually no data on the psychological toll that obsessional following takes on the victims. Mullen and Pathé (1994) gathered the only systematic information in this area of victimization, and repeatedly noted disruption at home and work, marital friction, fear and distress, a need for psychiatric treatment, embarrassment, and occasionally a need to relocate. They wrote that victims, "describe their escalating fear as the stalking proceeds. It is the constant presence of the stalker which unnerves them, particularly when their sudden appearance reveals a knowledge of the victim's plans and movements which they had believed was confidential" (p. 472). It is likely that victims of obsessional following would be vulnerable to symptoms of both anxiety and depression, and the psychological sequelae of trauma, both acute and chronic (van der Kolk, 1987). There is, as yet, no research to support this hypothesis.

PATTERNS OF VIOLENCE AND THREATS

Although stalking laws have often been passed in response to public outrage over a single or multiple homicide, violence research (Monahan & Steadman, 1994) would predict that most obsessional followers are not violent. Such is the case (see Table 7–1).

Zona et al. (1993) found that none of their "love obsessional" or "erotomanic" subgroups engaged in physically harmful acts, and only two of their simple obsessionals "acted to bodily harm their victim" (p. 900). The overall incidence of personal violence was 2.7 percent. Property destruction was more frequent, and 8 percent (N = 6) of their entire sample "destroyed the victim's property" (p. 900).

Mullen and Pathé (1994) reported a much higher frequency of violence in their study of erotomanic individuals who stalked their victims: 36 percent (N = 5) assaulted, another 43 percent (N = 6) sexually attacked, and 36 percent (N = 5) damaged property. Three of the latter subjects also assaulted, for an overall violence frequency of 50 percent. The most likely recipient of the violence was the stalking victim, and the "assaults" ranged from pushing and shoving to homicide (stabbing). The Mullen and Pathé (1994) data, however, should be treated with caution. Their sample size is small (N = 14), and there are inconsistencies in findings between their tables and narrative (e.g., number of victims, unrelated offense history).

Meloy and Gothard (1995) reported a 25 percent (N = 5) incidence of physical assault, but only two of these individuals were formally charged with assault. Most of the victims were the objects of pursuit. None of the physical violence involved a weapon (S. Gothard, personal communication, April, 1995). Harmon et al. (1995) likewise reported a 21 percent (N = 10) incidence of assault in which four out of five victimized their object of pursuit. Two of these attacks involved a knife; none involved a firearm. Most of the perpetrators used their hands to grab, strike, punch, or fondle their victim.

There were four homicides committed as a direct result of obsessional following by the 180 subjects in this research review, for an incidence of 2 percent. The weapons of choice were two knives, a .357 magnum revolver, and gasoline. This figure is likely elevated since two of these subjects were selected for study because of their violence (Meloy, 1992).

The relationship between threats and violence is controversial, characterized by much speculation and little research. One of the few empirical studies ever done found that only 3 percent of individuals who threatened homicide actually committed the act, and another 4 percent committed suicide instead (MacDonald, 1968). Dietz (1991a, 1991b) found that threatening letters had no relationship to approach behavior when the victims were Hollywood celebrities, and diminished the risk of approach to a United States Congressman.

Threats to person, property, or both are common among obsessional followers:

Table 7–2 outlines the frequency of threats in the three largest studies reviewed (N = 142), the proportion of individuals who threaten that are subsequently violent, and the false positive rate. Approximately one-half of obsessional followers will threaten, and one-fourth of these subjects will act on their threat, for a mean false positive rate of 75 percent.[5] Threats are likely underreported across these studies, however, which would tend to decrease the false positive rate.

---

[5] Two studies further refine this relationship. Meloy & Gothard (1995) found a significant relation (p = .004) between threats and prior intimacy, and Harmon et al. (1995) found a significant relation (p = .05) between threats and assaults in their "affectionate/amorous" subgroup. The magnitude or strength of these relationships is unknown.

Table 7–2.
Incidence of threats and subsequent violence
(person and property) by obsessional followers.

Study	Threats	Violence (true positive)	False positive
Zona et al.	45% (33)	25% (8)	75% (25)
Meloy & Gothard	60% (12)	17% (2)	83% (10)
Harmon et al.	46% (22)	32% (7)	68% (15)
Mean	50%	25%	75%

The investigator should be careful, however, to not overlook the false negatives: the obsessional followers who do not threaten, but are subsequently violent. Harmon et al. (1995) reported three such individuals (6% of their sample) and Meloy and Gothard (1995) found three (15% of their sample). The sensible approach would suggest that the subject's history of threats and their relationship to subsequent violence is the best source of data for assessing future risk subsequent to a threat. Threats may inhibit, disinhibit, or have no relationship to actual violence in any one subject.

Although the targets of the obsessional followers' threats and violence are most likely to be the objects of pursuit, Mullen and Pathé (1994) noted three other groups that may be at risk: third parties believed to be impeding access to the object, innocent bystanders, or the obsessional follower himself (suicide or attack by others). Their observations are consistent with other opinion (Meloy, 1989).

An overview of the violence risk among obsessional followers leads me to several conclusions:

1. Approximately one half of obsessional followers will threaten, and are more likely to do so if there was a prior intimate relationship (Meloy & Gothard, 1995) or a real or imagined injury related to a business or professional relationship (Harmon et al., 1995).

2. Three-fourths of those who threaten will not subsequently be violent toward person or property.

3. Violence may be committed by those who don't threaten, but this is usual.

4. The frequency of personal violence varies between 3-36 percent. Most obsessional followers are not violent toward person or property. Incidence rates vary widely, and will likely do so in future studies until researchers control for duration of the pursuit. The relation between

this latter factor and violence risk is unknown.

5. Violence is most likely to be a physical assault and battery without a weapon, the victim being grabbed, punched, struck, or fondled by the obsessional follower.

6. The incidence of homicide is less than 2 percent.

7. The most likely victim of the violence is the object of pursuit, probably at least 80 percent of the time.

8. Third parties perceived as impeding access to the object of pursuit are the next most likely victim pool.

9. The violence is usually "affective" (Meloy, 1988), and is often fueled by narcissistic rage, the result of acutely or chronically perceived rejection.

SUBTYPES OF OBSESSIONAL FOLLOWERS

There are two typologies of obsessional followers which have been subjected to empirical study. Zona et al. (1993) divided them into three groups: the erotomanics, the love obsessionals, and the simple obsessionals. Their typology is based on both offender characteristics and the relationship to the victim. They provided some discriminant validity for their typology, finding significant differences among at least two of the three subgroups in victim sex ratio, perpetrator sex ratio, foreign born status, presence of a mental disorder, telephone contact, letter writing, fax transmissions, and frequency of threats. These findings suggest that the typology may be useful to both clinicians and law enforcement. The major problems with the Zona typology are twofold: the potential presence of erotomanic delusion in the love obsessional group, and the idiosyncratic use of the term obsessional.

Harmon et al. (1995) developed a "two axis classification system" (p. 189) focusing on the nature of the obsessional attachment and the nature of the prior interaction. The first axis was divided into affectionate/amorous and persecutory/angry. Statistical analysis of eight demographic, criminal, and psychiatric variables found no significant differences, other than marital status. The affectionate/amorous group was more likely to be single. No inferential statistics were applied to the second axis, probably because of the small sample size in each of the six prior relationship classes: personal, professional, employment, media, acquaintance, and none known. Although their first axis showed virtually no discriminant validity, larger sample sizes and multivariate analyses that look for both main effects and interaction effects may prove useful. The major problems with the Harmon typology are the virtual lack of discriminant validity in their first study and the likely temporal instability of the first axis: the nature of the obsessional attachment.

PSYCHODYNAMIC FINDINGS

The reasons for obsessional following are not readily discernable through the quantification of data, but I would like to offer some thoughts concerning the psychodynamics of obsessional following after reviewing these studies. Patterns do emerge, and my assertions may be treated as testable hypotheses that may exist in any one particular case. Clinical interviewing, psychological testing, and scrutiny of the behavior of the individual independent of his self-report will likely support or refute these clinical insights.

Obsessional following is a pathology of attachment. It can be behaviorally described as proximity seeking toward an angry or frightened object that usually responds aversively to the act of pursuit. By definition, this is an abnormal attachment (Meloy, 1992). It fits most closely into the *preoccupied* attachment pattern developed by Bartholomew (1990) in his four-type model of attachment styles. Preoccupied individuals "actively seek to gain their attachment figure's approval in order to validate their tenuous sense of self-worth. Their feelings of unworthiness and strong approach orientation are expected to be associated with high levels of intimacy-anger" (Dutton, 1995, p. 153). This preoccupied attachment pattern is consistent with the obsessional thought of these subjects and the borderline nature of their affects and defenses. The abnormal attachment behavior of obsessional followers suggests the need for clinical probes into the childhood and adolescent attachment histories of these individuals, with a particular focus on developmental disturbances during the differentiation and practicing subphases of separation-individuation (Mahler et al., 1975).

The obsessional follower may be either psychotic or nonpsychotic during the pursuit. If psychotic, the primary symptom is likely to be a delusion characterized by erotomanic or persecutory beliefs. If nonpsychotic, reality testing is still likely to be seriously impaired, and will be clinically evident in the obsessional follower's confusion regarding the origin of feelings, thoughts, and impulses. He will often attribute his own internal stimuli to the victim, and vice versa, a marker for borderline personality organization (Meloy, 1992).

The psychopathology of obsessional following is, in part, a maladaptive response to social incompetence, social isolation, and loneliness. What differentiates these individuals from others, however, appears to be their aggression and pathological narcissism. The acting-out of their obsession in pursuit, and in a few cases eventual violence, is likely due to a disturbance in their narcissistic economy. A real event, such as acute or chronic rejection, challenges the compensatory narcissistic fantasy that the obsessional follower is special, loved, idealized, admired, superior to, or in some way linked or destined to be with the object of pursuit. The disturbance of this narcissistic fantasy, imbued with both a sense of grandiosity and a feeling of pride, triggers feelings of shame or humiliation that are defended against with rage. This intense anger also fends off any feeling of sadness, since the capacity to grieve the loss of a whole, real, and meaningful person is not available to the obsessional follower. Instead, from a self-psychology perspective (Kohut, 1971), a merging narcissistic transference is apparent, characterized by rage toward a selfobject and attempts to control it.

Borderline defenses serve this narcissistic economy well. Denial, splitting, initial idealization, eventual devaluation, projection, and projective identification are explicitly mentioned, or implicitly referenced, in most of the reviewed cases. Some neurotic defenses are also apparent, including minimization and rationalization, the latter most evident in a plausible, but false explanation for the pursuit.

Overt paranoia in the obsessional follower will likely be directed toward third parties perceived as standing in the way of the object, and is usually both a projection of annihilatory rage (displaced from the object of pursuit) and a symptom of increased vulnerability. Paranoia in these cases may range from suspicious beliefs to overt delusion. Paradoxically, intervention by third parties (spouse, psychotherapist, police officer, attorney, etc.) to help or protect the victim may exacerbate paranoid beliefs by providing a vehicle which can carry the paranoid projection.

This may be unavoidable, but should be noted as a social triangulation that may increase the risk of violence.

The most obvious interpersonal dynamic in obsessional following cases is a principle gleaned from behavioral psychology. Any real contact between the victim and the perpetrator is likely to increase the frequency of subsequent approaches. Such contact is an intermittent positive reinforcer, and attempts should not be made to reason with such an unreasonable individual.

FUTURE DIRECTIONS AND CONCLUSIONS

The clinical investigation of the obsessional follower, completed through the review of ten studies published between 1978 and 1995, and yielding 180 subjects, provides a detailed picture of the likely demographics, psychiatric diagnoses, pursuit patterns, victim characteristics, violence risk and its relationship to threats, subtyping validity, and psychodynamics of these individuals. The reader should keep in mind, however, that profiling attempts such as this, even when gleaned from empirical research, rarely describe all the facts apparent in any one case of obsessional following. The map is never the territory, but only serves as a guide for the traveler.

Future research concerning obsessional followers is clearly necessary, and should develop larger samples of individuals in different geographical areas to cross-validate the findings of this review. Samples of obsessional followers should be compared to random samples of other criminal and psychiatric populations. The Zona typology appears to be the most promising, although victim data could more usefully be grouped into the three categories I have suggested.

Research content areas that await study include victim reactions (both adaptive and maladaptive), psychological test characteristics of the obsessional follower, the longitudinal course of obsessional following, immigration as a stressor, epidemiological studies, precipitants of both pursuit and violence, differential risk factors between personal and property violence, psychiatric and psychological treatment, and effective risk management.

> A mighty pain to love it is,
> And 'tis a pain that pain to miss;
> But of all pains, the greatest pain
> It is to love, but love in vain.

Abraham Crowley, "Gold" *From Anacreon,* 1656

REFERENCES

American Psychiatric Association (1994). *Diagnostic and statistical manual of mental disorders. Fourth Edition.* Washington, D.C.

Bartholomew, K. (1990). Avoidance of intimacy: An attachment perspective. *Journal of Social and Personal Relationships, 7,* 147.

California Penal Code, Section 646. 9, 1995.

de Clérambault, C. (1942). Les psychoses passionelles. In *Qeuvres Psychiatriques.* Paris: Presses Universitaires de France, pp. 315–322.

Dietz, P., Matthews, D., Van Duyne, C., Martell, D., Parry, C., Stewart, T., Warren, J., & Crowder, J. (199 la). Threatening and otherwise inappropriate letters to Hollywood celebrities. *Journal of Forensic Sciences, 36,* 185.

Dietz, P., Matthews, D., Martell, D., Stewart, T., Hrouda, D., & Warren, J. (1991b). Threatening and otherwise inappropriate letters to members of the United States Congress. *Journal of Forensic Sciences, 36,* 1445.

Dutton, D. (1995). *The domestic assault of women.* Vancouver: University of British Columbia Press.

Freund, K., Scher, H., & Hucker, S. (1983). The courtship disorders. *Archives of Sexual Behavior, 12,* 369.

Goldstein, R. (1978). De Clérambault in court: A forensic romance. T*he Bulletin of the Amencan Academy of Psychiatry and the Law, 6,* 36.

Goldstein, R. (1986). Erotomania in men (letter to the editor). *American Journal of Psychiatry, 143,* 6.

Goldstein, R. (1987). More forensic romances: de Clérambault's syndrome in men. *The Bulletin of the American Academy of Psychiatry and the Law, 15,* 267.

Harmon, R., Rosner, R., & Owens, H. (1995). Obsessional harassment and erotomania in a criminal court population. *Journal of Forensic Sciences, 40,* 188.

Hinsie, L., & Campbell, R. (1974). *Psychiatric Dictionary, Fourth Edition.* New York: Oxford University Press.

Kohut, H. (1971). *Analysis of the self.* New York: International Universities Press.

Leong, G. (1994). De Clérambault syndrome (erotomania) in the criminal justice system: Another look at this recurring problem. *Journal of Forensic Sciences, 39,* 378.

Leong, G., & Silva, M. (1992). The physician as erotomanic object. *Western Journal of Medicine, 156,* 77.

Mahler, M., Pine, F., & Bergman, A. (1975). *The psychological birth of the human infant.* New York: Basic Books.

McAnaney, K., Curliss, L., & Abeyta-Price, C. (1993). From imprudence to crime: Anti-stalking laws. *Notre Dame Law Review, 68,* 819.

MacDonald, J. (1968). *Homicidal threats.* Springfield, IL: Charles C Thomas.

Meloy, R. (1988). *The psychopathic mind: Origins, dynamics and treatment.* Northvale, NJ: Jason Aronson.

Meloy, R. (1989). Unrequited love and the wish to kill: The diagnosis and treatment of borderline erotomania. *Bulletin of the Menninger Clinic, 53,* 477.

Meloy, R. (1992). *Violent attachments.* Northvale, NJ: Jason Aronson.

Meloy, R., & Gothard, S. (1995). Demographic and clinical comparison of obsessional followers and offenders with mental disorders. *Amencan Journal of Psychiatry, 152,* 258.

Meyers, J., & Meloy, R. (1994). Discussion of "a comparative study of erotomanic and obsessional subjects in a forensic sample" (letter to the editor). *Journal of Forensic Sciences, 39,* 906.

Monahan, J., & Steadman, H. (1994). *Violence and mental disorder: Developments in risk assessment.* Chicago: University of Chicago Press.

Mullen, P., & Pathé, M. (1994a). Stalking and the pathologies of love. *Australian and New Zealand Journal of Psychiatry, 28,* 469.

Mullen, P., & Pathé, M. (1994b). The pathological extensions of love. *British Journal of Psychiatry, 165,* 61.

Nietzsche, F. (1883–92). *Thus spoke Zarathustra.* New York: Penguin Books (1969 edition).

Noone, J., & Cockhill, L. (1987). Erotomania: The delusion of being loved. *American Journal of Forensic Psychiatry, 8,* 23.

Raskin, D., & Sullivan, K. (1974). Erotomania. *American Journal of Psychiatry, 131,* 1033.

Rudden, M., Sweeney, J., & Frances, A. (1990). Diagnosis and clinical course of erotomanic and other delusional patients. *American Journal of Psychiatry, 147,* 625.

Segal, J. (1989). Erotomania revisited: From Kraepelin to *DSM–III–R. American Journal of Psychiatry, 146,* 1261.

Segal, J. (1990). Reply to JR Meloy: Nondelusional or borderline erotomania (letter to the editor). *American Journal of Psychiatry, 147,* 820.

Taylor, P., Mahendra, B., & Gunn, J. (1983). Erotomania in males. *Psychological Medicine, 13,* 645.

van der Kolk, B. (1987). *Psychological trauma.* Washington, D.C.: American Psychiatric Press.

Wilson, J., & Herrnstein, R. (1985). *Crime and human nature.* New York: Simon and Schuster.

Zona, M., Sharma, K., & Lane, J. (1993). A comparative study of erotomanic and obsessional subjects in a forensic sample. *Journal of Forensic Sciences, 38,* 894.

Chapter 8

FORENSIC ASPECTS
OF FACTITIOUS DISORDER

Robert D. Miller

I. FACTITIOUS DISORDER WITH PHYSICAL SYMPTOMS

What is now called "Factitious Disorder" in the American Psychiatric Association's diagnostic manuals was initially described by Asher (1951), under the name of "Munchausen's Syndrome" based on Rudolf Erich Raspe's 1784 book *Baron Munchausen's Narrative of His Marvelous Travels and Campaigns in Russia.* The initial description was of patients with medical complaints which the "patients" either fabricated entirely, or due to patient actions, such as causing actual bleeding or infections in themselves. In addition to the simulation of physical symptoms, such patients were described as commonly telling "tall tales" unrelated to their medical complaints (hence, the allusion to Baron Munchausen, a real person who did in fact love to tell such tales, but had no history of simulating medical complaints). The early papers were written by internists and surgeons, and clearly demonstrated the frustration and anger at people who spent their time deceiving medical professionals. The very language and energy of their papers, unusual in medical publications, indicated their emotional investment in uncovering and casting out these fakers. The "tall tales" were dubbed "pseudologia fantastica;" subtypes were given names such as Neurologica Diabolica, Laparotomorphia Migrans, and Hemorrhagia Terrifica. Some authors expended significant energy tracking patients across a country, documenting their tendency to leave medical facilities as soon as they are discovered, only to admit themselves to others with the same, or different, complaints. This behavior led to further colorful labels, such as "hospital hoboes," (Clark & Melnich, 1958), "hospital addicts," (Barker, 1962), "metabolic malingerers," (Gorman, Wahner & Tauxe, 1970) and "perigrinating problem patients," (Chapman, 1977).

Mental health professionals subsequently assumed hegemony over the diagnosis, arguing that the behavior was caused by a mental disorder, and also reporting that there were patients who simulated psychological as well as physical symptoms. From its inception, Munchausen's syndrome has been conceptualized psychodynamically as involving the conscious production of false symptoms, which are based on unconscious motives. Unlike frank malingerers, factitious patients do not appear to be motivated by financial advantage, disability, or relief from dangerous or onerous duties; rather they appear to want to assume the "sick role." (Plewes & Fagan, 1994)

Spiro (1968) recommended that the name of the syndrome be changed to "chronic factitious illness," to avoid the focus on lying and swindling and the pejorative connotations of those behaviors. More recent reports demonstrate that factitious patients are no longer likely to invent fantastic stories or wander from hospital to hospital (Eisendrath, 1984; Humphries, 1988; Rumans & Vosti, 1978). That recommendation was adopted by the American Psychiatric Association (1980) in its *DSM-III*; but Munchausen's syndrome remains in active use because, as Nadelson (1979, p. 11) "the Baron's name is a more charming, evocative, antique, and noble reference and makes a more mouth-filling phrase." With the third edition of the *Diagnostic and Statistical Manual of Mental Disorders (DSM-III)* (American Psychiatric Association, 1980), the nonetiological format of that Manual reduced the criteria to observable symptoms, without comment on the etiology, except to state that "The individual's goal is apparently to assume the 'patient role' and is not otherwise understandable in light of the individual's environmental circumstances (as is the case in Malingering)."

Despite the atheoretical orientation of the official diagnostic manual, many clinicians continue to conceptualize factitious disorder in psychodynamic terms. Nadelson (1985) proposes that factitious disorder is a manifestation of borderline character pathology, in which the patient becomes both victim and victimizer by receiving medical attention from health care providers while at the same time devaluing and defying them. They project hostility and worthlessness onto caretakers, who are both desired and rejected. Viederman (1985) argues that early life experience, such as a history of abuse, emotional deprivation, childhood illness and hospitalization, abandonment in childhood, or lack of nurturance may contribute to a personality structure which lends itself to factitious behaviors. The history of abuse by parental or authority figures leads to masochistic tendencies in which caring is associated with submissiveness and pain.

DIFFERENTIAL DIAGNOSIS OF FACTITIOUS DISORDER

1. Malingering

The major diagnosis which must be differentiated from factitious disorder is malingering. The *DSM–IV* criteria for malingering are rather nonspecific; *DSM–IV* defines as "the intentional production of grossly exaggerated physical or psychological symptoms, motivated by external incentives such as avoiding military duty, avoiding work, obtaining financial compensation, evading criminal prosecution, or obtaining drugs. Under some circumstances, malingering may represent adaptive behavior, for example feigning illness while a captive of the enemy during wartime." Malingering should be suspected in the following situations: (1) medicolegal presentation, (2) marked discrepancy between the person's claimed stress.

Yudofsky (1985) suggests that any combination of the following behaviors should alert a physician to the possibility of malingering: (1) staged events, (2) data tampering, (3) opportunistic malingering, and (4) symptom intervention. Stoudemire (1988, pp. 533–556.) would add a fifth form of malingering: self-destructive behavior. Overholser (1990) argues that the differentiation between malingering and factitious disorder cannot be made on observed behavior alone, but must take psychological factors into account. The differential must examine the course of the disorder, response to treatment, and possible etiologic factors.

Overholser categorized factitious patients on the basis of the level of deception involved: (1) symptom invention; (2) data tampering; (3) opportunistic malingering–exaggeration of existing illness (more frequent in malingering); (4) and staged events leading to injury (more frequent in malingering); (5) Verifiable pathology by creation of tissue damage (more frequent in factitious disorder–see Reich & Gottfried, 1983, Shafer & Shafer, 1980). Differences between malingering and factitious disorder can be detected in the following areas: (1) observed symptomatology: both present with dramatic symptoms, although malingerers more frequently overact because they lack the medical experience of many factitious patients), and infrequently present with tissue damage (more common in factitious disorder) and guarded behavior. Malingerers are seen more frequently in outpatient settings, while factitious patients are usually seen in inpatient settings. Spiro (1968) argues that malingering should be diagnosed only in the absence of other psychiatric disorder and in the presence of socio-pathic behavior adaptive to a long-term goal. Janofsky (1994) argues that while both malingerers and factitious patients will fabricate symptoms, only factitious patients will lie and fake symptoms and historical details unrelated to the understandable goals in their cases.

A. Course Over Time.

The onset of malingering is more frequently sudden. Malingered symptoms are usually time-limited, to the time necessary to achieve goals (Eisendrath, 1984; Sussman & Hyler, 1985). Malingered episodes are usually brief, because of the difficulty maintaining the simulation (Clark, 1988). Factitious symptoms are more chronic, but erratic, often lasting until the patient is discharged from the hospital (Ford, 1973; Ries, 1980; Stone, 1977; Swanson, 1981). Factitious patients discharge themselves against medical advice approximately 42 percent of the time (Pankrantz, 1981). Malingerers less frequently leave AMA or antagonize medical personnel. Factitious patients may indirectly reveal their simulations to demonstrate their superiority over physicians (Swanson, 1981). Malingerers rarely have previous episodes of psychiatric problems (Clark, 1988; Miller & Cartlidge, 1972), and rarely have repeated episodes of falsified symptoms (Hyler & Sussman, 1981), while factitious patients almost always have had previous episodes (Ananth, 1977; Humphries, 1988; Ireland, Sapira & Templeton, 1967;Justus, Kreutziger & Kitchens, 1980; Klonoff, Younger, Moore & Hershey, 1983; Kooiman 1987; Pankrantz, 1981; Ries, 1980; Stone, 1977; Swanson, 1981). If they do repeat, malingerers are more likely to display the same symptoms, while factitious patients are more likely to change symptoms (Klonoff et al., 1983; Kooiman, 1987). Factitious patients are also likely to elaborate on the

symptoms and signs of previous illnesses from which they have suffered (Ford, 1986).

B. Response to Treatment.

Malingerers are usually satisfied with more benign treatments than
are factitious patients. (Ananth, 1977 Shafer & Shafer, 1980). Neither
typically responds well to treatment, although malingerers are likely to
improve quickly once their external goals have been achieved.
Placebo response may be dramatic (Miller, 1988; Miller, Blancke,
Doren & Maier, 1985). Direct confrontation of factitious patients may
produce a temporary decrease in symptoms (Cramer, Gershberg &
Stern, 1971; Reich & Gottfried, 1983). Malingerers are more likely to
be initially uncooperative with thorough examinations, while factitious
patients are likely to welcome examinations initially, but then become
hostile when no improvement results from treatment.

C. Proposed Etiology.

Both disorders involve conscious production of false symptoms,
and therefore involve deception of others. Both freely improvise histories, and there are thus frequently inconsistencies between patient
reports and observed symptoms (which also may be true with genuine
patients, of course). Factitious patients' motivation is assumed to be
unconscious (Reich & Gottfried, 1983; Jonas & Pope, 1985). Thus,
malingerers can stop producing symptoms at will, but factitious
patients cannot. Voluntariness must be demonstrated by (1) the
patient's admission of deceit, (2) physiologically impossible symptoms,
(3) observable evidence (such as a patient moving a "paralyzed" arm),
(4) symptoms that contradict laboratory tests, (5) physical evidence, or
(6) an unusual response to treatment. Motivation for the factitious
patient is to assume the sick role; Folks & Freeman (1985) argue that
secondary gain, such as receiving attention, support, sympathy, and
relief from responsibility, may underlie the need to assume the sick
role. Carney (1980) reported that 74 percent of his factitious patients
experienced severe sexual or marital stress prior to the development
of their signs or symptoms. Some propose a masochistic tendency in
factitious patients (Bursten, 1965; Ford, 1973; Spiro, 1968). These
patients' actions differ from suicidal acts in that the purpose is to transfer responsibility to medical staff (Menninger, 1934). Others (Cramer

et al., 1971; Justus et al., 1980; Stone, 1977) view factitious disorder as manipulative behavior–but more assertive than the less aggressive methods typically discussed. Cramer et al. (1971) argue that factitious behavior serves to reenact the relationship with parents; physicians have often served as parental figures for such patients when they were young. While malingerers are likely to satisfy criteria for Antisocial Personality Disorder, Factitious patients are more likely to satisfy criteria for Borderline Personality Disorder (Aduan, Fauci, Dale, Herzberg & Wolff, 1979; Folks & Freeman, 1985; Nadelson, 1979; Ries, 1980; Stone, 1977).

Pankrantz and Lezak (1987) report that although factitious patients generally tested in the normal range of intelligence, formal neuropsychological evaluation revealed deficits in conceptual organization, management of complex information, and judgment, suggesting that subtle but important neuropsychological impairment may contribute to their aberrant behavior. Personality testing did not reveal psychosis, but did produce patterns suggestive that they were immature, impulsive, histrionic, and narcissistic. Patients were passive, had poor body images and sexual identities, and tended to see physicians as parent-equivalents who could or would not help them. The patients were preoccupied with death and morbid thoughts, and appeared depressed with some having suicidal ideation.

Overholser concluded that longitudinal data are crucial to the diagnosis of Munchausen's syndrome, as are objective data such as the stability of the problems over time, the recurrence of symptomatic episodes, and observed response to treatment.

2. Other Disorders

The differential diagnosis should also include true psychoses such as schizophrenia, mood disorders, and antisocial personality disorder. It may be difficult to tell factitious disorder from psychosis, but continued observation of behaviors and of response to test doses on antipsychotic medication in an inpatient setting may reveal inconsistencies. Antisocial patients may exhibit pseudologia fantastica, few close relationships, and a history of criminal behavior and substance abuse; but these behaviors usually have an earlier onset than in factitious disorder, and antisocial patients rarely seek unneeded medical treatment (Overholser, 1990). Pope, Jonas and Jones (1982) discuss the problems in distinguishing among factitious, malingering, and somatizing patient presentations; they proposed that the three disorders are closely related, and should be studied as a group. They suggest that somatization disorder or conversion disorder in a female patient with underlying histrionic personality is equivalent to factitious disorder or malingering in a male patient with underlying antisocial personality. Therefore, factitious symptoms and signs seen in various disorders may represent gender- and culture-specific manifestations of a single disorder. They further argue that to distinguish factitious disorders from the others, the diagnostic focus should be on more objective factors such as demographics, associated phenomenology, biological findings (if any), family history, treatment response, and long-term outcome, rather than on evaluating a patient's motivation in conscious or unconscious terms.

PREVALENCE

It is difficult to collect reliable data on incidence and prevalence rates, course of the disorder, and efficacy of treatment, because of the unreliable and deceptive nature of the patients and the changeability of their histories. As patients who repeatedly engage in suicidal "gestures" may accidentally die as a result of such actions, Munchausen patients may be at risk for genuine and serious medical or surgical conditions as a result of prior treatments for factitious illnesses. Reports of the disorder remain infrequent, in part perhaps due to a low index of suspicion among clinicians. But Sutherland and Rodin (1990) reported that of 1,288 medical inpatients referred for psychiatric consultation, only 0.8 percent warranted the diagnosis of factitious disorder, and only one qualified for Factitious Disorder with Psychological Symptoms.

Carney (1980) and Reich and Gottfried (1983) demonstrated a bimodal distribution of factitious patients: (1) Classic Munchausen patients: mostly males with criminal and/or psychopathic traits, drug or alcohol abuse, multisystem complaints, and wandering behavior with multiple hospitalizations. Many have dramatic presentations, with histories of many hospitalizations over a wide geographic area, several discharges against medical advice, multiple abdominal scars, and evidence of selfmutilation. They often seek care at times when emergency rooms are staffed with less experienced doctors. (2) "Neoclassic" Munchausen patients are mostly young women with conforming life styles and more family support and involvement. They have been described as passive, immature, and hypochondriacal; about half have health-related jobs (Ford, 1986). They are typically not wanderers, have single-system complaints, and generate fewer hospitalizations than classic Munchausen patients.

TREATMENT/MANAGEMENT

The management of factitious disorder is complicated, often requiring the physician to deviate significantly from the traditional doctor-patient relationship by adopting an adversarial relationship with patients; this exacerbates the patient's existing tendency to be truculent, and frequently leads to premature disruption of medical care. The diagnostic process also raises questions about medical ethics and patients' right to confidentiality (Plewes & Fagan, 1994) which will be discussed in more detail below.

Plewes and Fagan (1994) also argue that treatment for factitious patients with physical symptoms patients should usually be carried out by a team of psychiatrist plus internist. Effort should be made to de-emphasize the confrontational approach which the patient often elicits. The approach should initially be aimed at preventing the patient from leaving the hospital and terminating treatment. Then transfer to an inpatient psychiatry unit should be recommended.

The major problem with this approach is that factitious patients adamantly reject the possibility that they are suffering from psychological disorders, and leave as soon as the legitimacy of their physical symptoms is challenged. This prevents not only effective treatment, but even collection of the past history which is essential to diagnosis and treatment. The forensic context actually provides some advantages in these areas, as will be discussed below.

II. FACTITIOUS DISORDER WITH PSYCHOLOGICAL SYMPTOMS

After the existence of Factitious Disorder with physical symptoms became better known, clinicians began to discover that patients presenting with traditional psychiatric symptoms also fit the pattern.

Initially, such patients had to be diagnosed as suffering from conditions other than factitious disorder (Miller, 1978), but with *DSM–III*, Factitious Disorder with Psychological Symptoms (FDPS) became recognized as a subtype of factitious disorder. Such patients are less likely than those with physical symptoms to have formal medical training, but they often have histories of previous psychiatric hospitalizations or treatment, usually for less severe disorders than those with which they currently present. Although they present to (or are committed to) psychiatric facilities, they are just as resistant to interpretation of their disorders as factitious as are factitious patients with physical symptoms. Even if committed, once the validity of their presenting symptoms is challenged, the symptoms frequently remit quickly, thus removing the basis for the commitment.

The diagnosis is even more difficult to make than in the case of physical symptoms, since there are no objective tests to demonstrate the falsity of the symptoms. As demonstrated in Rosenhan's (1973) classical article, psychiatrists too rarely challenge the validity of reported severe symptoms, such as psychosis or major depression, and are thus less likely than their physical medicine colleagues to suspect the factitious nature of such symptoms. In addition, since the symptoms frequently remit spontaneously once the stress that precipitated them is removed by hospitalization, psychiatrists may be deceived into thinking that their treatment (typically with psychotropic medications) has been responsible for the remission, thus reinforcing the (erroneous) diagnosis.

Several authors have challenged both the reliability and the validity of the diagnosis of FDPS. Rogers and colleagues argue that it is difficult to assess intrapsychic motivation in an uncooperative patient. The focus of the literature has been to further our understanding of the etiology and intrapsychic mechanisms involved in FDPS. The creative attempt to "have it both ways," i.e., both voluntary and involuntary, appears diagnostically indefensible. There are three unresolved issues surrounding the motivation question: (1) Because of the individual's deception of others and possible self-deception, the specific motivations for a "factitious presentation," while probably multidetermined, may not be knowable. (2) Given our assumptions about multicausality, the thesis that intrapsychic phenomena alone would account for a complex set of interpersonal behaviors is an insufficient explanation. (3) The diagnosis of factitious disorder with psychological symptoms appears to be based on the implicit assumption that such motivation for dissimulation, whether intrapsychic or not, is necessarily maladaptive.

The authors argue that FDPS lacks reliable inclusion, exclusion, and outcome criteria. They present case examples, and argue that even in "classical" cases, there may be many potential motives in addition to a wish to assume the sick role. The validity of factitious disorder is questionable: (1) *DSM–III* achieved unacceptably low kappa coefficients (0.66 and -0.005) on seven patients with factitious disorder (*DSM–III*, p. 470) (Rogers, Bagby & Rector, 1989). The field trials for *DSM–III* yielded very few FDPS cases, and those they found had unacceptable interrater reliability (Spitzer, Forman & Nee (1979).

Rogers, Bagby and Vincent (1994) followed-up on their previous theoretical article with a study drawing on a data base of 700 patients referred for forensic evaluation. They compared 9 patients with FDPS, 25 suspected malingerers, and 26 psychiatric inpatients, using the Structured Interview of Reported Symptoms (SIRS). No significant differences were found between malingerers and FDPS patients. Discriminant analysis yielded a classification rate of 60 percent, and correctly identified only 22.2 percent of FDPS patients. Two SIRS items (word opposites and thought broadcasting) were significantly different between the 2 groups. Discriminant analysis using 7 significant items increased the hit rate to 75 percent; 77.8 percent of the FDPS patients were correctly identified, but 7/25 suspected malingerers were also classified as FDPS by this method. The 8 items were taken from 4 separate SIRS scales, and the findings, in the absence of a clinical framework is a weak argument for diagnostic validity.

The authors questioned diagnoses which are face valid, particularly FDPS. They also question the concept of conscious behavior based on unconscious motives, as have other authors (Cunnien, 1988; Pope et al., 1982). A second conceptual problem is the insistence that the patient is solely motivated by the need to assume the sick role in the absence of any external incentives. FDPS appears to have a sociocultural dimension–factitious PTSD cases began appearing after the Viet Nam war, and more recently, factitious AIDS cases have appeared. In addition, disorders such as depression, mania, and somatic disorders have been reported to coexist with FDPS. The use of standard psychometric instruments to detect malingering have not been well studied, in part because of the small numbers of FDPS patients.

While Rogers restricts his criticisms to the FDPS, many of his criticisms are equally applicable to factitious disorder with physical symptoms as well; these criticisms become especially important in the forensic context.

III. FACTITIOUS DISORDER
IN THE FORENSIC CONTEXT

A. Criminal

Factitious disorder itself is rarely directly involved in criminal cases. A computerized search revealed only one reported case in which it figured in an insanity defense; in *Olivier v. State* (1993), despite the fact that the defendant was found by all the experts to be suffering from both factitious disorder and schizoaffective disorder, the jury found him sane. On appeal, the court reversed the jury's finding. It appears, however, that the major diagnosis relevant to insanity was schizoaffective disorder, not factitious disorder. Unlike Munchausen's syndrome by proxy (discussed below), in which the disorder is by definition frequently associated with criminal behavior, the acts committed by factitious patients are rarely criminal per se. It is possible that factitious patients could be charged with fraud if they attempt to collect medical insurance, or sue providers over their medical conditions, but the author is not aware of any such cases at this point.

Because of the proposed repression of the acts which create the fictitious signs, it is possible to conceive of situations in which factitious disorder could interfere with competency to proceed, but the author is again not aware of any such cases in practice.

Rogers' criticisms of the validity of factitious disorder are highly relevant here. Clinicians who have had the opportunity to treat factitious patients on a long-term basis (Miller et al., 1985) have often come to accept the psychodynamic explanations proposed above, but clinical validity does not necessarily equate with the factual validity required in court. As is the case with other controversial diagnoses, such as multiple personality disorder, the lack of objective verifiability, not of the *behavior* in question, but of the unconscious factors purportedly involved in its genesis, makes convincing a jury or judge that a defendant lacks responsibility or competency extremely difficult. Any expert attempting to provide exculpatory opinions thus faces a formidable task.

B. Civil

Factitious disorder has used as part of the basis for involuntary hospitalization. In *In the Matter of an Application for the Commitment of an Alleged Mentally Disordered Person* (1985), a patient diagnosed as suffering from chronic schizophrenia and factitious disorder and opined to be dangerous to others was committed. He appealed, and the appeals court affirmed the commitment, holding that the testimony satisfied the statutory requirements. It appears from the material cited in the opinion, however, that the dangerousness to others was not based on the factitious disorder. The case does appear to establish, however, that factitious disorder may satisfy the mental disorder criterion for commitment; if the factitious acts represent a sufficient threat to the person's health, commitment based solely on factitious disorder may well be appropriate. Here, unlike the situation in criminal cases, it is sufficient to base opinions on the observed behavior, and the validity of proposed unconscious etiologies is not in question.

Factitious patients would seem to be most likely to become involved in other types of civil litigation, although there are still few reported cases. In *Cohen v. Albert Einstein Medical Center, Northern Division* (1991), Ms. Cohen sued the hospital and its staff, alleging that a negligent intramuscular injection caused neurological damage to her arm. At trial, the judge refused to allow testimony that she suffered from factitious disorder, and the jury found for the plaintiff. On appeal, the court reversed the verdict, holding that Dr. Janofsky's proposed testimony was probative because it could explain to the jury how the plaintiff could have sustained the injuries without negligence on the part of the hospital staff, and also because it was material to the issue of the plaintiff's credibility (*not* competence, on which courts typically do not accept expert testimony) as a witness. After the appeals court ruled that the expert testimony should have been admitted, Ms. Cohen dropped the suit.

Janofsky (1994) discusses this case in detail. Ms. Cohen was a 63-year-old woman with at least 22 years of multiple hospitalizations and medically unexplained pain and other symptoms, who claimed to have been injured by an injection which could not be verified. The diagnosis of factitious disorder was based in part on Dr. Janofsky's review of 180,000 pages of medical records, going back over 20 years, which documented numerous hospitalizations for treatment of unexplained symptoms.

Janofsky emphasizes the important point that forensic psychiatrists called in to review cases in litigation often have time and resources not available to treating clinicians. Accumulation and review of medical records, and verification of historical data, require a great deal of time. As factitious patients are rarely cooperative with attempts to trace past medical histories, it may be necessary to have the court order release of those records. Even with authorization, receipt of requested records may take months. Examiners should suspect factitious disorder when presented with litigants reporting histories of multiple unexplained medical problems unrelated to the current litigation, and when attempts to verify personal or historical data are met with resistance.

TREATMENT IN THE FORENSIC CONTEXT

Since factitious patients almost universally deny creating their medical problems, and leave medical facilities AMA as soon as the validity of their symptoms and signs is challenged, treatment is virtually impossible under voluntary conditions. There are two major avenues to involuntary treatment. One is involuntary hospitalization, with factitious disorder satisfying the mental disorder requirement, and the creation of serious medical conditions satisfying the danger-to-self requirement. The other situation involves forensic commitments. While it is unlikely that a defendant suffering solely from MSP would be found incompetent to proceed or insane, factitious patients suffering from other disorders may be. Miller et al. (1985) reported on the treatment of a factitious patient committed under a state sex crimes law. His factitious disorder had nothing to do with his sexual behavior, but made his management in the hospital quite difficult. He had a documented history of severe and continuing physical and sexual abuse as a child, and experienced a number of brief hospitalizations in which he looked upon health care personnel as his only support, but ultimately blamed them for discharging him back to his abusing family. He enlisted in the army, but was discharged after a few months because of complaints of knee and back pain.

He was quite litigious, setting state records for number of grievances filed, most of which involved complaints of inadequate medical care for a wide variety of reported symptoms. He also claimed to have won a number of medical malpractice lawsuits, none of which could be verified. In response to his complaints, he was evaluated extensively by university hospital specialists, with little evidence to support his complaints. He was also placed under close observation on the ward; extensive evidence of verbally fabricating symptoms was obtained, as well as evidence of the physical production of faked signs (e.g., blood placed into his urine). He also attempted to use his symptoms as a method to split medical and psychiatric staff. Because of his extended commitment (15 years), there was ample time to monitor his medical condition, and to control his access to medical evaluation and treatment. Separating the medical from the psychological treatment, and interpreting the use of grievances as resistance allowed the unit psychiatrist to concentrate on traditional psychotherapeutic goals. The patient never directly admitted to fabricating symptoms, but he did come to acknowledge that his physical symptoms became worse when he was emotionally upset, which was recognized as a face-saving maneuver, but was not interpreted. The number and intensity of his physical complaints decreased significantly. Interpretation of his threats of litigation, treated as would be any other resistance to therapy, resulted in a 75 percent decrease in the number of grievances filed.

IV. MUNCHAUSEN'S SYNDROME BY PROXY

A. Characteristics

In 1977, Meadow described a new variant of factitious disorder, in which one person persistently fabricates symptoms or signs of illness in another person for the purpose of indirectly assuming the sick role. In most situations, the disorder involves a caretaker/victim (e.g., parent/child) relationship. If the victim colludes in the production of the symptoms or signs, then the victim is also diagnosed as suffering from factitious disorder. Meadow (1982) proposed that Munchausen's syndrome by proxy (MSP) should be suspected with: (1) Persistent or recurrent illness with no explanation; (2) Discrepancies between history, clinical findings, and general health of the child; (3) Discrepancies between parents or between parent and child as to symptoms or events; (4) Signs and symptoms witnessed only by parents, or that disappear when parents are absent; (5) Unusual medical findings; (6) Routine treatments repeatedly fail or are poorly tolerated; (7) A parent who is constantly at the bedside, or who seems less concerned about the illness than are staff; (8) A parent who welcomes invasive testing, or displays considerable medical knowledge and becomes highly involved in the care of other patients; (9) A parent who has repeated hospitalizations or illnesses without diagnoses, or who has unexplained symptoms similar to those of the child. Fisher and Mitchell (1992) state that clues to the presence of MSP include discrepancies between history and physical findings, and overinsistent mothers. The most informative clue is when symptoms only occur in the presence of the mother or can only be reported by her. Once suspicions are aroused, they should be shared with as few persons as possible. Case histories by Sullivan, Francis, Bain and Hartz (1991) and Sugar, Belfer, Israel and Herzog (1991) refer to the splitting and personal/interpersonal conflict between physicians and nurses that is so common in cases of Munchausen's syndrome by proxy, and typical of the mothers' enmeshment with clinicians.

Fisher and Mitchell (1992) state that some diseases may be directly induced: skin conditions with caustic solutions, fever by heating thermometers, bleeding by cutting, and bacteremias by contaminating intravenous sites. Anemia may be created by depriving children of dietary iron. Other conditions can be simulated: specimens may be altered by adding chemicals, and bleeding can be fabricated by using blood from others. Fecal vomiting can be simulated by feeding children a mixture of chlordiaz-epoxide and feces. One mother simulated cystic fibrosis by altering sweat tests and obtaining sputum from patients with cystic fibrosis (Orenstein and Wasserman, 1986). Reports of MSP to date have all been of physical illness, although Fisher, Mitchell and Murdoch (unpublished) have recently described the possible fabrication of psychosis.

Mothers are the perpetrators in nearly every case, although fathers have been implicated (Makar & Squier, 1990; Meadow, 1984; Zohar, Avidan, Shvili & Laurian, 1987), as has a foster mother (Frederick, Luedecke, Barret, Hixson & Burch, 1990) and even a babysitter (Richardson, 1987). In many cases, more than one child in a family may be victimized (Alexander, Smith & Stevenson, 1990; Mehl, Coble & Johnson, 1990). The mothers are typically socially skilled and overly attentive to their children. Their whole lives rotate around illness, with almost continuous contact with clinicians. Many are experts at resuscitation and some acquire sophisticated medical knowledge. The fathers are typically absent, disengaged, undemonstrative, and rarely visit their children in hospitals. There are usually strong indicators of family and marital discord. Most mothers have significant past psychiatric histories, and many have histories of abuse (Fisher & Mitchell, 1992).

Some affected children have histories of actual illness, but their parents exaggerate the severity of symptoms, making it difficult for physicians to verify the diagnoses. As with direct factitious patients, many parents suffering from MSP also engage in "doctor shopping" (Fisher & Mitchell, 1992).

Libow and Schreier (1986) list three categories of MSP perpetrators: (1) active inducers of dramatic symptoms. Little is known about their intrapsychic functioning, since they rarely cooperate with assessment. The most consistent pattern is that of an anxious and depressed mother who uses an extreme degree of denial, dissociation of affect, and paranoid projection. (2) Help seekers: these appear like "classical" MSP patients, but the children are presented less frequently, and the mothers are more open to psychiatric intervention. (3) Doctor addicts: mothers who are driven to seek treatment for nonexistent illnesses. They are antagonistic, suspicious, paranoid, and their children are older. Waller (1983) hypothesizes that the child's illness serves to express the parent's need for attention or help.

Rosenberg (1987) described four features of the syndrome: (1) An illness in the child that is simulated and/or produced by a parent or significant other; (2) Presentation of the child for medical assessment and care, usually persistently; (3) Denial of knowledge by the perpetrator of the etiology of the illness; (4) Acute symptoms and signs that abate when the child is separated from the perpetrator. The perpetrator is usually female and usually the mother. There is also a greater incidence of factitious disorder or personality disorder in the perpetrator. He reported that the largest impediment to early discovery of MSP was omission of factitious illness from the differential diagnosis.

B. Prevalence

Rosenberg's (1987) review of the literature found only 117 cases of MSP in the ten years since it was first described by Meadow in 1977 Other authors also reported a low incidence: Of the 1,648 asthma patients studied by Godding and Kruth (1991) over three years, 17 were identified as having MSP. In a survey of apnea monitoring centers by Sheridan (1989), only 0.27 percent of parents with a child in treatment were strongly suspected of MSP. More recently, as the diagnosis has become more widely known, and clinicians have been more likely to suspect it, the number of reported cases has increased. Plewes and Fagan (1994) stated that there are now over 200 cases in the literature. Warner & Hathaway (1984) report that as many as 5 percent of children referred for allergy evaluation may be victims of MSP. Schreier and Libow (1993) surveyed pediatric gastroenterologists and neurologists; 315 of the 1258 surveys were returned, with respondents reporting 465 cases of possible MSP. Two hundred seventy-three were confirmed and 192 were seriously suspected. Despite the increased awareness, Fisher and Mitchell (1992) state that MSP is still underreported.

The average age of the child victim at the time of the perpetrator's diagnosis was 4–5, and there were equal numbers of girls and boys Rosenberg (1987) estimated that the overall mortality in MSP was 9 percent. Of those killed, 20 percent had been removed from the home and then returned. Rosenberg's (1987) review of the literature found only 117 cases of MSP in the ten years since it was first described by Meadow in 1977.

Diagnosis often requires external information–husband's reports mother's own medical history, relationship of observed symptoms or signs to presence of parent. Eminson and Postelthwaite (1992) report that MSP children have the tendency to experience somatic symptoms, possible histrionic traits, and coexisting serious illnesses. MSP parents may be impaired in their abilities to distinguish their own needs from those of their children; and the parents put their own needs first (Kahan & Yorker, 1991).

Fisher and Mitchell (1992) propose that the diagnosis should be made behaviorally by pediatricians, and that confusing behaviors and etiological considerations must be avoided. Authors do not believe that mothers "have" MSP, since there are many pathways leading to the behavior in question. One-third of the mothers in their review also have symptoms of Munchausen's syndrome. Enmeshment between mother and child is often noted. Leeder (1990) suggests that the father's absence is crucial to the development of Munchausen's syndrome by proxy. Gender role theory highlights the chronic powerlessness that women experience that may lead to feelings of inadequacy, especially in relation to parenting. Preliminary data on in-depth phenomenological and psychodynamic exploration with two of Fisher and Mitchell's active inducers revealed histories of extensive sexual abuse leading to severe personality distortion, and the possibility of psychosis or dissociation.

Rand (1990) has recently described a "contemporary" version of MSP which is a variation of the classic condition in which a parent or other adult caretaker fabricates or induces the idea that a child has been abused and then gains recognition from professionals as the protector of the abused child. Rand suggests that this contemporary version is likely to increase with the rising divorce rate. Rand (1993) reports that physical symptoms may occur, but emotional symptoms are much more common in the contemporary version of MSP. Meadow (1993) suggests that in classical MSP, abuse seems to begin in the child's first year, while in the contemporary version, the children are typically older. Therefore, an integral part of the contemporary version is the indoctrination of the child into the "story." Characteristics of families with contemporary MSP include (1) a lack of appropriate language and detail in the reports; (2) The children did not express the feelings which would be expected to accompany the alleged abuse; (3) The mothers were the most active in repeating the story and insisting on further assessment; and (4) The mothers demonstrated inappropriate empathy and concern.

C. Etiology

In their review of the literature on MSP, Plewes and Fagan (1994) found that mothers were the perpetrators in 99 percent of the cases; fathers were seen as uninvolved with the families. Mothers were most frequently diagnosed as suffering from personality disorders and/or depression; they were diagnosed as suffering from factitious disorder themselves in 10 percent of cases, and suspected of it in an additional 14 percent; one-third worked in the health care field. The average age of victims at the onset of symptoms was a little over 3 years. Psychological evaluation of the victims revealed severe withdrawal, preoccupation with bodily integrity and with being poisoned or attacked, and concern with their relationships with their mothers, loss, death, and vulnerability. The overall mortality rate for victims was 8.5 percent. Nineteen cases were reviewed in depth, based on availability of extensive details in the reports. In those cases, mothers suffered from factitious disorder in 50 percent of the cases.

The perpetrators are cunning in their deceptions, and (like factitious patients) often have a medical connection to give them knowledge of how to simulate the illnesses (Senner & Ott, 1989). Common presentations include infant apnea, diarrhea, and neurological illness, including seizures, ataxia, hyperactivity, chorea, nystagmus, headache, delirium, drowsiness, sleep disorder, and vague symptoms such as limb paralysis. Chronic conditions such as spine bifida, mental disorder, and defects of vision and hearing may also be produced (Fisher & Mitchell, 1992).

Kahan and Yorker (1991) hypothesized that there is a lack of differentiation between mother and child, which accounts for the powerful effects of the vicarious reinforcement of the attention given to the child on the mother. As children get older, some begin to cooperate actively in the production of symptoms (McGuire & Feldman, 1989).

D. Treatment/Management

Unlike simple factitious disorder, MSP involves injury to those other than the disordered person. For that reason, the initial response must be to protect the child victims. Once the diagnosis is confirmed, there must be regular communication among those involved with the child's welfare (Kahan & Yorker, 1991). Waller (1983) hypothesizes that the child's illness serves to express the parent's need for attention or help. To diagnose MSP, it is useful to appoint one long-term case supervisor to see the case through to completion. Barker and Howell (1994) agree, arguing that the value of having one case manager is that the doctor shopping can be uncovered over time.

The first step in protecting victims is recognition of the syndrome. Many professionals don't consider the possibility when faced with apparently solicitous parents (Kaufman, Coury, Pickrel & McCleery, 1989). Protective agencies depend on health professionals for evidence, but waiting for such evidence may place the victim at increasing risk (Kahan & Yorker, 1991).

When professionals have reason to suspect that a child is being abused, through MSP or for any other reason, they have an obligation in every state to take action to prevent further harm to the child, or other children who might be at risk. Fisher and Mitchell (1992) state that action should be taken when the diagnosis is suspected; physicians cannot wait until it is proven. Amassing complete medical history from as many sources as possible is crucial to making the diagnosis, but this should be done without alerting the parents that investigation is underway. Sheridan (1989) states that aggressive investigation is often required, and says that psychiatrists are often not helpful in practice. By far the greatest barrier to diagnosis and management is the attitudes and knowledge of psychiatrists and pediatricians. Psychiatrists may not be important for diagnosis, but they can be useful to help the clinical team to devise a management plan. Since the mother may be suspicious, the approach may have to be circumspect. If trust with the family can be established, the chances of engaging the perpetrator are increased.

Treatment of persons who themselves suffer from MSP is as difficult as with patients suffering from direct factitious disorder, since they are also quite likely to deny fabricating signs in their children. As with direct factitious patients, a lengthy period of involuntary treatment appears to offer the only chance of success. Such commitments should be easier to obtain with MSP patients, however, since their actions endanger children not just themselves. Courts have the power to order treatment, either as part of the disposition of a criminal case, or as a requirement before an MSP mother can be granted access or custody of her child.

V. MUNCHAUSEN'S SYNDROME BY PROXY IN THE FORENSIC CONTEXT

As discussed above, the major legal issues in MSP cases are protection of child victims and, secondarily, prosecution of parents who abuse their children because of their disorders. The first goal is accomplished through traditional child protective services mechanisms, including temporary removal of the potential victim from the mother's custody, and if necessary permanent termination of parental rights. The major difficulty is recognizing that the injuries to the child are due to abuse, and not to unexplained medical causes, and obtaining sufficient evidence to provide the basis for protecting the child. There are still few reported appellate cases, but MSP is becoming more and more common at the trial court level. Barker and Howell (1994) state that experts may be used in the following situations in MSP cases: (1) Refutation of defense counsel's challenges to the credibility of the child witness; (2) Expert testimony offered as direct evidence of abuse.

Courts have begun to recognize MSP as providing such evidence. In *In the Interest of M.A.V.* (1992), although the Georgia Court of Appeals reversed the juvenile court's decision to terminate parental rights to a child, because the evidence showed that M.A.V. had not yet been abused, and was living with a grandparent, it noted that another child had been removed from the family because it had been established that the mother suffered from MSP, and had been abusing the child

The difficulties of correctly diagnosing MSP, and the issue of admissibility of testimony concerning its characteristics, are well illustrated in *People v. Phillips* (1981). Ms. Phillips was described as kind, helpful, and loving. She had a masters in social work, and had been employed in that capacity by Marin County, California. After the birth of her son, she volunteered her time to the Child Protective Services Unit. She had a hysterectomy in 1975 following the birth of her second son, but wished to have a daughter, so she adopted a Korean girl in 1975. The child was initially healthy, but subsequently began to demonstrate severe GI symptoms, and was hospitalized repeatedly for diagnostic tests, which were normal except for high sodium and bicarbonate levels. She always improved in hospitals, then relapsed when she was returned home. She ultimately died in the hospital secondary to cerebral damage. Still, no one suspected MSP. Several months later, Ms. Phillips adopted another Korean infant, Mindy. On the anniversary of the first child's death, she brought Mindy to the hospital with the same GI symptoms, and the same pattern began to emerge. The treatment team finally suspected poisoning. They were given a copy of Meadow's 1977 paper on MSP. A nurse reported that Ms. Phillips had asked about Mindy's formula. When it was later checked, it was found to contain 30 times the sodium it was supposed to have. Ms. Phillips was then barred from feeding Mindy, or even being in the room with her without a nurse present. Mindy returned to normal.

Ms. Phillips was then charged with the murder of her first daughter and abuse of Mindy. At trial, Dr. Martin Blinder testified, over defense objections, to a hypothetical containing the facts in the case, and stated that they were consistent with MSP. Ms. Phillips denied all the allegations defense experts testified that she suffered no mental disorder, and that her mental status was not consistent with MSP. She was convicted; on appeal the court ruled that it was not error to admit Dr. Blinder's testimony, even though it was apparently novel for the prosecution to present mental state testimony when the defense had not raised the issue. While the prosecution need not prove motive, in this case it was essential to provide the jury with one, to explain why this otherwise perfect mother could do what she was charged with. The court held that since Dr. Blinder made it clear that he had never interviewed Ms. Phillips, he did not mislead the jury, nor did he intro-duce any incriminating statements made by her. Ms. Phillips also argued that MSP was not accepted by the medical profession, and therefore testimony concerning it should not have been admitted. The appeals court held that although Dr. Blinder's testimony might have been somewhat speculative, and there was therefore some risk of prej-udice and confusion of the jury, it was based on reports in scientific journals, and therefore admissible. The fact that MSP is not yet in the *DSM* was not dispositive of its admissibility. The court also held that it was not error for the judge not to present jury instructions *sua sponte* on diminished capacity, since the defense did not request it, and in fact based its defense on the theory that Ms. Phillips did not commit the acts and suffered from no mental illness. Although generally a prose-cutor is not allowed to establish a person's guilt through evidence that the person has a particular character trait or propensity (Myers, 1992), in the case of MSP, those characteristics define criminal behavior, rather than being merely consistent with it, as in the case of other types of child abuse.

MSP is more frequently placed at issue by the defense, as the basis for an insanity or diminished capacity defense to child abuse, assault, or murder charges. Defendants argue that because their motives for creating medical problems in their children are unconscious, and therefore not under their volitional control, they lack the intent neces-sary for conviction. There are no reported appellate decisions in this area as of yet, but anecdotal information from practitioners indicates that this approach has met with little success.

Unlike the much-discussed situation with the more usual types of physical or sexual abuse, the focus of the evaluation has been on the parent, rather than the victim, but there is no reason why the children should not also be examined. In such examinations, the same caveats obtain as in physical or sexual abuse cases, including examiner bias and lack of training, suggestive and leading interview techniques, use of questionable materials for evaluation, and the multiple roles and goals of evaluators (Jenkins and Howell, 1994). Jenkins and Howell (1994) have proposed a set of guidelines to be used in interviewing children who may have been sexually abused: (1) The examiner must have adequate specialized training, which includes knowledge of child development, techniques used to interview children, childhood sexu-ality, trends in sexual abuse, and basic social psychology. Examiners should be appointed by the court to reduce bias. (2) There need to be guidelines for the process of evaluation, such as the guidelines promulgated by the American Academy of Child and Adolescent Psychiatry (1988). (3) All interviews should be videotaped. (4) A complete psychosocial family history needs to be taken, and all relevant external documents should be reviewed. (5) Interviews of the alleged victim should be done as soon as possible, and the interviewer should take every precaution to minimize verbal and nonverbal cues to the child. The child should be interviewed alone. Hypnosis should be avoided. Open-ended questions are to be preferred. (6) Evaluators should also interview all those in significant relationships with the child. In particular, accused perpetrators should be given an opportunity to tell their stories. Burton and Myers (1992) also list factors which may lead to incorrect assessments and overdiagnosis of child sexual abuse: (1) lack of professional resources and training on the part of evaluators; (2) lack of investigatory independence; (3) improper interview techniques (e.g., leading questions); (4) inadequate data base; (5) contamination by external influences (e.g., media coverage, parent-child communications); (6) failure to consider the possibility that allegations may be false. Many of these criticisms apply with equal force to evaluations of MSP victims.

Because of the difficulty in proving that parents with MSP are responsible for medical problems in their children, several authors have suggested the use of video monitoring in hospital rooms where the children are being evaluated. Epstein, Markowitz, Gallo, Holmes and Gryboski (1987) and Foreman and Farsides (1993) argue that such techniques are both appropriate and necessary in such cases. But Zitelli, Seltman and Shannon (1988) question the practicality, legality, and ethics of video surveillance. It should be pointed out that since the patients in question are the children, not the parents, confidentiality is not at issue and the standard legal and clinical exceptions to confidentiality in suspected child abuse situations should govern.

While there are not reported cases directly on point as of yet, previous court decisions appear to sanction such techniques. In *Burdeau v. McDowell* (1921), the U.S. Supreme Court held that evidence obtained by a private party, not acting under the direction of the state, is admissible, even if the private party obtained the evidence illegally. In the case before the court, the government did nothing illegal, so that the 4th and 5th Amendments were not violated, and the government could therefore use the evidence in court.

When applied to hospital use of video to observe children suspected of being abused, a major legal issue is whether or not a parent has a reasonable expectation of privacy in a hospital room in which her child resides. The U.S. Supreme Court held in *Katz v. United States* (1967) that electronic surveillance which would violate that expectation requires a warrant. But it also held there was an exception to 4th Amendment prohibitions to search and seizure in emergency situations, which could be interpreted to include hospital surveillance of suspected MSP parents.

Courts have been willing to relax 4th Amendment protections when the safety of children is involved. In *State v. Hunt* (1965), the defendant parents were convicted of aggravated assault on their daughter, and of child abuse and neglect. The parents challenged the admission of evidence obtained through a police search of the Hunts' house, based on a report made by a person doing housework who discovered the child tied up in the furnace room. The officer had no arrest or search warrants when he entered the Hunts' house. The trial court held, and the Arizona appeals court affirmed, that (1) a child is not "property" and therefore the requirements for a search warrant (which explicitly refer to property) are not triggered; (2) the officer had the legal authority (and in fact the *duty*) to enter the house in order to protect a minor under state law; his actions were civil, not criminal; and (3) since the officer had obtained the evidence (his observations of the child, and subsequent medical evaluation) legally, it was therefore admissible at the subsequent criminal trial. If such evidence, obtained by a police officer entering a defendant's house without a warrant, is admissible, it would certainly seem that video surveillance in a hospital would be permissible, and any evidence obtained admissible.

REFERENCES

Aduan, R., Fauci, A., Dale, D., Herzberg, J., & Wolff, S. (1979). Factitious fever and self-induced infection: a report of 32 cases and review of the literature. *Annals of Internal Medicine, 90,* 230.

Alexander, R., Smith, W., & Stevenson, R. (1990). Serial Munchausen's syndrome by proxy. *Pediatrics, 86,* 581.

American Academy of Child and Adolescent Psychiatry (1988). Guidelines for the clinical evaluation of child and adolescent sexual abuse. *Journal of the American Academy of Child and Adolescent Psychiatry, 27,* 655.

American Psychiatric Association (1980). *Diagnostic and Statistical Manual of Mental Disorders, 3rd edition.* Washington, D.C.: American Psychiatric Press.

American Psychiatric Association (1994). *Diagnostic and Statistical Manual of Mental Disorders, 4th edition.* Washington, D.C.: American Psychiatric Press.

Ananth, J. (1977). Munchausen syndrome: Problematic diagnosis. *New York State Journal of Medicine, 77,* 115.

Asher, R. (1951). Munchausen's Syndrome. *Lancet, 1,* 339.

Barker, J. C. (1962). The syndrome of hospital addiction (Munchausen's syndrome): A report on the investigation of seven cases. *Journal of Mental Sciences, 177.*

Barker, L. H., & Howell, R. J. (1994). Munchausen's syndrome by proxy in false allegations of child sexual abuse: Legal implications. *Bulletin of the American Academy of Psychiatry and the Law, 22,* 499.

Burdeau v. McDowell, 256 U. S. 465 (1921).

Bursten, B. (1965). On Munchausen's syndrome. *Archives of General Psychiatry, 13,* 261.

Burton, K., & Myers, W. (1992). Child sexual abuse and forensic psychiatry: evolving and controversial issues. *Bulletin of the American Academy of Psychiatry and the Law, 20,* 439.

Carney, M. W. P. (1980). Artefactual illness to attract medical attention. *British Journal of Psychiatry, 136,* 542.

Chapman, J. (1977). Perigrinating problem patients–Munchausen's syndrome. *Journal of the American Medical Association, 16,* 927.

Cohen v. Albert Einstein Medical Center, Northern Division, 405 Pa. Super. 382, 592 A. 2d 720 (1991).

Clark, C. (1988). Sociopathy, malingering, and defensiveness. In R. Rogers (ed.) *Clinical assessment of malingering and deception.* New York: Guilford Press.

Clark, E. J., & Melnich, S. C. (1958). Munchausen's syndrome or the problem of hospital hoboes. *American Journal of Medicine, 25,* 6.

Cramer, B., Gershberg, M., & Stern, M. (1971). Munchausen's syndrome: Its relationship to malingering, hysteria, and the physician-patient relationship. *Archives of General Psychiatry, 24,* 573.

Cunnien, A. J. (1988). Psychiatric and medical syndromes associated with deception. In R. Rogers (ed.) *Clinical assessment of malingering and deception.* New York: Guilford Press.

Eisendrath, S. (1984). Factitious illness: A clarification. *Psychosomatics, 25,* 110.

Eminson, D., & Postelthwaite, R. (1992). Factitious illness: Recognition and management. *Archives of Diseases of Children, 67,* 1510.

Epstein, M., Markowitz, R., Gallo, D., Holmes, J., & Gryboski, J. (1987). Munchausen's syndrome by proxy: Considerations in diagnosis and confirmation by video surveillance. *Pediatrics, 80*(2), 220.

Finklehor, D. (1986). *Sourcebook on child sexual abuse.* Beverly Hills, CA: Sage Publications.

Fisher, G. C., Mitchell, I., & Murdoch, D. Munchausen's syndrome by proxy: The question of psychiatric illness. [submitted for publication].

Fisher, G. C., & Mitchell, I. (1992). Munchausen's syndrome by proxy (factitious illness by proxy). *Current Opinion in Psychiatry, 5,* 224.

Folks, D. G., & Freeman, A. M. (1985). Munchausen's syndrome and other factitious illness. *Psychiatric Clinics of North America, 8,* 263.

Ford, C. V. (1973). The Munchausen syndrome: A report of four new cases and a review of psychodynamic consideration. *Psychiatry in Medicine, 4,* 31.

Ford, C. V. (1986). The somatizing disorders. *Psychosomatics, 27,* 327.

Foreman, D., & Farsides, C. (1993). Ethical use of covert videoing techniques in detecting Munchausen's syndrome by proxy. *British Medical Journal, 307,* 611.

Frederick, V., Luedecke, G., Barret, F., Hixson, S., & Burch, K. (1990). Munchausen's syndrome by proxy: Recurrent central catheter sepsis. *Pediatric Infectious Disease Journal, 9,* 440.

Godding, V., & Kruth, M. (1991). Compliance with treatment in asthma and Munchausen's syndrome by proxy. *Archives of Diseases of Children, 66,* 956.

Gorman, C. A., Wahner, H. W., & Tauxe, W. N. (1970). Metabolic malingerers: Patients who deliberately induce or perpetuate a hypermetabolic or hypometabolic state. *American Journal of Medicine, 48,* 708.

Humphries, S. (1988). Munchausen's syndrome: Motives and the relation to deliberate self harm. *British Journal of Psychiatry, 152,* 416.

Hyler, S., & Sussman, N. (1981). Chronic factitious disorder with physical symptoms (the Munchausen's syndrome). *Psychiatric Clinics of North America, 4,* 365.

In the Interest of M.A.V., 206 Ga. App. 299, 425 S. E. 2d 377 (Ga. App., 1992).

In the Matter of an Application for the Commitment of an Alleged Mentally Disordered Person, 147 Ariz. 313, 709 P. 2d 1372 (Ariz. App. 1985).

Ireland, P., Sapira, J., & Templeton, B. (1967). Munchausen's syndrome: Review and report of an additional case. *American Journal of Medicine, 43,* 579.

Janofsky, J. S. (1994). The Munchausen syndrome in civil forensic psychiatry. *Bulletin of the American Academy of Psychiatry and the Law, 22,* 489.

Jenkins, P., & Howell, R. (1994). Child sexual abuse examinations: Proposed guidelines for a standard of care. *Bulletin of the American Academy of Psychiatry and the Law, 22,* 5.

Jonas, J., & Pope, H. (1985). The dissimulating disorders: A single diagnostic entity? *Comprehensive Psychiatry, 26,* 58.

Justus, P., Kreutziger, S., & Kitchens, C. (1980). Probing the dynamics of Munchausen's syndrome: Detailed analysis of a case. *Annals of Internal Medicine, 93,* 120.

Kahan, B., & Yorker, B. C. (1991). Munchausen's syndrome by proxy: Clinical review and legal issues. *Behavioral Science and the Law, 9,* 73.

Kaufman, K. L., Coury, D., Pickrel, E., & McCleery, J. (1989). Munchausen's syndrome by proxy: A survey of professional's knowledge. *Child Abuse and Neglect, 13,* 141.

Katz v. United States, 398 U. S. 347 (1967).

Klonoff, E., Younger, S., Moore, D., & Hershey, L. (1983). Chronic factitious illness: A behavioral approach. *International Journal of Psychiatry in Medicine, 13,* 173.

Kooiman, C. G. (1987). Neglected phenomena in factitious illness: A case study and review of literature. *Comprehensive Psychiatry, 28,* 499.

Lasky, R. (1982). *Evaluation of criminal responsibility in multiple personality and the related dissociative disorders.* Springfield, IL: Charles C Thomas.

Leeder, E. (1990). Supermom or child abuser? Treatment of the Munchausen mother. *Women and Therapy, 9,* 69.

Libow, J. A., & Schreiber, H. A. (1986). Three forms of factitious illness in children: When is it Munchausen's syndrome by proxy? *American Journal of Orthopsychiatry, 56,* 602.

McGuire, T. L., & Feldman, K. W. (1989). Psychological morbidity of children subjected to Munchausen's syndrome by proxy. *Pediatrics, 83,* 289.

Makar, A. F., & Squier, P. J. (1990). Munchausen's syndrome by proxy: Father as perpetrator. *Pediatrics, 85,* 370.

Meadow, R. (1977). Munchausen by proxy—the hinterland of child abuse. *Lancet, ii,* 343.

Meadow, R. (1982). Munchausen's syndrome by proxy. *Archives of Diseases of Children, 57,* 92.

Meadow, R. (1984). Fictitious epilepsy. *Lancet, ii,* 25.

Meadow, R. (1993). False allegations of abuse and Munchausen's syndrome by proxy. *Archives of Diseases of Children, 68,* 444.

Mehl, A. L., Coble, L., & Johnson, S. (1990). Munchausen's syndrome by proxy: A family affair. *Child Abuse and Neglect, 14,* 577.

Menninger, K. (1934). Polysurgery and polysurgical addiction. *Psychoanalytic Quarterly, 3,* 173.

Miller, H., & Cartlidge, N. (1972). Simulation and malingering after injuries to the spinal cord. *Lancet, 1*, 58.

Miller, R. D. (1978). Pseudohomosexuality in male patients with hysterical psychosis: A preliminary report. *American Journal of Psychiatry, 135*, 112.

Miller, R. D. (1988). The use of placebo trials as part of a forensic assessment. *Journal of Psychiatry and Law, 16*, 219.

Miller, R. D., Blancke, F. W., Doren, D. M., & Maier, G.J. (1985). The Munchausen patient in a forensic facility. *Psychiatric Quarterly, 57*, 72.

Myers, J. E. B. (1992). *Legal issues in child abuse and neglect practice.* Newbury Park, CA: Sage Publications.

Nadelson, T. (1979). The Munchausen spectrum: Borderline character features. *General Hospital Psychiatry, 1*, 11.

Nadelson, T. (1985). The false patient: Chronic factitious disease, Munchausen's syndrome, and malingering. In J. O. Cavenar (Ed.), *Psychiatry, Vol. 2*, Philadelphia: JB Lippincott.

Olivier v. State, 850 S. W. 2d 742 (Text App. 1993).

Orenstein, D. M., & Wasserman, A. L. (1986). Munchausen's syndrome by proxy: Simulating cystic fibrosis. *Pediatrics, 78*, 621.

Overholser, J. C. (1990). Differential diagnosis of malingering and factitious disorder with physical symptoms. *Behavioral Sciences and the Law, 8*, 55.

Pankrantz, L. (1981). A review of the Munchausen syndrome. *Clinical Psychology Review, 1*, 65.

Pankrantz, L., & Lezak, M. D. (1987). Cerebral dysfunction in Munchausen syndrome. *Hillside Journal of Clinical Psychiatry, 9*, 195.

People v. Phillips, 122 Cal. App. 3d 69 (1981).

Plewes, J. M., & Fagan, J. G. (1994). Factitious disorders and malingering. In R. E. Hales, S. C. Yudofsky, and J. A. Talbott, (Eds.). *Textbook of psychiatry.* Washington, D.C.: American Psychiatric Press.

Pope, H. G., Jr., Jonas, J. M., & Jones, B. (1982). Factitious psychosis: Phenomenology, family history, and long-term outcome of nine patients. *American Journal of Psychiatry, 139*, 1480.

Rand, D. (1990). Munchausen's syndrome by proxy: Integration of classic and contemporary issues. *Issues in Child Abuse Allegations, 2*, 83.

Rand, D. (1993). Munchausen's syndrome by proxy—a complex type of emotional abuse responsible for some false allegations of child abuse. *Issues in Child Abuse Allegations, 5*, 135.

Reich, P., & Gottfried, L. (1983). Factitious disorders in a teaching hospital. *Annals of Internal Medicine, 99*, 240.

Richardson, G. (1987). Munchausen's syndrome by proxy. *American Family Physician, July*, 119.

Ries, R. (1980). *DSM–III* differential diagnosis of Munchausen's syndrome. *Journal of Nervous and Mental Disease, 168*, 629.

Robbins, P. M., & Sesan, R. (1991). Munchausen's syndrome by proxy: Another women's disorder? *Professional Psychology Research Practice, 22*, 285.

Rogers, R., Bagby, R. M., & Rector, N. (1989). Diagnostic legitimacy of factitious disorder with psychological symptoms. *American Journal of Psychiatry, 146*, 1312.

Rogers, R., Bagby, R. M., & Vincent, A. (1994). Factitious disorders with predominantly psychological signs and symptoms: A conundrum for forensic experts. *Journal of Psychiatry and Law, 22*, 91.

Rosenberg, D. A. (1987). Web of deceit: A literature review of Munchausen's syndrome by proxy. *Child Abuse and Neglect, 11*, 547.

Rosenhan, D. L. (1973). On being sane in insane places. *Science, 179*, 250.

Rumans, L., & Vosti, K. (1978). Factitious and fraudulent fever. *American Journal of Medicine, 65,* 745.

Samuels, M., McClaughlin, W., Jacobson, R., et al. (1992). Fourteen cases of imposed upper airway obstruction. *Archives of Diseases of Children, 67,* 162.

Schreier, H., & Libow, J. (1993). Munchausen's syndrome by proxy: Diagnosis and prevalence. *American Journal of Orthopsychiatry, 63,* 318.

Senner, A., & Ott, M. (1989). Munchausen's syndrome by proxy. *Issues in Comprehensive Pediatric Nursing, 12,* 345.

Shafer, N., & Shafer, R. (1980). Factitious diseases including Munchausen's syndrome. *New York State Journal of Medicine, 80,* 594.

Sheridan, M. S. (1989). Munchausen's syndrome by proxy. *Health and Social Work, 14,* 53.

Spiro, H. R. (1968). Chronic factitious illness: Munchausen's syndrome. *Archives of General Psychiatry, 18,* 569.

Spitzer, R. L., Forman, J. B. W., & Nee, J. (1979). Initial interrater diagnostic reliability. *American Journal of Psychiatry, 136,* 815.

State v. Hunt, 406 P. 2d 208 (Ariz. 1965).

Stone, M. (1977). Factitious illness: Psychological findings and treatment recommendations. *Bulletin of the Menninger Clinic, 41,* 239.

Stoudemire, G. A. (1988). Somatoform disorders, factitious disorders, and malingering. In J. A. Talbott, R. E. Hales, and S. C. Yudofsky, (Eds.) *The American Psychiatric Press Textbook of Psychiatry,* Washington, D.C.: American Psychiatric Press.

Sugar, J. A., Belfer, M., Israel, E., & Herzog, D. B. (1991). A 3-year-old boy's chronic diarrhea and unexplained death. *Journal of the American Academy of Child and Adolescent Psychiatry, 30,* 1015.

Sullivan, C. A., Francis, G. L., Bain, M. W., & Hartz, J. (1991). Munchausen's syndrome by proxy: 1990, a portent for problems. *Clinical Pediatrics (Phila.), 30,* 112.

Sussman, N., & Hyler, S. (1985). Factitious disorders. In H. Kaplan, and B. Sadock (Eds.) *Comprehensive textbook of psychiatry, 4th Edition.* Baltimore: Williams & Wilkins.

Sutherland, A. J., & Rodin, G. M. (1990). Factitious disorders in a general hospital setting: Clinical features and a review of the literature. *Psychosomatics, 31,* 392.

Swanson, D. (1981). The Munchausen syndrome. *American Journal of Psychotherapy, 35,* 436.

Viederman, M. (1985). Somatoform and factitious disorders. In J. O. Cavenar (Ed.), *Psychiatry, Vol. 1,* Philadelphia: JB Lippincott.

Waller, D. (1983). Obstacles to the treatment of Munchausen's syndrome by proxy syndrome. *Journal of the American Academy of Child and Adolescent Psychiatry, 22,* 80.

Warner, J. & Hathaway, M. (1984). Allergic form of Meadow's Syndrome (Munchausen's syndrome by proxy). *Archives of Diseases of Childhood, 59,* 151.

Yudofsky, S. C. (1985). Conditions not attributable to a mental disorder. In H. I. Kaplan, and B. J. Sadock (Eds.) *Comprehensive textbook of psychiatry, 4th Edition.* Baltimore: Williams & Wilkins.

Zitelli, B., Seltman, M., & Shannon, R. (1988). Munchausen's syndrome by proxy and video surveillance. *American Journal of Diseases of Childhood, 142,* 918.

Zohar, Y., Avidan, G., Shvili, Y., & Laurian, N. (1987). Otolaryngologic cases of Munchausen's syndrome. *Laryngoscope, 97,* 201.

Chapter 9

MORBID JEALOUSY
AND CRIMINAL CONDUCT

BARRY MORENZ AND STEVEN HERRON

> . . . all manner of actions from which hitherto he would of recoiled in shame such as spying, putting adroitly provocative questions to casual witness . . . listening at doors, seemed to him now on a level with . . . the methods of scientific investigation, with a genuine intellectual value and legitimately employable in the search for truth
>
> Marcel Proust

INTRODUCTION

Smith, a forty-year-old man, employed as a farrier and ranch hand, had no history of violence. He had fallen deeply in love with one of the patrons, Sara, at the dude ranch where he worked. Although married in the past, Smith had never fallen so deeply in love with a woman since his mother left him with his father and brother when he was a boy. His mother had met another man and Smith no longer fit into her life. Smith's new love was consuming. Smith and Sara wrote each other numerous love letters. Sara left her husband and son to come live with Smith. It was a time of ecstasy for both of them. There were signs of trouble though. Smith became possessive; he was irritable if she showed attention to another man. He always wanted to know where she was. She started to resent his monitoring her. When she demanded some time to herself and refused to tell him where she was, he searched all night for her. He was in a state of exhaustion and virtual panic when she appeared at their apartment the next morning.

She announced that she was returning to her husband. Sara went to take a shower. Smith was dazed, he had no feeling, but he knew he could not let Sara go. He took a knife from the kitchen, went to the bathroom, pulled back the shower curtain and stabbed Sara numerous times. He then attempted to disembowel himself. He managed to call his father before he lost consciousness. He remembered the pressure of the knife penetrating Sara but could remember no feelings; he was in a depersonalized state.

Sara died but Smith lived and continues to love Sara. He's a rational man with no major psychiatric disorders. Extreme jealousy was probably at the heart of his murder and attempted suicide. The Smith vignette is based on an actual case. One of the authors (BM) had been consultant to defense counsel regarding Smith's mental state at the time of his acts.

In this chapter we will explore the many dimensions that constitute the emotion of jealousy and its extreme manifestations in morbid jealousy. And we will describe the relation of jealousy and morbid jealousy to criminal conduct. To achieve our aims in this chapter we will (1) define morbid jealousy; (2) discuss the emotion of jealousy from a sociological viewpoint; (3) review psychological and psychoanalytic constructs that have been used to understand jealousy; (4) describe the clinical characteristics, phenomenology and epidemiology of morbid jealousy; (5) discuss the treatment of morbid jealousy; (6) discuss the effect that morbid jealousy may have on; predilection for violence, competence to stand trial, insanity pleas and sentencing; and (7) give recommendations for further research on morbid jealousy.

Jealousy has been a favorite subject of authors, playwrights and other thinkers for centuries. It has been the subject of psychoanalytic writings and is associated with a variety of medical and psychiatric disorders. Jealousy is virtually a universal human experience and can be seen in all cultures. Unfortunately, there have been few systematic scientific studies of jealousy. One possible explanation for the absence of such studies is the lack of a clear definition of what constitutes abnormal jealousy. The dividing line between normal, socially desirable jealousy and pathological, socially objectionable jealousy changes between cultures and within cultures over time. In its more extreme manifestations, jealousy is associated with violence, turbulent emotional states, and psychotic thought processes. Thus, jealousy is a regular issue in legal proceedings.

DEFINITION

Morbid jealousy has been used to describe a variety of abnormal jealous states. The terms pathological jealousy and the Othello syndrome refer to the same abnormal jealous states as morbid jealousy. We will use the terms interchangeably in this chapter. Descriptions of "platonic jealousy" have recently been described in relation to childbirth, between parents and children or siblings or friends but will not be emphasized in this review (Hill & Davis, 2000).

The *Diagnostic and Statistical Manual of Mental Disorders, 4th edition, text revision (DSM–IV–TR)* (American Psychiatric Association, 2000) diagnosis of delusional disorder, jealous type provides one definition of morbid or pathological jealousy. The *DSM–IV–TR* diagnostic criteria for this disorder are as follows:

A. Nonbizarre delusions (i.e., involving situations that occur in real life, such as being followed, poisoned, infected, loved at a distance, or deceived by spouse or lover, or having a disease) of at least one month's duration.

B. Criterion A for Schizophrenia has never been met. **Note:** Tactile and olfactory hallucinations may be present in Delusional Disorder if they are related to the delusional theme.

C. Apart from the impact of the delusion(s) or its ramifications, functioning is not markedly impaired and behavior is not obviously odd or bizarre.

D. If mood episodes have occurred concurrently with delusions, their total duration has been brief relative to the duration of the delusional periods.

E. The disturbance is not due to the direct physiological effects of a substance (e.g., a drug of abuse, a medication) or a general medical condition.

Jealous Type: delusions that the individual's sexual partner is unfaithful.

The *DSM–IV–TR* definition of delusional disorder, jealous type describes an extreme form of morbid jealousy. It does not reflect the range of abnormal jealous states that have been associated with the concept of morbid jealousy. Morbid jealousy has been described not only as delusional, but also as the result of an overvalued idea, obsession or neurotic conflict. It has been associated with a number of medical and psychiatric syndromes. Enoch (1991) provides a cogent discussion of the ambiguities surrounding the term morbid jealousy. He provides the following definition,

> . . . morbid jealousy covers a wide range of unacceptable disturbed behaviour associated with distressing irrational thoughts and disordered emotions, all of which show an underlying dominant theme of consuming preoccupation with the partner's sexual unfaithfulness.

Later he comments, "The borderline between even, so-called, normal jealousy and morbid jealousy is blurred." Thus, morbid jealousy can be seen as covering a spectrum from slightly excessive (almost normal) to delusional jealousy. Although the *DSM–IV–TR* definition of delusional disorder, jealous type has the advantage of clarity, it is too narrow. Enoch's definition allows for a broader range of disturbed behaviors and thoughts to be included in the concept of pathological jealousy and is the one we will use in this chapter.

SOCIOLOGIC PERSPECTIVE

The first question we must address is whether jealousy is ever normal? If a man becomes suspicious that his wife is having an affair; begins to read her mail, asks questions of her friends and hires a private detective to follow her; is he jealous? Does it depend on whether the wife is actually having sexual relations with someone else? Or is it enough that the wife is thinking of an affair or flirting with other men? Is any measure of jealousy considered legitimate? Pam and Pearson (1994), describe the following consideration regarding the cuckolded man, "Did A contribute to the affair by her or his own inadequacies, or by neglecting B's needs, thereby making affair B–C an inevitability?" This indicates that any measure of jealousy suggests a flawed personality in need of treatment.

Jealousy has not always had such negative connotations. Mullen (1991) portrays jealousy in the seventeenth century as ". . . a passion which had a role in maintaining individual and social values . . .". Saint Augustine (354–430) said ". . . who is not jealous does not love. . . ."Thus, in different cultural constructions, jealousy was seen as necessary and desirable in preserving social order. It conveyed an emotion of total commitment and devotion. Adultery, real or imagined, is often the ultimate fear of the jealous person. Legal codes in most cultures address the issue of adultery as a type of property violation in which the injured husband may collect damages; violent revenge, divorce, or monetary compensation. In the Yanomamo tribal culture of Venezuela the following practice has been described (Chagnon, 1992):

> A particularly nasty husband might hit his wife with the sharp edge of a machete or axe or shoot a barbed arrow into some nonvital area, such as the buttocks or the leg. Another brutal punishment is to hold the glowing end of a piece of firewood against the wife's body, producing painful and serious burns. Normally, however, the husband's reprimands are consistent with the perceived seriousness of the wife's shortcomings, his more drastic measures being reserved for infidelity or suspicion of infidelity. It is not uncommon for a man to seriously injure a sexually errant wife, and some husbands have shot and killed unfaithful wives.

Such zealous protection of a wife's sexuality may be part of an evolved masculine psychology used by a man to insure his reproductive success. Without access to a woman's reproductive tract, a man cannot pass on his genes (Wilson & Daly, 1993; Daly & Wilson, 1988). The state of jealousy is accompanied by heightened attention and arousal to a perceived threat from a rival and an inclination to fight to protect one's "property." Some type of marital alliance is universal in human cultures with varying patterns of shared responsibility for raising children. A man's reproductive success is doubly threatened if he uses his energies and resources to raise a rival's child who is the result of his wife's adultery. Harris describes possible subtle evolutionary differences in the character of jealousy among men and women (Harris, 2003; Harris, 2004). Tort actions for "loss of consortium" and "alienation of affection" among others may once have been reflective of the social legitimacy of jealousy and masculine sexual proprietariness. Today, such actions are considered anachronistic in many industrialized cultures.

The purpose of love, of sexual union, of marriage has shifted in twentieth century industrialized cultures. The emphasis in marriage has moved from family and children or masculine sexual proprietariness to the quality of the relationship. Modern love relations reflect a greater concern with excitement and novelty than with sustained commitment. The important marital question is whether the relationship is satisfying individual emotional and psychological needs. Excessive demands for commitment and exclusivity are likely to be met with rejection. Individual needs often take ascendancy over family or community needs in modern industrialized cultures. Mullen (1991) makes the following plea for the rehabilitation of jealousy:

> . . . if we are human, all too human, members of a tradition which still seeks to realize some of their potential through intimate relationships, then jealousy cannot yet be relegated entirely to a pathology of the passions.

Despite this plea, almost any level of jealousy carries negative connotations today. It is usually seen as a reflection of a disturbed personality. Nevertheless, to perceive jealousy as just a character flaw would be to ignore its cultural heritage and complexity and its possible biologic underpinnings as an evolved characteristic of the male mind.

PSYCHOLOGICAL AND PSYCHOANALYTIC PERSPECTIVE

The emotion of jealousy is closely related to that of envy. A recent study has empirically explored this distinction (Parrott & Smith, 1993). The authors defined envy as an emotion which ". . . occurs when a person: lacks another's superior quality, achievement, or possession and either desires it or wishes that the other lacked it." The envious person defines his own worth relative to another based on their own personal subjective values. A variety of affects may be included in the experience of envy; longing, ill will towards the envied person, guilt and denial. Jealousy always occurs in relationships and is like the experience of envy with the additional fear of loss of a loved object. This fear is usually combined with anger about betrayal. Parrott and Smith's work support this concept and make some interesting observations. The envious person is always able to describe what is better, in their opinion, about the person they envy. However, "A jealous man may envy his rival despite being unable to answer the question 'What does she see in him?'" This may be due to envy of the attention the rival is receiving from the valued person or that the judgment of superiority is being made by a person whose opinion is valued a great deal. Another conclusion from the study is that envy is generally associated with concern about public disapproval and guilt but jealousy showed a different pattern. As the authors state, "Overall, one might say that envy tended to elicit concern about public disapproval, whereas jealousy tended to elicit self-righteousness."

Several psychoanalysts, beginning with Freud have discussed the origins of envy and jealousy. Freud believed an unconscious homosexual wish was projected on to the heterosexual partner in delusional jealousy and in the "neurotic" forms of jealousy he believed an unconscious or preconscious heterosexual wish to be unfaithful was projected on to the partner (Freud, 1922). Melanie Klein relied heavily on the concept of envy in her work. She carefully describes the differences between envy, greed and jealousy (Klein, 1957). Klein looked further into the issue of jealousy and believed it stemmed from her definition of envy which had its origins in the death instinct. Both Freud and Klein believed that jealousy stemmed from the triangular relationship of the Oedipus complex. Freeman, describes his psychoanalytic treatment of four women with morbid jealousy (1990), two with delusional jealousy and the other two with neurotic jealousy ("overvalued ideas" (McKenna, 1984)). He postulated elements of envy in combination with unconscious externalizations of homosexual and heterosexual wishes leading to delusional or neurotic jealousy. A thorough psychoanalytic discussion of envy and jealousy is beyond the scope of this chapter, however, excellent works on this topic have appeared in the psychoanalytic literature (Spillius, 1993; Feldman & De Paola, 1994; Coen, 1987).

Nonanalytic theorists have suggested that paranoid individuals lacking in interpersonal skills are not able to accurately check their thoughts about others making them more prone to jealous interpretations (Cameron, 1943). Other authors have postulated that jealousy represents a means of exercising extreme control over a partner (Morgan, 1975).

NOSOLOGY AND EPIDEMIOLOGY

Until Mullen's (1994) random survey, most empirical research on jealousy was done with college students. Besides the narrow age and education range of the college student subjects these studies also tended to ask students to project themselves into the role of a jealous individual by asking "what if" questions. Thus, earlier studies did not have actual jealous subjects and had other serious methodological limitations which Mullen has attempted to correct. He surveyed 351 individuals selected at random from a moderate-sized community in New

Zealand. His response rate was 62 percent after removing subjects unable to respond because of death or infirmity. He used a 50-item jealousy scale along with several other measures in his study. However, he acknowledges that his subjects were often relying on their memories instead of reporting current experience with jealousy and that autobiographical memories are not always reliable (Barclay, 1986). He also makes the observation that "Jealousy is private and isolating, and its very existence may be hidden out of shame or embarrassment" which may tend to make it difficult for subjects to accurately report to a random mail survey.

All of his subjects indicated having experienced jealousy by a positive response to at least one question on his 50-item jealousy scale helping to confirm the universality of jealous emotions. Almost half (46%) considered jealousy inevitable if you truly loved someone. Only 10 percent of subjects admitted that their jealousy had caused significant relationship problems. However, 15 percent of men and 19 percent of women thought their partner's jealousy had caused relationship difficulties. This suggests that partners of jealous individuals are more likely to perceive jealousy as a problem in relationships than the jealous individuals themselves.

Fear of loss of partner was reported by 65 percent of the subjects (70% of men 59% of women) and was the most commonly reported jealous fear. The second most common concern expressed by 21 percent of both sexes was loss of attention and time. Additional fears expressed equally by both sexes are the following: loss of sexual exclusivity (14%), infidelity causing shame and humiliation (12%) and financial insecurity (10%). Mullen found that men and women in equal proportion responded to fears of infidelity with anger, sadness, agitation and restlessness.

Mullen found the following behaviors associated with jealousy: questioning partners about their whereabouts (~30% of men and women), checking on the whereabouts of partners by phone (10% of men and women), searching through partner's belongings (7% of women and 1% of men), opening the partner's mail (3.8% of women and 1% of men), following partners to see where they went and who they met with (2% of men and women) and one man and six women checked their partner's clothing for signs of sexual contact with others.

Men and women tended to use different coping strategies for their jealous feelings. Women were more likely to (1) confront their partners and ask for an explanation (27% versus 19%), (2) openly express tearfulness and anger (32% versus 11%), and (3) attempt to make themselves more attractive to their partners (20% versus 10%). Men tried to ignore the problem (21% versus 13%). Both sexes demanded future commitment to the relationship (13%), contemplated ending the relationship (12–14%), and confided in family or friends (12–18%). Approximately 12–15 percent of subjects went on spending sprees, drank more alcohol than usual, or ate more than usual. Unusual coping strategies included confronting or criticizing an actual or supposed rival. Only 12 subjects asked for professional help. Threats of violence to the partner occurred with 13 subjects and threats to the rival occurred with five subjects. Actual violence directed towards the partner and rival happened in eight and three subjects respectively. In contrast, 15 percent of subjects reported physical aggression towards them as a result of jealousy.

The greatest difficulties with jealousy occurred among both sexes in their late teens and early twenties and decreased with age. Those who had never married, were not living with a partner, or married at an early age were at greater risk for problems with jealousy. Those with low self-esteem particularly among women had greater problems with jealousy. Subjects of both sexes with higher scores on the Spielberger Anger Expression Scale, which measures overt and suppressed anger, were more likely to be jealous. Further, those with outward anger tended to fear loss of intimacy and were more likely to confront or threaten their partners. Those with greater inwardly directed anger were more likely to try to obtain greater commitment from their partners or to make use of excessive food or alcohol.

Mullen also identified a group of 66 subjects (19%) who had high levels of jealousy defined by having scores greater than one standard deviation above the mean on his 50-item jealousy scale. Younger ages, not living with a partner and to a lesser extent social class were risk factors in the high levels of jealousy group among both sexes. Subjects with chronic scores over 11 (38 men and 41 women) on the General Health Questionnaire (a screening instrument for the presence of psychiatric disorders), suggesting they had a diagnosable psychiatric disorder (Romans-Clarkson, 1989), were almost three times as likely to have high jealousy concerns and were more likely to be threatening or physically aggressive. For men, marrying before age 20, being divorced or separated, or having an older sibling were risk factors for being in this group. Among women, those who lacked a confidante or were in relationships in which they did not confide were at risk for having high jealousy concerns.

Many of Mullen's findings are not congruent with findings from other studies or folklore. For instance, women do not appear to be the jealous sex as is commonly believed, men and women show an equal proclivity to jealousy. Women do not appear to be more concerned with financial security than men when jealous. Fear of loss of sexual exclusivity was not a major concern among either sex and was equal in both sexes. Mullen's study did not show frequent efforts to criticize the alleged rival, which was thought common in jealous individuals. Another study (Mashes & Verstraete, 1993) also shows that the object of the jealous individual's anger is usually the partner, not the rival. However, Mullen's study did confirm that the greater number and intensity of jealous behaviors such as; questioning a partner, opening their mail, following them and checking for physical evidence of sexual activity was indicative of pathological jealousy. The study also showed greater evidence for psychiatric disorders and heavy drinking in those with high levels of jealousy. Unfortunately, there was no attempt to discover the incidence of specific psychiatric disorders.

To determine the prevalence of delusional jealousy in specific psychiatric disorders, a retrospective study of the case histories of all inpatients treated from 1981 to 1985–numbering 8,134, mean age 41.8, 55.6 percent women–was conducted at the Psychiatric Hospital of the University of Munich (Soyka, Naber, & Volcker, 1991). The authors noted the confusion surrounding the terms morbid or pathological jealousy and were specifically interested in delusional jealousy which they defined as the unfounded "conviction of being deceived or betrayed by loved ones." The results showed a prevalence rate of 1.1 percent in these psychiatric inpatients. Delusional jealousy was found in the following psychiatric disorders diagnosed using the World Health Organization's ICD-9 criteria: organic psychosis (7.0%), paranoid disorders (6.7%), alcohol psychosis (5.6%), schizophrenia (2.5%), affective disorders (0.1%) and neuroses or psychopathy (0.6%). The sex distribution of delusions of jealousy was equal.

PHENOMENOLOGY, TREATMENT, AND OUTCOME

Morbid jealousy has been described in association with a wide range of psychiatric and medical disorders and has responded to a variety of treatments. Unfortunately, systematic data on the treatment and outcome of morbid jealousy remains sparse. However, techniques in neuroimaging and determination of neurochemical composition of the brain have progressed dramatically, creating an improved understanding of pathology behind the process of morbid jealousy. One of the major obstacles in the study of this condition is the varied presentation of the behavior, and the effect of physical and psychological conditions upon jealousy. For example, case reports indicate the appearance of morbid jealousy following a stroke (Westlake & Weeks, 1999), or as a result of alcoholism (Michael, Mirza, Mirza, Babu, & Vithayathil, 1995). Kingham and Gordon suggest the most common forms of psychopathology related to morbid jealousy include delusions, obsessions, and overvalued ideas, and much of the treatment literature indicates a focus in the areas of delusional or obsessional content (Kingham & Gordon, 2004). In order to appreciate the logic behind treatment considerations for patients with pathological jealousy, we must first explore the phenomenology of the condition. As mentioned, the most common forms of psychopathology related to morbid jealousy include delusions and obsessions. Since an overvalued idea is a difficult concept to quantify, and does not correlate well with specific types of pathology provided in the *DSM–IV–TR*, it will be excluded from the discussion here. However, obsessional thinking does translate well to the *DSM–IV–TR* diagnosis of Obsessive-Compulsive Disorder (OCD). As neuroimaging techniques have advanced and improved, researchers have been able to concentrate on smaller areas of the brain in an effort to localize certain disease processes. Techniques such as functional magnetic resonance imaging (fMRI), positron emission tomography (PET), and single photon emission computed tomography (SPECT) have allowed greater access to actual functioning of the brain, creating better opportunities to identify problem areas, and possibly suggest further targets for treatment. Research suggests those with OCD show increased activity in the orbitofrontal cortex, caudate nucleus, thalamus, and anterior cingulate cortex (Anderson & Savage, 2004, Fitzgerald et al., 2005), and reduced volumes in the areas of the orbitofrontal cortex and amygdala (Szezko et al., 1999) compared to controls. Some of these variations normalize with successful treatment. These areas of the brain are important for regulating various aspects of cognitive functioning, illustrating the importance of these structures for more normalized behavior. Similarly, individuals with delusional disorder have shown abnormalities in the anterior cingulate and the dorsolateral prefrontal cortex, which has connections to the substantia nigra, globus pallidus, caudate, and thalamus, (Su, Hsu, & Hsieh, 2001) though the authors point out the participants in this particular study suffered from significant cerebrovascular disease complicating the conclusiveness of the imaging. These authors also caution attributing any specific etiology to the development of delusions. While further imaging studies aimed primarily at those with morbid jealousy are not likely to produce a single diagnostic finding, these studies can assist in clarifying specific areas of pathology which could have implications in tailoring treatments for patients with these disorders.

Morbid jealousy has been reported as a symptom in a variant of an obsessive-compulsive disorder (Wright, 1994; Gross, 1991; Lane, 1990). In one of these cases (Lane, 1990), a family history revealed three relatives having excessive jealousy to a degree that impaired social relationships. In each of these cases the symptom of pathological jealousy was not believed to be psychotic in nature but to rather be obsessive in character, though the distinction was subtle. In each of these cases the patients developed a steadfast conviction of their spouses infidelity (the primary symptom, although other symptoms suggesting an obsessive-compulsive disorder were also present) which did not yield to reassurance and lasted for months or years and therefore could have been diagnosed as a delusional disorder, jealous type as well. Of note, however, is that each of these patients successfully responded to a course of fluoxetine at higher doses as would be expected when treating an obsessive-compulsive disorder. Unfortunately, a trial of neuroleptic medication had not been attempted with these patients—an effective response would have suggested that the jealousy was perhaps delusional as well as obsessive in nature.

A patient with Frégoli's syndrome (a disguised persecutor is believed to be following the patient) was reported to have prominent symptoms of pathological jealousy. The patient, a 51-year-old Iranian housewife was depressed, anxious and developed the belief that the wife of an ex-colleague of her husband had disguised herself and was trying to seduce her husband. The patient had a history of misidentifying strangers as familiar. She was diagnosed with a delusional disorder and successfully treated with trifluoperazine (Sanati & Mojtabai, 1993).

A wide range of medical disorders have been reported in association with pathological jealousy. Patients described in the following case histories were free of psychiatric problems prior to the development of their medical disorders. In one case of hyperthyroidism (Hodgson, Murray, & Woods, 1992), the symptoms of pathological jealousy completely remitted after successful treatment with carbimazole to bring his thyroid function back to normal. A 37-year-old Chinese man developed narcolepsy and morbid jealousy after a head injury (Wing, Lee, Dhiu, Ho, & Chen, 1994). He showed initial response to fluoxetine but refused further treatment. A 48-year-old hypertensive man suffered a left frontal stroke with the subsequent development of seizures and morbid jealousy (Silva & Leong, 1993). He responded to a course of phenytoin. Another man, 68 years old, suffered a right frontal lobe stroke and developed pathological jealousy but was unresponsive to phenytoin and haloperidol. A 66-year-old woman was withdrawn over a four-month period from the 10 mg of prednisone she had been taking for 26 years for asthma. Within a few weeks of discontinuing the prednisone she began to develop depression, memory problems and pathological jealousy. The patient responded successfully to prednisolone 3–4 mg a day. All of these patients would meet the *DSM–IV–TR* criteria for Psychotic Disorder Due to a General Medical Condition and were it not for their medical problems they would all meet the criteria for delusional disorder, jealous type.

Additional evidence that head injury can cause pathological jealousy was described in a preliminary study from Finland. Ten thousand war veterans who suffered brain injuries during World War II were reviewed (Achte, Jarho, Kyykka, & Vesterinen, 1991). About 3,000 of these veterans have had a psychiatric disturbance at some point after their head injury. About 26 percent of these are classified as psychotic. The first 100 of the 762 veterans classified as psychotic were studied in detail. "Delusional psychosis" was the most common primary diagnosis (68%) among this group. The jealous type of delusional psychosis was present in 28 percent of veterans diagnosed with delusional psychosis.

Various pharmacologic agents have been well documented to provide successful treatment for pathological jealousy (Pollack, 1982; Stein, Hollander, & Josephson, 1994; Lane, 1990). Yet there are few recent, well-controlled studies indicating the long term benefits to these strategies. Many clinicians argue the treatment of morbid jealousy should, in fact, be based on the underlying illness causing the symptomatology (Silva, Ferrari, Leong, & Penny, 1998). For example, there is ample evidence illustrating the presence of pathological jealousy in patients with schizophrenia. These symptoms have been noted to remit partially or completely with the use of various psychotropic medications, including older antipsychotics such as thiothixene (Navane) (Herceg, 1976; Mooney, 1965). Significant literature is now overwhelmingly positive for the use of newer, "atypical" antipsychotics which may have benefits over older, "classic" agents given the lower risk of potentially permanent side effects such as tardive dyskinesia, despite their own risk for weight gain and endocrine or metabolic abnormalities. In addition, newer agents have proven effective for aggression and impulsivity, two potentially disturbing symptoms which can be associated with psychotic illnesses such as schizophrenia or delusional disorder. Studies also are positive for the use of "selective serotonin reuptake inhibitors" (SSRI's) in the treatment of pathological jealousy, especially if the symptoms seem to align with obsessional thinking. There has even been a case report of a positive response to "obsessional jealousy" using Clomipramine (Lawrie, 1998), a tricyclic antidepressant. However, less information exists on the use of "mood stabilizers" or anticonvulsants for these disorders, though some evidence suggests improvements in the impulsivity related to types of morbid jealousy (Silva et al., 1998). Fortunately, with the ever-increasing number of pharmaceutical agents at the disposal of a psychiatrist, medication treatment for pathological jealousy is becoming much easier to tailor toward the specific needs and symptoms of an individual seeking, or sent for, assistance.

Some research also suggests the benefit of specific types of psychotherapy for individuals suffering from morbid jealousy. As mentioned earlier, the types of psychotherapy which may be useful in these patients likely depends upon the etiology of the symptoms. Obsessional thinking as an underlying cause of pathological jealousy has been treated effectively with cognitive therapy (Dolan & Bishay, 1996) in small numbers of nonpsychotic patients, though larger scale studies of this modality have not been accomplished at the time of this publication. In addition, some authors have suggested benefits in this condition with couples or individual dynamic psychotherapy. Yet, studies of these treatments are limited and caution must be used when interpreting their applicability for larger populations.

A retrospective study of patients hospitalized in Oslo, Norway for delusional disorder examined outcomes for this condition after 20 years (Retterstol, 1991). Though only 14 of the original 72 in the sample were available for interview, the study showed those with symptoms lasting six months or less had a more favorable outcome. In addition, there did not appear to be a difference in outcome when the etiology of the delusions was either the persecutory or jealous types of the disorder. However, patients with jealous delusions tended to have ordinary work and social contacts. Overall, about half of study subjects' jealous symptoms had resolved upon follow-up interview. In a more recent article, Kingham suggests prognosis is dependent upon the underlying etiology, co-morbid diagnoses, and the effectiveness of various types of therapy (Kingham et al., 2004). Without more well-controlled studies, conclusions about long-term prognosis are likely to be inaccurate, though some suggest approximately a third of the patients in their clinical sample showed "significant improvement" with treatment (Langfeldt, 1961; Mooney, 1965).

POTENTIAL FOR VIOLENCE

Jealous individuals can be threatening and aggressive (15%) toward their partners (Mullen & Martin, 1994; Leong et al., 1994) and are at an increased risk for spousal homicide and murder-suicide. The extent of such aggression is substantial, ten percent of homicides in Miami in 1980 were committed by individuals married to their victims (Wilbanks, 1984). The most common form of murder-suicide in the United States, one-half to three-fourths, involves jealousy and is estimated to account for 1,000 to 1,500 deaths each year. The murder-suicides are usually done by a male perpetrator (> 90%) between the ages of 18 and 60, who kills his partner and within minutes kills himself (Marzuk, Tardiff, & Hirsch, 1991; Currens, Fritsch, & Jones, 1991). The precipitating event is often the partner's rejection and immediate threat of withdrawal (as with Smith and Sara described above). The jealous concerns may range from the obsessive-ruminative to the delusional. While some murder-suicides may occur shortly after the onset of the morbid jealousy, there is often a period of several years of a troubled relationship before the fatal event occurs. Murder-suicides tend to have different characteristics from murders or suicides alone. Usually only a few minutes time elapses between the murder and suicide suggesting they were linked and planned to occur together. Murder-suicide occurs principally among young and middle-aged men in an intimate relationship with the female victim. In contrast, suicide is distributed from adolescence to the elderly. Finally, an intimate relationship is thought to protect against suicide and homicide (Lester, 1987) but is an essential ingredient in murder-suicide. Depression may be present in 75 percent of those committing murder-suicide, which is considerably greater than those committing homicide alone (Rosenbaum, 1990). Motives may relate to male sexual proprietariness and revenge (Daly et al., 1988; Danto, 1978). It's unusual for the alleged rival to be the object of aggression by jealous individuals (Mashes et al., 1993; Mullen et al., 1994; Leong et al., 1994). Although rare, female perpetrated murder-suicide has similar characteristics to male murder-suicide (Fishbain, Rao, & Aldrich, 1985).

Long-term outcomes in patients with morbid jealousy are, in many ways, related to these particular individuals potential for violence. Undoubtedly, if one is asked to evaluate such a person, the question of their risk for future acts of violence is inevitable. Unfortunately, once suspicions regarding the fidelity of a partner arise, it often becomes all-consuming for the patient, and in some cases creates a self-fulfilling prophecy (i.e., drives the partner to seek out another who is less suspicious, intrusive, and more trusting) which can be followed by violence. Jealousy may even be used to justify violent actions directed at partners, and has been used as the basis of a provocation defense in criminal trials (Kingham et al., 2004). Various areas of risk regarding patients with morbid jealousy should be addressed during an evaluation, and can include the risk of self-harm or harm to others (such as the spouse or significant other, the presumed rival, family of the significant other, or children cared for by the couple). Limited research exists regarding these questions, and there is even less to suggest the degree of risk for different ethnic and cultural groups, as well as the risk associated with morbid jealousy in homosexual couples. However, small studies have revealed certain trends important in appreciating the risk associated with these groups of individuals.

According to the United States Department of Justice–Bureau of Statistics, in 1996 just over 1,800 murders were committed by "intimates" (defined as "people who have an intimate relationship–spouses, ex-spouses, boyfriends, girlfriends, and former boyfriends and girlfriends"), with about three-fourths of the victims being women (Greenfeld et al., 2005). The percentage of female murder victims killed by a partner or significant other has remained at 30 percent since the mid-1970s, and about 840,000 women in 1996 were the victims of "nonlethal" forms of violence at the hands of a significant other. In comparison, about 150,000 men suffered the same type of intimate violence during the same period. The report indicates about one in ten women sought medical attention, suggesting a significantly higher prevalence rate of violence, but an inability to measure the true number of victims of these crimes, as only half of the incidents are ever reported to the authorities. The vast majority of perpetrators of female homicides were unknown, a relative, a friend, an acquaintance, or stranger (70.3%), but of the remaining intimate group (about 29.7%) of offenders, 18.9 percent were spouses. For men, the number is significantly lower, accounting for around 3.7 percent of intimate murders. These statistics illustrate clearly the elevated risk of violence against women associated with marriage or a common-law union.

Silva et al. conducted a small study examining the characteristics of 20 patients (19 males, 1 female) with delusional jealousy who were identified in hospital or forensic hospital settings between 1990 and 1995. Sixty-five percent of subjects threatened to kill their allegedly unfaithful spouse, while 60 percent had committed a physical act of harm to their partner (Silva et al., 1998). Two-thirds of the subjects who threatened their significant other later carried out at least one violent act, with the most common weapon their own hands. One-fourth of the subjects who harmed their partner had not threatened them prior to the violence. This study also stressed the common understanding that prior acts of violence suggest a higher likelihood of future violence because subjects with a history of violence unrelated to their jealousy all committed violent acts against their partners. In addition, while known rivals were occasionally the target of violent threats or actions of the morbidly jealous, spouses or significant others were statistically much more likely to become victims of violent acts. Command hallucinations were another noted risk factor, as individuals with morbid jealousy related to this psychotic symptom accounted for 95 percent of the population, though the presence of auditory hallucinations does not necessarily increase the risk of violence in all individuals.

Similarly, Muzinic and colleagues conducted a retrospective review between 1975 and 1999 of 200 male subjects who committed murder or attempted murder and were hospitalized for observation and treatment in Europe (Muzinic et al., 2003). They divided the sample into those with "psychotic symptoms of jealousy" (undefined) and those without, and determined the victims of the offenses for both groups were overwhelmingly the spouse (62%). The next highest group of victims was unwedded, heterosexual partners (19%). Offenders with psychotic jealousy were more likely to have a history of treatment for psychiatric disorders, while those with nonpsychotic jealousy had significantly higher rates of personality disorders. Twenty-three percent of the subjects in the combined group had been in contact with law enforcement previously due to a different crime related to their jealousy. In addition, offenders with nonpsychotic jealousy were two times more likely to be under the influence of alcohol than offenders with psychotic jealousy, 43.5 percent to 21.5 percent. These general trends indicate factors such as presence of a psychiatric condition, a history of prior contact with law enforcement, and use of alcohol increase the risk for potential violence, mainly directed at the spouse of the offender. Similarly, this data suggests clarification of the etiology for the jealousy (psychotic vs. nonpsychotic) might assist those in assessing these individuals with determining a more proper treatment regimen for their symptoms.

Assessing the risk of potential violence in patients with morbid jealousy is challenging but necessary. Statistically, these individuals have an increased risk of committing violence, primarily against their spouses or significant others, and are much more likely than the general population to have an underlying psychiatric condition. However, extensive research about this group of individuals has been neglected, meaning those assessing these patients are only able to make general comments regarding the presence of specific factors increasing their risk for violence. Further research might help elucidate cultural and ethnic differences in these populations, gender differences in the types of violence committed and the reasons for the acts, as well as differences in risk between heterosexual and homosexual couples. In addition, further research into the etiology and treatment of this condition is vital for a more thorough clinical understanding of the disorder, and an improved ability to successfully manage morbidly jealous patients.

The jealous individual is at risk of committing acts of extreme violence, most importantly murder-suicide. Perhaps the most important precipitant of violence is rejection by the partner. Overall, the incidence of violent acts in those with jealousy is low. Statistically, a low base rate makes prediction difficult. Even with very sensitive criteria clinicians will inevitably over predict violence in populations with low base rates for violence (Monahan, 1981). The challenge then is to try to select and intervene in those situations with the highest potential for violence. Volatile emotions are common and perhaps unavoidable as relationships dissolve. However, if a male partner is showing signs of high levels of jealousy as described by Mullen (1994) and warrants a psychiatric diagnosis, then precautions against violence probably should be taken. Treatment can sometimes significantly diminish or completely resolve symptoms of morbid jealousy as we described earlier. But in many cases treatment has little effect and the jealousy may continue and grow in intensity. Hospitalization may provide some temporary but no long term safety for the partner of the jealous individual. As with a related disorder, erotomania, a geographical cure may be the only solution (Leong et al., 1994). Implementing such physical separation may be difficult because of a network of relationships that the couple may have in common. Still, if the situation is serious enough the partner may need to be fully informed of the potential risk they run and be counseled to avoid all contact with their estranged jealous intimate. If the jealous person continues to attempt to come into contact with their partner, then the police can sometimes intervene utilizing stalker laws which are becoming increasingly common in many jurisdictions. The lack of contact with a jealous individual may help diffuse some of their volatile feelings and may help diminish their suicidal inclinations as well.

COMPETENCE TO STAND TRIAL

Probably the most common forensic psychiatric evaluation requested is for a determination of a defendant's competence to stand trial (CST). The issue of paramount importance for a CST determination is their "legally-relevant functional abilities" (Grisso, 1986). One study looked at other factors that may impact on CST determinations such as; demographics, type of offense, psychopathology and legal ability (Nicholson & Johnson, 1991). The study concluded that only legal ability and psychopathology were correlated with a CST determination. This is what would be expected since the mental health clinician is evaluating legal ability at the same time they are evaluating psychological factors that may impact on that ability. As we have already discussed morbid jealousy is associated with a wide variety of psychiatric disorders such as schizophrenia and depression, both of which may lead to a determination that a defendant is incompetent to stand trial if the symptoms significantly impair their legal ability. The next question is, can morbid jealousy on its own lead to a determination of incompetence?

The most important theoretical impairment (the authors are not aware of any cases in the literature or from their experience where morbid jealousy has been the focus of a CST determination) is a defendants ability to accurately disclose facts about the case to an attorney. A defendants perceptions about the "facts" may be grossly distorted or delusional as a result of their morbid jealousy which may seriously hamper their ability to assist their attorney and defend themselves (assuming their charges are related to their jealousy). Also, jealous misperceptions about the activities of an intimate may impair a defendant's decision-making ability in deciding how to plea or whether to accept a proffered plea arrangement with the prosecution. Similar subtle forms of incompetence have been described by Gutheil (1986). In view of the difficulty of treating morbid jealousy there is a plausible likelihood that some defendants could not be restored to competency resulting in a probable dismissal of the charges against them. The defendant may then face prolonged civil commitment in a psychiatric facility until they are no longer judged to be dangerous.

LEGAL INSANITY

Insanity pleas are used in only about one percent of felony trials and are successful in only one quarter of those cases (Callahan, Steadman, McGreevy, & Robbins, 1991). Although used infrequently, the insanity defense has received a disproportionate amount of media attention, especially in high profile or controversial trials. After John Hinckley was found not guilty by reason of insanity in 1984 (after shooting President Reagan) (Low, Jeffries, & Bonnie, 1986) there was a public outcry to reform or abolish the insanity defense. In recent years, several states have restricted or abolished the defense of insanity or have created alternative verdicts such as "Guilty but Mentally ill" (GBMI) (Rappeport, 1992; Miller, 1994a; Steadman et al., 1993). The Supreme Court has upheld the constitutionality of abolishing the insanity defense (Miller, 1994b). These changes have made it increasingly difficult to successfully plead insanity. And for those that do plead insanity some jurisdictions allow for an alternative verdict of GBMI which is essentially the same as a guilty verdict and has led to capital sentencing in a few cases. The GBMI verdict has an appeal to juries who believe they are taking a defendants mental illness into account with the verdict, yet the verdict sidesteps the crucial issue of criminal and moral culpability. Those that do successfully plead insanity today are more likely to face prolonged supervision by some form of "Psychiatry Review Board" modeled after that created in Oregon (Bloom & Williams, 1992). It is less common, as in the recent past, for those acquitted by reason of insanity to be released into the community with no further scrutiny. There have been several notorious trials in Arizona (Frondorf, 1988) which led to wholesale reform of the insanity defense in 1994 with a new verdict of "guilty except insane" (a variant of GBMI).

Morbid jealousy can theoretically be used as an insanity defense. The prototypical pathologically jealous individual is beset by delusions of infidelity and driven by irrational convictions and uncontrollable emotions. Such an individual may have an associated psychiatric or medical diagnosis. They may be employed and have no history of violence. Such an individual may become emotionally overwhelmed by the fear of losing the most important person in their life to a rival. Such arguments have been successfully used (*State v. Austin* in Pima County, Arizona was one notorious case that led to insanity defense reform) in the past, but are more difficult to use in most jurisdictions today because of the insanity defense reform that has occurred across the country since Hinckley. The test for legal insanity in most states is still the M'Naghten test, a cognitive "right-wrong" test (Goldstein & Rotter, 1988; Goldstein, 1989). In essence, legal insanity can only be proved if the individual did not know, in a cognitive sense, right from wrong at the time of their acts, understanding is not a part of the legal definition. Though a morbidly jealous individual may persuasively argue that they were emotionally overwhelmed by their jealousy, they would still probably have had a cognitive understanding of their acts. In other words, while they may not have emotionally appreciated the significance of their acts, they knew in a concrete legal sense or by an accepted community standard that their act (e.g., killing their wife) was wrong.

The narrowing of the legal test for insanity has led defense attorneys to be reluctant to raise an insanity defense. Defense attorneys may be more inclined to recommend accepting a plea agreement (to avoid capital sentencing or a life sentence) unless they have extremely strong evidence for their client meeting the test of legal insanity. For example, one of the authors (BM) was involved in a case where a middle-aged, employed mother with no legal or psychiatric history found her husband in a compromising situation with another woman and instantly shot and killed them both. The defense attorney believed he had an excellent case for acquittal by reason of insanity but the jury found her guilty of first degree murder. The primary reason for the conviction was probably that the jury believed the defendant, although overwhelmed with jealousy, still "knew" her acts were wrong. Morbid jealousy may provide a framework for an insanity defense, but with current legal standards and public opinion, proving legal insanity in an individual with morbid jealousy may be difficult. Nevertheless, cases may arise where there is compelling evidence for legal insanity, such as morbid jealousy associated with hyperthyroidism or extreme and bizarre jealousy in association with schizophrenia.

SENTENCING

A convicted individual's pathological jealousy can be used in mitigation of their sentence. After a defendant is convicted there is usually a separate hearing in which sentencing takes place. During this hearing, aggravating and mitigating circumstances will be raised by the prosecutor and defense counsel before the judge renders the final sentence. Most jurisdictions have guidelines, determined by law, regarding items which can be used in mitigation or aggravation. A person's mental state at the time of the offense and their likelihood to reoffend can usually be used for mitigation in sentencing. The complexity and intensity of emotions associated with a defendants pathological jealousy can be offered to the court to lessen an individuals sentence. Unfortunately, the court was unmoved by Smith's (case described in the introduction) problems and rendered an aggravated sentence for the second degree murder he pled guilty to.

SUMMARY

Jealousy has a rich literary, legal, and psychiatric history and is a universal human emotion closely related to envy. Morbid jealousy has been viewed as neurotic, delusional and as an overvalued idea. Its extreme manifestations have been associated with a variety of psychiatric and medical disorders. Psychotropic medications, psychotherapy and treatment of underlying medical disorders have sometimes produced marked improvement in jealous symptoms.

Several of the reports regarding morbid jealousy that we have reviewed suggest that jealousy may be "hard-wired" as a human emotion. The following observations support this hypothesis (1) morbid jealousy seems to run in some families; (2) head injuries, hyperthyroidism, strokes and other medical problems can cause morbid jealousy; and (3) pathological jealousy is sometimes responsive to psychotropic medication. Research to explore this possibility may further our understanding of the nature of jealousy. Using imaging techniques such as positron emission tomography to study the brain function of jealous patients might identify brain structures associated with Shakespeare's ". . . green eyed monster/which doth mock the meat it feeds on."

Finally, extreme violence such as murder-suicides and spousal homicides are commonly associated with jealousy. Such violence leads to the use of jealousy in criminal litigation, although no empirical studies exist delineating how frequently jealousy is raised in criminal proceedings. Empirical studies are needed to develop strategies to diminish the potential for violence in jealous individuals and to delineate how jealousy is used in criminal proceedings.

Jealousy and envy are intense human:emotions which are the epitome of the darker side of human relations. As the Spanish poet Calderon de la Barca wrote in 1647:

> There is no man so wretched
> That he is not envied by someone
> Nor is there anyone so fortunate
> That he envies no one.

REFERENCES

Achte, K., Jarho, L., Kyykka, T., & Vesterinen, E. (1991). Paranoid disorders following war brain damage. Preliminary report. *Psychopathology, 24,* 309–315.

American Psychiatric Association (2000). *Diagnostic and Statistical Manual of Mental Disorders, Fourth Edition, Text Revision.* (4 TR ea.) Washington, DC: American Psychiatric Association.

Anderson, K. E., & Savage, C. R. (2004). Cognitive and neurobiological findings in obsessive-compulsive disorder. *Psychiatric Clinics of North America, 27,* 37–47.

Barclay, C. R. (1986). Schematization of autobiographical memory. In D. C. Rubin (Ed.), *Autobiographical memory* (pp. 82–98). Cambridge: Cambridge University Press.

Bloom, J. D., & Williams, M. H. (1992). Oregon's experience with insanity acquittees. *Psychiatric Annals, 22,* 579–583.

Callahan, L. A., Steadman, H. J., McGreevy, M. A., & Robbins, P. C. (1991). The volume and characteristics of insanity defense pleas: An eight-state study. *Bulletin of the American Academy of Psychiatry and the Law, 19,* 331–338.

Cameron, N. (1943). The development of paranoic thinking. *Psychological Review, 50,* 219–233.

Chagnon, N. A. (1992). *Yanomamo. The last days of Eden.* San Diego, CA: Harcourt Brace Jovanovich.

Coen, S. J. (1987). Pathological jealousy. *International Journal of Psycho-Analysis, 68,* 99–108.

Currens, S., Fritsch, T., & Jones, D. (1991). Homicide followed by suicide–Kentucky, 1985–1990. *Morbidity and Mortality Weekly Reports, 40,* 652–659.

Daly, M., & Wilson, M. (1988). Evolutionary social psychology and homicide. *Science, 242,* 519–524.

Danto, B. L. (1978). Suicide among murderers. *International Journal of Offender Therapy and Comparative Criminology, 22,* 140–148.

Dolan, M., & Bishay, N. R. (1996). The effectiveness of cognitive therapy in the treatment of nonpsychotic morbid jealousy. *The British Journal of Psychiatry, 168,* 588–593.

Enoch, D. (1991). Delusional jealousy and awareness of reality. *British Journal of Psychiatry, 159,* 52–56.

Feldman, E., & De Paola, H. (1994). An investigation into the psychoanalytic concept of envy. (Review). *International Journal of Psycho-Analysis, 75,* 217–234.

Fishbain, D. A., Rao, V. J., & Aldrich, T. E. (1985). Female homicide-suicide perpetrators: A controlled study. *Journal of Forensic Sciences, 30,* 1148–1156.

Fitzgerald, K. D., Welsh, R. C., Gehring, W. J., Abelson, J. L., Himle, J. A., Liberzon, I. et al. (2005). Error-related hyperactivity of the anterior cingulate cortex in obsessive-compulsive disorder. *Biologic Psychiatry, 57,* 287–294.

Freeman, T. (1990). Psychoanalytical aspects of morbid jealousy in women. *British Journal of Psychiatry, 156,* 68–72.

Freud, S. (1922). Some neurotic mechanisms in jealousy, paranoia and homosexuality. In J. Strachey (Ed.), *Standard Edition* (pp. 221–232). London: Hogarth Press.

Frondorf, S. (1988). *Death of a "Jewish American princess."* New York: Berkley Books.

Goldstein, R. L. (1989). The psychiatrist's guide to right and wrong: Part II: A systematic analysis of exculpatory delusions. *Bulletin of the American Academy of Psychiatry and the Law, 17.*

Goldstein, R. L., & Rotter, M. (1988). The psychiatrist's guide to right and wrong: Judicial standards of wrongfulness since M'Naghten. *Bulletin of the American Academy of Psychiatry and the Law, 16,* 359–367.

Greenfeld, L. A., Rand, M. R., Craven, D., Klaus, P. A., Perkins, C. A., Ringel, C. et al. (2005). *Violence by intimates, analysis of data on crimes by current or former spouses, boyfriends and girlfriends.*

Grisso, T. (1986). *Evaluating competencies: Forensic assessments and instruments.* New York: Plenum Press.

Gross, M. D. (1991). Treatment of pathological jealousy by fluoxetine. *American Journal of Psychiatry, 148,* 683–684.

Gutheil, T. G. (1986). Clinicians' guidelines for assessing & presenting subtle forms of patient incompetence in legal settings. *American Journal of Psychiatry, 143.*

Harris, C. R. (2003). A review of sex differences in sexual jealousy, including self-report data, psychophysiological responses, interpersonal violence and morbid jealousy. *Personality and Social Psychology Bulletin, 7,* 102–128.

Harris, C. R. (2004). The evolution of jealousy. *American Scientist, 92,* 62–71.

Herceg, N. (1976). Successful use of thiothixene in two cases of pathological jealousy. *The Medical Journal of Australia, 1,* 569–570.

Hill, R., & Davis, P. (2000). Platonic jealousy: A conceptualization and review of the literature on non-romantic pathological jealousy. *British Journal of Medical Psychology, 73,* 505–517.

Hodgson, R. E., Murray, D., & Woods, M. R. (1992). Othello's Syndrome and hyperthyroidism. *Journal of Nervous and Mental Disease, 180,* 663–664.

Kingham, M., & Gordon, H. (2004). Aspects of morbid jealousy. *Advances in Psychiatric Treatment, 10,* 207–215.

Klein, M. (1957). *Envy and gratitude.* London: Tavistock.

Lane, R. D. (1990). Successful fluoxetine treatment of pathologic jealousy. *Journal of Clinical Psychiatry, 51,* 345–346.

Langfeldt, G. (1961). The erotic jealousy syndrome: A clinical study. *Acta Psychiatr Scand, 36,* 7–68.

Lawrie, S. M. (1998). Attacks of jealousy that responded to clomipramine. *Journal of Clinical Psychiatry, 59,* 317–318.

Leong, G. B., Silva, J. A., Garza-Treviño, E. S., Oliva, Jr. D., Ferrari, M. M., Komanduri, R. V. et al. (1994). The dangerousness of persons with the Othello Syndrome. *Journal of Forensic Sciences, 39,* 1445–1454.

Lester, D. (1987). Benefits of marriage for reducing risk of violent death from suicide and homicide for white and nonwhite persons: Generalizing Gove's findings. *Psychological Reports, 61,* 198.

Low, P. W., Jeffries, J. C., & Bonnie, R. J. (1986). *The trial of John W. Hinckley, Jr.: A case study in the insanity defense.* Mineola, NY: The Foundation Press, Inc.

Marzuk, P. M., Tardiff, K., & Hirsch, C. S. (1991). The epidemiology of murder-suicide. *Journal of the American Medical Association, 267,* 3179–3183.

Mashes, E. W., & Verstraete, C. (1993). Jealous aggression: Who is the target, the beloved or the rival? *Psychological Reports, 72,* 1071–1074.

McKenna, P. J. (1984). Disorders with overvalued ideas. *British Journal of Psychiatry*, *145*, 579–585.

Michael, A., Mirza, S., Mirza, K. A., Babu, V. S., & Vithayathil, E. (1995). Morbid jealousy in alcoholism. *The British Journal of Psychiatry*, *167*, 668–672.

Miller, R. D. (1994a). Abolition of the insanity defense. *Commentary: Insanity*, *19*, 55.

Miller, R. D. (1994b). U.S. Supreme Court allows abolition of insanity defense to stand. *AAPL Newsletter*, *19*, 35–36.

Monahan, J. (1981). *Predicting violent behavior. An assessment of clinical techniques*. Beverly Hills: Sage Publications.

Mooney, H. B. (1965). Pathological jealousy and psychochemotherapy. *British Journal of Psychiatry*, *111*, 1023–1042.

Morgan, D. H. (1975). The psychotherapy of jealousy. *Psychotherapy and Psychosomatics*, *25*, 43–47.

Mullen, P. E. (1991). Jealousy: The pathology of passion. *British Journal of Psychiatry*, *158*, 593–601.

Mullen, P. E., & Martin, J. (1994). Jealousy: A community study. *British Journal of Psychiatry*, *164*, 35–43.

Muzinic, L., Goreta, M., Jukic, V., Dordevic, V., Koic, E., & Herceg, M. (2003). Forensic importance of jealousy. *Collegium Antropologicum*, *27*, 293–300.

Nicholson, R. A., & Johnson, W. G. (1991). Prediction of competency to stand trial: Contribution of demographics, type of offense, clinical characteristics, and psycholegal ability. *International Journal of Law and Psychiatry*, *14*, 287–297.

Pam, A., & Pearson, J. (1994). The geometry of the eternal triangle. *Family Process*, *33*, 175–190.

Parrott, W. G., & Smith, R. H. (1993). Distinguishing the experiences of envy and jealousy. *Journal of Personality and Social Psychology*, *64*, 906–920.

Pollack, B. G. (1982). Successful treatment of pathological jealousy with pimozide. *Canadian Journal of Psychiatry*, *27*, 386–389.

Rappeport, J. R. (1992). Current status of the insanity plea. *Psychiatric Annals*, *22*, 550–555.

Retterstol, S. O. (1991). Delusional disorder: The predictive validity of the concept. *Acta Psychiatr Scand*, *84*, 250–254.

Romans-Clarkson, S. E. (1989). Validity of the GHQ-28 in New Zealand women. *Australian and New Zealand Journal of Psychiatry*, *23*, 187–196.

Rosenbaum, M. (1990). The role of depression in couples involved in murder-suicide and homicide. *American Journal of Psychiatry*, *147*, 1036–1039.

Sanati, M., & Mojtabai, R. (1993). Frégoli syndrome with a jealous theme. *Journal of Clinical Psychiatry*, *54*, 490–491.

Silva, J. A., Ferrari, M. M., Leong, G. B., & Penny, G. (1998). The dangerousness of persons with delusional jealousy. *Journal of the American Academy of Psychiatry and Law*, *26*, 607–623.

Silva, J. A., & Leong, G. B. (1993). A case of organic Othello Syndrome. *Journal of Clinical Psychiatry*, *54*, 277.

Soyka, M., Naber, G., & Volcker, A. (1991). Prevalence of delusional jealousy in different psychiatric disorders. An analysis of 93 cases. *British Journal of Psychiatry*, *158*, 549–553.

Spillius, E. B. (1993). Varieties of envious experience. *International Journal of Psycho-Analysis*, *74*, 1199–1212.

Steadman. H. J., McGreevy, M. A., Morrissey, M. P., Callahan, L. A., Robbins, P. C., & Cirincione, C. (1993). *Before and after Hinckley: Evaluating insanity defense reform*. New York: The Guilford Press.

Stein, D. J., Hollander, E., & Josephson, S. C. (1994). Serotonin reuptake blockers for the treatment of obsessional jealousy. *Journal of Clinical Psychiatry*, *55*, 30–33.

Su, K. P., Hsu, C. Y., & Hsieh, S. C. (2001). Magnetic resonance imaging findings in patients with delusional disorder due to diffuse cerebrovascular disease: A report of seven cases. *Psychiatry and Clinical Neurosciences, 55*, 121–126.

Szezko, P. R., Robinson, D., Alvir, J. M. J., Bilder, R. M., Lencz, T., Ashtari, M. et al. (1999). Orbital frontal and amygdala volume reductions in obsessive-compulsive disorder. *Archives of General Psychiatry, 56*, 913–919.

Westlake, R. J., & Weeks, S. M. (1999). Pathological jealousy appearing after cerebrovascular infarction in a 25-year-old woman. *Australian and New Zealand Journal of Psychiatry, 33*, 105–107.

Wilbanks, W. (1984). *Murder in Miami.* Lanham, MD: University Press of America.

Wilson, M., & Daly, M. (1993). An evolutionary psychological perspective on male sexual proprietariness and violence against wives. *Violence and Victims, 8*, 271–294.

Wing, Y. K., Lee, S., Dhiu, H. F. K., Ho, C. K. W., & Chen, C. N. (1994). The patient with coexisting narcolepsy and morbid jealousy showing favourable response to fluoxetine. *Postgrad Med J, 70*, 34–36.

Wright, S. (1994). Familial obsessive-compulsive disorder presenting as pathological jealousy successfully treated with fluoxetine. *Archives of General Psychiatry, 51*, 430–431.

Chapter 10

PSEUDOLOGIA FANTASTICA AND PATHOLOGICAL LYING: A FORENSIC ISSUE

W. A. WESTON

"And, after all, what is a lie?"
"Tis but the truth in masquerade."
Byron

The concept of Pseudologia Fantastica first appeared in the literature in 1891 in a paper by A. Delbreuck (1891) titled "Pathological Lying and Abnormal Swindling." It is a term which has been widely used in the psychiatric literature, but there does not appear to be a consensus as to its definition (King and Ford, 1988). It has been used interchangeably with pathological lying and mythomania. The dictionary definition of pseudologia fantastica and pathological lying is as follows:

> "Pseudologic fantastica, a tendency to tell extravagant and fantastic falsehood centered about one's self," Dorland's (1988).
> "Pseudologia [pseudo-false + Grk. logos-word +ia] lying; falsehood."
> "Pseud (o) [Grk. pseudes-false] combining form signifying false or spurious."

There appears to be no definition of pathological lying in Webster's Dictionary (1994). It defines pathological as;

1. of or related to pathology.
2. alter or caused by disease.

and a lie as lied; lying and defines it as;

1. to make an untrue statement with intent to deceive.
2. to create a false or misleading impression.

Lie is defined as;

1. (a) an assertion of something known or believed by the speaker to be untrue with intent to deceive.
   (b) an untrue or inaccurate statement that may or may not be believed true by the speaker.
2. something that misleads or deceives.
3. a charge of lying.

It would appear from these definitions that pathological lying is a lie which is created by underlying pathology. A definition of pathological lying was given by Healy and Healy (1917) and is as follows: "Pathological lying is falsification entirely disproportionate to any discernible end in view, engaged in by a person who, at the time of observation, cannot definitely be declared insane, feebleminded, or epileptic. Such lying rarely, if ever, centers about a single event; although exhibited in very occasional cases for a short time, it manifests itself most frequently by far over a period of years, or even a life time. It represents a trait rather than an episode. Extensive, very complicated fabrications may be evolved. This has led to the synonymous:–mythomania; pseudologia phantastica." A simpler definition was given by Selling (1942) as follows: "a pathological liar is a person having a constellation of symptoms caused by diseases of the total personality, characterized psychopathologically by a very definite tendency to tell untruths about matters which perhaps could be easily verified and which untruths may serve no obvious purpose either in the personality of the individual or in the situation which he finds himself. The pathological liar is characterized clinically by a constellation of traits which prevent him from giving full cooperation to the examiner and responding normally to treatment from the point of view having adequate insight and a normal truth-telling capacity. The definition of the pathological liar can be extended to include all those whose lying is seemingly purposeless and it can be limited to those who by virtue of obvious mental disease, particularly a diagnosable psychopathic personality of some type, exhibit as a major symptom the lack of ability to stick to the verifiable word."

Some authors have viewed pseudologia as a subtype of pathological lying (Karpman, 1949). Other authors have viewed pathological lying as the primary disorder and pseudologia as a subtype (Deutsch, 1982).

Honesty is considered an important virtue in modern civilization, and along with this goes truth–a serious human vice is lying. Yet, lying is used by most people during every aspect of their lives, from early childhood to old age (Ford, 1996; Lewis & Saarni, 1993). The legal test of insanity is the knowledge of the difference between right and wrong.

Lying appears to be a universal characteristic and it has been found in many cultures as an acceptable practice (Wigmore, 1913). It has been asserted that women deviate more readily from the truth than men (Mack Brunswick, 1943) and examples given are that women are permitted to lie about their age even in official documents, where they are allowed to state that they are over twenty-one years. A general observation noted by Healy and Healy (1917) is that students of conduct have found that women tend to deviate from the truth more readily than males.

The concept of lying is widespread in our society and has been present in some form in most cultures since early times. It would appear that lying has played an important part in human relationships according to Wile (1942). Liars, according to Georgiade (1938), developed the theme that the lie, while of biological origin, has taken on the characteristics of magic in the mind of prehistoric man. In the early stages, prehistoric man had both visual and special imagery and this became inimical and vocal. He was later able to abstract from immediate reality through the medium of language, to interiorize thought (imperceptible vocalization) and thus guard his own self-interest from his fellow man. After acquiring language, the magical power of images was substituted by verbal magic. By his use of laryngeal-oral images, this was equivalent to the manipulation of real objects. The verbal magic which resulted from this illusion, in turn led to lying in order to escape from difficulties which were encountered.

In nature, deceit is stated as a form of lying and is used for biological purposes (Wile, 1942). Color is used by plants, such as carnivorous plants, for the purpose of securing pollination. Animals show protective devices in deceit by assuming forms which are different (e.g., the leaf-butterfly). Color changes in animals, such as are seen in the chameleons, who also show exaggerated gait, helps to protect them. Many more such examples of biological lying can be found in the plant and animal kingdoms.

Acts similar to biological lying have been found in humans, such as pretending to be dead on the battlefield. The most common form of lying in humans is verbal: the telling of a lie. Different forms of lies have been differentiated by Anna Freud (1965). First, fantasy lying, in which the child engages in infantile forms of wishful thinking usually in response to intolerable realities. Second, there is a group of delinquent liars who lie for material advantage, such as to escape the consequences of their actions.

Lying appears to be implicit in the behavior of mankind and attempts to classify lying are enormous. Karpman (1949) made what he called a cursory attempt and outlined several areas, which are as follows: benign and salutary forms of lying, hysterical lying, defensive lying, compensatory lying, malicious lying, gossiping, implied lying, love intoxication type of lying, and finally pathological lying. He points out that an attempt to really classify lying would be a difficult and complex task.

DEVELOPMENTAL ISSUES

In early childhood, it is not possible for the child to lie because they have not developed any verbal skills which are the most common method by which humans lie. The child does not develop the skills to lie until it has a level of command of language. Piaget (1969) suggested that the child develops the concept of lying around the age of six years. He asked the following questions to a group of children from six to seven years of age, "What is a lie?" The definition which they gave appeared to be that a lie was a naughty word. They all stated, when asked, that not all "naughty words" were lies. In children aged six years, to tell a lie is to commit a moral fault by use of language. A more clear conception of a lie occurs around age six to ten years.

Current studies of preschool children indicate that they are unlikely to be successful in telling lies (Morency and Krauss, 1982). Their ability to lie becomes more proficient as they reach the fourth and fifth grades (Allen and Atkinson, 1978). The motives given for telling lies are to avoid punishment, to protect both themselves and their friends from getting into trouble, to keep them from harm, to get something that they would not otherwise get, to avoid embarrassment, and to maintain privacy. It appears, to the child, that lying is a way to demonstrate power over those in authority (Ekman, 1989).

The concept of lies and truth is developed in childhood as part of moral development. The child develops a moral sense by differentiating good from evil. This is connected with the teaching of "thou shalt" of "thou shalt not." The child, at first, is unable to differentiate between a lie and the truth and, in the early stages of development, these two concepts are firmly entwined and cannot exist without each other. As the child matures and its ego develops, the concept becomes differentiated, the child's inner world and outer world are distinguished, and reality testing occurs. Woolf (1966) stated that the child cannot lie before the age of four years because they do not know the truth. After the age of five years, the concept of lying becomes more defined and the ability to differentiate external reality from fantasy starts to occur.

It has been suggested that lying is essential for the psychic development of the individual (Goldberg, 1973; Ekstein and Caruth, 1972; Kohut, 1966 and Taausk, 1933). Lying may be an essential mechanism by which the child can test its own ego boundaries in order to define and establish its autonomy. Many authors have stressed that the concept of lying is important in establishing the child's autonomy and in developing its ego. Lying may also play a developmental role in the growth and self-regulation of the child (Goldberg, 1973).

The response to the child's fantasy can affect the development of lies, whether such fantasies are encouraged or repressed by the parents. The parent may deal with such fantasies either by helping the child to move from these into more creative reality, or by suppressing the fantasy, may push the child into unreality, leading to lying (Smith, 1968).

If the child is exposed to lying by others in his environment, then he is more likely to turn to using lies himself. If the child is given promises which are repeatedly broken, then he feels he is being deceived. If the expectation he is given differs from the reality that occurs, such as a promised visit to the movies, and the child is taken to the hospital for a procedure, which may turn out to be unpleasant, then this may be seen by the child as not fulfilling expectations. This deceit will eventually lead to lying.

If the milieu of the household contains many secrets, such as past incidents which are hidden from the child, this may produce an environment conducive to the development of lying. Such secrets may be found in multiple marriages which are more prevalent now than in the past. Six focal concerns or ideals were identified by Miller (1958) in lower class culture: trouble, toughness, smartness, excitement, fate and autonomy. Smartness was specifically defined as the ability to "dupe" or "con" others successfully. Such an outlook extols the virtues of clever deceit and regards it shameful to be so incompetent as to be caught in a lie.

The case of two individuals who were diagnosed as pathological liars was reported by Healy and Healy (1917), and it was felt their lying was in part due to "contagion from long continued untruthfulness." In one case, after they had been removed from the home, their lying partially remitted.

The psychic stress encountered in adolescence may result in the fragmentation of the self, and the manifestation of further lying occurs. The parent may be viewed as hypocritical, corrupt or deceitful by the adolescent. The adolescent may struggle over separation and so reactivate behavior such as secrecy and deceit in an effort to become an autonomous person.

According to Woolf (1966), lying and stealing are the two main offenses characteristic of childhood. The child is taught he must not lie, but he must tell the truth. It is not possible for the child to do this until he has learned what the truth is. Truth is a statement of reality, and before the age of about four years, the child cannot differentiate external reality from his own inner experiences, desires, fantasies and aspirations. Around the age of five years, the child is able to differentiate between external reality and the products of inner fantasy. It appears that, around this time, the concept of lying becomes clearer and the child is aware of the conscious lies. For the first time the child realizes the demands not to lie but tell the truth. The child has to learn how to lie as lies are used by human society especially in areas such as sexual behavior. Such lies have been learned as necessary social lies. From six years on, the child starts to lie with the same motives as adults, namely for the sake of convenience.

DIAGNOSTIC ISSUES

Diagnosis in psychiatric practice has always created a problem, and many attempts have and are being made to clarify the criterion for all disorders. The use of the *International Classification of Diseases* (1979) and the American Psychiatric Association's *Diagnostic and Statistical*

Manual (1968, 1980, 1987, 1994, 2000) have been reviewed with regard to the diagnosis of pseudologia fantastica and pathological lying. Some diagnoses have been widely accepted and appear with little, if any, change in each revision of the *Diagnostic and Statistical Manual*, but others have shown variation of the criteria. Some have never been recognized and others have been removed. Pseudologia fantastica and pathological lying are such diagnoses. The diagnosis of pathological lying, pseudologia fantastica and mythomania do not appear in any of the editions of *Diagnostic and Statistical Manual.* In the second edition, no mention is found of these conditions. It may be that these were dealt with by considering them under the umbrella of personality disorders.

In the *Diagnostic and Statistical Manual III, III–R* and *IV*, under the heading of Factitious Disorders, there are a number of conditions listed which include deceit as a major symptom. In *DSM–III–R*, 301.51 Factitious Disorder with Physical Symptoms, is as follows:

A. Intentional production of feigning of physical (but not psychological) symptoms.
B. A psychological need to assume the sick role, as evidenced by the absence of external incentives for the behavior, such as economic gain, better care, or physical well-being.
C. Occurrence not exclusively during the course of another Axis I disorder, such as Schizophrenia.

300.16 Factitious Disorder with Psychological Symptoms.

A. Intentional production of feigning of psychological (but not physical) symptoms.
B. A psychological need to assume the sick role, as evidenced by the absence of external incentive for behavior, such as economic gain, better care, or physical well-being.
C. Occurrence not exclusively during the course of another Axis I disorder, such as Schizophrenia.

In *DSM–IV* the diagnostic criteria for Factitious Disorder is as follows:

A. Intentional production or feigning of physical or psychological signs or symptoms.
B. External incentives for the behavior (such as economic gain, avoiding legal responsibility, or improving psychial well-being, as in Malingering) are absent.

Although the criteria does not specify lying, there is the intent of deception present in this diagnostic criteria, and pathological lying may not have been necessary as a separate diagnostic category.

In *The International Classification of Diseases 9th Revision*, Liar, pathological, is found in the index and the *ICD* No. 301.7 which is defined as follows:

301.7 Antisocial personality disorder
Amoral personality
Asocial personality
Dyssocial personality
Personality disorder with predominantly sociopathic or asocial manifestations.

A paper entitled "Pseudologia Fantastica" by Hoyer (1959) cited the case of a thirty-six-year-old male who had many admissions to hospital during 1943 to 1950. The following diagnoses were made:

1. Psychosis, unclassified–CDD Army Discharge. 1943
2. No psychosis found–first Veterans Administration examination. 1944.
3. Immature reaction, emotional instability type, with pseudologia fantastica. 1948.
4. Paranoid personality, manifested by emotional instability and pseudologia fantastica, ideas of persecution. 1948.
5. Psychosis with constitutional psychopathic states. 1948.
6. Personality defect, unclassified. 1949.
7. Neuropsychiatric diagnosis undetermined after 44 days of hospitalization. 1949.
8. Psychopathic personality, pathological liar. 1950.
9. Schizophrenic reaction, paranoid type. 1950.

One of the difficulties in making the diagnosis of pseudologia fantastica and pathological lying is that there is a need for objective data about the subject's early life. If he has previous hospital admissions, there is a need to obtain this information in order to develop a clear and precise history of these earlier events. Such data is difficult to get because it may take a long time to obtain histories from other facilities. By the time the information is received, the patient has invariably moved on to add another page to his life history. Second, it is often difficult, if not impossible, to obtain accurate family histories, as these patients have often been cut off from their families for many years and it is not possible to contact any family member.

SOCIAL ISSUES AND EARLY IDEAS

Social issues that are connected with lying have been discussed, and child rearing may play a part in the propensity to be able to tell the truth and to differentiate a lie from the truth. Parental and cultural attitudes towards lying will affect how the child is reared to view the use of lies in their everyday interactions. It appears that in certain cultures, lying is part of their cultural development (Wigmore, 1913).

When the concept of pathological lying and pseudologia fantastica were first described by Delbreuck (1891), there appears to have been a fascination with the whole concept of pathological lying, and a substantial amount of literature was then published. Delbreuck stressed that lying occurred in both normal and abnormal cases and in every conceivable form as part of a mental disturbance, even in general paralysis and mania.

Koeppen (1898) stated that pathological lying was always for some purpose and the lies bore an obviously active character. One of the first reported cases was by Joerger (1904), who published the case of Georg Gruen, a high school boy who became a swindler on a grand scale. The account does not cover some of the aspects that Schneider (1958) felt were essential, such as personality vanity, the role the subject wanted to play, and the craving for attention.

The same case was reported by Wenger-Kunz (1920). The subject hand prefaced a second edition of a handbook of psychology, with a bogus recommendation by a Professor W. Egleman. Gruen later played the roles of a theologian, a man of means, a director of a sanatorium, and finally an obscure and shady lawyer.

There are several other cases quoted in the early literature, and one of the patients described by Wendt (1911) is said to have written that the "tragi-comedy or comedy of my life, lies in the battle between reality and dream. I cannot keep my real and imaginary acts apart and I mix up being and pretending to be." Wendt, in this case, excluded mania and paranoia. He did support the nonculpability of his subjects in court. The leading motif in this, and many cases, appeared to be personal vanity, the need for attention, the insistent bent to be seen by others to be other than what one really was.

In the early literature, the writers speculated whether pathological liars believed their lies or not. In the German literature, Wendt (1911) did not give a clear indication whether he had found this, but

Aschaffenburg (1908) thinks that the lies were believed and that the personality is carried away by the lies. This is also the opinion held by both Jasper (1948) and Zeihan (1905).

Other authors such as Koeppen (1898) have stated that patients have flashes of insight in the middle of the fabrications. Wendt (1911) suggested that pseudologia phantastica occurs only when the patient truly believes the lie, but the awareness of what is fabricated is never lost and he suggests that a kind of double consciousness exists. It has been postulated by Kraepelin (1906) that patients know when they have left reality, but in their confabulatory gusto they begin to weave a more intricate web of lies. There always appear to be a motive in such pathological lying but material gain may not be the primary motive. In early reported cases, it is worth noting that the personality bearing is likeable, indeed often charming, the manner is easy, and they have self-assurance which commands success. Kraepelin (1906) reported that his liars and swindlers were attention-seeking and about three-quarters were male. Nearly 50 percent were under the age of 25 years. They were mostly single, their attention-seeking behavior had been noted in early childhood by their boasting to others about having rich relations, receiving handsome parents, that they had suffered from dangerous illness, and they related tales of death.

BIOLOGICAL AND COGNITIVE ISSUES

The biological issues associated with lying can be examined as a cognitive dysfunction. Some authors seem to suggest that there is a clear relationship between pseudologia fantastica and confabulation (Ford et al., 1988). Bonhoeffer (1901) stated that in Korsakoff's syndrome confabulation could take two forms:

1. confabulation of embarrassment, which is the direct result of memory loss and depended for its presence on a certain attentiveness and activity and
2. confabulation exceeds the need of memory impairment, the patient describes spontaneously adventurous activities.

In a later paper, Bonhoeffer (1904) described this as momentary confabulation. He also described cases in which the patient exceeds the need of the memory impairment and describes experiences of a fantastic nature. He felt such states developed out of dream like states and had a relationship to delirious states which he called fantastic confabulations.

In a later study, Whitty and Lewin (1957) described vivid day-dreaming and difficulty distinguishing reality from fantasy following an anterior cingulectomy. They also noted symptoms similar to Korsakoff's syndrome following cingulectomy (Whitty & Lewin, 1961).

Memory falsification can be found in such conditions as schizophrenia, depressive illness, in prestige-seeking psychopaths, and even compulsive states (Schneider, 1928). There may be an element of wish fulfillment in the fantastic confabulation associated with organic brain disorder, and Kahn (1931) felt that a similar mechanism may be present in "fantast" and "pseudologue" psychopaths. These conditions were described by Berlyne (1972). The relationship of confabulation and lies is not clear and the definition of confabulation has been poorly defined and variously interpreted (Berlyne, 1972). There does not appear to be a conscious willfulness to deceive in confabulation, whereas this appears to occur in lying

CLASSIFICATION, INCIDENCE, I.Q., GENETICS AND OTHER ISSUES

A classification of pathological lying has been made by Selling (1942) who considers that there are two general types of pathological lying, the first by degree and the second by process. He considered there were five stages of pathological lying. The least significant and the first stage he called the amusing stage. Following this, he described the ludicrous stage and then the third stage as annoying. He called the fourth stage pathetic and the final stage vicious. In discussing the classification by process, Selling suggested that pathological lying was a symptom of psychosis. His second category was psychotoid lying, where the psychopathic personality is very close to a psychosis but does not have the characteristic malignancy of the psychosis. He then describes compulsive lying, or lying as found in the neuroses. Then there is lying as habit and finally lying as a symptom of psychopathic personality. He cites cases to support his classification.

The defensive role of pseudology in denying unpleasant realities and replacing them with better ones, as if it was a movie screen, is described by Fenichel (1939). Both Winnicott (1960) and Kahn (1983) felt that pseudologia could be viewed as the elaboration and exploitation of the false self, ensuring a cloak of secrecy and privacy in the realm of the undeveloped and vulnerable true self. It protected the patient's true self from intrusion and impingement.

It is very difficult to get a clear picture on the incidence of pathological lying, mythomania, and pseudologia fantastica. The number of cases reported in the early German literature was stated to be very large as there was a certain fascination in describing these interesting cases (Schneider, 1950). There are no clear references to the number of cases which were reported. Healy and Healy (1969) evaluated 1,000 repeat juvenile offenders and found that lying was excessive and notoriously characteristic. In their population, 15 percent were male and 26 percent female; out of these, they identified 104 males and 80 females as liars, but of the total population only eight or ten were considered as pathological hers.

There are fewer cases reported in the more recent literature and this may be because the *Diagnostic and Statistical Manual* does not recognize pathological lying as a separate entity. It has been recognized that pathological lying may occur in some cases of Factitious Disorders. The sex distribution of cases in the early literature is difficult to assess but Kraepelin (1906), in his liars and swindlers, found about three-quarters were male, but no exact numbers of cases are reported. Of the total 72 cases identified by King and Ford (1988), half were male and half were female. This is at variance with the cases of both Healy and Healy (1969) and Burt (1938) in which there was a preponderance of females. Kraepelin (1906) reported that nearly 50 percent were under 25 years of age. Burt (1938) suggested that the pseudologue was pubescent. Of the 55 cases for which information was available to King and Ford (1988), the mean age was 22, with an onset at approximately 16 years.

The level of intelligence has been discussed, and a number of references in the early literature has been made to their ability to use colorful language which may suggest a reasonably high level of intelligence, but no statistics are available. The subjects have been described as generally having normal intelligence (Wiersma, 1933). The majority of cases in the work of Healy and Healy (1969) are also described as being of normal intelligence. They further state that they appear to have linguistic ability and are especially good at verbal composition. A number of cases are reported with superior intelligence by both Wile (1942) and Risch (1908). In a case reported by Weston and Dalby (1991), it was found that the patient was functioning overall at an average level of intelligence (with a verbal IQ of 96 and a performance IQ of 121, giving a full scale IQ of 107). Memory skills were found to be in the high average range, but academic skills were lower than general cognitive abilities (reading = 25th percentile, spelling = second percentile and arithmetic = fourth percentile). No neuropsychological deficit was discovered. In a case entitled "an unusual variant of folie a deux?", the patient was found to have an IQ of 92 and her husband an IQ of 104 (Casey and Corcoran, 1989).

King and Ford (1988) suggested that there appeared to be a bimodal grouping of patients, with average or slightly below average intelligence, and another group of superior intellect. They stated that in only eight cases was verbal and performance ability reported, and five of these patients had significantly better verbal ability than performance scores. The importance of this is that, when there is a significant difference between verbal and performance IQ's, it is sometimes accepted as suggesting nondominant hemispheric dysfunction (Kaufman, 1979).

In a number of cases, neurological abnormalities have been found such as epilepsy, a history of head trauma, infection of the central nervous system, and abnormal electroencephalograms. The overall incidence is not significantly different between the sexes. It has been reported that at least 25 percent of all males with pseudologia have epilepsy (King and Ford, 1988). Pankrantz (1981) suggested a relationship between pseudologia and brain dysfunction in patients diagnosed with Munchausen's syndrome.

Hereditary factors in pathological lying were researched by Lutz (1929) and he found no homogenous family history. A similar finding was made by Stumpfl (1935) and by von Baeyer (1935). Among the siblings of liars and swindlers, von Baeyer (1935) found many drifters, weak-willed personalities, oversuggestible, unstable individuals, addicts, attention-seekers, dishonest and unrealistic people. In the recent literature, there are no reports about hereditary or environmental factors. Yet in the discussion of the development of lying in the child, the environmental factors are discussed.

Amongst the siblings of pathological liars there were found many drifters, addicts, attention-seekers, dishonest and unrealistic people which was reported by von Baeyer (1935). On an examination of the children of pathological liars, Riedel (1937) found the same traits commonly appeared. King and Ford (1988) reported that in their sample, over 10 percent of the pseudologue's parents had a history of alcoholism, and a great number of their homes had a chaotic environment. They also found that 30 percent presented with a history of neuropsychiatric illness, such as "insanity," epilepsy, sociopathy, "nervousness" and neurosyphilis, amongst the parents and siblings. The overall incidence of either alcoholism or neuropsychiatric illness was 35 percent. One case was reported by Healy and Healy (1917) in which the parent of the patient also suffered from pseudologia, and this case had an excellent outcome when they were separated.

In a paper by Casey and Corcoran (1989) entitled "An unusual variant of folie a deux?", they described a case which at first appeared to be a psychosis in the wife with the husband believing what appeared to be delusion. When they separated, their folie a deux remitted, and it was eventually felt this was a case of pathological lying by the wife, with the husband accepting the lies.

The relationship of pseudologia fantastica and Munchausen's syndrome was discussed in an original paper by Asher (1951), in which he described the syndrome and pathological lying was a significant feature. In a recent paper by Geracioti et al. (1987), they stated that the eponym, Munchausen's syndrome, was applied by Asher to describe a syndrome complex characterized by the dramatic but plausible presentation of acute illness that is found to be factitious, and is accompanied by pathological lying and rootless wandering from hospital to hospital. In several other reports of Munchausen's syndrome, the authors emphasize pathological lying as a syndrome.

The relationship between daydreaming, pathological lying, confabulation and delusion needs to be further researched. Kronfeld (1927) concluded that the daydreamer falsifies the environment for himself, whilst the pathological liar falsifies himself for the environment. The daydreamer deceives himself alone, but the pathological liar deceives others and he deceives himself as a secondary effect. Many authors have suggested that pathological lying requires a good deal of personal vigor as well as imagination. Daydreaming has been described by Kaplan et al. (1975) as a fantasy which is a mental representation of a scene or occurrence that is recognized as unreal but is either expected or hoped for. It has been divided into two types: creative fantasy that prepares for some later action (i.e., becoming a reality), and daydream fantasy which is a refuge for wishes that cannot be fulfilled. The daydreamer is aware that his fantasy is not real.

Pathological lying is falsification disproportionate to any discernible end in view. Confabulation is the unconscious filling in of memory gaps by imagined experience. Their recollections change from moment to moment and are easily influenced by suggestion. Delusion is a false belief that arises without appropriate external stimulation and that is maintained unshakably in the face of reason. The belief is not held by other members of the patient's sociocultural and educational group. In those four different areas of psychopathology, the common factor is the falsification of mental content. The difference may be the underlying reason for this (e.g., the daydreamer has wishes that could be fulfilled); the delusion is the result of a psychotic process. The question to be asked is whether there is a link between these processes, and further research is needed to explore this more adequately.

PSEUDOLOGIA FANTASTICA AND OTHER DISORDERS

Another question that has to be asked is whether pathological lying is an entity in its own right, or whether it is a co-morbid process or even a symptom of another diagnosis. If the literature is reviewed, it will be seen that from the early German literature, there has nearly always been another diagnosis associated with pathological lying. Delbreuck (1891) stated that pathological lying could be found in every conceivable form of mental disturbance, even in general paralysis and mania. Pseudologia fantastica, in the borderline patient, was reported by Snyder (1986), and four cases were reported. The *Diagnostic and Statistical Manual III* and *IV*, state that the diagnosis of antisocial personality disorder, includes as criteria deceitfulness and repeated lying. This suggests that pathological lying may be a symptom of a disease entity and not a disease in its own right.

A similar argument could be made regarding Munchausen's syndrome, where it is stated that it is part of the syndrome. In a paper entitled "A case of pseudologia fantastica with antisocial personality disorder," Weston & Dalby (1991) described a male subject who had both of these conditions. Other cases have been reported associated with histrionic personality (Kernberg, 1986). Goldberg (1973) suggested that the narcissistic personalities often rearrange the facts of the external world to meet their internal needs. It could be assumed that lying would not be expected in compulsive personality disorders; however, Dickes (1968) pointed out that there is a close relationship between secrecy and lying, and the keeping of secrets can be viewed as a compulsive withholding of mental activity.

Pseudologia fantastica is a fascinating disorder with many forensic implications, as the telling of truth is so important in court cases. Since 1891, when it was first reported, until the present, the disorder has not achieved the type of recognition and amount of research and study it deserves. It is possible that it may become an historic concept reflective of psychiatric practice in the twentieth century, or it could become better understood and used regularly in understanding some types of criminal defendants in the twenty-first century. Hopefully this chapter will make a modest contribution towards the latter.

REFERENCES

Allen, V. L., & Atkinson, M. L. (1978). Encoding of nonverbal behavior by high achieving and low-achieving children. *Journal of Educational Psychology, 70,* 298.

Aschaffenburg, G. (1914). Pseudologia phantastica. *Archives of Psychiatry and Neurology, 54,* 89.

Asher, R. (1951). Munchausen's syndrome. *Lancet, February,* 339.

Baeyer, W. von. (1935). *Family histories of psychopathic liars and swindlers.* Leipzig.

Berlyne, N. (1972). Confabulation. *British Journal of Psychiatry, 120,* 31.

Bonhoeffer, K. (1904, 1972). Der Korsakowsche Symptomenkomplex in seinen Beziehungen zu den verschiedenen Krankheitsformen. *Allg. Z. Psychiat, 61,* 744.

Burt, C. (1938). Children's lies. *Burt, C. the young delinquent.* New York: Appleton Century.

Casey, P., & Corcoran, F. (1989). An unusual variant of folie a deux?. *Irish Journal of Psychological Medicine, 6,* 44.

Delbreuck, A. (1891). *Pathological lying and abnormal swindling.* Stuttgart.

Deutsch, H. (1982). On the pathological lie (Pseudologia Phantastica). *Journal of the American Academy of Psychoanalysis, 10,* 369.

Diagnostic and Statistical Manual of Mental Disorders, Second Edition (1968). Washington, D.C.: American Psychiatric Association.

Diagnostic and Statistical Manual of Mental Disorders III, Third Edition (1980). Washington, D.C.: American Psychiatric Association.

Diagnostic and Statistical Manual of Mental Disorders, Third Edition, Revised (1987). Washington, D.C.: American Psychiatric Association.

Diagnostic and Statistical Manual of Mental Disorders IV (1994). Washington, D.C.: American Psychiatric Association.

Diagnostic and Statistical Manual of Mental Disorders IV–TR (2000). Washington, D.C.: American Psychiatric Association.

Dickes, R. (1986). Some observations on lying, a derivative of secrecy. *Journal of Hillside Hospital*, *17*, 93.

Dorland's Illustrated Medical Dictionary, 27th Edition (1988). New York: Harcourt Brace Jovanovich.

Ekman, P. (1989). *Why kids lie: How parents can encourage truthfulness*. New York: Charles Scribner & Sons.

Ekstein, R., & Caruth, E. (1972). Keeping secrets. *Tactics and Techniques in Psychoanalytic Therapy*. P. L. Giovacchini, (Ed.). New York: Science House.

Fenichel, O. (1955). The economics of pseudologia fantastica. *The Collected Paper of Otto Fenichel*. New York: Norton.

Ford, C. V. (1996). *Lies, lies, lies: The psychology of deceit*. Washington D.C.: American Psychiatric Association Press.

Ford, C. V., King, B. H., & Hollender, M. H. (1988). Lies and liars: Psychiatric aspects of prevarication. *American Journal of Psychiatry*, *145*, 5.

Freud, A. (1972). *Normality and pathology in childhood: Assessment and development*. New York: International Universities Press.

Georgiade, C. (1938). Originile magice ale minciunii si geneza gandirii (Magic as the origin of lying and the genesis of thought) *Stud Cercet. Acad. Romana*, *34*, 294.

Geracioti, T. D., Van Dyke, C., Mueller, J., & Merrin, M. D. (1987). The onset of Munchausen's syndrome. *General Hospital Psychiatry*, *9*, 405.

Goldberg, A. (1973). On telling the truth. *Adolescent Psychiatry. Development and Clinical Studies*, *vol. II*, S. C. Feinstein and P. L. Giovacchini, (Eds.). New York: Basic Books.

Healy, W., & Healy, M. T. (1917). Pathological lying, accusation, and swindling. A study in Forensic Psychology. *Criminal Science Monograph. No. 1*. Boston: Little, Brown.

Healy, W., & Healy, M. T. (1969). Pathological lying, accusation, and swindling. In R. H. Gault, F. B. Crossley, and J. W. Garner (Eds.) *Patterson Smith reprint series in criminology, law enforcement, and social problems*. Montclair, New Jersey, Patterson Smith.

Hoyer, T. V. (1959). Pseudologia fantastica. A consideration of "The Lie" and a case presentation. *Psychiatric Quarterly*, *33*, 203.

Joerger, J. (1904). Pseudologia Phantastica. *Vjschr. gesichtl. Med. Series 3, Suppl. 27*, 189.

Kahn, E. (1931). *Psychopathic Personalities*. New Haven: Yale University Press.

Kahn, M. (1983). Secret as potential space. *Hidden Selves*. New York. International University Press.

Kaplan, H. I., Freedman, A. M., & Sadock, B. J. (1975). *Comprehensive Textbook of Psychiatry/III. Vol. 1*. Baltimore: Williams & Wilkins.

Karpman, B. (1949). Lying: A minor inquiry into the ethics of neurotic and psychopathic behavior. *Psychiatric Quarterly*, *23*, 3.

Kaufman, A. (1979). Interpreting testing, the IQ's and verbal-performance difference. *Intelligence testing with the WISC–R*. New York: John Wiley and Sons.

Kernberg, O. F. (1986). Hysterical and histrionic personality disorders in psychiatry. In J. O. Cadaver, R. Mickeys, and H. K. H. Brody (Eds.) *Psychiatry*. Philadelphia, PA: Lippincott.

King, B. H., & Ford, C. V. (1988). Pseudologia fantastica. *Acta Psychiatry of Scandanavia*, *77*, 1.

Kohut, H. (1966). Forms and transformation of narcissism. *Journal of the American Psychoanalytic Association*, *14*, 243.

Koeppen, M. (1898). Pathological lying. *Charte-Annalen*, *23*, 674.

Kraepelin, E. (1906). Swindling hysterics. *Allg. Z. Psychiat*, *63*, 902.

Kronfeld, A. (1927). Phenomenology and the psychopathology of will and impulse. *Charakterol*, *4*, 240.

Lewis, M., & Saarni, C. (Eds.) (1993). *Lying and deception in everyday life.* New York: Guilford.

Lutz, M. (1929). A case of pseudologia phantastica and its heredity. *Arch. Klaus-Stift. Vereb Forsch, 4,* 183.

Mack Brunswick, R. (1943). The accepted lie. *Psychoanalytic Quarterly, 12,* 4.

Merriam-Webster's Collegiate Dictionary, Tenth Edition (1994). Springfield, MA: Merriam-Webster.

Miller, W. B. (1958). Lower class culture as a generating milieu of gang delinquency. *Journal of Social Issues, 14,* 5.

Morency, N. L., & Krauss, R. M. (1982). Children's nonverbal encoding and decoding of affect. R. S. Feldman (ed.). *Development of Nonverbal Behavior in Children.* New York: Springer-Verlag.

Piaget, J. (1969). *The moral judgment of the child with the assistance of seven collaborators.* New York: Free Press.

Pankratz, L. (1981). A review of Munchausen's syndrome. *Clinical Psychology Review, 1,* 65.

Riedel, H. (1937). Hereditary indications in psychopathic prognosis. *Z. ges Neurol. Pschiat., 159,* 597.

Risch, B. (1908). Uber die phantastiche form des degenerativen irrseins, pseudologia phantastica. *Allgemeine Zeitschrift fur Psychiatric, 65,* 576.

Schneider, K. (1928). Storungen des Gedachtnisses. In O. Bumke (Ed.), *Handbuch der Geistestkrankheiten.* Berlin: Springer.

Schneider, K. (1958). *Psychopathic Personalities.* London: Cassell.

Selling, L. S. (1942). The psychiatric aspects of the pathological liar. *Nervous Child, 1,* 42.

Smith, J. H. (1968). The first lie. *Psychiatry, 31,* 61.

Stumpfl, F. (1935). *Heredity and Crime.* Berlin.

Snyder, S. (1986). Pseudologia fantastica in the borderline patient. *American Journal of Psychiatry, 143,* 1287.

Wendt, E. (1911). Pseudologia phantastica. *Allg. Z. Psychiat., 68,* 481.

Wenger-Kunz, M. (1920). Some case histories of pseudologia phantastica. *Z. ges Neurol. Psychiat., 53,* 263.

Weston, W. A., & Dalby, J. T. (1991). A case of pseudologia fantastica with antisocial personality disorder. *Canadian Journal of Psychiatry, 36,* 612.

Whitty, C. W. M., & Lewin, W. (1957). Vivid day dreaming: An unusual form of confusion following anterior cingulectomy. *Brain, 80,* 72.

Whitty, C. W. M., & Lewin, W. (1960). Korsakoff syndrome in the post-cingulectomy state. *Brain, 83,* 648.

Wiersma, D. (1933). On pathological lying. *Character and Personality, 1,* 48.

Wile, I. S. (1942). Lying as a biological and social phenomenon. *Nervous Child, 1,* 293.

Wigmore, J. H. (1913). *The principles of judicial proof.* Boston: Little, Brown.

Winnicott, D. W. (1960). Ego distortion in terms of true and false self. *The maturational processes and the facilitating environment.* London: Hogarth Press.

SECTION III
BORDERLINE AND
PSYCHOTIC DISORDERS

INTRODUCTION TO SECTION III

Section Three is comprised of five chapters that highlight different types of psychopathology often considered falling within the borderline or psychotic spectrum. In Chapter 11, James A. Cocores, Louis B. Schlesinger, and V. Blair Mesa review Ganser's syndrome (sometimes called prison psychosis). Ganser's syndrome, mainly noted by the symptom of giving approximate answers, was first described in 1897 and has been cited throughout the literature since then. The authors discuss the symptom of approximate answers versus malingering, and they also analyze the various symptoms of dissociation, delirium, hallucinations, conversion, and other associated features often found in individuals with Ganser's syndrome. Issues of classification are reviewed as well as possible etiological factors, including more recent research suggesting a strong neurobiological component. Brief case reports are included along with the discussion of differential diagnosis and some treatment issues.

In Chapter 12, Sheilagh Hodgins, Jari Tiihonen, and Deborah Ross, discuss the consequences of conduct disorder for males who develop schizophrenia. In this empirically oriented chapter, the authors review the accumulated evidence which indicate that individuals who develop schizophrenia are at increased risk for having conduct disorder as adolescents, at risk for nonviolent offending, at high risk for violent offending, and an even higher risk to commit homicide. Issues involving the childhood characteristics of the families of origin, the consequences of adolescent conduct disorder in adulthood, the implications for subsequent substance abuse, and how psychiatric services can interact with such individuals are all covered in this chapter. The authors believe that the results of the research suggests that conduct disorder is a distinct comorbid disorder that runs parallel to the cause of schizophrenia. Limitations of the research are reviewed, along with implications for further study.

George Serban examines dissociative identity disorder (multiple personality disorder) and its relationship to crime in Chapter 13. The author reviews the concept of dissociative identity disorder (i.e., the existence within one person of two or more distinct personalities) and the many problems with the diagnosis both in general clinical as well as forensic populations. Dr. Serban considers issues of hypnosis, sexual abuse, the psychodynamics of altered personalities, relationships between DID and psychiatric disorders, as well as a discussion of some unusual and atypical cases. The whole issue of malingering, so important in forensic cases, is covered throughout this interesting chapter. There is a concluding discussion of the necessary clinical skills of the practitioner which are needed in order to avoid possible pitfalls, so common in making an erroneous diagnosis, particularly within a forensic context.

In Chapter 14, Landy F. Sparr discusses forensic issues associated with post-traumatic stress disorder. Post-traumatic stress disorder is the development of characteristic symptoms following a severe trauma, such as reexperiencing the event through intrusive memories. Diagnostic problems are reviewed along with the relationship of PTSD to legal issues such as criminal responsibility, insanity, diminished capacity, and self-defense. PTSD and memory, mitigation used in sentencing, expert witness testimony, and the necessary use of retrospective forensic assessment are all covered. Like many other areas of forensic practice, the diagnosis of PTSD can be misused and those professionals who testify in PTSD cases must be aware of the potential abuses of the diagnosis in order for them to effectively aid in the judicial process.

The concluding chapter of the book is on the assessment of malingering in criminal settings, a major issue in forensic practice. The assessment of malingering is certainly a necessary component in all forensic evaluations, since the defendant frequently has a vested interest in portraying himself in one way or another. Karen L. Salekin and Richard Rogers review the importance of accurate clinical assessments within a forensic context, often compounded by the problems of malingering. The chapter covers the important issue of base rates, the overall assessment of malingering, and carefully reviews various measures of feigned mental disorders and feigned cognitive impairment. The authors also caution the forensic evaluator about overemphasiz-

ing malingering in criminal settings. The chapter concludes by applying the findings to the assessment of malingering in the evaluation of
competency. Chapter 15 is particularly appropriate to close this book
since so many prior chapters involved psychopathology where issues
of careful diagnosis and possible feigning of symptoms figured in so
prominently.

Chapter 11

GANSER'S SYNDROME, PRISON PSYCHOSIS, AND RARE DISSOCIATIVE STATES

JAMES A. COCORES, LOUIS B. SCHLESINGER, AND V. BLAIR MESA

Over a hundred years have passed since Dr. Siegbert Joseph Marie Ganser presented a lecture at the Assembly of Central German Psychiatrists and Neurologists in Halle. On the 23rd of October, 1897, Ganser described a unique cluster of symptoms that he had observed in a number of prisoners. The mosaic of psychological manifestations consisted of approximate answers, clouding of consciousness, somatic conversion, and hallucinations. The presentation of multiple and varied psychological symptoms followed severe psychological stress and was of brief duration with subsequent amnesia for the episode. Ganser believed the outstanding feature of his syndrome was the prisoners' giving approximate answers to questions.

APPROXIMATE ANSWERS

Giving approximate answers has always been the symptom most pathognomonic of Ganser's syndrome. Without the seemingly calculated near-miss responses to questions, the syndrome probably would not have been reported because the other manifestations are not that distinctive. Ganser (1898) described the symptom of approximate answers: [Giving approximate answers is] "the most obvious sign which [patients] present [and] consists of their inability to answer correctly the simplest questions which are asked of them, even though by

236

many of their answers they indicate that they have grasped, in a large part, the sense of the question, and in their answers they betray at once a baffling ignorance and a surprising lack of knowledge which they most assuredly once possessed, or still possess. . . ." The following are examples of questions and approximate answers: Question: $2 + 2 = ?$ Answer: 5, Question: watch shows 9:10–What time is it? Answer: 2:45, Question: How many legs does an elephant have? Answer: 5, Question: shows a key–What is this? Answer: a revolver, Question: $4 - 1 = ?$ Answer: 5. Approximate answers are often interspersed with correct responses, and the patient's affect is often incongruent with the near-miss, tongue-in-cheek responses. By 1904, Ganser had seen more than 20 such cases, which occurred more frequently than he had first thought. He reported that the patients were not surprised or irritated by the stupidest questions or at the low estimate of their intelligence implied by their answers.

Ganser believed such patients deliberately "pass over" the correct answer and choose a false, but close, amusing response. Ganser was aware that his peculiar patients may have been responding in an approximate fashion in order to avoid being transferred back to prison or, in one case, to an equally stressful environment. Although all Ganser's patients were male, giving approximate answers is not exclusive to male prisoners. Weiner and Braiman (1955) found approximate answers to be not as uncommon in civilian hospitals as had been believed, and their nonprisoners were predominantly female at a ratio of 4:1.

Many articles have described terminology related to approximate answers. Goldin and MacDonald (1955) stated that the symptom of approximate answers may have originally been identified five years before Ganser's report and labeled *Vorbeireden*, which translates as "talking past the point" and "talking beside the point." Goldin and MacDonald also pointed out that the word *Vorbeireden* does not appear in Ganser's original 1898 article or in his 1904 follow-up article. Ganser used the word *Vorbeigehen* which translates as "passing by" the correct answer and giving one near it. Tyndel (1956) added the term *paralogia* to the descriptive mix. He reviewed paralogia as a "condition in which the patient's reply shows the question has been understood, but in which the answer, because of defective reasoning, is erroneous, due to the . . . thinking to which the schizophrenic is particularly given."

The most prominent theory behind the etiology of approximate answers is that the patient is exhibiting his or her own generic conception or interpretation of mental illness without having accurate knowledge of the symptoms associated with specific types of mental disorders. Goldin and MacDonald (1955) considered approximate answers as "the layman's imperfect notion of madness." Whitlock (1967) found that Ganser's syndrome symptoms without clouding of consciousness are likely to occur in "intellectually dull persons [who find themselves] in social difficulties." Intellectually dull individuals are likely to lack sophistication in their conceptualization of mental illness, and their simple-minded understanding could, in part, explain the approximate answers given by Ganser's 1890s patients. It also may help explain the current low incidence of Ganser's syndrome despite the significant rise in the prison population and in post-traumatic stress in today's more populated world.

GIVING APPROXIMATE ANSWERS AS MALINGERING

Immediately after describing the symptom of approximate answers in his 1898 article, Ganser introduced the possibility of malingering. Ganser suspected malingering because most of the cases he isolated were criminals transferred to the hospital from prison. The approximate answers themselves seemed fabricated and raised the question of malingering more than any other symptom in the syndrome presentation. But the presence of approximate answers within animated individuals who seem to be responding to auditory and visual hallucinations can appear real. One of Ganser's patient's "vivid" affect fluctuated, as a result of hallucinations, from tense to anxious to insecure in a way "which absolutely could not arouse the suspicion of deliberateness or artificiality." Ganser's patients were also delirious, and many of their responses indicating disorientation to time, person, and place were not "approximately" incorrect. An obvious secondary gain was present in each of Ganser's original patients, but, according to Ganser, unquestionable mental illness was also present along with the approximate answers. Ganser did not believe any of his cases was malingering, and he was not inexperienced regarding prisoner manipulation as a way to transfer out of jail. Ganser believed this variety of prison psychosis was genuine. Also, as Schneuder and Klosinski (1989) astutely pointed out, Ganser was Emil Kraepelin's successor in Dresden.

Another argument against malingering is that all Ganser's patients were dissociated; they later had no recollection of the symptoms they had exhibited, and they had also lost a block of time. Ingraham and Moriarty (1967) believed that if Ganser's patients were malingering, they were "doing a terrible job of it in that their ludicrous childlike behavior and approximate answers immediately suggest the possibility of faking." They pointed out that Ganser's syndrome has been reported on numerous continents and in different cultures and that it would be an extraordinary coincidence if feigned illness from such diverse parts of the world and different times were so similar.

In addition to the symptom of approximate answers, Ganser's syndrome as an entity has been suspected of being a type of malingering. Tsoi (1973) studied 10 cases and was ambivalent, concluding that Ganser's syndrome belongs to a "hysteria-malingering dimension." Singh (1977) proposed definitions for the syndrome that distinguished between "hysteria" and "malingering." The *Diagnostic and Statistical Manual of Mental Disorders* (*DSM–III*, American Psychiatric Association, 1980) differentiated the symptoms of Ganser's syndrome from malingering by viewing the Ganser symptoms as "voluntary in the sense that they are deliberate and purposeful, but not in the sense that the acts can be controlled." Cocores, Santa, and Patel (1984) first suggested that the symptoms were not a product of malingering or a factitious disorder with psychological symptoms, as the *DSM–III* suggested, but rather part of a primary dissociative disorder, a position adopted by the *DSM–III–R*. The most recent edition of the *DSM* (*DSM–IV–TR*, American Psychiatric Association, 2000) again considers the syndrome to be a type of factitious disorder in that the patient gives approximate answers intentionally, in order to assume the sick role; however, the manual also notes that Ganser's syndrome is found in dissociative states as well.

Cosgray and Fawley (1989) remind us that the syndrome-versus-malingering debate continues in both psychiatric and judicial systems. These authors address such issues by identifying useful guidelines for the assessment and recognition of common malingering behaviors displayed by Ganser's syndrome patients. As with other psychiatric conditions, Ganser's syndrome can blend with malingering for secondary gain. For example, it is not uncommon for individuals with a documented schizophrenic disorder to feign psychosis for multiple reasons, including a desire to be hospitalized.

ACCOMPANYING SYMPTOMS

Dissociation

All Ganser's patients suddenly improved completely and had no recollection of any of their symptoms, including their approximate answers. One of Goldin and MacDonald's (1955) patients even experienced a fugue state. Although these authors realized that Ganser symptoms are "dissociated from normal memory," they considered the syndrome to be a hysterical disturbance of consciousness because a hysterical element is generally apparent. Weiner and Braiman (1955) reported that only two symptoms were uniformly present in their cases: approximate answers and "amnesia with loss of personal identity." Dissociation is often termed psychogenic amnesia in older case reports. Also, the amnesia is more specifically referred to as local, selective, or general in older papers. Other terms appearing in case reports include posttraumatic amnesia and fugue. Dissociation is the symptom most commonly associated with approximate answers in Ganser's syndrome.

Delirium

Ganser (1898) described the presence of approximate answers within a "clouding of consciousness." His patients were disoriented for place, date, time, and sometimes person. After dissociation, disorientation is the symptom most commonly associated with approximate answers in Ganser's syndrome. However, it is not unusual for individuals in dissociative states to exhibit disorientation or a clouded sensorium; they often coexist outside of Ganser's syndrome.

Hallucinations

All Ganser's patients were hallucinating. Ganser (1898) described them as being "in acute hallucinatory delirium" and reported both auditory and visual hallucinations. He described their affect as emotionally reactive to what must have been "the most vivid hallucinations." Goldin and MacDonald (1955) reported visual, olfactory, and auditory hallucinations in their cases. Auditory hallucinations were most commonly reported (81% of cases) prior to 1984. In addition, visual hallucinations were reported in about 50 percent and olfactory hallucinations in about 19 percent of Ganser's syndrome cases.

Conversion

Ganser (1898) reported hysterical analgesia or hyperaesthesia in his four original cases. Weiner and Braiman (1955) reported that conversion symptoms of the anesthetic, hypesthetic, or paralytic type were present in their cases. The most common conversion symptoms in published cases prior to 1984 were sensory in nature (70% of cases). Twenty percent experienced hysterical-type seizures. As with hallucinations, the conversion symptoms associated with Ganser's syndrome are in no way approximate and do not have features of malingering.

Other Associated Features

- Ganser (1898; 1904)–attention deficit, headache, catatonic negativism
- Goldin and MacDonald (1955)–depression, mania, depersonalization, derealization, ideas of reference, delusions, obsessive behavior, neurotic behavior, head injury
- Ingraham and Moriarty (1967)–alcohol abuse
- Whitlock (1967)–meningiona, postpartum schizophreniform illness, neuro-syphilis, hypomania, brain vascular defects, typhus, EEG abnormalities, Korsakoff syndrome
- Burd and Kerbeshian (1985)–mental retardation, visual impairment
- Feinstein and Hattersley (1988)–dysprosody
- Grieger and Clayton (1990)–major depression
- Mahadevappa (1990)–prosopagnosia
- Epstein (1991)–symptom duration of 21 days or less, catalepsy, echolalia, echopraxia, echokinesis, perseveration, factitious disorder, malingering
- Heron, Kritchevsky, and Delis (1991)–neuropsychological testing used as diagnostic adjunct

- Apter, Ratzoni, Iancu, Weizman, and Tyano (1993)–Ganser syndrome in two adolescent brothers
- Haddad (1993)–followed by major depression
- Cohen and Cocores (1997)–dissociative identity disorder, Ecstasy abuse
- Miller, Bramble, and Buxton (1997)–head injury
- Snyder, Buchsbaum, and Krishna (1998)–positive neurological findings on PET scan
- Refaat, Firth, and Robertson (2002)–Tourette's syndrome
- Ladowsky-Brooks and Fisher (2003)–frontal-temporal lobe involvement

THE CLASSIFICATION AND ETIOLOGY DEBATE

Ganser admitted in the second sentence of his paper "A Peculiar Hysterical State" (1898) that he neglected to study his cases in a "systematic manner." He probably would not have been concerned had he known that his syndrome would not be systematically studied for another 86 years. Ganser's guess was that the peculiar constellation of symptoms including approximate answers was a "hysterical twilight state." Ganser (1904) later took up the dilemma of whether his cases were a hysterical reaction or a catatonic negativism. In fact, the debate as to the proper classification of the syndrome has persisted since Ganser's initial description of the condition.

Cameron (1947) stated that "no matter what symptoms are being investigated, the differentiation between hysteria and malingering must finally rest on the criterion of self-deception. If the patient accepts and believes in his symptom as evidence of disability or disease, we must accept and believe in him as a hysterical patient; if he does not, we must consider him a malingerer." Here are the early roots of what later became the *DSM-III* classification of Ganser's syndrome as a form of factitious disorder with psychological symptoms.

Wertham (1949) pronounced that a "Ganser reaction is a hysterical pseudostupidity which occurs almost exclusively in jails and in old fashioned German psychiatric textbooks" and that "it is now known to be almost always due more to conscious malingering than to unconscious stupefaction." However, Goldin and MacDonald (1955) argued that Ganser's syndrome was in a position between malingering and hysteria of more unconscious motivation. This view is also similar to the *DSM* classification of factitious disorder with psychological symptoms. Goldin and MacDonald (1955) pointed out that Eugen Bleuler believed that twilight states, including Ganser's syndrome, could be produced on a neurotic, psychotic, organic, or psychopathic foundation. Weiner and Braiman (1955) emphasized the difference between the symptom of approximate answers and the syndrome. This viewpoint, although useful and accurate, may have contributed to additional obscurity regarding the classification of Ganser's syndrome as it revives the malingering-versus-disorder debate. A good general rule when differentiating between the two is that the isolated symptom of approximate answers is usually associated with malingering while the symptom within dissociation is suggestive of Ganser's syndrome.

Tyndel (1956) found no sharp delineation between unconscious and conscious mental process as did Goldin and MacDonald (1955). Tyndel described the "borderland or no-mans land" between conscious and unconscious as nonexistent; rather, he believed they are intermingled. He pointed out that the human being is a dynamic personality, constantly being motivated by two levels of cerebral activity, conscious and unconscious, and the final performance is the result of their interaction. This line of thinking makes sense when assuming that Ganser's syndrome is fundamentally a dissociative disorder. Each dissociative state has a consciousness that registers in the unconscious of the nondissociated person.

Nyiro and Iranyi (1965) interpreted their seven Ganser patients as manifesting a "psychotic state." They claimed that the psychotic symptomatology was the result of regression as the symptoms correspond to behavior in an early stage of development. Ingraham and Moriarty (1967) observed that the symptom of hallucinations and the symptom of approximate answers can occur in psychosis, neurosis, or addictions. They also believed that Ganser's syndrome represents a thought disorder caused by regression and disturbances in perception.

Whitlock (1967) found that previous head injury or acute psychosis was conducive to the development of Ganser's syndrome in many of the cases he reviewed. He rejected the notion of classifying Ganser's syndrome as a hysterical disorder and believed it to be a psychotic disorder. Enoch, Trethowan, and Barker (1967) viewed Ganser's syndrome as a hysterical dissociative reaction which occurs as a result of an unconscious effort by the subject to escape from an intolerable situation.

Tsoi (1973) classified Ganser's syndrome as nonpsychotic and lying somewhere between hysteria and malingering. Latcham, White, and Sims (1978) described a case of Ganser's syndrome and concluded that abundant evidence supported both an organic and a hysterical etiology. Reiger and Billings (1978) presented a useful discussion of differential diagnosis of their case and agreed with the majority that Ganser's syndrome is a "hysterical twilight state." De la Fuente, Hanson, and Duncan (1980) believed Ganser's syndrome reflects a hysteric phenomenon. Adler (1981) and Adler and Touyz (1989) suggested that the focus of the debate about whether the syndrome is hysteria, malingering, or hysterical psychosis be redirected by viewing it as a form of "abnormal illness behaviour" instead of a psychiatric disorder. They also clarified the confusion surrounding the terms pseudodementia and Ganser's syndrome.

Knobloch (1986) objected to the *DSM–III* description and stated that it describes "a different syndrome." Bromberg (1986) also believed Ganser's syndrome is a valid illness that should be classified as a separate entity. Cocores, Santa, and Patel (1984) presented two new case reports and systematically reviewed an additional 41 case reports in the literature. These authors suggested that Ganser's syndrome may have been linked inappropriately to the concept of factitious illness and proposed that approximate answers and related psychological symptoms are better classified as associated features of an atypical dissociative disorder.

Cocores, Schlesinger, and Gold (1986) reexplored the possibility of an underlying organic etiology and included CT scan and EEG results for one case and reviewed EEG data for several patients with Ganser's syndrome. They found that although all cases of Ganser's syndrome may be clinically suggestive of seizures, only two EEGs were indicative of seizure disorder. These authors found that most of the EEG data presented were not suggestive of any specific organic illness. Kerbeshian and Burd (1987) viewed including Ganser's syndrome under the heading of factitious disorder as "reductionistic."

The *DSM–III–R* (American Psychiatric Association, 1987) and the *DSM–IV–TR* (2000) followed the lead of Cocores, Santa, and Patel (1984), who concluded that Ganser's syndrome is best classified as an atypical dissociative disorder. Dabholkar (1987) disinterred the notion that Ganser's syndrome should be regarded as a hysterical state and should not be confused with the similar picture observed in organic brain syndromes and psychoses. Feinstein and Hattersley (1988) supported the *DSM–III–R* classification of Ganser's syndrome as a dissociative disorder. Parker (1989) believed Ganser's syndrome is being used to describe so many different disorders that it has lost all specificity: "continuing to use this term no longer serves any useful purpose, if indeed it ever did." This position sounds similar to the one taken by Wertham (1949).

The more recent literature emphasizes the connection between Ganser's syndrome and an organic component. For example, Miller, Bramble and Buxton (1997) reported the case of a 12-year-old male who, after receiving a minor head injury, developed some unusual symptoms of confusion and dissociative amnesia, with features of Ganser's syndrome. A six-month follow-up found that he still gave approximate answers to questions and was unable to perform some simple tasks (such as swimming) which he was previously able to do. This case is interesting since it occurred in an adolescent outside of a criminal justice setting, and it seems that the symptoms were triggered by the head injury and not of brief duration.

Another unusual case of Ganser-like syndrome due to cerebral injury was reported by Snyder, Buchsbaum and Krishna (1998), involving a 32-year-old male who presented with neurological symptoms and had positive neurological findings on a PET scan. He also displayed conversion symptoms and gave approximate answers to questions. This case raised questions about the boundary between Ganser's syndrome and "Ganser-like states," particularly when the symptoms follow some type of cerebral injury.

Dalfen and Feinstein (2000) studied 512 patients who were referred to a traumatic brain injury clinic during a one-year period. The authors found four cases of Ganser's syndrome following head injury, all with typical Ganser-like symptoms including approximate answers. Brain scans were normal in all four cases; little posttraumatic amnesia was found, and all patients had symptoms of postconcussion disorder after the injury. Lee and Koenig (2001) reported another case of Ganser's syndrome following some type of organic condition. These authors could find no secondary gain and no premorbid history of hysterical traits; they concluded that a "micro-embolic shower during a coronary artery bypass" triggered Ganser's syndrome in their 54-year-old male patient. Ladowsky-Brooks and Fisher (2003) reported the case of a 50-year-old male who presented with features of Ganser's syndrome, which they considered the result of neurological problems. The authors believed this case illustrates the role of the frontal-temporal lobes in the production of the symptoms of Ganser's syndrome. Dwyer and Reid (2004) presented a brief case of a 45-year-old South African man admitted to a neurology unit with a left hemiparesis and Ganser's syndrome. His symptoms improved with no specific treatment, and he was quickly discharged.

Several papers note the adaptive function of Ganser's syndrome when one wants to escape an intolerable situation. For instance, Williams (1999) described a case of an individual who gave approximate answers and, over the course of several weeks, improved. It was concluded that the patient's inability to deal with the death of his parents triggered his symptoms. Andersen, Sestoft, and Lillebaek (2001) found a typical case of Ganser's syndrome triggered by solitary confinement in a Danish prison after having been charged with having sexual relations with a 9-year-old child. The authors concluded that the cause of Ganser's syndrome was the difficulty of coping with solitary confinement as well as the stigmatizing nature of the alleged crime. They also found Ganser's syndrome to be quite rare, inasmuch as this was the only case in their study of 173 inmates who were in solitary confinement. Deibler, Hacker, and Rough (2003) reported Ganser's syndrome in a man with AIDS. They believed that there was no connection between his HIV infection and the Ganser's syndrome; however, they noted that the intolerable situation of contracting AIDS, transmitting it to his wife, and then having her leave him caused the man to be unable to cope and may have triggered Ganser's syndrome as a means of escape from the situation.

Another interesting case of Ganser's syndrome in a 15-year-old female was reported by Refaat, Firth and Robertson (2002). This adolescent had Tourette's syndrome, which made it difficult for her to fit in at school and produced an intolerable situation for her. In addition, her discovery that she was homosexual was thought to be another precipitating factor. Her display of Ganser's syndrome symptoms was so bizarre that she was no longer able to attend school, and thereby avoided the difficult situation. Eventually the disorder cleared, but not until she was in her early 20's.

Most indicators continue to suggest that Ganser's syndrome is still best classified as an atypical dissociative disorder. De la Fuente, Hanson and Duncan (1980) highlight additional important themes that are consistently reported in major papers on Ganser's syndrome: (1) the syndrome is more commonly seen in males than in females; (2) it has a sudden onset and termination; (3) it is usually of short duration; (4) the patients are not judged as malingering; (5) a history of head trauma–or some type of organicity–is common; (6) there is no history of psychotic illness; and (7) all psychiatric symptoms terminate abruptly with subsequent amnesia for the episodes. Added to this list should be Ganser's original contention that the subjects are trying to escape an intolerable situation, and therefore the syndrome seems to be adaptive in this regard.

The symptom of approximate answers needs to be reanalyzed because the world population, including the prison population, has become larger and more sophisticated in its understanding of mental illness, but Ganser's syndrome seems to remain relatively rare. Drob and Meehan (2000) argued that Ganser's syndrome is more common than thought and individuals with these symptoms complicate forensic assessments. These authors noted that pseudodementia must be differentiated from malingering, factitious disorder, and Ganser's syndrome on a number of different dimensions. The authors believed that Ganser's syndrome is unconsciously generated but could come under the individual's control over time.

Perhaps the unconscious and conscious conceptualization of psychiatric illness has become more accurate over the years. As a result, contemporary appearances of Ganser's syndrome may not always include approximate answers, a situation that leads to the underdiagnosis of the disorder. One of the authors (JAC) evaluated a 53-year-old woman with dissociative identity disorder that involved Ganser's syndrome without approximate answers but with a personality posing as mentally ill. In this case, the stress stemmed from the patient's history of severe sexual abuse. This case raises the possibility of Ganser's syndrome as an atypical dissociative disorder that is similar, in some ways, to dissociative identity disorder. However, a case evaluated by one of us (LBS) involved a 62-year-old male with Ganser's syndrome including approximate answers. He was incarcerated for murdering his boss during a dispute. He presented with a dazed sensorium and gave approximate answers to questions; he provided the wrong date (day and year), the wrong time, and the wrong color of the judge's robe. He had not been arrested previously and the stress of being in the county jail was enormous for him. These factors may have triggered the episode, which cleared after a brief transfer to the hospital.

DIFFERENTIAL DIAGNOSIS AND TREATMENT

Sigal, Altmark, Alfici, and Gelkopf (1992) demonstrated the importance of personality, psychological and organic aspects, and their interaction in the development of Ganser's syndrome. Accordingly, the clinician should avoid using only the symptom of approximate answers as a primary navigational tool, as focus on this symptom has been the cause of much controversy, debate, and confusion in the literature. When the symptom is present, Tyndel (1956) suggests not repeating more than necessary those questions calling for approximate answers to emerge.

Clinicians should also explore psychosocial stresses that may have precipitated the dissociative episode. As previous (or distant) traumatic stress triggers a dissociative state in multiple personality, recent stress triggers Ganserian dissociation. This dissociative state is often incapacitating and cannot be treated in an outpatient or partial-hospitalization setting. Enoch, Trethowan and Barker (1967) believed that the acute phase of the condition causes so much distress that inpatient hospitalization is inevitable.

Tyndel (1956) cautions that many Ganser patients have been found subsequently to be epileptic, schizophrenic, or suffering from "organic cerebral disease" and highlights the importance of EEG testing in these patients. Cocores, Schlesinger, and Gold (1986) recommended additional neurological testing including a CT scan and Brain Electron Activity Mapping (BEAM). Although neurological testing is an important adjunct, the clinical history remains of paramount importance. Reiger and Billings (1978) ruled out organic brain syndrome in their case report only because the patient was sufficiently oriented in all spheres. Schizophrenia was ruled out because of a negative family history, good premorbid adjustment, rapid recovery, and the absence of hallucinations and delusions. Ganser's syndrome can occur on any diagnostic axis. For example, Ganser's syndrome superimposed on a depressive disorder is not uncommon. Cocores (1991) referred to several case reports that described a depressive foundation, and Haddad (1993) reported one case of post-Ganser syndrome major depression.

Carney, Chary, Robotis, and Childs (1987) recommended a brief hospital stay and underscored the need for planning and persuasion. They also suggested that Ganser's syndrome has diverse causes and that the underlying illness or problem needs to be identified. Primary treatment of Ganser's syndrome involves treatment of the triggering traumatic stress. Most of these data are collected from significant others while the patient is dissociated. Tyndel (1956) suggested that prolonged sleep proves beneficial. Once the dissociative state has passed, treatment can continue in an outpatient form. The dissociation associated with Ganser's syndrome seems somewhat adaptive; the individual's coping skills and goal orientation are usually much more stable shortly after the dissociation ends. Antidepressants, antiseizure, and antipsychotics have been prescribed, but their use in these individuals remains controversial. Medication is probably best reserved for patient safety rather than for treatment.

COMMENT

More prisoners and more people are suffering from posttraumatic stress a hundred years after Ganser's report. Therefore, we need to consider why we do not see an exponential rise in the incidence of the symptom of approximate answers in Ganser's syndrome. Ganser's prisoners likely had no formal psychological training and may have been projecting their best guess–either conscious or unconscious–of a "generic mental illness." Perhaps giving approximate answers was more commonly considered a symptom of mental illness in 1898 than it is today, when prisoners have a more sophisticated general understanding of mental illness. Perhaps the beacon of approximate answers has been replaced by other, more accurate symptoms in prisoners and others who assume a sick role in order to be temporarily absolved from responsibility. Or perhaps, as implied by Drob and Meehan (2000), contemporary clinicians are unfamiliar with the significance of approximate answers and Ganser's syndrome; after all, the disorder has not been given its own diagnostic spot in the recent editions of the *DSM.*

Multiple personality disorder was relatively rare in the early 1980s, with only a little over 100 cases reported (Cocores, Bender, and McBride, 1984). Today, case reports of dissociative identity disorder are numerous. Similarly, the prevalence of Ganser's dissociative disorder may rise as our understanding–and recognition–of it increases.

REFERENCES

Adler, R. (1981). Pseudodementia or Ganser syndrome in a ten-year-old boy. *Australian and New Zealand Journal of Psychiatry, 15,* 339.

Adler, R., & Touyz, S. (1989). Ganser syndrome in a 10-year-old—An 8-year follow up. *Australian and New Zealand Journal of Psychiatry, 23,* 124.

American Psychiatric Association (1980). *Diagnostic and statistical manual of mental disorders (3rd Ed.).* Washington, DC: Author.

American Psychiatric Association. (1987). *Diagnostic and statistical manual of mental disorders (3rd Ed., rev.).* Washington, DC: Author.

American Psychiatric Association Press. (2000). *Diagnostic and statistical manual of mental disorders (4th Ed., text rev.).* Washington, DC: Author.

Andersen, H. S., Sestoft, D., & Lillebaek, T. (2001). Ganser syndrome after solitary confinement in prison: A short review and case report. *Nordic Journal of Psychiatry, 55,* 199.

Apter, A., Ratzoni, G., Iancu, J., Weizman, R., & Tyano, S. (1993). The Ganser syndrome in two adolescent brothers. *Journal of the American Academy of Child and Adolescent Psychiatry, 32,* 582.

Bromberg, W. (1986). The neglect of Ganser's syndrome [Letter]. *American Journal of Psychiatry, 143,* 937.

Burd, L., & Kerbeshian, J. (1985). Tourette syndrome, atypical pervasive developmental disorder Ganser syndrome in a 15-year-old, visually impaired, mentally retarded boy. *Canadian Journal of Psychiatry, 30,* 74.

Bustamante, J. P., & Ford, C. V. (1977). Ganser's syndrome. *Psychiatric Opinion, 9,* 39.

Cameron, N. (1947). *The psychology of behavior disease.* New York: Houghton Mifflin.

Carney, M.W. P., Chary, T. K. N., Robotis, P., & Childs, A. (1987). Ganser syndrome and its management. *British Journal of Psychiatry, 161,* 697.

Cocores, J. A. (1991). Ganser's syndrome clarification [Letter]. *Journal of Clinical Psychiatry, 3,* 1.

Cocores, J. A., Bender, A. L., & McBride, E. (1984). Multiple personality, seizure disorder, and the electroencephalogram. *Journal of Nervous and Mental Disease, 171,* 7.

Cocores, J. A., Santa, W. G., & Patel, M. D. (1984). The Ganser syndrome: Evidence suggesting its classification as a dissociative disorder. *International Journal of Psychiatry in Medicine, 14,* 47.

Cocores, J. A., Schlesinger, L. B., & Gold, M. S. (1986). A review of the EEG literature on Ganser's syndrome. *International Journal of Psychiatry in Medicine, 167,* 59.

Cohen, R. S., & Cocores, J. A. (1997). Neuropsychiatric manifestations following the use of 3,4-methylenedioxymethamphetamine (MDMA: "Ecstasy"). *Progress in Neuropsychopharmacology, Biology, and Psychiatry, 21,* 727.

Cosgray, R. E., & Fawley, R. W. (1989). Could it be Ganser's syndrome? *Archives of Psychiatric Nursing, 3,* 241.

Dabholkar, P. D. (1987). Ganser's syndrome. *British Journal of Psychiatry, 155,* 256.

Dalfen, A. K., & Feinstein, A. (2000). Head injury, dissociation, and the Ganser syndrome. *Brain Injury, 14,* 1101–1105.

Deibler, M. W., Hacker, C., & Rough, J. (2003). Ganser's syndrome in a man with AIDS. *Psychosomatics: Journal of Consultation Liaison Psychiatry, 44,* 342–345.

De la Fuente, J. R., Hanson, N. P., & Duncan, G. M. (1980). A new look at Ganser's syndrome. *Psychiatric Annals, 10,* 434.

Drob, S. L., & Meehan, K. B. (2000). The diagnosis of Ganser syndrome in the practice of forensic psychology. *American Journal of Forensic Psychology, 18,* 37.

Dwyer, J., & Reid, S. (2004). Ganser's syndrome. *Lancet, 364*, np.

Enoch, M. D., Trethowan, W. H., & Barker, J. C. (1967). *Some uncommon psychiatric syndromes.* New York: Bristol.

Epstein, R. E. (1991). Ganser syndrome, trance logic and the question of malingering. *Psychiatric Annals, 21*, 238.

Feinstein, A., & Hattersley, A. (1988). Ganser symptoms, dissociation, and dysprosody. *Journal of Nervous and Mental Disease, 176*, 692.

Ganser, S. J. (1898). A peculiar hysterical state. *Archiv für Psychiatrie and Nervenkrankheiten, 30*, 633.

Ganser, S. J. (1904). A peculiar hysterical state. *Archiv für Psychiatrie and Nervenkrankheiten, 38*, 34.

Goldin, S., & MacDonald, J. E. (1955). The Ganser state. *Journal of Mental Science, 101*, 267.

Grieger, T. A., & Clayton, A. H. (1990). A possible association of Ganser's syndrome and major depression [Letter]. *Journal of Clinical Psychiatry, 51*, 437.

Haddad, P. M. (1993). Ganser syndrome followed by major depressive episode. *British Journal of Psychiatry, 162*, 251.

Heron, E. A., Kritchevsky, M., & Delis, D. C. (1991). Neuropsychological presentation of Ganser symptoms. *Journal of Clinical and Experimental Neuropsychology, 13*, 652.

Ingraham, M. R., & Moriarty, D. M. (1967). A contribution to the understanding of the Ganser syndrome. *Comprehensive Psychiatry, 8*, 35.

Kerbeshian, J., & Burd, L. (1987). More on Ganser's syndrome and *DSM-III* [Letter]. *American Journal of Psychiatry, 144*, 119.

Knobloch, F. (1986). Ganser syndrome and *DSM-III* [Letter]. *American Journal of Psychiatry, 143*, 393.

Ladowsky-Brooks, R. L., & Fisher, C. E. (2003). Ganser symptoms in a case of frontal temporal lobe dementia: Is there a common neural substrate? *Journal of Clinical and Experimental Neuropsychology, 25*, 761–768.

Latcham, R., White, A., & Sims, A. (1978). Ganser syndrome: The aetiological argument. *Journal of Neurology, Neurosurgery, and Psychiatry, 41*, 851.

Lee, H. B., & Koenig, T. (2001). A case of Ganser syndrome: Organic or hysterical? *General Hospital Psychiatry, 23*, 230–231.

Mahadevappa, H. (1990). Ganser syndrome: A case report [Letter]. *Journal of Clinical Psychiatry, 51*, 167.

Margetts, E. L. (1960). Ganser syndrome in a native African criminal. *East African Medical Journal, 37*, 32.

May, R., Voegele, G., & Paolino, A. (1960). The Ganser syndrome: A report of 3 cases. *Journal of Nervous and Mental Disease, 130*, 331.

Miller, P., Bramble, D., & Buxton, N. (1997). Case study: Ganser syndrome in children and adolescents. *Journal of the American Academy of Child and Adolescent Psychiatry, 36*, 112–115.

Nyiro, J., & Iranyi, C. (1965). A contribution to the interpretation of Ganser symptoms. *Psychiatric Neurology, 150*, 66.

Parker, N. (1989). Ganser syndrome [Letter]. *Australian and New Zealand Journal of Psychiatry, 23*, 308.

Refaat, R., Firth, D. A., & Robertson, M. M. (2002). Uncomplicated Gilles de la Tourette syndrome and probable Ganser syndrome: A case report and review of the literature. *European Child and Adolescent Psychiatry, 11*, 234–239.

Reiger, W., & Billings, C. K. (1978). Ganser's syndrome associated with litigation. *Comprehensive Psychiatry, 4*, 371.

Schneuder, R., & Klosinski, G. (1989). Travelers in five worlds: Adolescents with Ganser's syndrome. *Acta Paedopsychiatrica, 52*, 150.

Sigal, M., Altmark, D., Alfici, S., & Gelkopf, M. (1992). Ganser's syndrome: A review of 15 cases. *Comprehensive Psychiatry, 33*, 134.

Singh, R. (1977). Experimental analysis of Ganser syndrome. *Indian Journal of Clinical Psychology, 4*, 19.

Snyder, S. L., Buchsbaum, M. S., & Krishna, R. C. (1998). Unusual visual symptoms and Ganser-like state due to cerebral injury: A case study using 18-F-deoxyglucose position emission tomography. *Behavioral Neurology, 11*, 51–54.

Tsoi, W. F. (1973). The Ganser syndrome in Singapore: A report on ten cases. *British Journal of Psychiatry, 123*, 567.

Tyndel, M. (1956). Some aspects of the Ganser state. *Journal of Mental Science, 102*, 324.

Weiner, H., & Braiman, A. (1955). The Ganser syndrome. *American Journal of Psychiatry, 111*, 676.

Wertham, F. (1949). *The show of violence*. New York: Doubleday.

Whitlock, F. A. (1967). The Ganser syndrome. *British Journal of Psychiatry, 113*, 19.

Williams, K. (1999). Ganser syndrome: 100 years on. *Irish Journal of Psychological Medicine, 16*, 115–117.

Chapter 12

THE CONSEQUENCES OF CONDUCT DISORDER FOR MALES WHO DEVELOP SCHIZOPHRENIA: ASSOCIATIONS WITH CRIMINALITY, AGGRESSIVE BEHAVIOR, SUBSTANCE USE, AND PSYCHIATRIC SERVICES

SHEILAGH HODGINS, JARI TIIHONEN, AND DEBORAH ROSS

Evidence has accumulated indicating that persons who develop schizophrenia are at increased risk for nonviolent offending, at higher risk for violent offending, and at even higher risk to commit homicide. This evidence derives from investigations of large birth cohorts (Arseneault et al., 2000; Brennan et al., 2000; Tiihonen et al., 1997) and population cohorts (Wallace et al., 2004) in which the criminality of persons who developed schizophrenia is compared to that of other cohort members, from studies comparing the criminality of persons with schizophrenia living in the community to that of their neighbors (Lindquist and Allebeck, 1999), and from diagnostic studies of random samples of convicted offenders (Fazel & Danesh, 2002) and of complete cohorts of homicide offenders (Erb et al., 2001). The increased risk of nonviolent and violent crime among persons who develop schizophrenia has been observed using different types of investigations, conducted in different countries, by different research teams. These consistent findings impel us to discover why persons with schizophrenia engage in criminal behaviors and to develop interventions to prevent it.

Recently, a report from a prospective investigation of a New Zealand birth cohort indicated that as many as 40 percent of the cohort members who developed schizophreniform disorders by age 26 met the criteria for Conduct Disorder (CD) by age 15 (Kim-Cohen et al., 2003). This finding replicates an older report from a prospective US study indicating that children with antisocial behavior were at an increased risk for schizophrenia (Robins, 1966). These observations from prospective investigations concur with results from a cross-sectional study of a large, representative sample of U.S. adults (Robins, 1993; Robins and Price, 1991; Robins et al., 1991) again indicating an increased prevalence of CD among individuals who develop schizophrenia. Consistent with these findings are results showing that among children of parents with schizophrenia, there is a subgroup, larger among males than females, who display persistent behavior problems in childhood and adolescence prior to the onset of schizophrenia (Asnarow, 1988; Olin et al., 1997).

In general population samples, CD has very negative consequences for adult life, either by leading to persistent criminality or to other serious forms of maladjustment. Longitudinal investigations suggest that few, if any, individuals who display CD by adolescence become healthy autonomous adults (Farrington et al., 1988; Moffitt, et al., 2002). Little is known about the consequences of CD among individuals who develop schizophrenia. We have found four previous studies and they all suggest a link between CD and violence. But one included only 39 men and women, aged 21, with schizophrenia-spectrum disorders and participants with schizophrenia (Arseneault et al., 2000); one did not present results separately for participants with schizophrenia (Fulwiler and Ruthazer, 1999); one examined only participants with co-morbid substance use disorders (Mueser et al., 1997); and a fourth included only offenders with schizophrenia and assessed the link with childhood problems and not CD (Tengström et al., 2001).

Conduct disorder precedes the onset of substance misuse both in general population samples (Armstrong & Costello, 2002; Robins & McEvoy, 1990) and in patients with severe mental illness (Mueser et al., 1999). Two studies, one prospective and one cross-sectional, reported that among patients with major mental disorders, substance misuse in childhood or early adolescence was a more powerful predictor of adult violence than substance misuse in adulthood (Fulwiler et al., 1997); Hodgins and Janson, 2002). While CD and childhood onset substance misuse overlap, they have been shown to be at least partially independent in predicting violence in adulthood (Fulwiler et al., 1997). Most studies that have identified substance misuse as a correlate of violence among persons with schizophrenia (Eronen et al., 1996; Monahan et al., 2001; Swartz et al., 1998) have not measured CD or Antisocial Personality Disorder (APD). Yet, one study has shown that among male offenders with schizophrenia, substance misuse was associated with criminality only among those men who did not have a childhood history of antisocial behavior (Tengström et al., 2004).

One view posits that CD is distinct from schizophrenia and that the courses of the two disorders run in parallel across the life span. This view suggests that adult criminality is a consequence of CD among individuals who develop schizophrenia as among those without a psychotic illness. We reasoned that if CD is distinct from schizophrenia, then it would not be associated with features of schizophrenia, such as age of onset and symptom presentation. However, since CD is associated with antisocial attitudes and behaviors, it may be associated with noncompliance with medication and substance misuse and thereby with symptoms. There is a good deal of evidence that the parents of individuals with persistent antisocial behavior are themselves characterized by antisocial behavior (Rhee & Waldman, 2002), substance misuse (Krueger et al., 2002), and poor parenting practices (Hodgins et al., 2001). We therefore reasoned that if CD is a distinct comorbid disorder among those who develop schizophrenia, then elevations in the prevalence of antisocial behavior and poor parenting practices such as physical abuse would be evident among their parents as among those with CD who do not develop a psychotic illness. Antisocial behavior, defined in different ways, is elevated among the relatives of persons with schizophrenia as compared to relatives of nondisordered persons (Bleuler, 1978; Brennan et al., 1996; Kendler et al., 1993; Kety et al., 1968; Landau et al., 1972; Lewis & Bälla, 1970; Lindelius, 1970; Robins, 1966; Silverton, 1988). We hypothesized that among persons with schizophrenia, it is the relatives of those with CD who are characterized by antisocial behavior. We therefore examined criminality, substance misuse, and mental illness among the parents and siblings of the participants with and without CD, and physical abuse of the participants in childhood.

The alternate view posits that CD is not a comorbid disorder as such, but rather an early consequence of the abnormalities characterizing a subgroup of individuals who are developing schizophrenia. This view is based largely on the findings that CD is more prevalent among persons who develop schizophrenia than in the general population. If what is labeled CD is an early feature of the developing schizophrenia, then it is reasonable to suggest that individuals who presented so-called CD in childhood may have a different presentation of the illness than those without a childhood history of conduct problems. This hypothesis is supported by findings from the Copenhagen High Risk Project showing that a pattern of disruptive behavior prior to mid-adolescence was associated with the development of schizophrenia with predominant positive symptoms and less brain abnormality as indexed by smaller ventricles (Cannon et al., 1990). This alternate view is consistent with the idea that after the onset of schizophrenia, CD is associated with aggressive behavior, indirectly, via its impact on factors known to be associated with aggressive behavior such as positive symptoms, noncompliance with medication, lack of care, and substance misuse (Swartz et al., 1998). This view implies that the parents and siblings of men with schizophrenia with and without CD would present similar rates of antisocial behavior, that a history of CD would be associated with positive symptoms, and that positive symptoms would be associated with aggressive behavior.

The present analyses used data from "The Comparative Study of the Prevention of Crime and Violence by Mentally Ill Persons" to examine the associations between CD before age 15 and criminality in adulthood in a sample of men with schizophrenia and schizo-affective disorder aged, on average, 39 years old. In addition, we closely tracked the participants for 24 months while they were living in the community and assessed aggressive behavior while taking account of objective and subjective reports of substance misuse. Unlike previous studies, the present investigation included a relatively large sample that is homogeneous with respect to principal diagnosis and well characterized by information collected from multiple sources. In addition, while a cross-sectional study of adults with schizophrenia cannot identify causal mechanisms related to the development of schizophrenia, we aimed to provide descriptive information useful for the development of etiological hypotheses to be tested with appropriate experimental designs. To this end, we examined the associations of CD with characteristics of first-degree relatives, age of onset of schizophrenia, levels of positive and negative symptoms, medication noncompliance, and substance misuse at discharge from hospital at six-month intervals during a two-year follow-up period. The availability of complete psychiatric records allowed us to examine the association of CD with inpatient care. Since many studies have reported dose-response relationships between the number of CD symptoms and adult outcomes such as schizophrenia (Robins & Price, 1991), antisocial behavior (Robins et al., 1991), and drug use (Robins & McEvoy, 1990), we examined the associations of both the diagnosis of CD and the number of CD symptoms and our outcomes of interest.

METHOD

Details of the method have been reported (Hodgins et al., 2003, and, in press) elsewhere. The sample included 248 men with schizophrenic disorders recruited from forensic and general psychiatric hospitals in four sites. Participants were assessed in the weeks preceding discharge and at six-month intervals for two years thereafter. Multiple sources of information were available including interviews with the participants, family members and treatment staff, complete records of psychiatric treatment, social service files, and official criminal records. Throughout, the term "convictions" is used to include judgments of nonresponsibility due to a mental disorder. Lifetime and current diagnoses were made using the Structured Clinical Interview for *DSM–IV* (SCID) for both axis I and II disorders (Spitzer et al., 1992) by psychiatrists trained to use this instrument by its authors. The CD diagnosis, however, was made using *DSM–III–R* criteria that include only behaviors and are thus more reliably diagnosed retrospectively. At discharge and at each follow-up interview, symptoms were assessed by research team psychiatrists using Positive and Negative Symptom Scale (PANSS) (Kay et al., 1987). Information on the first-degree relatives of the participants was collected from the participants and at least one family member.

Aggressive behavior in each six-month period was reported by the participant and a collateral who was in regular contact with the participant using a protocol developed for the MacArthur Risk Assessment Project. Aggressive behavior was defined as throwing something at someone, pushing, shoving, grabbing, slapping, kicking, biting, choking, or hitting someone, trying to physically force someone to have sex against his/her will, threatening someone with a knife, gun or other weapon, and any other violent act towards another person as reported by either the participant and/or the collateral. In addition, at each follow-up interview, participants were asked a series of questions concerning daily intake of medication, alcohol and illicit drugs during the past seven days and were asked to provide urine and hair samples.

Participants included 248 men with a principal diagnosis of schizophrenia (n = 201) or schizo-affective disorder (n = 46), and schizophreniform disorder (n = 1). Participants' characteristics are presented in Table 12–1.

Fifty-two of the 28 men received a *DSM–III–R* diagnosis of Conduct Disorder, 43/201 with schizophrenia and 8/46 with schizo-affective disorder. The diagnoses were made using information from psychiatric and social service files, in some cases school records, from family members, and from the participant. Of the 52 participants with CD, 43 received a *DSM–IV* diagnosis of APD.

At each follow-up, an increasing number of participants (8.9%, 13.4%, 20.6%, 24.6%) either refused to complete the interview, were too ill to be interviewed, or had died. Importantly, the proportion of participants with CD who were interviewed remained stable over the four periods (22.1%, 22.3%, 22.3%, 23.6%).

RESULTS

Childhood Characteristics and the Family of Origin

More of the participants with CD (51.0%) than those without CD (19.8%) had obtained below average marks in elementary school and only 15.7 percent of those with CD completed high school as compared to 38.4 percent of those without CD. Substance misuse before age 18 was recorded for 80.4 percent of those with CD and for 41.5 percent of those without. A greater proportion of the participants with CD (77.6%) than without (54.0%) reported experiencing physical abuse before age 12, and more of those with CD (54.0%) than without CD (21.2%) were institutionalized at least once before age 18.

As presented in Table 12–2, rates of mental illness among mothers and fathers and sisters and brothers did not differ for those with and without CD. Participants with CD had more male relatives with a his-

Table 12–1. Characteristics of participants at discharge.

	(*n* = 248)
Mean age in years	38.6 (SD = 11.1)
Comorbid diagnoses	
% With diagnoses of alcohol abuse and/or dependence	56.5
% With diagnoses of drug abuse and/or dependence	45.2
% With antisocial personality disorder	21.8
Psychosocial functioning	
Mean GAF scale score (raw score)	48.6 (SD = 12.9)
% Ever in a relationship	39.5
% Employed at least once	94.4
% Employed Full-time, not protected workshop	75.0
% Completed high-school	33.5
Psychiatric history	
Mean age at first admission (years)	24.8 (SD = 8.4)
% With previous admissions	94.8
Mean number of admissions	8.1 (SD = 7.1)
% Recruited from a forensic hospital	60.5
Criminal history	
% With a conviction for at least one nonviolent crime	57.3
Mean number of nonviolent crimes	7.4 (SD = 17.3)
% With a conviction for at least one violent crime	66.0
Mean number of violent crimes	2.7 (SD = 5.0)
% With a conviction for at least one homicide	15.8

tory of crime, substance misuse, and with either criminality or substance misuse, than those without CD. Female relatives of patients with CD were not found to have higher rates of criminality, but they did have higher rates of substance misuse. Not only the diagnosis of CD, but also the number of CD symptoms was related to the number of male relatives with a history of crime or substance abuse. The odds ratios are calculated taking account of the number of relatives. The presence of one CD symptom increased the risk of a male relative with crime by a factor of 1.2, two symptoms by a factor of 1.22, three symptoms by 1.23, etc.

Is CD an Antecedent of Criminal Offending in Adulthood?

As can be observed in Table 12–3, the diagnosis of CD increased the number of nonviolent offenses 3.7 times. The increase in risk remained significant after adjusting for lifetime diagnoses of alcohol or drug abuse/dependence or both. There is a significant interaction effect between CD and alcohol abuse/dependence such that the increase in the number of nonviolent offenses is higher for participants without than with alcohol abuse/dependence. The diagnosis of CD also increased the number of violent crimes by 2.6 times and the increase in risk again remained significant after adjusting for lifetime diagnoses of alcohol or drug abuse/dependence, or both. None of the interaction terms were significant.

Each CD symptom increased the number of nonviolent offenses 1.3 times (Fig. 12–1). The increase in risk remained significant after adjusting for lifetime diagnoses of alcohol or drug abuse/dependence or both. There is a significant interaction effect between CD and a lifetime diagnosis of alcohol abuse/dependence such that the increase in the number of nonviolent offenses is higher for participants without than with alcohol abuse/dependence.

The number of violent offenses increased 1.2 times with each CD symptom and the increase in risk remained significant after adjusting for lifetime diagnoses of alcohol and/or drug abuse/dependence or both. There were significant interaction effects between the number of CD symptoms and lifetime diagnoses of drug abuse/dependence indicating stronger associations between the number of CD symptoms and number of violent offenses in the absence than in the presence of drug misuse disorders. Participants with CD (5/52) were no more likely than those without CD (33/189) to have committed a homicide.

The mean age at first conviction for a nonviolent offense for participants with CD was 20.0 and for those without CD 26.5. The mean age at first conviction for a violent offense was also significantly younger for those with CD (21.9, SD = 6.49) than those without CD (29.7, SD = 9.75).

Is CD Associated with Substance Misuse?

More of those with CD (73.1%) than those without met life-time criteria for alcohol abuse and/or dependence (52.0%) and for abuse and/or dependence on at least one drug (with CD 69.2%, without CD

Table 12-2. Characteristics of First-degree relatives of participants with and without Conduct Disorder

	Diagnosis of Conduct Disorder			Odds ratio for number of Conduct Disorder symptoms
	Present	Absent		
Mean number of fathers and brothers with				
Criminal record	0.51 (SD = 0.71)	0.20 (SD = 0.59)	X^2 (1, N = 231) = 6.75[a], p = .009	1.20[b] (1.08, 1.33)
Substance abuse	0.90 (SD = 0.94)	0.50 (SD = 0.80)	X^2 (1, N = 234) = 6.49[a], p = .011	1.12[c] (1.03–1.22)
% With relatives with either a criminal record and/or substance abuse	32.7%	13.0%	X^2 (1, N = 233) = 7.85, p = .005	1.246[d] (1.078, 1.441)
Mean numbers of mothers and sisters with				
Criminal record	0.15 (SD = 0.46)	0.05 (SD = 0.23)	X^2 (1, N = 235) = 3.11[a], p = .078	1.14[e] (0.95, 1.37)
Substance abuse	0.46 (SD = 0.68)	0.20 (SD = 0.58)	X^2 (1, N = 238) = 5.43[a], p = .020	1.11[f] (1.00, 1.23)
% With relatives with either a criminal record and/or substance abuse	6.0%	4.3%	X^2 (1, N = 238) = 0.20, p = .656	1.131[g] (0.893, 1.432)
Father mentally ill	15.4%	15.3%	X^2 (1, N = 248) = 0.00, p = .989	1.019[h] (0.870, 1.193)
Mother mentally ill	30.8%	26.5%	X^2 (1, N = 248) = 0.36, p = .546	1.070[i] (0.943, 1.215)
Brothers mentally ill	18.6%	18.4%	X^2 (1, N = 156) = 0.05, p = .820	
Sisters mentally ill	19.4%	14.2%	X^2 (1, N = 177) = 0.40, p = .528	

[a] Likelihood ratio test.
[b] Likelihood ratio test X^2 (1, N = 224) = 11.20, p = 0.001.
[c] Likelihood ratio test X^2 (1, N = 227) = 6.48, p = 0.011.
[d] Likelihood ratio test X^2 (1, N = 226) = 8.41, p = 0.004.
[e] Likelihood ratio test X^2 (1, N = 228) = 1.69, p = 0.194.
[f] Likelihood ratio test X^2 (1, N = 231) = 3.60, p = 0.058.
[g] Likelihood ratio test X^2 (1, N = 231) = 0.94, p = 0.332.
[h] Likelihood ratio test X^2 (1, N = 241) = 0.05, p = 0.818.
[i] Likelihood ratio test X^2 (1, N = 241) = 1.07, p = 0.300.

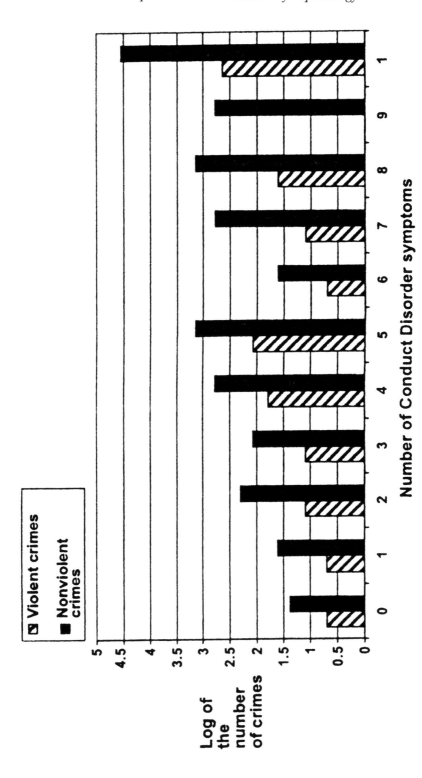

Figure 12–1. Number of nonviolent and violent crimes in adulthood
as a function of the number of Conduct Disorder symptoms before age 15.

38.8%).

During the two-year period under study, alcohol use was defined by self-report. Illicit drug use was defined very strictly, by self-report or drugs detected in urine or hair, or refusals to provide samples of urine or hair in any of the four interviews. Neither the diagnosis of CD nor the number of CD symptoms was related to either alcohol or drug use. In the fourth six-month period, there was initially a weak association of the number of CD symptoms and drug use. These associations disappeared once the Bonferonni correction was applied to adjust for multiple comparisons, as did one association with the CD diagnosis and drug use at the fourth interview.

Is CD an Antecedent of Aggressive Behavior in Adulthood?

The percentages of participants who were reported to have engaged in aggressive behavior during each six-month period was low (7.5%, 8.9%, 8.3%, 10.3%). There was no evidence that aggressive behavior in one period was related to participation in the subsequent interview. As presented in Table 12–4, the diagnosis of CD and the number of CD symptoms increased the risk of aggressive behavior during the 24-month follow-up period. The diagnosis of CD increased the risk of aggressive behavior by a factor of 2, and the increase remained after controlling for lifetime diagnosis of alcohol abuse and/or dependence, alcohol and drug use during the follow-up period, depot medication or self-reported medication compliance, and obligatory care. The diagnosis of CD did not predict aggressive behavior, however, once we controlled for lifetime diagnosis of drug abuse and/or dependence diagnosis. Each CD symptom increased the risk of aggressive behavior by a factor of 1.2, and this remained significant after controlling for lifetime diagnoses of alcohol and drug use disorders, self-reported alcohol and drug use, drug detected in urine or hair or a refusal to provide a sample, depot medication or self-reported compliance, and a court order to comply with treatment.

Is CD Associated With Age of Onset of Schizophrenia,

Table 12–3. Predictions (incidence risk ratios) of the numbers of nonviolent and violent crimes by diagnosis and symptoms of Conduct Disorder.

	Incidence risk ratios (95% confidence intervals)	
	Number of nonviolent comes	Number of Violent crimes
Diagnosis of Conduct Disorder	3.704[a] (2.112, 6.496)	2.636[m] (1.630, 4.261)
Adjusted for		
Lifetime diagnoses of alcohol abuse/dependence	3.170[b] (1.755, 5.728)	2.407[n] (1.508, 3.843)
Lifetime diagnoses of drug abuse/dependence	3.157[c] (1.760, 5.663)	2.441[o] (1.352, 4.406)
Lifetime diagnoses of alcohol and drug abuse/dependence	2.841[d] (1.555, 5.193)	2.292[p] (1.305, 4.026)
CD X alcohol abuse/dependence	0.287[e] (0.107, 0.765)	0.958[q] (0.405, 2.267)
CD X drug abuse/dependence	0.576[f] (0.201, 1.650)	0.382[r] (0.132, 1.109)
Number of CD symptoms	1.280[g] (1.179, 1.390)	1.184[s] (1.105, 1.269)
Adjusted for		
Lifetime diagnoses of alcohol abuse/dependence	1.243[h] (1.137, 1.358)	1.164[t] (1.090, 1.243)
Lifetime diagnoses of drug abuse/dependence	1.251[i] (1.148, 1.362)	1.165[u] (1.067, 1.272)
Lifetime diagnoses of alcohol and drug abuse/dependence	1.223[j] (1.116, 1.340)	1.151[v] (1.060, 1.249)
CD X alcohol abuse/dependence	0.828[k] (0.709, 0.967)	0.995[w] (0.870, 1.138)
CD X drug abuse/dependence	0.936[l] (0.792, 1.106)	0.833[x] (0.707, 0.981)

a. Wald $z = 4.57$, $p = .000$; b. Wald $z = 3.82$, $p = .000$; c. Wald $z = 3.86$, $p = .000$; d. Wald $z = 3.39$, $p = .001$;

e. Wald $z = -2.49$, $p = .013$; f. Wald $z = -1.03$, $p = .304$; g. Wald $z = 5.89$, $p = .000$; h. Wald $z = 4.81$, $p = .000$;

i. Wald $z = 5.14$, $p = .000$; j. Wald $z = 4.30$, $p = .000$; k. Wald $z = -2.38$, $p = .017$; l. Wald $z = -0.77$, $p = .439$;

m. Wald $z = 3.95$, $p = .000$; n. Wald $z = 3.68$, $p = .000$; o. Wald $z = 2.96$, $p = .003$; p. Wald $z = 2.89$, $p = .004$;

q. Wald $z = -0.10$, $p = .922$; r. Wald $z = -1.77$, $p = .077$; s. Wald $z = 4.81$, $p = .000$; t. Wald $z = 4.54$, $p = .000$;

u. Wald $z = 3.41$, $p = .001$; v. Wald $z = 3.34$, $p = .001$; w. Wald $z = -0.07$, $p = .946$; x. Wald $z = -2.19$, $p = .028$.

Table 12–4. Predictions (odds ratios) of aggressive behavior during the follow-up period by diagnosis and symptoms of Conduct Disorder.

	Odds ratio (95% confidence interval)		Wald statistic
CD diagnosis	2.39	(1.18, 4.83)	$z = 2.50$, $p = 0.012$
Adjusted for			
Lifetime diagnoses of alcohol abuse/dependence	2.15	(1.06, 4.38)	$z = 2.12$, $p = 0.034$
Lifetime drug abuse/dependence	1.81	(0.88, 3.76)	$z = 1.60$, $p = 0.109$
Self-reported alcohol use	2.64	(1.29, 5.41)	$z = 2.65$, $p = 0.008$
Drug in urine or hair or refused to provide sample	2.35	(1.15, 4.78)	$z = 2.35$, $p = 0.019$
Self-reported compliance with medication or depot medication	2.10	(0.97, 4.55)	$z = 2.80$, $p = 0.005$
Obligatory outpatient care	2.42	(1.19, 4.92)	$z = 2.44$, $p = 0.015$
Number of CD symptoms	1.23	(1.09, 1.40)	$z = 3.24$, $p = 0.001$
Adjusted for			
Lifetime alcohol abuse/dependence	1.21	(1.06, 1.37)	$z = 2.86$, $p = 0.004$
Lifetime drug abuse/dependence	1.18	(1.04, 1.35)	$z = 2.49$, $p = 0.013$
Self-reported alcohol use	1.24	(1.09, 1.41)	$z = 3.28$, $p = 0.001$
Drug in urine or hair or refused to provide sample	1.23	(1.08, 1.40)	$z = 3.15$, $p = 0.002$
Self-reported compliance with medication or depot medication	1.22	(1.06, 1.40)	$z = 2.85$, $p = 0.004$
Obligatory outpatient care	1.24	(1.09, 1.41)	$z = 3.28$, $p = 0.001$

Duration of Untreated Psychosis, or Positive or Negative Symptoms?

The age of onset of schizophrenia was earlier among participants with CD (20.6, SD = 6.02) than without CD (24.4, SD = 7.91) after adjusting for age at study entry. The difference in the duration of untreated psychosis, however, was not statistically significant (with CD, M = 0.00 years, SD = 4.49, without CD, M = 0.85 years, SD = 5.57).

At study entry, the mean number of positive symptoms did not differ for participants with CD (2.45, SD = 1.90) and without CD (2.36, SD = 2.18). Similarly, the number of negative symptoms was similar for those with CD (3.73, SD = 2.25) and without CD (3.95, SD = 2.29). The diagnosis of CD was not associated with either the number of positive symptoms at discharge or any of the four follow-up interviews. The number of CD symptoms slightly increased the risk of symptoms by a factor of 1.07 (1.012–1.127) during the second period and 1.07 (1.000–1.135) during the third period, but after applying the Bonferonni correction to adjust for multiple comparisons, the increases were no longer statistically significant. Neither the diagnosis of CD nor the number of CD symptoms were associated with the number of negative symptoms.

Is CD Associated With Medication Noncompliance?

Medication compliance was defined as a report from the participant that he took his medication as prescribed or received medication by injection. CD was not associated with medication noncompliance at any of the four follow-up interviews, neither alone nor after controlling for substance use and obligatory care.

Is CD Associated With Inpatient Care?

Participants with CD were first hospitalized, on average, at a younger age (21.5, SD = 6.61) than participants without CD (25.6, SD = 8.65). The presence of CD increased the number of hospitalizations (odds 1.33, 1.01–1.76) and the number of hospitalizations with civil orders (odds 1.53, 1.01–2.32) to a small degree, it increased the number of hospitalizations with criminal orders to a greater degree (odds

2.21, 1.6–3.03). These results remain significant after controlling for age at study entry, and despite the fact that the participants with CD spent significantly more time in hospital (101.9 months, SD = 95.3) than those without CD (57.6 months, SD = 66.37) after controlling for age. Neither the diagnosis of CD nor the number of CD symptoms was related to the number of readmissions during the two-year period under study.

DISCUSSION

This study is the first to our knowledge to examine the consequences of CD during adult life among a large sample of men with schizophrenia and schizo-affective disorder. In childhood and adolescence, CD was associated with poor academic performance, physical abuse, substance misuse, institutionalization, and being raised in a family characterized by criminality and substance misuse. CD was an antecedent of both nonviolent and violent criminal offending, aggressive behavior, diagnoses of alcohol and drug abuse and dependence, an early onset of schizophrenia, and long stays in the hospital during adulthood.

Not only the diagnosis of CD, but also each symptom, was associated with an increased risk of both violent and nonviolent offending. This suggests that even at a very low level of severity, antisocial behavior is stable over the life span among men who develop schizophrenia. The increases in risk for nonviolent and violent offending associated with CD diagnosis and symptoms were all adjusted for lifetime diagnoses of substance misuse disorders. CD was also associated with a younger age at first conviction for both violent and nonviolent offenses (Hodgins, 2004).

CD was not associated with homicide. This finding is consistent with results of studies indicating that significant proportions of homicide offenders with schizophrenia have no previous history of violent crime or antisocial behavior (Erb et al., 2001), and with studies showing that CD and APD, both among those with and those without major mental disorders, are associated primarily with nonviolent rather than violent offending (Hodgins & Côté, 1993).

More of the participants with than without CD had begun to abuse substances before age 18, in middle age more of them met criteria for lifetime diagnosis of alcohol abuse/dependence and drug abuse/dependence. These results concur with those from other studies indicating that CD is an antecedent of substance misuse in adulthood, both among persons who develop severe mental illness (Mueser et al., 1999) and persons without psychoses (Robins & McEvoy, 1990).

The diagnosis of CD and each CD symptom were associated with increases in risk for aggressive behavior during a 24 month period when participants were aged on average 39 years old and living in the community. The diagnosis of CD was associated with a two-fold increase in the risk of engaging in aggressive behavior towards others and each CD symptom with an increased risk of 1.2. These associations remained after controlling for current substance misuse, medication compliance, and obligatory care. The association between the diagnosis of CD and aggressive behavior disappeared after controlling for lifetime diagnosis of drug abuse/dependence but remained after controlling for lifetime alcohol abuse/dependence. The association of CD symptoms and aggressive behavior remained after controlling for lifetime diagnoses of both alcohol and drug abuse/dependence. Three conclusions are drawn. One, among men who develop schizophrenia, conduct problems in childhood and early adolescence are antecedents of physical aggression towards others throughout adulthood. Two, despite treatment and management aimed at preventing aggressive behavior, CD symptoms before age 15 continued to impact on aggressive behavior decades later. Three, studies that suggest that violence among patients with schizophrenia is largely the result of substance abuse may be misleading, for the present results suggest that even if the substance misuse is effectively treated, antisocial behavior would remain.

Despite the association between CD and lifetime substance misuse, at their current age (average age of 39 years), neither the diagnosis of CD nor the number of CD symptoms was associated with levels of positive and negative symptoms measured five times during a two-year period. Consistent with the lack of association between CD and psychotic symptoms was the lack of association with compliance with medication. Although compliance was measured by self-report, the similarity in symptom levels of those with and without CD suggests that the veracity of the reports of compliance did not vary as a function of CD. Consistent with these findings, CD was not associated with substance misuse nor with readmissions. The lack of association between CD and current drug use could be due to a lack of statistical power, the strict definition of use that included refusals to provide urine and hair samples, or the failure of hair analyses to detect cannabis. Yet during the two-year period studied, CD continued to be associated with aggressive behavior despite not being associated with symptoms, compliance with medication, substance use, or readmission.

Taken together, the results of the present study suggest that CD is directly associated with criminal offending and substance abuse that begins in adolescence and persists across the life span and that the course of antisocial behavior runs parallel to schizophrenia. This interpretation of the findings supports the view that among persons with schizophrenia, CD is a distinct comorbid disorder and not a consequence of abnormalities associated with the developing schizophrenia. The findings of elevated rates of criminality and substance misuse among the parents and siblings of those with CD are consistent with the notion that CD has an etiology that is distinct from the causes of schizophrenia. Yet, the elevated prevalence of CD among persons with schizophrenia (Kim-Cohen et al., 2003) suggests that individuals at genetic risk for schizophrenia are more vulnerable than others to these etiological factors. Given the elevated rates of criminality, substance misuse, and aggressive behavior towards their own children evidenced by the parents of participants with CD, it is reasonable to speculate that these parents modeled inappropriate behaviors, especially for coping with stress (Jaffee et al., 2003). When the participants with CD reached adolescence and began to experience prodromal symptoms such as anxiety, they may have lacked, even more than other adolescents developing schizophrenia, effective cognitive and behavioral coping skills. The CD participants may then have taken elicit drugs, such as cannabis, in an effort to diminish prodromal symptoms. Since heavy cannabis use has been associated with an increase in risk for schizophrenia (Arseneault et al., 2002; Zammit et al., 2002), the presence of CD may have actually contributed to the development of schizophrenia. The diagnosis of CD was associated with a younger age at onset of schizophrenia, a younger age at first admission, and a non-statistically significant shorter duration of untreated psychosis. The earlier age at onset may have resulted from early substance misuse. Increasingly, a recent Dutch study (Veen et al., 2004) reported that male cannabis users were younger at onset than nonusers.

We hypothesize that the association between CD and schizophrenia exists because children who carry the susceptibility genes for schizophrenia are more likely than other children to be exposed to specific environmental events, for example physical abuse, than in interaction with highly prevalent genes, for example, the polymorphism encoding monoamine oxidase A, confer vulnerability for antisocial behavior (Caspi et al., 2002; Foley et al., 2004). An alternate hypothesis is that the elevated rates of CD among individuals who develop schizophrenia are due, in part, to elevated rates of assortative mating between women with schizophrenia and men with antisocial behavior (Parnas, 1988) such that their offspring inherit susceptibility genes for both schizophrenia and antisocial behavior (Rhee & Waldman, 2002).

Implications for Services

The results of the present study have implications for services, both for children and adults. There are a number of interventions that have been shown to be effective in reducing the disruptive behaviors characteristic of CD (Farmer et al., 2002). It is presently not known if children with CD who are developing schizophrenia would respond positively to such interventions. Reducing CD and increasing pro-social skills in children vulnerable for schizophrenia could prevent substance misuse and possibly lessen the risk of schizophrenia. Were schizophrenia to develop, the absence of criminality and the presence of pro-social skills would nonetheless improve quality of life.

The present study demonstrated that among men with schizophrenia, those with a childhood history of CD had earlier and more frequent interventions by mental health services than those without CD, primarily as a consequence of their antisocial behavior. Despite having spent so much time in the hospital, they committed more criminal offenses in the community. At first contact with mental health services, it is relatively easy to identify patients who have a history of CD. They continue to display antisocial behavior, and as well, antisocial attitudes and ways of thinking, lack of pro-social and employment skills, and prefer antisocial associates. They are usually treated in general psychiatric services, often for lengthy periods, before committing the offense that leads to admission to a forensic hospital (Hodgins & Müller-Isberner, 2004). Interventions designed to target antisocial be-haviors, attitudes, and ways of thinking have been found to be effective with offenders who do not have psychotic illnesses (McGuire, 1995), and they are currently being adapted and tested with men with schizophrenia. If successful, such interventions would not only positively impact the lives of patients and their potential victims, but also significantly reduce costs to health and criminal justice systems.

Limitations and Strengths

The present study is characterized by a number of weaknesses. Diagnoses of CD were made retrospectively. However, the criteria for CD are largely behavioral and multiple sources of information were used. Further, almost all of the participants with CD and none of those without, met criteria for APD. The numbers of patients who refused to participate was relatively high, and while record information was available for all, at each follow-up the proportion of participants who were not interviewed grew larger. No women were included. In addition, alcohol misuse was only measured by self-report for the week prior to each interview, illicit drug intake was only detectable for approximately four weeks prior to each interview, and hair samples were often insufficient to detect cannabis. Knowledge of relatives was not based on face-to-face interviews and childhood physical abuse was often only based on self-reports. The study is also characterized by a number of strengths, including a relatively large sample size, official records of crime, complete records of hospitalizations, multiple sources of information, and objective measures of illicit drug use.

ACKNOWLEDGMENTS

The authors would like to thank the patients and their families who participated in this study. We would also like to thank the following colleagues for their participation in obtaining funding for the project and in data collection.

Canada: Derek Eaves, M.D. Vancouver; Christopher Webster, Ph.D., Simon Fraser University and McMaster University.

Finland: Markku Eronen, M.D., Ph.D., Vanha Vaasa Hospital, Vaasa and Niuvanniemi Hospital, Kuopio; Aija Räsänen, Eila Repo-Tiihonen, M.D., Ph.D., Kirsi Väänänen, Niuvanniemi Hospital, Kuopio; Päivi Toivonen, M.D., Aila Vokkolainen, MSc., Vanha Vaasa

Hospital, Vaasa; Irma Kotilainen, M.D., National Authority for Medicolegal Affairs, Helsinki; Heikki Vartiainen, M.D., Ph.D., Helsinki Central University Hospital, Helsinki.

Germany: Roland Freese, M.D., Dieter, Jöckel, Dr.med., Rüdiger Müller-Isberner, Dr.med., Klinik für Forensiche Psychiatrie Haina, Haina (Kloster).

Sweden: Robert Kronstrand, Ph.D., Rättsmedicinalverket and Linköping University, Linköping, Sten Levander, M.D., Ph.D., Eva Tuninger, M.D., Universitetssjukhuset i Lund, Lund.

We would also like to thank Tim Mak, Institute of Psychiatry, King's College, London, for his help with the data analyses.

Grants to support this study have been awarded by the BIO-MED-II programme of the European Union; Canada: the Forensic Psychiatric Services Commission of British Columbia, the Mental Health, Law and Policy Institute, Simon Fraser University, Riverview Hospital; Finland: Niuvanniemi and Vanha Vaasa State mental Hospitals; Germany: Deutsche Forschungagemeinschaft, Institut für forensische Psychiatrie Haina; Sweden: Medicinske Forskningrådet, Vårdalstiftelsen, National Board of Forensic Medicine, Forensic Science Center, Linköping University, and Linköping University.

Sheilagh Hodgins is a holder of a Wolfson Merit Award from the Royal Society.

This chapter is, in large part, reprinted (with permission) from *Schizophrenia Research*, 2005, *78*, 323–335.

REFERENCES

Armstrong, T., & Costello, E. J. (2002). Community studies on adolescent substance use, abuse, or dependence and psychiatric comorbidity. *Journal of Consulting and Clinical Psychology, 70*, 1224.

Arseneault, L., Moffit, T. E., Caspi, A., Taylor, P. J., & Silva, P. A. (2000). Mental disorders and violence in a total birth cohort. *Archives of General Psychiatry, 57*, 979.

Arseneault, L., Cannon, M., Poulton, R., Murray, R., Caspi, A., & Moffitt, T. E. (2002). Cannabis use in adolescence and risk for adult psychosis: Longitudinal prospective study. *British Medical Journal, 325*, 1212.

Asnarow, J. R. (1988). Children at risk for schizophrenia: Converging lines of evidence. *Schizophrenia Bulletin, 14*, 613.

Bleuler, M. (1978). *The Schizophrenic disorders: Long term patient and family studies*. New Haven: Yale University Press.

Brennan, P. A., Mednick, S. A., & Jacobsen, B. (1996). Assessing the role of genetics in crime using adoption cohorts. In: G. R. Bock, & J. A. Goode (Eds.), *Genetics of criminal and anti-social behavior.* (pp. 115–124.) Chichester, United Kingdom; John Wiley.

Brennan, A., Mednick, S. A., & Hodgins, S. (2000). Major mental disorders and criminal violence in a Danish birth cohort. *Archives of General Psychiatry, 57,* 494.

Cannon, T. D., Mednick, S. A., & Parnas, J. (1990). Antecedents of predominantly negative and predominantly positive symptom schizophrenia in a high risk population. *Archives of General Psychiatry, 47,* 622.

Caspi, A., McClay, J., Moffitt, T. E., Mill, J., Martin, J., Craig, I. W., Taylor, A., & Poulton, R. (2002). Role of genotype in the cycle of violence in maltreated children. *Science, 297,* 851.

Erb, M., Hodgins, S., Freese, R., Müller-Isberner, R., & Jöckel, D. (2001). Homicide and schizophrenia: Maybe treatment does have a preventive effect. *Criminal Behavior and Health, 11,* 6.

Eronen, M., Tiihonen, J., & Hakola, P. (1996). Schizophrenia and homicidal behavior. *Schizophrenia Bulletin, 22,* 83.

Farmer, E. M. Z., Compton, S. N., Burns, B. J., & Robertson, E. (2002). Review of the evidence base for treatment of childhood psychopathology: Externalizing disorders. *Journal of Consulting and Clinical Psychology, 70,* 1267.

Farrington, D. P., Gallagher, B. B., Morley, L., St. Leger, R. J., & West, D. (1988). Are there any successful men from crimogenic backgrounds? *Psychiatry, 51,* 116.

Fazel, S., & Danesh, J. (2002). Serious mental disorder in 23,000 prisoners: A systematic review of 62 surveys. *Lancet, 359,* 545.

Foley, D. L., Eaves, L. J., Wormley, B., Silberg, J. L., Maes, H. H., & Riley, B. (2004). Childhood adversity, monoamine oxidase A genotype, and risk for conduct disorder. *Archive of General Psychiatry, 61,* 738.

Fulwiler, C., & Ruthazer, R. (1999). Premorbid risk factors for violence in adult mental illness. *Comprehensive Psychiatry, 40,* 96.

Fulwiler, C., Grossman, H., Forbes, C., & Ruthazer, R. (1997). Early-onset substance abuse and community violence by outpatients with chronic mental illness. *Psychiatric Services, 48,* 1181.

Hodgins, S. (2004). Criminal and antisocial behaviors and schizophrenia: A neglected topic. In: W. F. Gattaz, & H. Häfner (Eds.), *Search for the causes of Schizophrenia, vol. V.* (pp. 315–341). Darmstadt, Germany: Steinkopff Verlag.

Hodgins, S., & Côté, G. (1993). The criminality of mentally disordered offenders. *Criminal Justice and Behavior, 28,* 115.

Hodgins, S., & Janson, C. G. (2002). *Criminality and violence among the mentally disordered: The Stockholm metropolitan project.* Cambridge: Cambridge University Press.

Hodgins, S., & Müller-Isberner, R. (2004). Preventing crime by people with schizophrenia: The role of psychiatric services. *British Journal of Psychiatry, 185,* 245.

Hodgins, S., Kratzer, L., & McNeil, T. F. (2001). Obstetrical complications, parenting, and risk of criminal behavior. *Archives of General Psychiatry, 58,* 746.

Hodgins, S., Hiscoke, U. L., & Freese, R. (2003). The antecedents of aggressive behavior among men with schizophrenia: A prospective investigation of patients in community treatment. *Behavioral Sciences and Law, 21,* 523.

Hodgins, S., Tengström, A., Eaves, D., Hart, S., Konstrand, R., Levander, S., Müller-Isberner, R., Tiihonen, J., Webster, C. D., Eronen, M., Freese, R., Jöckel, D., Kreuzer, A., Levin, A., Maas, S., Repo, E., Tuniger, E., Kotilainen, I., Väänänen, H., & Vokkolainen, A. An international comparison of community treatment programs for mentally ill persons who have committed criminal offenses. *Criminal Justice and Behavior,* in press.

Jaffee, S., Moffitt, T., Caspi, A., & Taylor, A. (2003). Life with (or without) father: The benefits of living with two biological parents depend on the father's antisocial behavior. *Child Development, 74*, 109.

Kay, S. R., Fiszbein, A., & Opler, A. (1987). The positive and negative syndrome scale (PANSS) for schizophrenia. *Schizophrenia Bulletin, 13*, 261.

Kendler, K. S., McGuire, M., Gruenberg, A. M., O'Hare, A., Spellman, M., & Walsh, D. (1993). The Roscommon family study: III. Schizophrenia-related personality disorders in relatives. *Archives of General Psychiatry, 50*, 781.

Kety, S. F., Rosenthal, D., Wender, P. H., & Schulisnger, F. (1968). The types and prevalences of mental illness in the biological and adoptive families of adopted schizophrenics. In: D. Rosenthal, & S. S. Kety, (Eds.), *The transmission of schizophrenia.* (pp. 345–362). London: Pergamon Press.

Kim-Cohen, J., Caspi, A., Moffitt, T. E., Harrington, H., Milne, B. J., & Poulton, R. (2003). Prior juvenile diagnoses in adults with mental disorder: Developmental follow-back of a prospective-longitudinal cohort. *Archives of General Psychiatry, 60*, 709.

Krueger, R., Hicks, B., Patrick, C., Carlson, S., Iacono, W., & McGue, M. (2002). Etiologic connections among substance dependence, antisocial behavior, and personality: Modeling the exermalizing spectrum. *Journal of Abnormal Psychology, 111*, 411.

Landau, R., Harth, P., Othnay, N., & Sharthertz, C. (1972). The influence of psychotic parents on their children's development. *American Journal of Psychiatry, 129*, 38.

Lewis, D. O., & Bälla, D. A. (1970). *Delinquency and Psychopathology.* New York: Grune Stratten.

Lindelius, R. (Ed.), A study of schizophrenia: A clinical, prognostic, and family investigation. *Acta Psychiatrica, Scandinavica*, Supplement 216.

Lindquist, P., & Allebeck, P. (1999). Criminality among Stockholm mental patients. *British Journal of Criminology, Delinquency, and Deviant Social Behavior, 139*, 450.

McGuire, J. (1995). *What works: Reducing reoffending-guidelines from research and practice.* Chichester, UK: Wiley.

Moffit, T. E., Caspi, A., Harrington, H., & Milne, B. J. (2002). Males on the life-course-persistent and adolescence-limited antisocial pathways: Follow up at age 26 years. *Deviant Psychopathology, 14*, 179.

Monahan, J., Steadman, H. J., Silver, E., Appelbaum, P. S., Robbins, P. C., Mulvey, E. P., Roth, L. H., Grisso, T., & Banks, S. (2001). *Rethinking risk assessment: The MacArthur study of mental disorder and violence.* New York: Oxford University Press.

Mueser, K. T., Drake, R. E., Ackerson, T. H., Alterman, A. I., Miles, K. M., & Noordsy, D. L. (1997). Antisocial personality disorder, conduct disorder, and substance abuse in schizophrenia. *Journal of Abnormal Psychology, 106*, 473.

Mueser, K. T., Rosenberg, S. D., Drake, R. E., Miles, K. M., Wolford, G., Vidaver, R., & Carrieri, K. (1999). Conduct disorder, antisocial personality disorder and substance use disorders in schizophrenia and major affective disorders. *Journal of Studies on Alcohol, 60*, 278.

Olin, S. S., Raine, A., Cannon, T. D., Parnas, J., Schulsinger, F., & Melnick, S. A. (1997). Childhood behavior precursors of schizotypal personality disorder. *Schizophrenia Bulletin, 23*, 93.

Parnas, J. (1988). Assortative mating in schizophrenia: Results from the Copenhagen high-risk study. *Psychiatry, 51*, 58.

Rhee, S. H., & Waldman, I. D. (2002). Genetic and environmental influences on antisocial behavior: A meta-analysis of twin and adoption studies. *Psychological Bulletin, 128*, 490.

Robins, L. (1966). *Deviant children grown up.* Baltimore: Williams and Wilkins.

Robins, L. N. (1993). Childhood conduct problems, adult psychopathology and crime. In: S. Hodgins, (Ed.), *Mental disorder and crime.* (pp. 173–193). Newbury Park, Canada: Sage.

Robins, L. N., & McEvoy, L. (1990). Conduct problems as predictors of substance abuse. In:

L. N. Robins, & M. Rutter, (Eds.), *Straight and deviant pathways from childhood to adulthood.* (pp. 182–204). Cambridge, England: Cambridge University Press.

Robins, L. N., & Price, R. K., (1991). Adult disorders predicted by childhood conduct problems: Results from the NIMH epidemiologic catchment area project. *Psychiatry, 54,* 116.

Robins, L. N., Tipp, J., & Przybeck, T. (1991). Antisocial personality. In: L. N. Robins, & D. Regier, (Eds.), *Psychiatric disorders in America: The epidemiologic catchment area study.* (pp. 258–290). New York: MacMillan/Free Press.

Silverton, L. (1988). Crime and the schizophrenia spectrum: A diathesis-stress model. *Acta Psychiatry Scandanavia, 78,* 72.

Spitzer, R. L., Williams, J. B. W., Gibbon, M., & First, M. B. (1992). The structured clinical interview for *DSM–III–R* (SCID) I: History, rationale, and description. *Archives of General Psychiatry, 49,* 624.

Swartz, M. S., Swanson, J. W., Hiday, V. A., Borum, R., Wagner, R., & Burns, B. J. (1998). Taking the wrong drugs: The role of substance abuse and medication noncompliance in violence among severely mentally ill individuals. *Social Psychiatry and Psychiatric Epidemiology, 33* (suppl. 1), 75.

Tengström, A., Hodgins, S., & Kullgren, G. (2001). Men with schizophrenia who behave violently: The usefulness of an early versus late starters typology. *Schizophrenia Bulletin, 27,* 205.

Tengström, A., Hodgins, S., Grann, M., Långström, N., & Kullgren, G. (2004). Schizophrenia and criminal offending: The role of psychopathy and substance misuse. *Criminal Justice and Behavior, 31,* (4), 1–25.

Tiihonen, J., Isohanni, M., Räsänen, P., Koiranen, M., & Moring, J. (1997). Specific major mental disorders and criminality: A 26-year prospective study of the 1966 Northern Finland birth cohort. *American Journal of Psychiatry, 154,* 840.

Veen, N. D., Selten, J. P., Van der Tweel, I., Feller, W. G., Hoek, H. W., & Kahn, R. S. (2004). Cannabis use and age at onset of schizophrenia. *American Journal of Psychiatry, 161,* 501.

Wallace, C., Mullen, P. E., & Burgess, P. (2004). Criminal offending in schizophrenia over a 25-year period marked by deinstitutionalization and increasing prevalence of comorbid substance use disorders. *American Journal of Psychiatry, 161,* 716.

Zammit, S., Allebeck, P., Andreasson, S., Lundberg, I., & Lewis, G. (2002). Self-reported cannabis use as a risk factor for schizophrenia in Swedish conscripts of 1969: Historical cohort study. *British Medical Journal, 325,* 1199.

Chapter 13

DISSOCIATIVE IDENTITY DISORDER (MULTIPLE PERSONALITY DISORDER) AND CRIME: A FORENSIC ISSUE

George Serban

Since multiple personality disorder (MPD) has been reappraised by *DSM-IV* (1994) and *DSM-IV-TR* (2000), it has received a fancier name, that of dissociative identity disorder (DID), and a freer interpretation of its symptoms. Concomitantly, its incidence grew phenomenally to the delight of criminal lawyers, some unscrupulous clients, and self-declared expert witnesses. From over 300 cases reported in the 1980s, mostly in USA, there are estimated now, by some questionable surveys, that the diagnosis represents 12 percent of the inpatient population and 3.3 percent of the general population (Walker & Ross, 1977). In fact, according to these estimates the incidence of DID rivals that of schizophrenia and of anorexia nervosa (Gleaves & Williams, 2005). The growing interest in MPD/DID is reflected in the continuous debates about its validity as a separate entity, but also in its use by lawyers as a criminal defense strategy. Increasingly, various dissociative disorders (DD) tend to be used as a defense of the last resort in otherwise indefensible criminal cases, particularly those of rape or murder.

Basically, these defendants plead to have been not responsible for their criminal acts, either due to amnesia, lack of recollection of the act, or alleged lack of conscious control because of "another person inside of them" committed it. In the past, most of them were considered by the Court to have faked DID and were found guilty. And for good reasons, it had been difficult raising a defense based on a DID diagnosis (Coons, 1991). The main problem for the rejection of the defense has been that the validation of the diagnosis in Court presents serious psychiatric and legal issues. In order to understand the legal difficulty of a DID defense, we have to briefly review the concept of the insanity plea as formulated by the judicial system.

LEGAL STANDARDS

In general, two types of mental defenses are accepted in most of the United States courts for a defendant who wants to plead not guilty for a committed criminal act: either to offer proof of insanity at the time of committing the crime, or to demonstrate that he/she acted at that time under the influence of an extreme emotional disturbance, which amounts to a form of temporary insanity or diminished mental capacity. In cases of an insanity plea, the defendant must prove lack of substantial capacity to appreciate the wrongfulness of his/her conduct; in the case of diminished capacity, the defendant has to demonstrate not only "extreme emotional disturbance" at the time of the crime, but also that the "disturbance was a reasonable response to circumstances as they were perceived by the defendant, however irrational his/her perception might have been" (New York, Penal Law, Part 40). In the latter case, the diminished capacity defense, if accepted, represents mitigating circumstances which, at best, reduces the punishment. A plea of insanity, however, absolves the defendant of his/her crime.

The MPD/DID defense is based on a very expanded interpretation of the M'Naghten rule which permits the assumption of nonresponsibility for a crime in cases where the defendant could offer proof "of not having been himself" at the time of the crime, and yet not necessarily "insane." This assumption removes the responsibility from the defendant based on the idea of being "someone else inside of him/her" for allegedly committing the crime about which he/she does not have any knowledge.

Interestingly, in many jurisdictions the alter personality, "the other person inside of him/her," does not need to prove insanity. It could act in a perfectly conscious manner at the time of the crime. The only issue required to be proven is the lack of knowledge of the host personality about the criminal actions of the "alter." But, it is the burden of the defense to prove that "the culpable mental state" was acting without the knowledge of the person charged with the offense. This is most often supported by the statements of the defendant claiming some questionable past amnesia episodes or, inexplicably out-of-character behaviors. These alleged symptoms, when interpreted by a biased or inexperienced clinician as sufficient demonstration of presence of alter personalities, starts the problem of validating the diagnosis of MPD/DID.

Problems in Diagnosis

Clinically, establishing the diagnosis of DID is a challenging undertaking due to the difficulty to document beyond the claims of the patient or defendant of his/her extensive inability to recall significant past events, or to support the more pressing issue of alleged existence of two or more distinct identities-alters. In a forensic evaluation, this task can become truly daunting. Why should it be so difficult?

The basic ingredient present in the therapeutic interaction, that of honest mutual cooperation and trust between therapist and patient, is missing in forensic psychiatry. Defendant's motives are quite apart, if not antagonistic, to those of the clinician. The clinician, as an expert witness for the prosecution, wants to establish the truth, while the defendant, for self-protection, often attempts to distort, mislead or fabricate his own version of the truth. The situation might get sticky when the clinician testifies for a defendant in criminal case or a plaintiff in malpractice case. In this case, establishing the truth becomes more chancy, depending on many variables from clinical experience and biased position of the clinician to that of misplaced empathy.

This controversy would not be present if it were not for the subtle manifestations of the MPD/DID symptoms. In fact, according to Putnam (1991) it may take an average of 6.8 years between the first contact with the patient and the final diagnosis of DID, during which time his diagnosis had been changed many times. This diagnostic problem has been attributed to the lack of familiarity of mental health clinicians with DID and their skepticism about the validity of the existence of the disorder itself.

Yet, the doubts remain, outside of a small group of clinicians specializing in the treatment of DID. This explains why this condition, until recently, has been rarely diagnosed. Its sudden increase in frequency raises the issue of a strong iatrogenic component. The possibility of a biased selective reinforcement by the therapist of symptoms presented by the patient as suggesting DID should not be excluded. It can particularly happen when hypnosis is used for the exploration of alleged amnesic episodes or alters by either an inexperienced clinician or one too eager to prove the finding of a rare case (Orne, 1984; Serban, 1992).

In one case reviewed by the author for the Court, the treating therapist unwittingly became an accomplice of the patient, by providing him with books and literature about DID, while at the same time reinforcing the emergence of the alleged alter personalities by using leading questions during hypnosis. Researchers have shown that the reinforcement of one alternate personality could result in an increase in its presentation (Kohlenberg, 1973). However, the attempts to create alternate personalities in normal hypnotized volunteers produced inconclusive results except for inducing age regressed alternates (Kampman, 1976), but not fully developed personalities. Such changes were only transient in nature.

Problems with Hypnosis

If the consensus is that hypnosis can only create multiple personality phenomena, but not genuine multiple personalities, this does not exclude the possibility for the misuse of hypnosis in the diagnosis of DID or of other dissociative states. The false positive diagnosis of MPD/DID could be induced by the misguided belief of the hypnotist of his infallible skills in this area, compounded by the deliberate intent of the defendant to distort, lie, fabricate symptoms or amnesic states in order to mimic DID. In other cases, the misdiagnosis could be created by the leading questions of the hypnotist and the high suggestibility of the defendant. In this case, the defendant, responding to the cues inadvertently given by the hypnotist, fabricates or confabulates, with results either diminishing or removing his responsibility in the crime.

Such a situation would not occur if the hypnotist had been an experienced clinician, who had paid attention to a few basic principles of forensic hypnosis. To the extent to which the evaluation of DID offers the clinician only a discrete window of diagnosibility, the hypnotist is even more at risk than other forensic experts of producing a false positive diagnosis. If the hypnotist is unfamiliar with factitious disorders or ignores the possibility of malingering, then he might disregard the fact that the defendant could fabricate symptoms based on his own acquired knowledge of DID. Furthermore, if the clinician does not have available hard corroborative data about the defendant's alleged alters, his exploration of alternate personalities under hypnosis is handicapped. Indeed, his ability to differentiate between the true and false findings under hypnosis is drastically compromised. In view of this fact, the issue remains whether hypnosis has any place in the legal evaluation of the diagnosis of MPD/DID.

Ironically, more recently, the role of hypnosis in forensic psychiatry has been tremendously expanded. From its initial use in helping to determine legal responsibility of the defendant, hypnosis has lately enlarged its domain to that of attempting to improve a defendant's memory about events for which he claims amnesia. It is also used for improving the memory of witnesses or victims who may not remember events related to a crime, under the erroneous assumption that hypnosis has the ability to elicit truthful information, regardless of the motivation or cooperation of the hypnotized party. This approach has been touted by many hypnotists, working with the assumption that under hypnosis, the critical judgment of the defendant is diminished to the extent to which truthful information can be obtained. But this is not always true, and the Courts doubt quite often the hypnotist's testimony as not being a quite reliable way of ascertaining the truth. The reality is that people can simulate a state of hypnosis, not to mention that even under deep hypnosis they still can lie (Orne, 1989).

Furthermore, when hypnosis is used in cases of refreshing the memories of defendants about events related to crimes, the claims made by them under hypnosis could be false. The fact remains that all defendants intentionally or due to high suggestibility, distort or, fabricate for the simple reason of survival. Unfortunately, not only criminal defendants or plaintiffs in malpractice suits are manipulating the truth, but also DID patients under treatment often do so, although their motives might be different. Clinicians treating DID cases have found, to their dismay, that many of their patients are unprincipled. They may lie, manipulate, attempt to control, mislead or tell half-truths. The therapeutic alliance between the therapist and the patient may easily crumble. The therapist is pushed from acceptance to skepticism (Kluft, 1994). In forensic psychiatry, the clinician-expert witness has to proceed unbiased and review facts with a detective's mind. Most often this is not the case, when the expert witness works for the defense.

To reduce the possibility of faking by the defendant, expert witnesses thought to use hypnotic age regression that might increase the chances for elimination of false positive results. It was assumed that age regression will make it harder to fake a child's personality as an alter, while at the same time will bring out hidden alter personalities from childhood. Regrettably, it was proven that some defendant could fake the display of child-like alters, regardless of how dramatic they might appear to the outside observer. In one of my cases, a woman in her late thirties was parading as a child of seven, asking for lollipops in a chanting voice, jumping rope and behaving in a like manner in order, later on, to deny the existence of any alter. She voluntarily admitted that her behavior was faked, but she displayed it in order to please her therapist.

The most important fact to keep in mind is that the use of hypnosis in MPD/DID cases may work, only when there is evidence of dissociative identity disorder from outside sources, prior to the hypnotic exploration. This means that the defendant has to have, at least, a history of unexplainable changes in his behavior and identity for which he does not have any recollection, even though those events had been noticed by others. In this situation, the role of hypnosis is to find out whether the amnesia is faked or due to a dissociative state, or possibly caused by an alternate personality. If the defendant does not have an independently proven history of "appearance" of other alters, the hypnotist has a difficult task to establish the nature or veracity of defendant's alleged amnesia, particularly when the stakes for survival are high for him. In many cases, the defendant claims a loss of memory for events related to the crime for which he is accused for obvious reasons of denying responsibility for the act. Under this circumstance, it is naively assumed that the hypnotist will help the defendant to relive the forgotten events. To compound the error, the same approach to establish the diagnosis is used to bring back to consciousness long forgotten alleged traumatic events of childhood, which are viewed as responsible for the development of DID. Their retrieval is supposed to free the individual from the emotional trauma experienced in his childhood.

Sexual Abuse and DID

A psychiatric history may suggest that a sexually or physically abused child, unable to fight the aggressor, retreats into a world of fantasy, and gradually detaches him (her) self from the unpleasant events, which then are experienced, like happening in a dream to another self. This is thought to be the beginning of the development of an alternate personality. The hypothetical mental dynamics behind this personality fragmentation process is based on the need for the child to provide an emotional defense against the traumatic events which he/she has to live with. It is also assumed that the child is unable to cope with the emotional conflict created by the traumatic situation which, otherwise, would have torn him/her apart, as a result of feeling polarized between love or dependency and fear or hate towards the aggressor. It is not explained how this dissociation take place only in some children, when it creates patterns of bizarre behavior attributed to alters but unknown to the host, producing the possibility of DID.

In other cases, the claims of physical or sexual abuse surface later on in life and most often emerge during a therapeutic process "discovered" by the therapist. In this case, it is quite possible that both the patient may have coinciding ulterior motives of an emotional or financial nature to misinterpret facts, thereby suggesting MPD. For instance, a woman in her late forties sued her therapist of six months for alleged poor psychiatric care and sexual misconduct. She claimed to have a history of extensive sexual abuse by her father and brother in her childhood. She also claimed to have realized this fact when she suddenly regressed to the age of two to three years old. She could not offer any other proof of this regression, except the confirmation of her husband who claimed that she sometimes behaved at home like a child and who, by the way, was a co-plaintiff in the suit. Furthermore, she became fully aware of her regressive state to the age in the process of psychotherapy. However, during various depositions, she admitted seducing her therapist despite his misgivings. At the same time, she claimed that the host personality did not have any knowledge of the child alter. The host was informed later on, by another alternate personality, who she described as a girl of 16-year-old, Nancy. Interestingly, there was no evidence from any source to support her claims of either personality.

As a matter of fact, the etiological concept of sex abuse in childhood, while plausible, most often lacks objective documentation and verification and it is hard to conclude that it is the causative factor for DID. These psychosocial events attempt to explain the alleged psychodynamics responsible for the fragmentation of the personality. This is assumed to help the child cope with traumatic events which otherwise are frightening, but also it allegedly leads to the development of DID as an epiphenomenon that has its own consequences for the individual's life.

Dynamics of Alter Personalities

Another assumption is that alter personalities are taking on a life of their own, as dictated by the emotional needs that are unacceptable to the host personality. More exactly, one might say that in adulthood one might continue to operate with his childhood magical thinking by attempting to separate the good self from the bad self responsible for cooperating in the abuse (Serban, 1982). The magical pretense of being someone else is assumed to become gradually organized as an alter who has a life of his own. The alters are considered to function as relatively stable independent entities which sometimes interact with each other, but free from the host personality. These alters enact a limited role, determined by specific intrapsychic, interpersonal, or outside stimuli. They always operate within the same framework of behavior and respond to a specific set of needs, mostly alien or unacceptable to the host. It is also assumed that they process events with their own memories, reasoning, affective, and behavioral responses. *DSM-IV -TR* (2000) considers the alters autonomous personalities with their separate psychodynamics. They surface when circumstances favor their presence, to the total exclusion of the host personality from their field of consciousness. This condition is experienced by the host personality as an amnestic state.

The problem gets more complex with the broadening of the concept of DID by some experts who have suggested that quite often the alters not only lack continuity or consistency, by appearing and disappearing for long periods of time, but also they are able to give commands to the host on how to act in particular situations. The host is not aware of its own motives behind the actions. Furthermore, alters may develop inner alliances or enmities, interacting with each other like the members of a secret society or neurotic family. In this way, they can influence other alters, and they can create intrapsychic conflict affecting overt behavior. This means that the host personality, or any alter acting as the dominant personality, might behave in a manner contrary to usual beliefs of the core-self, inducing out of ordinary self-destructive acts. Furthermore, according to this theory, the conflict between alters may be experienced by the individual as psychotic symptoms.

Interestingly, this broader view of DID psychodynamics includes almost the whole range of human psychopathology as part of the manifestation of this illness. From obsessive-compulsive disorders, to phobic reactions, to schizophrenia or substance abuse, all have been considered as possible alter states of DID (Kluft, 2005). In this context, while the host personality may be healthy, it can switch to other pathological states of the alters such as obsessive-compulsive, phobic, alcohol abuse, drug addiction or outright psychosis. In fact, an expert clinician in DID has described the existence of Schneider's first rank symptoms, mostly identified with schizophrenia, as an expression of the alter's identity (Kluft, 1987). According to this view, the DID patient may become psychotic when the battle between the host personality and the antagonistic alters creates an inner conflict resulting in psychosis. In less dramatic cases, the alters may refuse to cooperate with the host personality, secretly sabotaging his/her actions.

Basically, the whole psychoanalytic concept of intrapsychic conflict is reworked around the arbitrarily conceived psychodynamics of alters which, without any warning, can come out of the recesses of the subconscious to take over the host's consciousness. The host is assumed to be unaware of what goes on at that time. Unfortunately, there are not any independent proofs to psychologically validate these fancy assumptions.

The old mythical concept of "little demons" inside an individual which are responsible for his irrational or immoral behaviors have reemerged with the explanation of convoluted psychopathological states, identified as alters. The only difference is that the host and its alters are not socially and (allegedly) legally responsible for their aberrant behaviors caused by various emotionally forbidden or socially incongruous acts with the host personality's alleged moral code. However, some alters, fixated at a particular painful period of the individual's life, may simply relive or react to those hurting experiences.

If the old concept of unconscious psychodynamics makes the individual unaware of his/her overpowering drives-needs, but aware of his actions, the new broadened concept of psychopathology and psychodynamics not only makes the individual unaware of episodes of his behavior, but absolves him/her of any responsibility by delegating it to hidden "others" within him/herself. Conveniently, the defendant or plaintiff, claiming amnesia for his action, dispenses with its unpleasant consequences by refusing to take responsibility for it. He denies any knowledge, as if the conscious alter which committed the illegal act had been an unknown guest. From the legal point of view, this is a better defense than invoking the Fifth Amendment by refusing to incriminate oneself while not disputing the criminal act.

These theoretical assumptions about the psychopathology and psychodynamics of MPD/DID may be used, at best, as a working hypothesis in the therapeutic process until proven otherwise, but they are most often of dubious validity in the support of any legal defense. If the condition is in itself "well hidden and difficult to discern" (Kluft, 2005), then how could it be the basis for a legal defense? Furthermore, if they cannot be independently documented during the therapeutic sessions, then the alleged amnestic events due to alters are legally meaningless.

Yet, what is interesting, is the fact that, in a successful therapy of DID, a seasoned therapist does not accept "the multiple realities of the patient" as a given. On the contrary, the therapist demands that the whole human being, across all alters that are brought to consciousness, accepts responsibility for the actions of all alters. In fact, actions of any alters is accessible to consciousness through another alter of the personality. The therapist attempts to address himself to the knowing part which is brought to the attention of the host (Kluft, 1994).

MPD/DID and Psychiatric Disorders

Another debatable issue is the role of various psychiatric disorders considered by some DID clinicians as part of the dissociative identity disorder. DID might be associated with phobia (60%), panic attacks (55%), obsessive-compulsive behavior (35%), depression (15–73%), sexual dysfunctions (60–89%), substance abuse (40–45%), eating disorders (16–40%), and post traumatic stress disorder (70–85%); but this does not mean that these conditions are part of the alters (Ross et al., 1989). However, some of these conditions may become a legal issue in a case when the defense attempts to use them as being part of the alter's functioning. The acceptable clinical judgment is that these disorders may coexist with DID, but not necessarily be part of the alter (Fink, 1991). For instance, imagine a drug abuser or drug dealer claiming that any time when he/she used or sold drugs he had been a different person, an addicted alter unknown to the core personality.

Legally, it also raises the question whether the alleged alter personality who was taking executive control, at the time of committing the illegal act, wasn't the host himself? If one alter is a drug abuser, while another claims to be suicidal-homicidal, and another is a pimp/prostitute, which one is the true host personality? It is interesting that all illegal acts are committed by alters without the knowledge of the host personality which happens always to act properly. To the extent to which the host personality was allegedly pushed out of the field of consciousness, and as such becoming amnesic, he is not responsible for the actions of alters. This is the routine explanation of a biased expert witness used as a major piece of evidence by the defendant or plaintiff. But this self-serving defense is hardly acceptable to the Court. Corroborative documentation by independent witnesses is necessary to support the ascertations of the claimant of DID. The arguments of some expert witnesses, that the person invoking MPD/DID as a defense, may not be able to produce past evidence of his (her) condition—due to the prior failures by treating mental health clinicians to realize his (her) emotional problems as being part of MPD/DID pathology—is highly arguable.

Atypical Cases

As if it is not hard enough to establish a valid diagnosis of DID, its problems are greatly compounded when the expert and the Court may deal with atypical cases. The most unusual problems in a legal defense are created by alleged atypical or rare variants of DID. For instance, there is a "latent" MPD/DID, when alters are only activated by a recent stressful event, which may raise serious doubts for the Court, since it appears to be too obviously self-serving. Certainly, the sudden appearance of a latent alter, supported by vague allegations childhood abusers or memory losses, is too subjective to constitute a solid legal argument.

One of the most troublesome forms of DID is one described as "epochal." In this case, one of the alters takes over the host personality for a long time, determining the daily life of the individual as if it was organized by the host itself. From the legal point of view, the question is whether it makes a difference which one of the personalities—

the alleged alter or the host personality—is responsible for the criminal act, since the clinical distinction is highly arguable. In reality, their possible co-existence makes their separation legally impossible.

A case history may illustrate this situation: John X., thirty-two years old, by profession an insurance man, suddenly disappeared, leaving behind an unrewarding job and a penniless wife with two children. A couple of years later, he is recognized by someone in a different location, living under an assumed name. John X., when confronted with his real identity, claimed amnesia particularly since he was accused of practicing bigamy. The question was whether John X. suffered from multiple personality disorder or, was he faking it? This might have been considered a typical case of an epochal alter, except he was not able to prove his case independent of his self-serving statements. Since he was functioning, fully aware of his activities during that period when the executive control was under the alleged alter, it did not make too much difference whether his behavior was claimed to be caused by one facet or another of the same personality.

The support of an MPD/DID diagnosis becomes even more difficult in the cases in which the alters are allegedly aware of each other, and the main feature is a vague loss of memory and a fuzzy relationship with the host personality with which they identify to a great extent. In this case, regardless of the alter who takes responsibility for a criminal act, in reality, the act was committed in a state of consciousness that was fully knowledgeable of its antisocial meaning, so that it makes harder to prove that the host personality was not involved. The argument that the host did not have any control over the act is questionable. It seems more likely a case of "bad faith" of the host personality, who refuses to take responsibility and pay for the consequences by invoking "another inside person" as committing the crime. It is interesting that most often the "bad" alters get in "trouble," whereas the host personality acts shocked and indignant when he/she finds out what he/she is charged with.

A case in point is the famous Billy Milligan, who was the first multiple personality case to be found not guilty by reason of insanity after raping and burglarizing three young women. Billy Milligan was a 23-year-old drifter who kidnapped, at gun point, over a period of three weeks, three students from Ohio State University and raped and robbed them. When he was caught, he claimed to be a friend of Billy named Danny, who displayed teenage behavior and denied any knowledge of the crimes. He could not explain the presence of a gun and the credit cards of the victims in the apartment where he allegedly was a guest. During his detention, Billy exhibited, from the beginning of the therapy, ten different personalities, some displaying unusual physical or intellectual skills which were known to some of the alters.

There were a few controversial issues about the existence of these multiple alters. Three alters–Allen (a con-artist), Ragen (keeper of rage and hate), a thief, and a third one Arthur (an alleged Englishmen who was the holder of the conscience who controlled for years his behavior)–claimed to protect Billy by keeping him asleep for the last seven years because he was afraid to face life. The story gets confusing when Ragen took responsibility for robbing the students but indignantly denied any involvement in raping them. Suddenly, unknown to him, another alter came out, a 19-year-old lesbian woman, named Adalanda, who confessed to raping them because of her craving for love. But the student-victim claimed to had been raped by penetration by a male. Yet the four psychiatrists who had evaluated his behavior in two hospitals, consulting with a famous expert on DID (Dr. Cornelia Wilbur), agreed on the diagnosis of DID, but they did not explain these discrepancies in his story. Furthermore, after the acquittal by reason of insanity, in the course of therapy, came out another alter who was the sum of all other 23 alters and who was the fused Billy (Keyes, 1981).

Assuming that indeed Billy had 23 alters, as they finally came out during therapy, how was it possible for him to teach the alters the range of skills–from speaking English with Slavic accent (Ragen), to knowledge of physics, chemistry or electronics, weapons or drawing– if he was asleep for seven years? And if he taught them all these skills, one can assume that he was aware of their existence and used them as a front for his illegal behavior. There are too many unanswered issues in this case that question the finding of insanity.

In another more recent case, the defendant (Thomas Dee Kuskey, a 32-year-old from Knoxville, Tennessee) invoked multiple personality as defense after killing four prostitutes. He was unable to convince the whole jury and his trial was declared a mistrial in 1999. Like Billy Milligan, he claimed to have been sexually abused in childhood with the result of developing a later alter, Kyle, a protector, Philip (speaking with a British accent), and a somewhat cultured third alter,

Tommy, a homosexual. However, in this case, the expert witness for the defense clashed with those for the prosecution about the validity of the diagnosis of DID (Bass & Jefferson, 2000).

Let us not forget that dissociative processes can take place in certain types of personalities under stressful situations. This fact weakens further the special status of "atypical or epochal" forms of DID, gratuitously offered by poorly trained clinicians. Indeed, this dissociative process can be triggered by histrionic or borderline personality. For instance, we already know that borderline personality presents many features in common with DID. Horevitz and Braun (1984) found, in a sample of thirty-three subjects diagnosed as having MPD, that 70 percent also met the criteria for borderline personality. In some cases, the borderline features are mixed with histrionic ones, showing a flair for dramatization, high suggestibility, and easy hypnotizability. The combination of these personality traits could, under stressful situations, lead to temporary dissociative states, appearing as alter personalities to an inexperienced clinician. It is also possible that these dissociative states might start in childhood as a coping response to overwhelmingly stressful events, and continue in adulthood mainly as transient states. However, is it more common for the individual with a fragile self-image to try to escape in a world of fantasy and daydreaming, or to lie when confronted by threatening or unacceptable situations?

There are other types of personality traits, particularly from Group B in *DSM–IV*, which may also lead, as a result of repeated traumatic events in childhood, to the development of dissociative responses. Some clinicians believe that dissociation could become part of the individual's coping style, in an attempt to manipulate the environment and become a permanent feature of the personality, identified later as alters. However, from either a clinical or a legal point of view, the main issue is that of establishing criteria that distinguish between true alters and transient dissociative states or outright faked alters.

Diagnostic Criteria for MPD

In order to be able to verify the true existence of alters, some MPD specialists have suggested a set of eight diagnostic criteria for identifying DID (Greaves, 1980; Larmore et al., 1977; Kluft, 2005). These criteria attempt to reduce the subjectivism of the patient or any prejudice of the clinician. Let us see if, indeed, they have solved our diagnostic concern. In order to identify the existence of two or more distinctive personalities states which recurrently take control of the host behavior, the following clinical signs should alert the clinician: (1) reports of time distortions and blackouts; (2) reports of being told of behavioral episodes by others; (3) reports of notable changes in the patient's behavior during which the patient calls him/herself by a different name; (4) history of severe headaches accompanied by blackouts, seizures, dreams, visions; (5) the use of self-referent "we" in the course of an interview; (6) discovery of writings and drawings unrecognized by the patient as his/hers; (7) elicitation of other personalities through hypnosis; and (8) the hearing of internal voices.

The main question, from a legal point of view, is which of the above criteria are subjective and which are objective. A closer study of their meaning suggests that, at least, five out of eight criteria are subjective (1, 4, 5, 6, 8), and could be claimed by the defendant without solid outside evidence. Criteria four is nonspecific for a diagnosis of DID, although, in combination with other symptoms might suggest the possibility of the existence of alters. The remaining three criteria are meaningful only if validated by other people with no vested interest in the litigation or the defendant. Criteria seven, which should confirm the diagnosis, depends heavily on the experience and good faith of the hypnotist. Important to note is the fact that most of the symptoms could be successfully faked! As previously mentioned, in a case evaluated by the author, the defendant voluntarily paraded as a little girl in front of a nurse, during the period of hospital observation, in order to conform with the expectation of her therapist, and also for "the fun of it, by fooling the professionals."

This means that a relatively intelligent person, familiar with the symptoms of MPD/DID, well motivated to succeed, could fake five to six out of eight diagnostic criteria of DID. Certainly, this is not an encouraging result for identifying DID. Apparently, this is one of the main reasons why expert-witnesses and lawyers have been attracted to the use of hypnosis as an allegedly more objective and reliable source of validation of the existence of the alters. It is still debated whether or not a patient, or in our case a defendant, could simulate a deep state of hypnosis and present alters to the hypnotist. Unfortunately, in the famous court case of the "Hillside Strangler," the defendant, with knowledge of DID, exhibited during deep hypnosis an alter personality responsible for his serial murders, and he succeeded in convincing an experienced hypnotist of the authenticity of his claims (Allison, 1984; Orne, 1984).

Further Issues of Malingering

A defendant, accused of a serious crime, from embezzlement to murder, and facing long imprisonment, if not capital punishment, may be ready to claim, fake, or play any psychiatric role which will relieve him of the responsibility for the crime. The argument that any malingerer could be detected by an experienced hypnotist-clinician is valid, but with serious reservations, as documented by the Hillside Strangler, and other cases when experienced hypnotists have argued this issue from opposite position. In addition, what is interesting in the Hillside case, is the fact that an experienced clinician was misled by some vague recalls of spells of amnesia in childhood, unverifiable otherwise, and displayed by the defendant during the course of an interview. These statements of the defendant became the basis for the hypnotic exploration of an alleged case of multiple personality.

The issue of amnesic episodes, in the past history of a defendant, or at the time of the crime, raises another set of legal questions. In most cases, it is highly questionable, the extent to which it can be ascertained, the reliability of these claims representing hearsay, without documented medical and/or other official records. The testimony of the family or of the acquaintances may be biased, or at least inaccurate. If the issue is amnesia related to the events of the committed crime, chances are that the defendant will lie to avoid any responsibility for his act.

In some cases, the alleged amnesia, misinterpreted by the therapist, has been exploited as a basis for personal gains. A case in point is Betty, a woman in her forties, unmarried, a high school graduate without a steady job who, in the course of therapeutic sessions, brought to the attention of the therapist the experience of episodes of amnesia about events of childhood. This had been "found" by the therapist to be related to alleged sexual abuse by an adult friend of the family. This "therapeutic discovery," was based on some recurrent dreams with sexual symbolism, interpreted by the therapist as related to alleged sexual molestation. The case reached the court where the accused successfully defended his innocence, mainly by debunking the validity of her dreams as supporting her sex abuse allegations and amnesic episodes. Later on, Betty admitted that her accusations were formulated during the therapeutic sessions and she never entertained these thoughts before. Now, she also thought that her amnesic periods were more likely related to the bad interactions with her mother.

Additional Indicators of DID

If hypnosis is unable, most often, to tell us with certitude the existence of an alter state, and if amnesia is difficult to prove without independent official records, then what other type of documentation is available in support of MPD/DID? There are several psychometric rating scales, such as Dissociative Disorders Interview Schedule (DDIS) (Ross et al., 1989), and the Structured Clinical Interview for dissociative disorders (SCID–D) (Ross et al., 1990), which can be of help. The latter two are interview questionnaires for helping the clinician evaluate a patient with specific symptom-verification in mind. However, as we may see, these inventories do not solve the problem of patient subjectivity, although, they may help to reduce a clinician's biases. Their main use may be in epidemiological studies. Psychological tests, like the Rorschach and Minnesota Multiphasic Personality Inventory, have also been used to evaluate multiple personality. The main purpose here has been to explore differences in psychological functioning and personality orientation of various alters. In general, the results have been unrewarding due to various intervening problems, from rapid shifting of alters, to alleged copresence of coconsciousness which is practically unexplainable. A researcher, circumventing these issues, was able to differentiate between borderline personality disorder, schizophrenia, and DID (Armstrong & Loewenstein, 1990); yet, the results did not offer independent, objective proof of the DID diagnosis free of clinician's expertise.

Some researchers believe that it is possible to have an independent evaluation of symptoms of DID by measuring various physiological reactions of the individual's body. They found that there are statistical differences between the alter personalities of a DID sample and a normal control group who stimulate alters under hypnosis. For instance, it was found that visual functioning of DID subjects and normal controls, simulating alter personalities under deep hypnosis, were different in the variability of their visual accommodation (Miller, 1989). The DID sample indicated a significantly greater changeability across alters than the controls. It was also stated that the DID individuals showed specific fluctuations not present in the control group. The most important finding related to visual functioning (esotropia) is the accommodative type of vision found only in young children, but also in child-alter states, which, if true, will confirm the age regression of the individual with DID. It seems that the changes in accommodative vision vary with different alter personalities exhibited by the individual. But until the data are replicated on a larger sample (the study sample included only nine DID patients), the results remains uncertain.

Another test which may differentiate DID subjects and normal controls simulating alters under hypnosis is that of skin galvanic reaction, skin temperature, heart rate, etc. A variability in the activity of the autonomic nervous system between different alter states was found. It suggests that the control group showed distinctive physiologic differences between simulated alter states and the host; but according to the researcher, they were different than those presented by DID alters (Putnam, 1991). In addition, DID subjects presented idiosyncratic phenomena not noticeable in the controls. Other researchers have studied visual evoked potentials and found differences across the alter personalities in response to the same stimulus (Putnam, 1984). While these physiological measures may prove the existence of DID as a separate entity, they are of little value in forensic psychiatry for establishing the diagnosis of DID. They are unreliable due to their lack of consistency and their inability to establish criteria that differentiate DID from malingering. The variability of the autonomic nervous system's response to instant emotional states created by outside stressors, or inner conflicts, has made the skin galvanic reaction and the measuring of other autonomic functions unreliable and unacceptable in courts.

CONCLUDING COMMENTS

It seems, in the final analysis, that the clinical judgment of an experienced clinician, able to verify by the defendant's history of claimed amnesia episodes, supported by observations of independent others, is what is needed to offer a credible diagnosis. The documentation of unusual, out-of-character behavior for which the claimant is unaware, might be the most reliable way of establishing the diagnosis of multiple personality disorder. The main difficulty that remains is the inability of most therapists to separate between the lax criteria for evaluating the symptoms in a therapeutic setting and the rigorous requirements of evidence demanded by the court.

For instance, in a clinical setting, a woman in her late thirties presented to her therapist with a history of childhood molestation by a brother and a rape at the age of fourteen by a brother-in-law for whose children she was baby-sitting. The therapist accepted her statements as facts and integrated them in the therapeutic process. When the alleged facts were discussed in court, after she sued her therapist for malpractice, another story emerged. According to her sister, for whose children she was baby-sitting, the defendant was found in bed with her husband. In fact, after she was thrown out of their home, she attempted to contact him again. It also came out that her whole family reprimanded her for her behavior. These distorted facts, plus other gross misrepresentations of events, constituted the basis for a clinical diagnosis of MPD/DID, rejected by the expert appointed by the Court (Serban, 1992).

Interestingly, this patient did not go into therapy with clear-cut symptoms of DID; they were discovered during the therapeutic process and integrated by the patient into her life story. This is why many experienced clinicians are skeptical when faced with patients who claim to have been diagnosed with DID based on questionable histories. If the patient is highly suggestionable, as many of them are, then the symptoms had been iatrogenically induced. In this case, the patient may not fake consciously the symptoms, yet the disease is just as fictional. This condition may require the therapeutic attention of a good clinician in order to bring the patient back to the reality of his/her true problems and emotional conflicts. But for the Court, what counts is the objective validation of the diagnosis. The justification of the criminal act cannot be supported by iatrogenically-induced symptoms or questionable interpretations of the defendant's past history that favors the defense. Any departure from an objective documentation, recorded by independent observers, makes the evaluation of a defendant's history and events vulnerable to severe criticism, thereby reducing the credibility of the expert witness.

Ultimately, to support the diagnosis of DID, the existence of the following proofs are required: a substantial history of amnesic periods related to significant experiences unexplainable by simple forgetfulness, and for which there are corroborative testimonies of disinterested, neutral parties, and also the presence of other distinctive identities, repeatedly taking control of the individual's behavior, noticeable to others but not to himself. Clinically, this can only be realized by a skilled, experienced, unbiased clinician who uses all of the available legitimate methods of establishing the diagnosis from a detailed past history and observation of the patient during sessions, to documentation based on other people's testimony who had known him and noticed his/her behavior at variance with the ordinary self. The thorniest problem, that of ulterior motives determining behavior, can only be solved in the context of the subject's life history, which might show various degrees of inconsistencies and discrepancies, irreconcilable with the criteria for a DID diagnosis.

REFERENCES

Allison, B. R. (1984). Difficulties diagnosing the multiple personality syndrome in a death penalty case. *International Journal of Clinical and Experimental Hypnosis, 32.*

American Psychiatric Association, *Diagnostic and Statistical Manual of Mental Disorders* (*DSM–IV* 1994; *IV–TR* (2000); Washington D. C.; American Psychiatric Association Press.

Armstrong, J. G., & Loewenstein, R. J. (1990). Characteristics of patients with multiple personality and dissociative disorders on psychological testing. *Journal of Nervous and Mental Disorders, 78,* 448.

Bass, B., & Jefferson, J. (2003). *Death's Acre.* New York: Putnam.

Boor, M. (1982). The multiple personality epidemic. *Journal of Nervous and Mental Disorders, 170,* 302.

Coons, P. M. (1991). Iatrogenesis and malingering of multiple personality disorder in the forensic evaluation of homicide defendants. *Psychiatric Clinics of North America, 14,* 757.

Fink, D. (1991). The co-morbidity of multiple personality disorder and *DSM–III–R* axis II disorders. *Psychiatric Clinics of North America, 14,* 547.

Greaves, G. (1980). Multiple personality, 165 years after Mary Reynolds. *Journal of Nervous and Mental Disorders, 168,* 577.

Harriman, P. L. (1943). The experimental induction of multiple personality. *Psychiatry, 5,* 179.

Keyes, D. (1981). *The Mind of Billy Milligan.* New York: Random House.

Horevitz, R. P., & Braun, B. G. (1984). Are multiple personality disorder patients borderline? An analysis of 33 patients. *Psychiatric Clinics of North America, 7,* 69.

Kampman, R. (1976). Hypnotically induced multiple personality: An experimental study. *International Journal of Clinical and Experimental Hypnosis, 3,* 215.

Kluft, R. P. (1987). First rank symptoms as a diagnostic clue to multiple personality disorder. *American Journal of Psychiatry, 144,* 293.

Kluft, R. P. (1987). Making the diagnosis of multiple personality. In Flach, F. F. (Ed.), *Diagnostics and psychopathology.* (pp. 207–225). New York: Norton.

Kluft, R. P. (1991). Clinical presentation of multiple personality disorder. *Psychiatric Clinics of North America, 14,* 605.

Kluft, R. P. (2005). Diagnosing Dissociate Identity Disorder. *Psychiatric Annals,* 633.

Kohlenberg, R. J. (1973). Behavioristic approach to multiple personality: A case study. *Behavior Therapy, 4,* 173.

Larmore, K., Ludwig, A., & Cain, R. (1977). Multiple personality: An objective study. *British Journal of Psychiatry, 131,* 35.

Miller, R. S. (1989). Optical differences in cases of multiple personality disorder. *Journal of Nervous and Mental Disease, 177,* 480.

New York State Penal Law, 1965. art. 30.05 c1030.

Orne, T. (1985). The use and misuse of hypnosis. In R. Rosner, (Ed.). *Critical issues in American Psychiatry and the Law.* (pp. 211–245). New York: Plenum Press.

Orne, T., Dinges, R. D., Carota, & Orne, E. (1984). On the different diagnosis of multiple personality in the forensic context. *International Journal of Experimental Hypnosis, 32,* 118.

Putnam, F. W. (1984). The psychophysiologic investigation of multiple personality disorder. *Psychiatric Clinics of North America, 7,* 31.

Putnam, F. W. (1991). Recent research on multiple personality disorder. *Psychiatric Clinics of North America, 14,* 489.

Ross, C. A., Heber, S., & Norton, G. (1989). The dissociative disorders interview schedule: A structured interview. *Dissociation, 2,* 169.

Ross, C. A., Norton, G. R., & Wozney, K. (1989). Multiple personality disorder: An analysis of 236 cases. *Canadian Journal of Psychiatry, 34,* 413.

Ross, C. A., Miller, S., & Bjornson, L. (1990). Structured interview data on 102 cases of multiple personality disorder from four centers. *American Journal of Psychiatry, 147,* 596.

Serban, G. (1982). *The Tyranny of magical thinking.* New York: E.P. Dutton.

Serban, G. (1992). Multiple personality: An issue for forensic psychiatry. *American Journal of Psychotherapy, XLVI,* 269.

Walker, N. G., & Ross, C. A. (1997). The prevalence and biometric structure of psychological dissociation in the general population, taxometric and behavior genetic findings. *Abnormal Psychology, 106,* 499.

Chapter 14

FORENSIC ISSUES ASSOCIATED WITH POST-TRAUMATIC STRESS DISORDER: TWENTY-FIVE YEARS LATER

LANDY F. SPARR

Since its formal introduction into psychiatric nomenclature twenty-five years ago, post-traumatic stress disorder (PTSD) remains firmly entrenched in the legal landscape and, by all accounts, continues to be a forensic growth industry. Simon has observed that "no diagnosis in American psychiatry has had such a profound influence on civil and criminal law" (Simon, 1995a, p. xv). In part, this is because PTSD seems easy to understand. It is one of only a few mental disorders for which the psychiatric *Diagnostic and Statistical Manual (DSM)* describes a known cause. In contrast, for example, a diagnosis of depression opens the issue of causation to many factors other than the stated cause of action. Since PTSD is usually based on patients' self-report, however, it creates the possibility of distortion aimed at avoidance of criminal punishment. Edwards (1998) has suggested that the PTSD diagnosis "was never intended to support litigation." PTSD was included in the *DSM* upon insistence of clinicians who were confronted by people with symptoms of puzzling etiology. Often, says Edwards, "these individuals had difficulty being taken seriously because family, friends and officials doubted whether they had experienced anything at all which would justify the alleged symptoms" (p. 144).

Although PTSD has received a generally enthusiastic reception in the legal community, it has achieved mixed success as a criminal defense. In the American criminal justice system, individuals are considered responsible and thus accountable or culpable for their behavior if there are two necessary ingredients: (1) a criminal act (*actus reus*); and (2) criminal intention (*mens rea*). If serious mental illness eliminates *mens rea* (or "culpable mind"), only the *actus reus* is left, and the individual may be deemed not criminally responsible (Sadoff, 1992). A defendant who is mentally ill may plead not guilty by reason of insanity (excuse defense), but alternatively may meet the requirements for a *mens rea* defense (failure-of-proof) or, if PTSD is the diagnosis and the facts fit, a self-defense defense (justification).

There has been some difficulty establishing PTSD as a criminal defense because generally those with PTSD have not lost touch with reality and can appreciate wrongfulness. Despite the drawbacks, however, some observers believe that the number of claims of mental incapacity because of the alleged effects of PTSD have steadily increased since 1980 (Speir, 1989; Bursztajn, Scherr and Brodsky, 1994). A search of WestLaw from 11/16/02 to 11/15/05 found 950 State Appellate decisions and 951 Federal cases where PTSD was a factor.

The framers of *DSM–III* (1980) were aware of the problems of using psychiatric diagnoses for nonclinical purposes and issued a disclaimer regarding determinations of legal responsibility. Attorneys, because they lack clinical perspective, have often approached *DSM–III* and *DSM–IV* (1994) in a formalistic and literal fashion (Simon, 1995b). Under "Issues in the Use of *DSM–IV*" the manual clearly warns, "It is important that *DSM–IV* not be applied mechanically by untrained individuals. The specific diagnostic criteria included in *DSM–IV* are meant to serve as guidelines to be informed by clinical judgment and are not meant to be used in a cookbook fashion" (*DSM–IV*, 1994; p. xxiii). Because it is a disorder that can be malingered, a PTSD diagnosis is vulnerable to legal challenge on several grounds. Specifically, symptom causation may be contested on the basis of prior susceptibility or intervening factors, and symptom assessment and/or stressor identification may be troublesome and called into question (Motherway, 1987). There have been suggestions that criminal behavior is linked with PTSD in Vietnam Veterans (Dondershine, 1989; Walker, 1981), but a study by Shaw (1987) found that PTSD was no more prevalent among incarcerated veterans than among a control group of nonincarcerated veterans.

In addition to the use of PTSD as a basis for reduction of charges, it has also been used to arrange pre-trial plea bargaining agreements, as a self-defense defense, in mitigation of post-trial sentencing determinations, and, recently, to question the reliability of a defendant's memory. Finally, in certain criminal cases there has been controversial expert witness testimony specifying that symptoms that match known psychological profiles of incest, battered women, or rape victims provides strong evidence that these events have actually occurred (Slovenko, 1984). Thus it is safe to conclude that although courts are increasingly recognizing psychological aspects of criminal behavior, the use of mental health testimony, particularly regarding stress disorders, has been controversial.

CRIMINAL INTENT

Criminal law constitutes a description of harms that society seeks to prohibit by threat of criminal punishment. At the same time, the criminal law includes an elaborate body of qualifications to these prohibitions and threats based on absence of fault. A common usage is to express these qualifications to liability in terms of the *mens rea* requirement. This usage is the thought behind the classic maxim, *actus non facit reum, nisi mens sit rea*, or in Blackstone's translation, "an unwarrantable act without a vicious will is no crime at all" (Kadish and Schulhofer, 2001, p. 203). One way in which the *mens rea* requirement may be rationalized is through a common sense view of justice that blame and punishment are inappropriate and unjust in the absence of choice (Hart, 1968). So viewed, a great variety of defenses to criminal liability may be characterized as presenting *mens rea* defenses–involuntary acts, duress, legal insanity, accident, or mistake, for example. This all-encompassing usage may be referred to as *mens rea* in its general sense.

There is, however, a narrower use of *mens rea* which may be referred to as *mens rea* in its special sense, that refers only to the mental state required by the definition of the offense that produces or threatens harm. Not all possible mental states are relevant to the law's purposes. Whether a defendant acted regretfully, arrogantly, eagerly, or hopefully may be pertinent for a judge contemplating a sentence, but mental states relevant to defining criminal conduct and differentiating degrees of culpability in legal systems are more limited. Indeed, mental state is something of a misnomer. The concern of criminal law is with the level of intentionality with which the defendant acted, in other words, with what the defendant intended, knew, or should have known (Kadish and Schulhofer, 2001).

In the twentieth century, in most U.S. jurisdictions, the idea of *mens rea* and the law has evolved from its earlier sense of guilty mind into a number of narrow and technically defined mental states (Roth, 1986). American law has employed an abundance of *mens rea* terms, such as general and specific intent, malice, willfulness, wantonness, recklessness, scienter, premeditation, criminal negligence, and the like, exhibiting what Justice Jackson, in a famous Supreme Court opinion, called, "the variety, disparity and confusion of definitions of the requisite elusive mental element" (*Morissette v. U.S.*, 1952). In the last century, *mens rea* terms have burgeoned in common law countries such as the United States and England.

In 1962, in the United States, with the release of the American Law Institute's Model Penal Code, the difficult task of articulating levels of culpability that may be required to establish liability was prescribed. The code delineated in descending order four levels of culpability: purpose, knowledge, recklessness, and negligence. The minimal concept was that one may not be convicted of a crime, unless he/she acted purposefully, knowingly, recklessly, or negligently, as the law may require, with respect to each material element of an offense (Wechsler, 1968; Model Penal Code, 2.02(1), 1962).

CONCEPTS OF JUSTIFICATION AND EXCUSE

There are three distinct defenses that can be invoked to bar conviction for an alleged crime. The first asserts that the prosecution has failed to establish one or more required elements of the offense. The defendant may deny, for example, that he was anywhere near the scene of the crime, or he may concede the fatal shot but deny that he acted intentionally. These are simply efforts to refute (or raise a reasonable doubt about) whatever the prosecution must prove (failure-of-proof defense). The defendant may attempt to put forth evidence to disprove either the mental elements and/or material elements of the crime. In the former, the defendant essentially states, "I did not commit the crime charged because I did not possess the requisite *mens rea*." Of course, the prosecution always retains the burden of proving its own case and of disproving any rebuttal efforts beyond a reasonable doubt (Compton, 1996).

The other two sorts of defenses are justifications and excuses, which do not seek to refute the required elements of the prosecution's case but rather suggest further considerations that negate culpability even when all elements of the offense are clearly present. The defendants admit they voluntarily committed the crime, with the relevant mental state, but still assert they are not guilty, based on what has been traditionally called an "affirmative defense" (e.g., insanity, self-defense, duress). This defense concedes that the prosecution has proven its case on the *actus reus* and *mens rea* elements but asserts that some justification or mitigating factor should lead to acquittal of the criminal charge (Melton, 1997). Thus, both self-defense and insanity claims suggest reasons to bar conviction even when it has been clearly proved that an act is intentional. It is customary, moreover, to distinguish sharply between these two groups of defenses (justifications and excuses). Self-defense, for example, is traditionally considered a justification, while insanity is considered an excuse. In one defense, the defendant accepts responsibility but denies bad behavior; in the other, the defendant admits that the behavior was bad but does not accept full responsibility (Austin, 1956).

INSANITY DEFENSE

Insanity is a legal term, not a medical term. The not guilty by reason of insanity (NGRI) defense has received so much public notoriety that most mental health professionals now know that it is rarely used as a criminal plea. It goes to trial even less frequently because when both sides agree, which is most of the time, there is no contest. Insanity defense trials only occur when there is disagreement (Rappeport, 1992). In an eight-state study of 967,209 felony indictments whose cases were collected from 1985 to 1990, there were insanity pleas in 8,953 instances (0.93%). Of those, the acquittal rate was 26.27 percent (Callahan, 1991). In a related study, data were collected on insanity pleas in 49 counties in 8 states from 1980 to 1986. The researchers found 8,135 defendants who pled NGRI. Of these, only 28 (0.30%) were based on a PTSD diagnosis (28.6% were successful) (Appelbaum,

1993). In another study in Baltimore, Maryland, the insanity defense plea was found 1.20 percent of the time, and only 10 percent of those were successful (Janofsky, 1989) and, finally, a successful insanity defense accounted for just 0.l0 percent of all criminal cases in Alaska from 1977–1981 (Phillips, Wolf, & Coons 1988). These data highlight two facts: the PTSD insanity defense is raised infrequently, and, like other insanity pleas, is not often successful when it is raised.

The two main American tests of insanity are the M'Naghten Rule and the American Law Institute (ALI) Model Penal Code (M'Naghten Case, 1843; Model Penal Code, 1962). The M'Naghten standard (also known as the right or wrong test) is the stricter of the two because the defendant must show that by virtue of mental disease or defect he did not know the nature and quality of his act or did not know the act was wrong. The ALI standard is a two-part test providing that a person is not responsible for criminal conduct if, as a result of mental disease, he lacks substantial capacity to appreciate the criminality (wrongfulness) of his conduct or conform his conduct to the requirements of the law. Superficially, this standard appears to draw on the M'Naghten rule in its first clause, and on the irresistible impulse rule in its second clause—the first part seems to aim at understanding (cognition), and the second at action (volition). Indeed, the disjunctive "or" allows more latitude to judges and juries because it permits either level of disturbance; lack of understanding or behavioral self-control (Gutheil, 1989).

A PTSD defense is most successful in these jurisdictions that have adopted the ALI test because a defendant could be judged insane even though he was able to appreciate the wrongfulness of his act. The phrase "to conform his conduct to the requirements of the law" seems most appropriate for defendants who may be acting involuntarily such as in a dissociative state. If the same defendant is tried in a state using M'Naghten, he has a greater burden of proof that he did not understand either the wrongfulness or the nature and quality of his act. For all practical purposes, a defendant must almost be totally deranged in order to be acquitted under the M'Naghten test (Brotherton, 1981).

In June 1982, a jury returned a verdict of NGRI in the case of John Hinckley, who had been tried for his attempt to assassinate then United States President Ronald Reagan (*U.S. v. Hinckley*, 1982). The jury in the Hinckley trial used the ALI test. Shortly afterwards the U.S. Congress held hearings on the insanity defense and passed the

Insanity Defense Reform Act in 1984 (18 U.S.C. § 20(a), 1985). Prior to the Reform Act, the vast majority of U.S. Federal courts followed the ALI standard. The Act created three basic changes in Federal insanity defense laws. First, the Federal system now limits the insanity defense to severe mental diseases or defects that make the accused "unable to appreciate the nature and quality of the wrongfulness of his acts. "Second, the Act eliminated the volitional portion of the cognitive-volitional test and eliminated the diminished capacity defense. These changes effectively resurrected M'Naghten in the federal courts. Finally, the Act placed on the defendant the burden of proving insanity by clear and convincing evidence (Davidson, 1988). Altogether, thirty-six states have imposed some form of insanity defense reform since Hinckley's acquittal. Five states–Idaho (1982), Kansas (1996), Montana (1979), Nevada (1995), and Utah (1983)–abolished the defense entirely (Giorgi-Guarnieri, 2002).

A pivotal question in the use of the PTSD insanity defense in U.S. Federal and most other courts is whether PTSD qualifies as a severe mental disease. Congress's purpose in imposing a severity requirement was to ensure that nonpsychotic behavior disorders, neuroses, or antisocial tendencies would not suffice as insanity defenses. Congress also intended to exclude voluntary drug or alcohol abuse as valid defenses, even though such abuse might prevent an accused from appreciating wrongfulness. The [Federal courts have not determined an exact standard for the severe mental illness requirement. As a minimum, however, PTSD dissociative states should qualify if an individual's cognitive abilities are completely altered (Davidson, 1988; *State v. Heads*, 1981; *State v. Mann*, 1983; *State v. Felde*, 1982; *State v. Cocuzza*, 1981, Stone, 1993). Nevertheless, the more restrictive nature of most current NGRI statutes has apparently worked against the use of PTSD as an insanity plea (*U.S. v. Whitehead*, 1990; *U.S. v. Cartagena-Carrasquillo*, 1995; *U.S. v. Rezaq*, 1998; *State v. Johnson*, 1998).

DIMINISHED CAPACITY

Evidence of a mental illness not amounting to a complete insanity defense is often ruled inadmissible. In about one-half the American states, however, evidence of abnormal mental condition is admissible on the question of whether the defendant had (or was capable of having) the requisite mental state pertinent to the crime charged. The doctrine by which this evidence is admitted is referred to as the *mens rea* variant and is the only mental incapacity variant explicitly adopted in U.S. jurisdictions (Compton, 1996). In this view, which is usually termed diminished capacity, evidence of mental abnormality is admitted to negate the required state of mind or mental element of the offense charged. Diminished capacity is called a "failure-of-proof" defense because it is used to show that the prosecution has not proved its case. This view recognizes that because the defendant must possess a certain state of mind to be convicted of certain crimes, any evidence showing the absence of that state of mind is admissible.

A sizeable number of states, as well as the federal courts, prohibit clinical testimony on any issue other than insanity, generally on the grounds that it is too speculative or comes too close to diminished responsibility testimony (a European concept whereby the defense seeks a charge reduction on the grounds of the alleged mental incapacity of the defendant). But many other states, perhaps twenty-five, permit clinical testimony on *mens rea* as well as insanity, at least under certain circumstances. Some of these courts merely state that principles of fairness and due process require that defendants be permitted to introduce any competent relevant evidence, including psychiatric testimony (Melton, 1997).

The insanity defense focuses on the defendant's responsibility for his criminal act and, if successful, involves a policy decision not to seek punishment. In contrast, the diminished capacity defense is admissible for the sole purpose of determining which crime was committed. A few states admit evidence of an abnormal mental condition for the purpose of mitigating punishment after a guilty verdict. Most formulations of the diminished capacity doctrine allow psychiatric testimony to show that the defendant was not capable of either premeditating or deliberating. Since insanity defense standards have been tightened, the use of PTSD in criminal proceedings has more applicability to diminished capacity, and in fact, has been used more often in that role (Sparr, 2005). Unlike NGRI, a claim of diminished capacity does not result in commitment to a hospital. Overall, the diminished capacity rule is used mainly in cases in which the defendant is charged with first-degree murder but has been used in lesser offenses and may be used to mitigate punishment (Morris, 1975).

In 1994, a Tennessee appeals court reversed a first-degree murder conviction because the jury was not instructed that PTSD evidence could be considered in deciding whether specific intent or diminished capacity had been shown (*State v. Phipps*, 1994). Four experts had testified that Phipps had major depression and PTSD, most of them agreeing that these conditions significantly affected his thought and reasoning at the time of the crime. The court had refused to instruct the jury on the defense theory that Phipps had been unable to formulate the specific intent required for first-degree murder and instead issued an instruction that the conditions noted were not to be considered as defenses to the charge.

New federal sentencing guidelines and mandatory minimum sentences and their counterpart in various states have given a lesser role to the concept of diminished responsibility in the post-trial phase of a prosecution. Reduced federal sentences (or downward departures) for diminished capacity are only allowed for "nonviolent crimes" (Pub. L. No. 98–596, 1984). The Ninth Circuit has held that PTSD is one type of mental disorder that can support a reduced sentence (*U.S. v. Cantu*, 1993), however, the exercise of discretion in considering mental state or mental incapacity defenses now occurs mostly in the pretrial or trial stages. In the pre-trial stage, the diminished capacity concept may influence prosecutorial judgment and play a role in charges brought against the defendant.

SELF-DEFENSE DEFENSE

Another possible legal theory to which PTSD is relevant is self-defense. The Modern Penal Code allows the defendant to demonstrate that his/her responses were subjectively reasonable (e.g., that he/she believed the use of force was necessary). The use of PTSD in this context is usually found when "battered woman syndrome" is employed to explain a female defendant's violent acts toward her spouse. For example, it might be possible to show that a particular type of provocation caused a PTSD-type reaction in which the defendant felt attacked and responded involuntarily or even reasonably given her background. In this circumstance, the existence of PTSD would make the whole of the defendant's life relevant to show her state of mind at the time of the crime (Erlinder, 1984). The battered woman syndrome is not a diagnosis unto itself but, rather, cuts across a spectrum of underlying diagnostic categories (Goodstein and Page, 1981). It is seen as a PTSD variation and draws upon the social science research of Lenore Walker (1980) among others. These theories help explain why more women simply do not leave their abusers (Lustberg & Jacobi, 1992).

Expert testimony may assist the jury to understand a woman's emotions and behavior in the years preceding the homicide, corroborating the history of violence in the relationship. It may also be used to explain that women may remain in abusive relationships because they may be terrified of leaving and believe they cannot survive on their own (Shuman, 2003). Increasing acceptance of battered woman syndrome has led some courts to hold that indigent defendants must be provided funds to retain a psychiatric or psychological expert to aid and assist in this defense (*Dunn v. Roberts*, 1992, *Lewis v. State*, 1995). The consequence of invoking a battered woman syndrome defense varies by jurisdiction. In some, evidence of the syndrome may be used to support a claim of self-defense (e.g., a normal response to a threat) (*State v. Kelly*, 1984; *State v. Grubbs*, 2003), whereas in others, it may be used to support an insanity defense (e.g ., a disordered response to a threat) (*State v. Necaise*, 1985).

In order to mount a successful self-defense claim, a woman must prove that she was operating under a reasonable belief of imminent danger. Further, the defendant must prove that the force she used was reasonable and necessary, that she was not the aggressor, and, depending on the jurisdiction, that she did not have an opportunity to retreat safely from confrontation. In particular, battered women have had a difficult time proving the two elements of reasonable belief and imminent harm. Most courts rely on an objective standard when assessing reasonableness that requires a judge or jury to assess the defendant's beliefs from the standpoint of a "reasonable man." The second element, imminent harm, presents difficulty when a woman kills in a nonconfrontational situation, for example, when the victim is sleeping or his back is turned (Blowers & Bjerregaard, 1994).

Expert testimony has been used to show that abused women often perceive their situation differently than a usual "reasonable (wo)man" would, because such abuse typically increases in both frequency and severity over time. Thus, it may be reasonable for an abused woman to believe that subsequent encounters may prove more deadly than preceding confrontations. The second characteristic of battered woman syndrome often involves learned helplessness. This theory posits that the woman's ability to control her situation is significantly impaired when she realizes that the abuse she receives is not contingent on her behavior or actions. Thus, an abused woman may develop the belief she is helpless to control her situation and will not perceive escape options (Walker, 2000).

In *State v. Kelly* (1984), it was held that in asserting self-defense the defendant may offer expert testimony on battered woman syndrome to aid a jury in understanding how a history of abuse may support a woman's claim that she believed she was in imminent danger and that her belief was reasonable. In particular, the *Kelly* court declared that the subject was "beyond the ken of the average juror and thus suitable for explanation through expert testimony." The court also held that the syndrome had sufficient scientific basis to fulfill an expert witness reliability requirement. In *State v. McClain* (1991), however, the court limited the applicability of battered woman syndrome evidence by holding that, because the defendant was not in imminent danger, such evidence was not relevant to the question of reasonableness (Lustberg & Jacobi, 1992). In *Bechtel v. State* (1992) the court defined self-defense as being based on reasonableness and imminence: "The key to the defense of self-defense is reasonableness. A defendant must show that she had a reasonable belief as to the imminence of great bodily harm or death. . . ."

In *State v. Allery* (1984), the defendant, who had been married for five years, experienced a consistent pattern of physical abuse at the hands of her husband. She had been hospitalized at one point because he had struck her in the head with a tire iron. Because the beatings increased in intensity and severity, she filed for divorce and served her husband with a restraining order. She testified that on the day of the shooting she had entered her house late at night, not expecting to find her husband home because of the restraining order. When she found him there, he allegedly threatened to kill her. After unsuccessfully trying to escape through a window, she fired one shot at him with a shotgun, killing him. The trial court refused to allow expert testimony on battered woman syndrome, and also refused to give self-defense instructions requested by the defense. Upon appeal, the Washington State Supreme Court reversed the defendant's conviction and remanded for a new trial concluding that the trial court erred in refusing to instruct the jury that the defendant had no duty to retreat, that instructions were defective in explaining self-defense law, and that testimony on battered woman syndrome should have been permitted.

Other U.S. courts have accepted battered woman syndrome as a scientifically recognized theory. Thirty-one (31) American states and the District of Columbia have allowed expert testimony on the subject. Five (5) states have acknowledged its validity but have held testimony inadmissible based on the facts of a particular case. In *Ibn-Tamas v. U.S.* (1979) expert testimony relating to "battered woman" in support of the defendant's claim of self-defense in the killing of her husband was ruled inadmissible on the grounds that it would invade the province of the jury and that its probative value was outweighed by its prejudicial impact. In contrast, in New Jersey, expert PTSD testimony was permitted to explain the inability of battered women to escape forced prostitution (*U.S. v. Winters*, 1984).

Ten state legislatures have passed statutes dealing with the battered woman syndrome conundrum. Several of them begin by resolving the admissibility issue explicitly as a matter of law; most statutes allow the concept as part of a self-defense defense. Battered woman syndrome may also be used in sentence mitigation, especially when the facts fall short of establishing a full legal defense (Brakel & Brooks, 2001). *State v. Pascal* (1987) is such a "downward departure" case. Furthermore, the concept has been, and continues to be, widely used to obtain executive clemency. In England, battered woman syndrome has been used as a plea of diminished responsibility in homicide cases while in Canada it is accepted as a legitimate extension of self-defense (Rix, 2001).

Unlike many novel defenses associated with PTSD, defenses based on battered woman syndrome continue to flourish both in number and success of outcome. One reason is that the concept dovetails with an increased societal awareness of domestic battery as a serious and pervasive problem. The law has moved toward greater protection of women in other ways as well, including anti-stalking laws and restraining orders. These developments are intended to combat a pattern of inadequate law enforcement response to domestic violence, which has been rationalized by pointing to the frequent ambiguity of such situations, including the unwillingness of some victims to pursue charges against their abusers (Brakel & Brooks, 2001).

PTSD AND MEMORY

The nature of remembrance of traumatic events has been particularly controversial during the past decade, as vigorous new research has reshaped thinking about trauma and memory. There are different types of memory, and empirical studies have associated PTSD with both a strengthening of some types and a weakening of others. Persons with PTSD form stronger conditioned fear responses, both of traumatic (Pitman, Orr, Forgue et al., 1987) and de novo (Orr, Metzger, Lasko et al., 2000) events. In contrast, deficiencies have been reported in their explicit, or declarative' memory, e.g., the ability to accurately report newly learned information (Gilbertson, Gurvits, Lasko et al., 2001; Bremner, Vermetten, Afzal et al., 2004), however, PTSD patients may have better explicit memory for trauma-related material (McNally, 1998). Recently, accuracy of memory has received particular scrutiny because considerable importance may be attached to victims' declarative recollections (Brown, Scheflin, & Hammond, 1998). In 1998, at the International War Crimes Tribunal in The Hague, a Bosnian-Croatian soldier (Anto Furundzija) was tried for aiding and abetting the rape of a Muslim woman (*Prosecutor v. Furundzija*, 1998). The defendant's lawyers suggested that the woman's memory was inaccurate because is had been adversely affected by her traumatic experiences, and that the defendant she identified was not actually present during her interrogation and abuse. The prosecution disagreed and argued that memories of traumatic experiences in individuals with PTSD are characteristically hyperaccessible. Expert witnesses on both sides were brought in to provide medicolegal testimony about the scientific parameters of stress and its long-term effects on brain regions associated with memory (Sparr & Bremner, 2005).

This case highlights on multiple levels the politics of psychological trauma and the law. PTSD researchers have identified psychological and biological markers that are characteristic of the disorder. This research has been used to champion PTSD as a real disorder, implying that trauma victims deserve financial compensation under the law and treatment from medical providers. The case of Anto Furundzija, however, turns the heretofore peaceful alignment of forces between trauma victims and clinicians/researchers on its head. The disruption this entails can be seen in the controversy related to this case in general, and the presentation and discussion of the scientific evidence in particular. The case taps into a recently evolving area of research that suggests that PTSD victims have more memory fallibility of a certain type than persons without the disorder. The same framework of physiological disturbances that was previously used in support of victims has now acquired the potential to undermine them in a fundamental way.

A controversial forensic question that emerges from the Furundzija case is whether testimony from PTSD patients should be thrown out of a court of law. Assuming for the moment that PTSD patients do have more fallible memories, at least in some areas, does that imply that all their memories are inherently suspect? There is now a wealth of evidence that memories in all individuals are subject to a range of inaccuracies, and much of this literature has been related to research on witness testimony in court. Does that mean that all witness testimony should be discounted? Perhaps this merely highlights the importance of obtaining collateral information for cases involving both PTSD and non-PTSD victims. The model of children's testimony could be used as an example. Although memory in children may not be as accurate or take the same form as memory in adults, children's testimony is allowed in court.

SENTENCE MITIGATION

In the United States, sentence mitigation based on the fact-finder's (or sentencer's) perception that the offender's criminal responsibility is diminished is unique in capital cases, in that mitigating reasons (or "factors") are typically set out in statute, and their consideration, if present, is mandatory (although nonenumerated mitigating factors may also be considered). Many states list mental impairment, by one designation or another, as among statutory mitigating factors. The complexity of the state's current death penalty schemes is a reaction to the case of *Furman v. Georgia* (1972). In *Furman*, the U.S. Supreme Court struck down Georgia's death penalty statute, because it left the jury with unfettered discretion in applying the statute. When the states redesigned their statutes in the wake of *Furman*, their dominant pattern was one in which the jury's discretion was now appropriately guided or "channeled" by explicitly stated sets of aggravating and mitigating circumstances (Brakel & Brooks, 2001).

Ten U.S. jurisdictions and the Model Penal Code allow for the admission of mental-abnormality evidence in sentencing by statute when deciding between imposing death or life imprisonment (Compton, 1996). At least one jurisdiction considers such evidence for imposing a probationary sentence (*State v. Spawr*, 1983). Contemporary death penalty jurisprudence requires the sentencing authority to consider any relevant mitigating evidence that a defendant offers as a basis for a sentence less than death (Perlin, 1994). Despite support for allowance of mitigating factors in *Lockett v. Ohio* (1978) and *Eddings v. Oklahoma* (1982), recent judicial trends have placed limitations on mitigation evidence (Kirchmeier, 1998).

In *Bell v. Cone* (2002) the Third District Court of Appeals concluded that during the penalty phase of a capital murder case counsel for the defense "entirely failed" to introduce available mitigating evidence demonstrating the presence of PTSD in Vietnam veteran defendant, Gary Cone. The Appellate finding was reversed and remanded by the U.S. Supreme Court with Justice John Paul Stevens dissenting. Justice Stevens cited defense counsel's significant misunderstanding and mishandling of PTSD evidence.

At the International War Crimes Tribunal for the former Yugoslavia in the Hague, Netherlands, Stevan Todorovic, former Chief of Police in the Serbian municipality of Bosanski Samac was charged with murder, rape and torture of non-Serbian civilians. Todorovic's legal defense team raised a plea of diminished responsibility (in mitigation of sentence only) and requested a psychiatric examination of the defendant. The Trial Chamber subsequently ordered the exam to be performed by two mental health experts. One expert concluded that the defendant did not have any psychiatric disorder during the period in question while the other found that Todorovic manifested both PTSD and alcohol abuse. The Trial Chamber in the final judgment determined that "Todorovic's condition at the time the crimes were committed was not one which would give rise to mitigation of sentence" (*Prosecutor v. Todorovic*, 2001, p. 27).

EXPERT WITNESS TESTIMONY

PTSD has provided fuel for the periodic firestorm about psychiatric and psychological expert testimony. In 1988, Faust and Ziskin took psychiatry to task for its difficulties in achieving "reliable" diagnostic classifications and for the gap between determination of clinical criteria and satisfaction of legal criteria. They maintained that there is generally considerable heterogeneity among individuals who fall within the same psychiatric diagnostic categories, which limits forensic value, and that, when a jury considers a criminal defense such as diminished capacity, "a diagnosis such as PTSD offers little guidance" (Faust & Ziskin, 1988, p. 32). Taking this notion to the extreme, the West Virginia Supreme Court held that despite expert opinion to the contrary, lay testimony was sufficient to find that a first degree murder defendant was sane beyond a reasonable doubt (*West Virginia v. Walls*, 1994). In this case, several witnesses testified that the defendant "appeared normal to them" before and after the crime, and the jury gave more weight to their testimony than to the three experts (two psychologists and a psychiatrist) who diagnosed paranoid schizophrenia and agreed that the defendant was not criminally responsible. This bias against psychiatric testimony is an example of frequently-held lay belief that ordinary common sense has more validity than "psychobabble." Psychiatric expert testimony has been assailed in other countries as well (Coles & Veiel, 2001; Rogers, 2004).

Most assuredly, the specific use of PTSD in the courtroom has been abused, but as Hoge and Grisso (1992) point out, the test in the courtroom is not scientific certainty but legal sufficiency. The fact that scientific experimentation would require more evidence before reaching a conclusion is irrelevant. In fact, the most common problem with the general acceptance of psychiatric testimony is that the judicial system seems to have an "unquenchable thirst" for its use, often asking mental health professionals to exceed their knowledge base. Indeed, in the current legal climate, psychiatric testimony is alternatively valued and devalued. On one hand it is seen as soft exculpatory and imprecise; on the other hand, it is in demand because it offers insight into criminal psychopathology (Perlin, 1994). Gutheil (1998) concludes that this ambivalence flows from the fact that the law both needs experts for its proper functioning yet resents their potential role in invading the province of the fact-finder. Mental health experts "do not have to answer legal questions of competence or criminal responsibility in order to provide valid assistance to courts. . . . Their proper role is to describe the relative abilities, disabilities, symptoms, and diagnostic conditions in clinical and behavioral terms, leaving the court to weigh the observation in the context of legal concepts and standards" (Hoge, 1992).

All scientific courtroom testimony including psychiatric evidence is governed by expert witness rules. The first important standard is called the Frye rule, which was laid down in a 1923 decision by a Federal Appellate Court in a case that involved a lie detector test. The Frye rule states that any scientific evidence given in trials must be "generally accepted by the scientific community." Since the 1920s, with the increasing litigation involving scientific issues and a broader appreciation of scientific controversy, lawyers and others have argued that a strict application of the Frye rule was becoming less relevant (Marwick, 1993a). One of the major problems with the Frye test is that the term "general acceptance" is vague and difficult to define. Because Frye is a relatively strict standard, there was concern that it could deprive courts of pertinent evidence, particularly new information that had not had a chance to diffuse throughout the scientific community. Some courts, however, see the conservative nature of the test as its primary advantage because it offers more protection against "junk science" testimony (Huber, 1991).

The U.S. Federal Rules of Evidence also apply to expert testimony. Rule 702 putatively broadens the Frye admissibility standard by allowing an expert witness to offer any evidence that will aid the trier-of-fact in determining a question. All evidence is relevant and admissible unless its probative value is "substantially outweighed by the danger of unfair prejudice, confusion of the issues, misleading the jury, or by considerations of undue delay, waste of time, or needless presentation of cumulative evidence" (Federal Rules of Evidence 403). The latest development comes from a 1993 U.S. Supreme Court decision, *Daubert v. Merrill Dow* when the Court granted certiorari in light of the sharp divisions among lower courts regarding the proper standard for admission of scientific expert testimony. The Court essentially handed down a strict interpretation of the Federal Rules of Evidence by rejecting the suggestion that Frye had been incorporated into the Federal Rules and requiring the Federal courts to make a "preliminary assessment of whether reasoning or methodology underlying the testimony is scientifically valid and . . . whether that reasoning properly can be applied to the facts at issue" (LeDoux, 2000, p. 4). To reach this assessment the court suggested a consideration of whether the underlying theory or technique can be and has been tested, whether it has been subject to scrutiny by others in the field through peer review and publication, whether the error rate and standards for controlling error are acceptable, and the degree of acceptance within the relevant scientific community (Steinberg, 1993; *Daubert v. Merrill Dow*, 1993, Marwick, 1993b). This was a more restrictive approach to the admissibility of expert testimony at the Federal level than has been taken at any time since the adoption of the Federal Rules twenty years ago (Shuman, 1995). The majority of states that have expressly addressed the issue have followed the Supreme Court's lead and have adopted *Daubert* as controlling the exercise of the "gatekeeper" function by the trial courts (LeDoux, 2000).

These standards have had variable influence on PTSD testimony which, although generally accepted, has been considered prejudicial, irrelevant, and/or non-probative by some courts, For example, an Alaska appeals court reversed a murder conviction because expert evidence about PTSD had been improperly excluded from the trial (*Shepard v. Alaska*, 1992). The defendant, a Vietnam veteran, had attempted to call two experts to bolster his case. One, a psychiatrist, was the director of a Veterans Administration (VA) PTSD treatment program and a specialist in PTSD. Outside the presence of the jury, he testified that PTSD is a generally accepted medical condition, discussed its technical definition, its causes, and its common symptoms. He noted that avoidance, denial, and fear or distrust of authority figures are among the symptoms. He indicated that the kind of stress the defendant experienced in Vietnam was typical of the stress that caused PTSD, and that members of his hospital staff had treated many such patients. He stated that physical attack is the type of event capable of bringing out recurrence of PTSD symptoms, and thought it plausible that the defendant's effort to cover up his crime resulted from PTSD. Although the trial court allowed another defense expert to testify generally about PTSD, it excluded the VA psychiatrist's testimony because it amounted to "questionable" psychological profile evidence that might induce a decision by the jury on a purely emotional basis. Prosecution experts, on the other hand, who had never served in Vietnam were allowed to testify about conditions there, to opine that the defendant's remaining expert was rather naïve about criminal defendants, and to assert that PTSD had become a fad in legal defenses. In contrast, in *Skidmore v. Precision Printing and Packaging Inc.* (1999), the Fifth Circuit Court of Appeals affirmed the trial court's admission of expert psychological testimony regarding PTSD suffered by the plaintiff as a result of sexual harassment and intentional infliction of emotional distress allegedly committed by the defendant.

Because PTSD has a specific, easily identifiable stressor causing equally identifiable symptoms, it is sometimes concluded that the existence or absence of the syndrome is well within the understanding of the ordinary man. PTSD expert testimony has usually been allowed when aspects of the post-traumatic behavior are thought to be outside the realm of common knowledge or when there are atypical considerations such as a dissociative state.

Finally, the risk of misuse of a psychiatric diagnosis is heightened when the diagnosis is based largely on subjective symptoms. Whenever a patient gains a great deal (either excuse from blame or monetary award) by receiving a diagnosis (such as PTSD) that is largely based on self-report, the use of that diagnosis in the courtroom requires scrutiny. Abuse of the PTSD diagnosis by forensic psychiatric experts stems from three major causes: (1) inadequate forensic evaluation of the claimant; (2) failure to properly apply the PTSD criteria to the claimant; and (3) advocacy or bias (Pitman, Sparr, Saunders et al., 1996). It is misleading for the expert to imply that making this diagnosis clarifies any legal issue unless the precise relationship between the symptoms and the stressful event is carefully documented (Halleck, Hoge, Miller, et al., 1992).

RETROSPECTIVE FORENSIC ASSESSMENT

PTSD assessment has been extensively covered in previous publications (Pitman, Sparr, Saunders, et al., 1996; Sparr, 1990; Sparr & Boehnlein, 1990; Sparr & Pitman, 1999). Many persons who seek redress in the legal system after a traumatic event have genuine claims. Others, however, come with the purpose of exaggerating a claim for compensation. In a forensic context, in particular, clinicians who evaluate patients after a major stressor must consider malingering in their differential diagnosis. As mentioned above, plaintiffs' attorneys strongly favor the diagnosis of PTSD because the diagnosis itself constitutes evidence that the symptoms are due to the traumatic event in question. Resnick (1998) who has observed that PTSD has been described by various names, many of which are pejorative and suggestive of malingering (e.g., litigation neurosis, compensation neurosis) has developed a list of clues to malingered PTSD: (1) malingerers are more likely to be marginal members of society with few binding ties or committed long-standing financial responsibilities such as home ownership; (2) the malingerer may have a history of spotty employment, previous incapacitating injuries, and extensive absences from work; (3) malingerers frequently depict themselves and their prior functioning in exclusively complementary terms; (4) the malingerer may incongruously assert an inability to work but retain the capacity for recreation. In contrast, the patient with genuine PTSD is more likely to withdraw from recreational activities as well as work; (5) the malingerer may pursue a legal claim with impressive tenacity, while at the same time alleging depression or incapacitation in other pursuits; (6) malingerers are unlikely to volunteer information about sexual dysfunction although they are generally eager to emphasize their physical complaints; and (7) malingerers are also unlikely to volunteer information about nightmares unless they have read the diagnostic criteria for PTSD. When they occur in PTSD, genuine nightmares typically show variations on the theme of the traumatic event. In contrast, the malingerer may claim repetitive dreams that always reenact the traumatic event in exactly the same way.

An evaluation process should begin with an attempt to sort claims into those that involve a PTSD diagnosis and those that do not. The plaintiff's condition may not meet PTSD criteria for any of several reasons generally related to a lack of severity of either the stressor or the symptoms. Does the plaintiff have another mental disorder? There are diagnoses in *DSM–IV* other than PTSD that should be considered before resorting to nonstandardized nomenclature such as "traumatic depression." The further from the PTSD diagnosis the evaluator strays, the more speculative the causation opinion will become and it is more likely that problems of pre-existing injury will be significant. The *DSM–IV* PTSD criteria are the starting point for psychiatric evaluation of a claim of negligent infliction of emotional distress whether the contest is criminal or civil (Spaulding, 1988).

It has been previously observed (Sparr & Atkinson, 1986) that, in criminal proceedings such as NGRI and diminished capacity, establishing a valid link between PTSD and criminal behavior is an imposing task. At least two levels of causation have to be investigated: (1) causal link between the traumatic stressor and the psychiatric symptoms; and (2) causal connection between psychiatric symptoms and the criminal act. No one argues whether or not mental health experts know the symptoms of PTSD. At issue is whether their professional abilities extend to deciding whether the stressor occurred, if it was sufficiently traumatizing, and whether the designated stressor or some preceding or subsequent stressor or provocation is the cause of the complainant's symptoms (Raifman, 1983). When PTSD is a factor in a criminal case, the diagnosis itself may not be questioned; however, the opposing attorneys will often point to secondary factors such as financial problems, interpersonal conflicts, or drug and alcohol abuse as proximate motivations for criminal activity. Although these factors may be related to PTSD, they are not generally regarded as sufficient to relieve an individual of criminal responsibility (Marciniak, 1986).

There are good reasons to place greater emphasis on outside information sources in legal evaluations than during other psychiatric examinations. For example, malingering is uncommon in routine clinical practice, but special care is needed to diagnose it in a forensic setting. The subject of evaluation often has something to gain by a finding of mental illness and may attempt to feign a psychiatric disturbance (Halleck, 1992). Ultimately, the most effective tool for detecting fabricated PTSD symptoms may be those that verify and quantify the stressor through eyewitness accounts or by other collateral sources. Direct psychiatric examination should always include a trauma history. Unresolved psychological reactions to previous trauma may predispose an individual to dissociative reactions to subsequent trauma. Because of the tendency of PTSD patients to avoid painful memories, superficial questioning may fail to elicit bona fide symptoms. On the other hand, direct inquiry regarding PTSD diagnostic criteria may be treated by motivated respondents as a series of leading questions evoking answers that too readily bring about a PTSD diagnosis.

These are formidable obstacles to reliable evaluation. The skilled evaluator, however, is not without tools to overcome them. The first device is nondirective interviewing. The interviewer should begin by asking the claimant to describe the problems he/she has been experiencing and then allow time to talk with as little interruption as possible. A claimant who talks for fifteen or thirty minutes hardly mentioning a PTSD symptom, but who answers positively to almost all PTSD queries should be regarded with suspicion. Another tool is insistence on detailed illustration. Knowledgeable or coached claimants may know which PTSD symptoms to report, but being able to illustrate them with convincing personal life details is another matter.

Invented symptoms have a vague and stilted quality. The interviewer must determine whether the history being presented has the quality of a personal autobiography, or merely a textbook. While eliciting the history, the evaluator should pay close attention to the claimant's behavior. Some PTSD symptoms (e.g., irritability, difficulty concentrating, or exaggerated startle) may be directly observed. Also relevant is whether the claimant's behavior and affect are consistent with the history he/she is providing. The display of genuine emotion, or lack of it, during rendition of a traumatic event and its sequelae can be revealing (Pitman, Sparr, Saunders et al., 1996). Bursztajn, Scherr and Brodsky (1994) point out that although standardized tests may be helpful, they are no substitute for an extended forensic psychiatric evaluation.

Following the nondirective portion of the interview, the evaluator should conduct a directive interview that inquires into each PTSD diagnostic criterion in turn, as well as into the criteria of other Axis IV mental disorders that could enter into the differential diagnosis. Psychiatric researchers are now required to determine the presence or absence of diagnostic criteria in a systematic manner, usually by means of structured interview instruments. Forensic evaluations may call for a similar approach. Recommended instruments include the Clinician-Administered PTSD Scale or CAPS (Blake et al., 1990), the Structured Clinical Interview for *DSM–IV* (SCID–I) (Spitzer, Williams, Gibbon, & First, 1995a) for Axis I mental disorders, and the SCID–II (Spitzer, Williams, Gibbon, & First, 1995b) for Axis II personality disorders. The CAPS has the additional advantage of incorporating a severity measure. An instrument available for the detection of malingering is the Structured Interview for Reported Symptoms, or SIRS (Rogers, Bagby, & Dickens, 1992).

A number of psychometric questionnaires yield numerical scores pertinent to the presence or absence, as well as severity, of PTSD. These include the Mississippi Scale for Combat-Related PTSD (Keane, Caddell, & Taylor, 1988) and its recent noncombat version the Civilian Mississippi; the Impact of Event Scale (Zilberg, 1982); and the Minnesota Multiphasic Personality Inventory–II (Litz et al., 1991). Of these questionnaires, only the MMPI–II incorporates validity scales as checks for symptom exaggeration. Moreover, research has indicated that even the MMPI can fail to detect fabricated PTSD (Lees-Haley, 1990; Perconte, & Goreczny, 1990).

The MMPI–II has two scales designed to assess combat related-PTSD (PK and PS scales). The more commonly used PK scale was developed by Keane, Malloy and Fairbank (1984) to determine the difference between those with a genuine PTSD diagnosis and those who had other diagnoses. The content of the PK scale is suggestive of emotional turmoil. The authors have indicated that caution should be used with the PK scale because it may be susceptible to faking by veterans who are motivated to appear to have PTSD in order to gain monetary compensation. Elhai, Gold, Frueh et al. (2000) used a clinical sample of combat-related war veterans to distinguish genuine from malingered PTSD on the MMPI–2. The scores of 124 male combat veterans were compared with those of 84 adult college students instructed and trained to malinger PTSD. Because neither discriminant function nor individual malingering predictors were able to correctly identify malingerers in all cases, the authors suggested that combat veteran profiles should not be ruled invalid solely on the basis of such factors as a high MMPI F score. Rather, MMPI–2 validity scales should be used as screening tools to determine advisability of more careful evaluation.

Raifman (1993) has proposed that expert witness testimony regarding PTSD should be "increasingly supported by empirically-based research data" (p. 115). Data obtained through laboratory testing has the potential to enhance expert testimony. Although this effort is in its infancy, objective measurement of psychophysiological responses during the structured (script-driven) recollection of the traumatic event has been shown to reliably distinguish trauma victims with and without PTSD (Pitman, Orr, Forgue et al., 1987), and it has been successfully used in the forensic setting (Pitman & Orr, 2003).

Laboratory measurement of physiologic responsivity during exposure to cues related to traumatic event has been described as "the best and most specific biological diagnostic test for PTSD" (Friedman, 1991, p. 74) and Pitman, Orr and Bursztajn (1993) have proposed that such measurement "has the potential to redeem the PTSD diagnosis from its current subjectivity and to help separate the wheat from the chaff in the forensic evaluation of PTSD claims" (p. 40). As with psychometric testing, those proposing the utility of psychophysiologic testing emphasize that the results do not stand on their own but serve as one component of a comprehensive forensic PTSD evaluation.

Simon (1995b) states that other options should be considered when PTSD symptoms do not rise to a level sufficient to meet *DSM–IV* criteria for a PTSD diagnosis. The examiner may decide to merely describe the existing symptoms while clearly stating that *DSM* criteria are not met fully for PTSD. Alternatively, the examiner may conclude that the claimant is suffering from a posttraumatic stress syndrome, which is not an official *DSM–IV* diagnosis (Blank, 1993). Moreover, some of the claimant's PTSD symptoms may have resolved over time, thus no longer meeting the parsimonious criteria for diagnosis of the disorder. Bursztajn, Scherr and Brodsky (1994) observe that contrary to popular opinion, a diagnosis of PTSD does not signify a simple ascription of causality to one event. Properly understood, PTSD results from an interaction between environmental stress (the traumatic event) and preexisting capacities. People are vulnerable in different degrees to different kinds of trauma on the basis of their past experience. The alleged victim may, on occasion, malinger, exaggerate, and/or misattribute symptoms, but also may deny, minimize, and/or discount the symptomatology in order to try to control the underlying distress as well as the shame secondary to experiencing it.

Finally, in evaluating a defendant with alleged PTSD who is charged with a crime (Auberry, 1985; Marciniak, 1986) the following factors (Blank, 1985) may have particular applicability to the determination of authenticity: (1) the criminal act should represent spontaneous unpremeditated behavior uncharacteristic of the individual; (2) the choice of a victim may be fortuitous or accidental; (3) the crimes should recreate in a psychologically meaningful way elements of the traumatic stressor; (4) the defendant is mostly unaware of the specific ways he has repeated and reenacted traumatic experiences; (5) seemingly benign incidents may result in bouts of violence; (6) there may be amnesia for all or part of the episode; (7) there is inability to explain the reason for the behavior; (8) there is no previous criminal record; (9) crimes are generally precipitated by events and circumstances that realistically or symbolically force the individual to face unresolved conflicts; (10) the behavior lacks current motivation; and (11) coherent dialogue appropriately related to time and place are not found in dissociative states. In assessment of combat trauma, discharge papers, combat history, and access to military records may be necessary. Evaluation protocols for Vietnam veterans have been offered by various authors (Sparr, 1986; Marciniak, 1986; *Physician's Guide*, 1985; Sparr & Pankratz, 1983). In addition, Simon (1995c) has established comprehensive guidelines for forensic PTSD assessment, and Motherway (1987) and Koch, O'Neill and Douglas (2005) have provided specific guidance to attorneys with PTSD clients.

CONCLUSION

When PTSD was formally accepted as a diagnostic entity in 1980, an unanticipated consequence was a favorable reception in the legal community. The diagnosis first gained notoriety when it was introduced as a new basis for the insanity defense. Since then, the use of PTSD in criminal law has been evolving steadily and has given new credibility to victims who come before the courts. Recent examples are the forensic manifestation of corollary PTSD conditions such as battered woman and rape trauma syndromes as PTSD becomes a tool of the prosecution as well as the defense. Yet, as Stone (1993) has observed, the diagnosis creates for psychiatrists some of the very problems it supposedly solves for legal purposes, including the illusory objectivity of the stressor and the expert's dependence upon the victim's subjective and unverifiable symptom report.

PTSD problems in criminal law have been compounded by its civilian counterpart. It has become apparent that public suspicion about PTSD may in large part be related to well-publicized frivolous civil lawsuits alleging stress disorders and to the recent increase in stress disability claims (Sparr, 1995). In either area (civil or criminal), self-reports of subjective PTSD symptoms have been difficult to verify. Despite these difficulties and despite pervasive public skepticism, legal advocates are expected to continue to request assistance from mental health professionals familiar with PTSD to provide opinions that will help their cases. The vicissitudes of PTSD in criminal law have been explored in this chapter. In the final analysis, only clinicians can misuse the diagnosis because only they can make it. Mental health professionals who testify in PTSD cases need to be aware of potential uses and abuses of the diagnosis in order to effectively aid the judicial process.

REFERENCES

American Psychiatric Association (1980). *Diagnostic and Statistical Manual of Mental Disorders, 3rd Edition*, Washington, D.C., American Psychiatric Association.

American Psychiatric Association (1994). *Diagnostic and Statistical Manual of Mental Disorders, 4th Edition*, Washington, D.C., American Psychiatric Association.

Appelbaum, P. S., Jick, R. Z., Grisso, T., Givelber, D., Silver, E., & Steadman, H. J. (1993). Use of post-traumatic stress disorder to support an insanity defense. *American Journal of Psychiatry, 150*, 229.

Auberry, A. R. (1985). PTSD: Effective representation of a Vietnam veteran in the criminal justice system. *Marquette Law Review, 68*, 648.

Austin, J. L. (1956-57). A plea for excuses. *Proceedings of the Aristotelian Society, 57*, 1.

Bechtel v. State, 840 P. 2d 1 (Oklahoma, 1992).

Bell v. Cone, 125 S. Ct. 847, petition for rehearing denied, 125 S. Ct. 1655 (2005).

Blake, D. D., Weathers, F. W., Nagy, L. M., et al. (1990). Clinical rating scale for assessing current and lifetime PTSD: The CAPO-I. *The Behavior Therapist, 18*, 197.

Blank, A. S. (1985). The unconscious flashback to the war in Viet Nam veterans: Clinical mystery, legal defense, and community problem. In S. M. Sonnenberg, A. S. Blank, and J. A. Talbott, (Eds.), *The trauma of war: Stress and recovery in Viet Nam veterans*. Washington, D.C.: American Psychiatric Press.

Blowers, A. N., & Bjerregaard, B. (1994). The admissibility of expert testimony on the battered woman syndrome in homicide cases. *Journal of Psychiatry and the Law, 22*, 527.

Brakel, S. J., & Brooks, A. D. (2001). *Law and psychiatry in the criminal justice system*. Littleton, CO: Rothman Publications.

Bremner, J. D., Vermetten, E., Afzal, N. et al. (2004). Deficits in verbal declarative memory function in women with childhood sexual abuse-related post-traumatic stress disorder. *Journal of Nervous and Mental Disease, 192*, 643.

Brotherton, G. L. (1981). Post-traumatic stress disorder–Opening Pandora's Box? *New England Law Review, 17*, 91.

Brown D., Scheflin A. W., & Hammond D.C. (1998). *Memory, trauma treatment, and the law*. New York: W. W. Norton.

Bursztajn, H. J., Scherr, A. E., & Brodsky A. (1994). The rebirth of forensic psychiatry in light of recent historical trends in criminal responsibility. *Psychiatric Clinics of North America, 17*, 611.

Callahan, L. A., Steadman, H. J., McGreevy, M. A., & Robbins, P. C. (1991). The volume and characteristics of insanity defense pleas: An eight-state study. *Bulletin of the American Academy of Psychiatry and the Law, 19*, 331.

Coles, E. M., & Veiel, H. O. F. (2001). Expert testimony and pseudoscience: How mental health professionals are taking over the courtroom. *International Journal of Law and Psychiatry, 24*(6), 607.

Compton, J. K. (1996). Expert witness testimony and the diminished capacity defense. *American Journal of Trial Advocacy, 20*, 381.

Daubert v. Merrill Dow, 92–102 U.S. S. Ct., 1993 125 L Ed 2d 469.

Davidson, M. J. (1988). Post-traumatic stress disorder: A controversial defense for veterans of a controversial war. *William and Mary Law Review, 29*, 415.

Dondershine, H. E. (1989). Criminal behavior and post-traumatic stress disorder. *Trauma, 31*, 31.

Dunn v. Roberts, 963 F2d 308 (10th Cir 1992).

Eddings v. Oklahoma, 55 U.S. 104, 114 (1982).

Edwards, C. N. (1998). Behavior and the law reconsidered: Psychological syndromes and profiles. *Journal of Forensic Sciences, 43*(1), 141.

Elhai, J. D., Gold, P. B., Frueh, C. B., & Gold, S. N. (2000). Cross-validation of the MMPI-2 in detecting malingered post-traumatic stress disorder. *Journal of Personality Assessment, 75*(3), 449.

Erlinder, C. P. (1984). Paying the price for Vietnam: Post-traumatic stress disorder and criminal behavior. *Boston College Law Review, 25*, 305.

Faust, D., & Ziskin, J. (1988). The expert witness in psychology and psychiatry. *Science, 241*, 31.

Federal Rules of Evidence 403.

Federal Rules of Evidence 702.

Friedman, M. J. (1991). Biological approaches to the diagnosis and treatment of post-traumatic stress disorder. *Journal of Traumatic Stress, 4*, 67.

Frye v. United States, 293 F, 1013 (D. C. Cir. 1923).

Furman v. Georgia, 408 U.S. 238 (1972).

Gilbertson, M. W., Gurvits, T. V., Lasko, N. B., et al. (2001). Multivariate assessment of explicit memory function in combat veterans with PTSD. *Journal of Traumatic Stress, 14*, 437.

Giorgi-Guarnieri, D, Janofsky, J, Keram, E., et al. (2002). AAPL Practice Guideline for forensic psychiatric evaluation of defendants raising the insanity defense. *Journal of the American Academy of Psychiatry and the Law, 30*(2) *Supplement*, S3.

Goodstein, R. K., & Page, A. W. (1981). Battered wife syndrome: Overview of dynamics and treatment. *American Journal of Psychiatry, 138*, 1036.

Gutheil, T. G. (1989). Legal issues in psychiatry. In *Comprehensive Textbook of Psychiatry/5th Ed., Vol. II, (Sect. 49.1)*, H. I. Kaplan, and B. J. Sadock, (Eds.) Baltimore, MD: Williams & Wilkins.

Gutheil, T. G. (1998). *The psychiatrist as expert witness.* Washington, D.C.: American Psychiatric Press.

Halleck, S. L., Hoge, S. K., Miller, R. D., Sadoff, R. L., & Halleck, N. H. (1992). The use of psychiatric diagnoses in the legal process: Task force report of the American Psychiatric Association. *Bulletin of the American Academy of Psychiatry and the Law, 20*, 481.

Hart, H. L. A. (1968). *Punishment and responsibility.* Oxford: Clarendon Press.

Hoge, S. K., & Grisso, T. (1992). Accuracy and expert testimony. *Bulletin of the American Academy of Psychiatry and the Law, 20*, 67.

Huber, P. W. (1991). *Galileo's revenge: Junk science in the courtroom.* New York, NY: Basic Books.

Ibn-Tamas v. U.S., 407 A 2d 626 (D.C. 1979).

Janofsky, J. S., Vandewalle, M. B., & Rappeport, J. R. (1989). Defendants pleading insanity: An analysis of outcome. *Bulletin of the American Academy of Psychiatry and the Law, 17*, 203.

Kadish, H., & Schulhofer, S. J. (2001). *Criminal law and its processes: Cases and materials (7th Edition).* New York: Aspen Publishers, Inc.

Keane, T. M., Caddell, J. M., & Taylor, K. L. (1988). Mississippi Scale for combat-related post-traumatic stress disorder: Three studies in reliability and validity. *Journal of Consulting and Clinical Psychology, 56*, 85.

Keane T. M., Malloy P. F., & Fairbank J. A. (1984). Empirical development of an MMPI subscale for the assessment of combat-related post-traumatic stress disorder. *Journal of Consulting and Clinical Psychology, 52*, 888.

Kirchmeier, J. L. (1998). Aggravating and mitigating factors: The paradox of today's arbitrary and mandatory capital punishment scheme. *William and Mary Bill of Rights Journal, 6*, 345.

Koch, W. J., O'Neill, M., & Douglas, K. S. (2005). Empirical limits for the forensic assessment of PTSD litigants. *Law and Human Behavior, 29*(1), 121.

LeDoux, D. A. (2000). Evidentiary concerns presented by proof of psychological injures due to Frye/Daubert: Getting past the "Gatekeeper." In *Psychological Injury Claims.* Minneapolis: Minnesota Institute Legal Education.

Lees-Haley, P. R. (1990). Malingering mental disorder on the Impact of Event (IES) Scale: Toxic exposure and cancerphobia. *Journal of Traumatic Stress, 3*, 315.

Lewis v. State, 1995 WL 296423 (Georgia, 1995).

Litz, B. T., Penk, W. E., Walsh, S., et al. (1991). Similarities and differences between MMPI and MMPI-2 applications to the assessment of post-traumatic stress disorder. *Journal of Personality Assessment, 57*, 238.

Lockett v. Ohio, 438 U.S. 586, 604 (1978).

Lustberg, L. S., & Jacobi, J. V. (1992). The battered woman as reasonable person: A critique of the Appellate Division Decision in *State v. McClain. Seton Hall Law Review, 22*, 365.

Marciniak, R. D. (1986). Implications to forensic psychiatry of post-traumatic stress disorder: A review. *Military Medicine, 151*, 434.

Marwick, C. (1993a). What constitutes an expert witness? *Journal of the American Medical Association, 269*, 2057.

Marwick, C. (1993b). Court ruling on 'Junk Science' gives judges more say about what expert witness testimony to allow. *Journal of the American Medical Association, 270*, 423.

McNally, F. J. (1998). Experimental approaches to cognitive abnormality in post-traumatic stress disorder. *Clinical Psychology Review, 18*, 971.

M'Naghten's Case, 10 Clark & Fin. 200, 8 Eng. Rep. 718 (1843).

Melton, G. B., Petrila, J., Poythress, N. G., & Slobogin, C. (1997). *Psychological evaluations for the courts (2nd Ed.).* New York: Guilford Press.

Model Penal Code (Official Draft, 1962)

Model Penal Code §2.02(1) (1962).

Morissette v. United States, 342 U.S. 246, 252 (1952).

Morris, G. H. (1975). *The insanity defense: A blueprint for legislative reform.* Lexington, Massachusetts: D.C. Heath and Company.

Motherway, J. J. (1987). Post-traumatic stress disorder. *American Jurisprudence Proof of Facts 2nd, 49*, 73.

Orr, S. P., Metzger, L. J., Lasko, N. B., et al. (2000). De Novo conditioning in trauma-exposed individuals with and without post-traumatic stress disorder. *Journal of Abnormal Psychology, 109*, 290.

Perconte, S. T., & Goreczny, A. J. (1990). Failure to detect fabricated post-traumatic stress disorder with the use of the MMPI in a clinical population. *American Journal of Psychiatry, 147*, 1057.

Perlin, M. L. (1994). *The jurisprudence of the insanity defense.* Carolina Academic Press.

Phillips, M. R., Wolf, A. S., & Coons, D. J. (1988). Psychiatry and the criminal justice system: Testing the myths. *American Journal of Psychiatry, 145*, 605.

"Psychiatric sequelae of military duty in a war zone" (Chapter 20) *Physician's Guide for Disability Evaluation Examinations,* 1985, Washington, D.C.: Department of Veterans Affairs.

Pitman, R. K., Orr, S. P., Forgue, D. F., et al. (1987). Psychophysiologic assessment of post-traumatic stress disorder imagery in Vietnam combat veterans. *Archives of General Psychiatry, 44*, 970.

Pitman, R. K., Orr, S. P., & Bursztajn, H. J. (1993). *Vinal v. New England Telephone:* Admission of PTSD psychophysiologic test results in a civil trial. *American Academy of Psychiatry and the Law Newsletter, 18*, 67.

Pitman, R. K., Sparr, L. F, Saunders, L. S., et al. (1996). Legal issues in post-traumatic stress disorder. In A. L. McFarlane, B. A. Vanderkolk, and L. Weisneth, (Eds.) *Comprehensive textbook on post-traumatic stress disorders.* New York: Guilford Publications.

Pitman, R. K., & Orr, S. P. (2003). Forensic laboratory testing for post-traumatic stress disorder, in *Post-traumatic stress disorder in litigation: Guidelines for forensic assessment, (2nd Ed.).* Edited by Simon R. I. Washington, D.C.: American Psychiatric Press, pp. 207–223.

Prosecutor v. Anto Furundzija, ICTY Case No. IT-95-17/1-T (1998). Available at www.un.org/icty

Prosecutor v. Stevan Todorovic, ICTY Case No. IT-95-9/1-S (2001). Available at www.un.org/icty

Pub. L. No. 98–596, §§ 402, 404, 406, 98 Stat. 3134 (Oct 12, 1984).

Raifman, L. J. (1993). Problems of diagnosis and legal causation in courtroom use of post-traumatic stress disorder. *Behavioral Sciences and the Law, 1,* 115.

Rappeport, J. R. (1992). Current status of the insanity plea. *Psychiatric Annals, 22,* 550.

Resnick, P. J. (1998). Malingering of post-traumatic stress disorders. *Journal of Practical Psychiatry and Behavioral Health, 4,* 329.

Rix, K. (2001). 'Battered woman syndrome' and the defense of provocation: Two women with something more in common. *Journal of Forensic Psychiatry, 12*(1), 131.

Rogers, R., Bagby, R. M., & Dickens, S. E. (1992). *Structured interview for reported symptoms.* Odessa, FL: Psychological Assessment Resources, Inc.

Rogers, T. (2004). Diagnostic validity and expert witness testimony. *International Journal of Law and Psychiatry, 27*(3), 281.

Roth, L. H. (1986). Preserve but limit the insanity defense. *Psychiatric Quarterly, 5,* 91.

Sadoff, R. L. (1992). In defense of the insanity defense. *Psychiatric Annals, 22,* 556.

Shaw, D. M., Churchill, C. M., Noyes, R, & Loeffelholz, P. L. (1987). Criminal behavior and post-traumatic stress disorder in Vietnam veterans. *Comprehensive Psychiatry, 28,* 403.

Shepard v. State, 457 P. 2d 75 (Alaska App. 1993).

Shuman, D. W. (1995). Persistent re-experiences in psychiatry and law: Current and future trends in post-traumatic stress disorder litigation. In *Post-traumatic stress disorder in litigation for forensic assessment.* R. I. Simon, (Ed.) Washington, D.C.: American Psychiatric Press.

Shuman, D. W. (2003). *Psychiatric and psychological evidence.* Chapter 12, (2nd Ed.), St. Paul, MN, West Group.

Simon, R. I. (1995a). Preface. *Post-traumatic stress disorder in litigation: Guidelines for forensic assessment.* R. I. Simon, (Ed.) Washington, D.C.: American Psychiatric Press.

Simon, R. I. (1995b). Toward the development of guidelines in the forensic psychiatric examination of post-traumatic stress disorder claimants. In *Post-traumatic stress disorder in litigation: Guidelines for forensic assessment.* R. I. Simon, (Ed.) Washington, D.C.: American Psychiatric Press.

Simon, R. I. (Ed.) (1995c). *Post-traumatic stress disorder in litigation: Guidelines for forensic assessment.* Washington, D.C.: American Psychiatric Press.

Skidmore v. Precision Printing and Packaging Inc., 188 F.3d 606 (5th Cir. 1999)

Slovenko, R. (1984). Syndrome evidence in establishing a stressor. *Journal of Psychiatry and the Law, 12,* 443.

Sparr, L. F., & Pankratz, L. D. (1983). Factitious post-traumatic stress disorder. *American Journal of Psychiatry, 140,* 1016.

Sparr, L. F., & Atkinson, R. M. (1986). Post-traumatic stress disorder as an insanity defense: Medicolegal quicksand. *American Journal of Psychiatry, 143,* 608.

Sparr, L. F. (1990). Legal aspects of post-traumatic stress disorder: Uses and abuses, In *Post-traumatic stress disorder: Ideology, phenomenology, and treatment.* Edited by Wolf, M. E., & Mosnaim, A. D. Washington, D.C.: American Psychiatric Press, pp. 239–264.

Sparr, L. F., & Boehnlein, J. K. (1990). Post-traumatic stress disorder and tort actions: Forensic minefield. *Bulletin American Academy of Psychiatry and the Law, 18*(3), 283.

Sparr. L. F. (1995). Post-traumatic stress disorder: Does it exist? *Neurologic Clinics of North America, 13*, 413.

Sparr, L. F., & Pitman, R. K. (1999). Forensic assessment of traumatized adults. In *Post-traumatic stress disorder: A comprehensive test.* Edited by Bremner, J. D., & Saigh, P. Boston: Allyn & Bacon, pp. 284–308.

Sparr, L. F. (2005). Mental incapacity defenses at the war crimes tribunal: Questions and controversy. *Journal of the American Academy of Psychiatry and the Law, 33*(1), 59.

Sparr, L. F., & Bremner, J. D. (2005). Post-traumatic stress disorder and memory: Prescient medicolegal testimony at the international war crimes tribunal. *Journal of American Academy of Psychiatry and the Law, 33*(1), 71.

Spaulding, W. J. (1988). Compensation for mental disability. In R. Michels (Ed.), *Psychiatry,* (Vol 3, Chapter 33, pp. 1–27). Philadelphia: J. B. Lippincott Co.

Speir, D. E. (1989). Application and use of post-traumatic stress disorder as a defense to criminal conduct. *Army Lawyer, June,* 17.

Spitzer, R. L., Williams, J. B., Gibbon, M., et al. (1990a). *Structured Clinical Interview for DSM–III–R.* Washington, D.C.: American Psychiatric Press.

Spitzer, R. L., Williams, J. B., Gibbon, M. et al. (1990b). *Structured Clinical Interview for DSM–III–R Personality Disorders.* Washington, D.C.: American Psychiatric Press.

State v. Allery, 101 Wn. 2d 591, 682 P. 2d 312 (1984).

State v. Cocuzza, No 1484–79 (Supp Ct. Middlesex Cty. N.J. 1981).

State v. Felde, 422 So. 2d 370 (La. 1982).

State v. Grubbs, 353 S.C. 374, 577 S.E. 2d 493 (Ct. App. 2003).

State v. Heads, 385 So. 2d 230 (La. Jun. 23, 1980).

State v. Johnson, 968 S.W. 2d 123 (Mo. S. Ct. 1998).

State v. Kelly, 97 N. J. 178, 478 A. 2d 364 (1984).

State v. Mann, No 82-CR-310 (Cir. Ct. Marinette Cty. WI, Aug. 1983).

State v. McClain, 248 N.J. Super. 409, 591 A. 2d b52 (N.J. Super. A.D. 1991).

State v. Necaise, 466 So. 2d 660 (La. Ct. App. 1985).

State v. Pascal, 736 P. 2d 1065 (Wash. 1987).

State v. Phipps, 883 S.W. 2d 138 (Tenn. Ct. App. 1994).

State v. Spawr, 653 S.W. 2d 404 (Tenn. 1983).

Steinberg, C. E. (1993). The Daubert decision: An update on the Frye rule. *American Academy of Psychiatry and the Law Newsletter, 18,* 66.

Stone, A. A. (1993). Post-traumatic stress disorder and the law: Critical review of the new frontier. *Bulletin of the American Academy of Psychiatry and the Law, 21,* 23.

United States v. Cantu, 12 F 3d 1506 (9th Cir. 1993).

United States v. Cartagena-Carrasquillo, 70 F.3d 706 (1st Circuit 1995).

United States v. Hinckley, 672 F. 3d 115 (D. C. Cir. 1982).

United States v. Rezaq, 134 F.3d 1121 (U.S. App. D.C. 1998).

United States v. Whitehead, 896 F.2d 432 (U.S. App. 9th Cir. 1990).

United States v. Winters, 729 F 2d 602 (9th Cir. 1984).

18 U. S. C. § 20 (a) (Supp, III 1985).

Walker, J. I. (1981). Vietnam combat veterans with legal difficulties: A psychiatric problem? *American Journal of Psychiatry, 138,* 1384.

Walker, L. E. (1980). *The battered woman.* New York, New York: HarperCollins.

Walker, L. E. (2000). *The battered woman syndrome.* (2nd Ed.) New York: Springer Publishing.

Wechsler, H. (1968). Codification of the criminal law in the United States: The Model Penal Code. *Columbia Law Review, 68,* 1425.

West Virginia v. Walls, 445 S.E. 2d 515 (W. Va. Sup. Ct. 1994).

Zilberg, N. J., Weiss, D. S., & Horowitz, M. J. (1982). Impact of Event Scale: A cross-validation study and some empirical evidence supporting a conceptual model of stress response syndromes. *Journal of Consulting and Clinical Psychology, 50,* 407.

Chapter 15

ASSESSMENT OF MALINGERING IN CRIMINAL SETTINGS

Karen L. Salekin and Richard Rogers

Malingering, as defined by the *Diagnostic and Statistical Manual, Fourth Edition, Text Revision* (*DSM–IV–TR*; American Psychiatric Association, 2000), is not a mental disorder, but instead it is considered a V code, specifically "a condition that may be the focus of clinical attention." According to the *DSM–IV–TR*, malingering involves the "intentional production of false or grossly exaggerated physical or psychological symptoms, motivated by external incentives such as avoiding military duty, avoiding work, obtaining financial compensation, evading criminal prosecution, or obtaining drugs" (American Psychiatric Association, p. 739). In the *DSM–IV–TR* the American Psychiatric Association recommends that malingering should be suspected if two or more of the following screening indices occur (a) an evaluation in a forensic context, (b) a marked discrepancies between claimed distress and the objective data, (c) uncooperativeness during the evaluation and treatment regimen, and (d) the presence of Antisocial Personality Disorder (APD).

As evident from above, the *DSM–IV–TR's* portrayal of the person who malingers is particularly pejorative and omits any discussion that a person feigning or exaggerating symptomatology could be genuinely distressed or suffer from a bona fide Axis I disorder. Furthermore, while acknowledging the potentially adaptive nature of the condition, the *DSM–IV–TR* conceptualization depicts the malingerer as a deceptive and likely corrupt individual who is taking liberties with the medical and/or judicial system. This viewpoint has been discussed in the literature and has been labeled the criminological model of malingering (Rogers, 1990a). Alternative conceptualizations (see Rogers, 1990a; Rogers, 1990b; Rogers; 2004) include the pathogenic and adaptational models. In brief, the pathogenic model assumes that malingering arises out of true pathology and that the intentional production of symptoms represents an ineffectual attempt to control symptoms associated with a bona fide mental disorder. In contrast, the adaptational model posits that malingered presentations originate from a decision-making process in which an individual weighs the potential costs and benefits of malingering. Faced with adversarial circumstances, an individual may choose to malinger based on potential benefits, potential costs, and perceived choices. Prototypicality studies (Rogers, Sewell, & Goldstein, 1994; Rogers, Salekin, Sewell, Goldstein, & Leonard, 1998) have demonstrated that forensic practitioners view the adaptational model as being most aligned with current conceptualizations of malingering.

An important concern with the criminological model is that it may overemphasize the likelihood of malingering, especially in criminal forensic cases, and underemphasize it in nonforensic referrals. The majority of criminal offenders are likely to meet at least two of the *DSM–IV* screening indices, simply because of the context (forensic setting) and their background (Antisocial Personality Disorder). In evaluating these indices, Rogers (1990b) found that they produce unacceptably high false-positive ratings, being wrong approximately four out of five times.

Researchers have not investigated the current conceptualizations of malingering, as considered by health care and legal professionals. For instance, some health care providers appear to equate medication seeking among inmates with malingering (Vitacco & Rogers, 2005). Such assumptions, combined with the criminological model, may subvert the accurate assessment of malingering and related response styles. Inaccuracies in the determination of malingering have far-reaching consequences for the verdicts and sentencing of criminal defendants. Regarding the latter, the U.S. Fifth Circuit Court of Appeals decision in *U.S. v. Greer* (1998) upheld the district court's decision to allow the government to increase the offense level of the purpose of sentencing. The sentence enhancement was justified because the defendant attempted to obstruct justice by malingering.

In this chapter we examine fundamental issues in the assessment of malingering, present a summary of current practices in the assessment of malingering, and apply this information to an area of concern in the legal arena; specifically, competency to stand trial. We begin with an overview of base rates.

THE ISSUE OF BASE RATES

For most people, understanding of base rates is largely intuitive; our expectations about what may, or may not occur, come from our estimations of its likelihood. For example, the saying "if you hear hoofs, think horse not zebra" rings true in most places of the world since it is far more likely that a person will encounter a horse than a zebra (Lane, 2003). When applying this principle to the assessment and classification of a disorder, two components must be known before a reasonably correct estimation of probability can occur. First, it is critical that the condition is accurately measured. Second, it is essential that the base rate remain relatively stable (Rogers & Salekin, 1998).

In recent years, much discussion has centered on the application mathematical principles to the classification of malingering (Mossman & Hart, 1996; Rogers & Salekin, 1998; Mossman, 2000; Rosenfeld, Sands, & Van Gorp, 2000). The thrust of the debate has focused on the applicability of Bayes theorem using base rates of malingering. Rogers and Salekin (1998) argue caution in the application of base rates, because of their instability. On this point, Rogers, Salekin, Sewell, Goldstein, and Leonard (1998) found marked variability in estimates of malingering. Across 220 experts, the standard deviation was 14.44 percent with a standard error of measurement of 1.08 percent. Such variability, by itself, argues against the assumption of a stable base rate. However, the issue is far more complicated. The prevalence of malingering is likely to vary with the type of referral (e.g., insanity vs. sexually violent predator) and individual circumstances, such as the offense (e.g., murder vs. drug possession). Of equal importance, the assessment process markedly affects base rates. When malingering screens are used, the prevalence rate is likely to triple. In summary, base rates *could* be a valuable tool for the classification of malingering. Before their use in forensic settings, base rates must be (a) established and replicated for the particular institution, (b) specific to the type of referral, (c) specific to the category of offense, and (d) applied to the same assessment process (i.e., screened or unscreened).

THE DAUBERT STANDARD

Prior to 1993, admissibility of expert testimony fell under the 1923 court ruling in *Frye v. United States*. Specifically, the threshold for admissibility hinged on whether or not the scientific theory or technique had "gained general acceptance in the particular field in which it belongs" (*Frye v. United States*, 1923, p. 1014). With the U.S. Supreme Court decision in *Daubert v. Merrell Dow Pharmaceuticals, Inc.* (1993), the threshold for admissibility was broadened. Briefly, the guidelines set forth in *Daubert* asked the judge to consider whether the theory or technique is (a) falsifiable, (b) subjected to peer review and publication, (c) has a known or potentially-known error rate and (d) has gained general acceptance in the scientific community. While the decision in *Daubert* addressed scientific testimony, the *Kumho* decision (*Kumho Tire Co. v. Carmichael*, 1999) expanded the guidelines to include all forms of expert witness testimony. The decisions in *Daubert* and *Kumho* placed the decision of admissibility squarely in the hands of the judiciary leaving judges in unenviable position of identifying invalid and unreliable expert evidence across multiple domains of science (see also *General Electric Company v. Joiner*, 1997). Not surprisingly, the ability of the judiciary to carry out this daunting task has been questioned (Kovera, Russano, & McAuliff, 2002). Krauss and Sales (1999) question how trial courts can understand complex scientific data and apply it consistently across jurisdictions.

Vallabhajosula and van Gorp (2001) examined the admissibility of three malingering measures in light of the *Daubert* criteria. The study focused on feigned cognitive impairment and the following measures: the Rey 15-Item Memory Test (REY–15; Lezak, 1995), the Validity Indicator Profile (VIP; Frederick, 1997), and the Test of Memory Malingering (TOMM; Tombaugh, 1996). Making assumptions about base rates, the authors concluded that only the TOMM was likely to meet the *Daubert* standards.

Data are limited in both the psychological literature and case law regarding the admissibility of malingering measures in light of *Daubert*. A recent Psycinfo search (December 2005) identified 18 articles for

Daubert and malingering. Of these, 14 specifically addressed malingering on psychological measures with a major emphasis on feigned cognitive impairment. Regarding case law, Mossman (2003) conducted a Lexis search and identified 18 published cases; only five pertained to *Daubert* admissibility issues (see *United States v. Gigante*, 1997a; *United States v. Gigante*, 1997b; *Downs v. Perstrop Components and ICI Americas*, 1999; *Coe v. Tennessee*, 2000; *Villalba v. Consolidated Freightways Corp.*, 2000). Four cases focused on cognitive malingering whereas the remaining case considered feigned psychopathology on three measures: the Minnesota Multiphasic Personality Inventory–2 (MMPI–2; Butcher, Williams, Graham, Tellegen, & Kaemmer, 1989), the Millon Clinical Multiaxial Inventory–III (MCMI–III; Millon, Davis, & Millon, 1997), and the Structured Interview of Reported Symptoms (SIRS; Rogers, Bagby, & Dickens, 1992).

Of the four cases evaluating the admissibility of cognitive measures of malingering, one case did not evaluate whether or not the testimony regarding four neuropsychological tests satisfied the guidelines put forth in *Daubert*, one stated directly that the expert testimony did satisfy the criteria, and two excluded expert testimony on the grounds that the conclusions did not meet one of more of the *Daubert* admissibility criteria. Use of the REY–15 was an instrument in *Gigante* (1997a) the validity of the REY–15 was not challenged, but it was deemed inadmissible in *Downs* because of inadequate validity. With general guidance from case law, forensic practitioners will need to establish their own reviews of malingering measures in light of *Daubert*.

THE ASSESSMENT OF MALINGERING

All psychological assessments depend on validity of the measures and the accurate interpretation of their results. Response styles and motivation must be ascertained for all evaluations because of their direct effects on test results. Clinicians should take great care in their assessment of malingering, irrespective of context or referral issue. They are obliged to choose measures with excellent reliability and validity that rely on multiple detection strategies to assess the potential for malingering (Rogers & Bender, 2003). In addition, malingering should be assessed with reference to one or more domains (e.g., mental disorders, cognitive impairment, and medical illness) and use detection strategies validated for that domain. Rogers (1997) summarized detection strategies for feigned mental disorders. They include an unexpected number of rare symptoms, improbable symptoms, erroneous stereotypes, and unusual symptom combinations. Other detection strategies capitalize on the severity of reported symptoms, indiscriminant symptom endorsement, disproportionate endorsement of obvious versus subtle symptoms, and the discrepancy between reported and observed symptoms.

Forensic evaluations of malingering are often challenging because of extensive records, conflicting reports, and variable findings on psychological measures. In addition, many measures of malingering have limited clinical value because of their emphasis on group differences rather than individual classification. Forensic practitioners must also take into account the accuracy of each measure and its applicability to forensic contexts. For example, validity scales on multiscale inventories are often elevated in forensic populations. However, these elevations rarely yield sufficient accuracy for the classification of malingering for individual forensic cases. The onus is on the clinician to objectively evaluate tests based on utility estimates (e.g., positive and negative predictive power) and their applicability to a particular criminal defendant (e.g., an individual with poor literacy and borderline intellectual functioning).

Forensic practitioners should also be alert for clinicians that mistakenly apply a false dichotomy to the assessment of malingering. Specifically, the determination of malingering does not preclude genuine disorder. Likewise, the presence of a genuine disorder offers no immunity against malingering or other response styles. In forensic assessments, the goal is to evaluate both malingering and bona fide disorders.

The literature is replete with measures either designed specifically to assess malingering or to have embedded scales to detect such response patterns. In his review of forensic practices, Lally (2003) identified validated measures for the evaluation of malingering. In the domain of feigned mental disorders, two measures were recommended (SIRS and MMPI–2) and one was deemed acceptable (PAI). For feigned cognitive impairment, three specialized measures were identified as acceptable (REY–15, TOMM, and VIP) that could be supplemented by special indices on the Wechsler Adult Intelligence Scale–3rd Edition (WAIS–III; Wechsler, 1997) and the Halstead-Reitan (Lezak, 1995).

MEASURES OF FEIGNED MENTAL DISORDERS

Structured Interview of Reported Symptoms (recommended). The SIRS is a structured interview that was designed to assess response styles such as malingering, defensiveness, irrelevant response style, and reliable response style (Rogers et al., 1992). The interview consists of 172 items that are organized into eight primary scales: (1) Rare Symptoms, (2) Symptom Combinations, (3) Improbable and Absurd Symptoms, (4) Blatant Symptoms, (5) Subtle Symptoms, (6) Selectivity of Symptoms, (7) Severity of Symptoms, and (8) Reported versus Observed Symptoms. Validation studies have been conducted using clinical, community, and correctional populations, and the instrument is appropriate for use with adults in both inpatient and outpatient evaluations, in both clinical and forensic settings.

The SIRS should be interpreted in conjunction with collateral interviews, clinical records, and test data on malingering (Rogers et al., 1992). Interpretation occurs at two levels: (1) descriptive analysis, and (2) classification of honest and feigned presentations. In brief, the scores on the eight primary scales of the SIRS are placed into classification levels based on certainty of the results. These levels have been termed honest responding, indeterminant, probable feigning, and definite feigning. The manual discusses the use of single scale score classifications, as well as the preferred multiple scale score classification.

Most classifications of feigning are based on use of multiple detection strategies with three or more primary scales being elevated to the "probable feigning" level. Occasionally, individuals will have such extreme elevations that the determination could rely on single detection strategy (i.e., one scale at the "definite feigning" level). In practice, however, such extreme elevations are typically accompanied by other SIRS scales at the "probable feigning" level.

Extensive research, both by Rogers and his colleagues and independent investigators, have established the SIRS as a well-validated measure (see Rogers, 1997; Rogers & Bender, 2003). As established through multiple studies, its decision rules produce very few false-positives (≤ 3%) thereby reducing the likelihood of genuine patients being misclassified as malingering. An important feature of the SIRS is its construct validity. Very recently, Rogers, Jackson, Sewell, and Salekin (2005) examined its latent dimensions via confirmatory factor analysis with multiple data sets. Using two latent dimensions, malingerers can be identified by highly atypical presentations and marked overreporting of plausible symptoms.

Minnesota Multiphasic Personality Inventory–2nd Edition (recommended). The MMPI–2 (Butcher et al., 1989) is a multiscale inventory designed to assess a broad range of psychopathology. Rogers, Sewell, Martin, and Vitacco (2003) conducted a comprehensive meta-analysis of the MMPI–2 that examined 65 feigning studies augmented with diagnostic research. This section relies heavily on the findings of this meta-analysis.

One caution regarding MMPI–2 interpretations with offender populations is its required reading level. According to Butcher et al. (1989), the MMPI–2 requires a reading level of approximately the sixth grade, although close to 10 percent of its items require at least some high school education. Butcher et al. caution that impaired comprehension may pose a problem for individuals who are young, intellectually limited, learning disabled, culturally deprived, and/or recent immigrants. Clearly, practitioners must use caution in their use of MMPI–2 with offenders that have limited comprehension due to cognitive abilities, reading comprehension, or cultural experiences.

Rogers et al. (2003) identified different detection strategies used by MMPI–2 validity scales. The Fp scale uses a true rare-symptom strategy comprised of MMPI–2 items that infrequently occur with genuine patients. In contrast, F and Fb rely on a quasi rare-symptom strategy; items on these scales rarely occur in presumably unimpaired individuals. In addition, erroneous stereotypes are utilized with by three validity scales: Ds, Dsr, and FBS. Other strategies include symptom severity (i.e., overendorsement on the Lachar-Wrobel critical items) and differences between obvious and subtle items.

Forensic practitioners should be very careful not to interpret elevated validity scales as necessarily evidence of malingering. As summarized by Rogers et al. (2003), marked elevations are common among genuine patients with Axis I disorders:

- Schizophrenia: average F = 80.10; average Fb = 79.36
- Major depression: average F = 71.68; average Fb = 82.02
- PTSD: average F = 86.31; average Fb = 92.31

With exceptionally large standard deviations, ranging from 21.58 to 24.55, genuine disorders cannot be ruled-out except in very extreme cases. In summary, elevations of F and Fb should be mostly used as a screen for potential cases of malingering.

Several scales have considerable promise for the evaluation of feigned mental disorders. The Fp scale, as a true rare-symptom strategy, does not produce such marked elevations among patients with genuine Axis I disorders. Based on the meta-analysis, Fp scores exceeding 98T are likely to produce very few false-positives in the determination of probable feigning. In addition, the Ds scale, using erroneous stereotypes, also appears effective when a high proportion of items are endorsed (feigning cut score > 35 raw). As an important caution, all inconsistent profiles must be removed before any MMPI–2 evaluation of feigning (Green, 1997). As with the SIRS, even such extreme elevations require further corroboration via a multi-method assessment.

Rogers and Bender (2003) summarized key missteps in the MMPI–2 interpretation of feigned profiles. In addition to interpreting inconsistent profiles, some practitioners attempt to infer feigning because the clinical profile is "incompatible" with other clinical data. This inference is a serious misuse of the MMPI–2 because no "signature" profiles exist for specific disorders. Indeed, the most common profile among genuine patients is a within-normal-limits profile (i.e., no clinical elevations). Rogers and Shuman (2005) provide sample cross-examination for addressing the vulnerabilities of MMPI–2 interpretations for the determination of feigning.

A major concern for all measures of response styles, is the ability of individuals to avoid detection after having been coached at how to foil the test or how to accurately feign a particular disorder. Rogers, Bagby, and Chakraborty (1993) found that knowledge of detection strategies incorporated into the MMPI–2 validity scales, but not knowledge of psychopathology, resulted in a decreased ability to detect feigned responding on the MMPI–2. Although the MMPI–2 is not recommended for the assessment of feigned head injury, Lamb, Berry, Wetter and Baer (1994) yielded results similar to Rogers et al.; information on the operation of the validity scales was valuable to feigners whereas facts about symptoms associated with head injuries were not. Even general instructions to avoid overendorsement of psychopathology may be sufficient to reduce detection (Viglione et al., 2001). One positive finding is that the Fp scale, may be less susceptible to coaching (Storm & Graham, 2000). The authors suggest that the Fp scale may be protected because its items are not obvious signs of psychopathology (i.e., they have low face validity). Taken together, coaching research indicates that MMPI–2 is clearly susceptible. In practical terms, its validity scales cannot be used as the primary indicator that individuals are genuine (i.e., nonfeigning) in their clinical presentations.

Personality Assessment Inventory (PAI) (acceptable). The PAI is a 344 item multiscale personality inventory that provides information regarding clinical symptoms, treatment needs, and interpersonal functioning (Morey, 1991). The test is comprised of 22 nonoverlapping scales including four validity scales, 11 clinical scales, five treatment scales, and two interpersonal scales. In criminal forensic settings, the PAI is especially useful given its relatively short length and easy reading comprehension (i.e., 4th grade). It capitalizes on two detection strategies: rare symptoms (NIM scale) and unlikely patterns of psychopathology. Regarding the latter strategy, the Malingering Index (MAL; see Morey, 1996) examines highly unusual patterns among PAI scales and subscales. A second effort to assess unlikely patterns of psychopathology is the RDF, a discriminant function for distinguishing feigned from genuine profiles. Other validity scales evaluate inconsistency (Inconsistency Scale or INC and Infrequency Scale or INF) and defensiveness (Positive Impression Index or PIM).

The NIM scale appears to be moderately effective as a screen for malingering. Focusing on the NIM, marked elevations (77T to 109T) indicate the need to evaluate feigning. Extreme elevations (NIM ≥ 110T) are infrequent, even in feigning populations; however, such elevations are likely to signify a feigned PAI profile.

The MAL index uses eight configural rules based on PAI scales and subscales. Given its complexity, the coaching of potential feigners would be difficult. Based on simulation research and known-groups comparisons, a MAL index > 5 indicates a high probability the individual is a feigning. This index has been validated with both clinical and forensic populations. In contrast to the MAL index, the RDF appears to be highly effective in clinical but not criminal forensic populations. Regarding the latter, its false-positive rate of approximately 36 percent is unacceptably high (Rogers, Sewell, Cruise, Wang, & Ustad, 1998).

Recently, Hopwood, Morey, Rogers, and Sewell (in press) reanalyzed the extensive data from PAI clinical samples and feigning research (Rogers, Sewell, Morey, & Salekin, 1996). By examining discrepancy scores, Hopwood et al. provide initial data on what type of disorder an individual may be feigning. While preliminary, these results have important implications to forensic practice. Because many malingerers have genuine disorders, these findings are an important first step in discriminating feigned from nonfeigned disorders.

MEASURES OF FEIGNED COGNITIVE IMPAIRMENT

Dozens of specialized measures have been developed during the last decade for the evaluation of feigned cognitive impairment. In the domain of criminal forensic practice, the potential malingering of mental retardation has become particularly salient in light of the Supreme Court decision in *Atkins v. Virginia* (2002) that prohibits the execution of inmates with mental retardation.

Rogers and Bender (2003) summarized the detection strategies that have been used and validated for the evaluation of feigned cognitive impairment. The *floor effect* is the most common strategy; it is composed of "too easy" items that can be completed by most cognitively impaired persons. Its primary limitation is its susceptibility to simple coaching (e.g., "try your best"). Two more sophisticated detection strategies are *performance curve* and *magnitude of error*. For *performance curve*, a genuinely impaired person evidences greater decrements in functioning as the item difficulty increases. Many malingerers are unaware of this pattern. The *magnitude of error* evaluates the plausibility of inaccurate responses. On complex measures, it appears to be very effective at detecting malingerers (Bender & Rogers, 2004).

Two detection strategies are often confused: *symptom validity testing (SVT)* and *forced choice testing (FCT)*. Both strategies are based on unexpectedly poor performance. The crucial difference is that *SVT* capitalizes on significantly below-chance performance. Such poor performances provide the most convincing evidence of cognitive feigning, although they occur in only a small percentage of malingerers. In contrast, *FCT* uses unexpectedly poor performances as measured against persons with genuine cognitive impairment. Unlike *SVT, FCT* is vulnerable to misclassifications because certain types of cognitive disorders (e.g., dementia) and comorbidity (e.g., dementia and depression) may produce lower than expected test results.

Two additional strategies include the *Consistency across Comparable Items (CACI)* and *violation of learning principles (VLP)*. The *CACI* requires a rigorous testing of item difficulty to ascertain whether the observed variability among similar items is expected in clinical populations, or whether it represents a marked departure associated with likely feigning. Frederick (1997) has refined this strategy and applied it to the Validity Indicator Profile. The *VLP* strategy relies on clear violations of learning principles. For example, performance on recognition should exceed recall on learning tasks.

Forensic practitioners should be well-grounded in methodology and validation of cognitive feigning measures (see Reynolds, 1998; Rogers, 1997). Hom and Denney (2002) provided a useful overview of the more popular measures with chapters contributed by test authors. This information should be supplemented by data on detection strategies (Rogers & Bender, 2003) including meta-analyses, such as *SVT* and *FCT* (see for example, Bianchini, Mathias, & Greve, 2001). Before using any specific measure, forensic practitioners should be versed in its validation, recommended uses, and psychometric limitations.

Because of space limitations, we present information on only those measures of cognitive malingering that were previously identified as recommended or acceptable in the Lally study. The intent is not to portray these measures as the most suitable for evaluations of malingered cognitive impairment; in fact, research would suggest that clinicians should use caution when using them in both forensic and clinical settings.

Test of Memory Malingering (TOMM). The TOMM is a forced-choice recognition task that utilizes *floor effect* and *SVT* to assess nonverbal memory recognition. The TOMM requires that the individual learn 50 line-drawn pictures of common objects (e.g., hat or birdhouse) and then choose the previously learned object from a set of two. Trial 1 and Trial 2 are identical in that they display for the examinee 50 pictures (the learning trial) and then immediately afterward present the forced choice alternatives. The retention trial is optional and occurs 15 minutes after the completion of the second trial.

The TOMM was validated on both clinical and nonclinical samples. The clinical sample included five groups who obtained the following diagnoses: (1) no cognitive impairment ($n = 13$), (2) cognitive impairment ($n = 42$), (3) aphasia ($n = 21$), (4) traumatic brain injury ($n = 45$), and (5) dementia ($n = 40$). The results indicated that the TOMM had high specificity. According to its author, the studies also demonstrated that the TOMM was "not sensitive to age or education" (Tombaugh, 1996, p. 12). However, a review of their findings suggests that further testing is needed for participants with low education; both the clinical and nonclinical samples have on average a high school education. In light of the modest clinical samples ($M = 32.2$ participants), we question whether the potential effects of age could be adequately tested.

Interpretation of the TOMM occurs at two levels. According to the manual, malingering should be suspected if the individual scores less than chance on any of the three trials (i.e., the SVT strategy), or if they score below 45/50 on Trial 2 or the retention trial (i.e., the floor-effect strategy). The author's choice of 45/50 was based on the finding that in the normative studies the TOMM correctly classified 95 percent of all nondemented individuals and 91 percent of all patients as not malingering (Tombaugh, 1996, p. 14).

Several studies (Weinborn, Orr, Wood, Conover, & Feix, 2003) employing a differential prevalence design provide evidence on construct validity for the TOMM. As expected, they found a higher proportion of "failed" TOMM protocols among forensic referrals. Because of the weakness of this research design, these studies cannot address the critical issue, specifically their accuracy of classification.

One critical issue that must be addressed with measures of malingered memory is whether their detection strategies are adversely affected by psychotic or mood disorders. Several studies (Ashendorf, Constantinou, & McCaffrey, 2004; Rees, Tombaugh, & Boulay, 2001) found that genuine patients with mood disorders performed adequately on the TOMM. However, inpatients with little motivation to malinger may be misclassified at rates exceeding 10 percent (see Weinborn, Orr, Wood, Conover, & Feix, 2003). Even more concerning are cases of dementia. According to Teichner and Wagner (2004), more than 70 percent of genuine patients with dementia "failed" the TOMM and were misclassified as malingerers. In summary, forensic practitioners need to rule out severe Axis I disorders, especially dementia, before using the TOMM.

Powell, Gfeller, Hendricks, and Sharland (2004) studied the effects of coaching on the TOMM via a simulation design. In examining both symptom and strategy coaching, the TOMM performed well excellent sensitivity and specificity. Given the simplicity of the floor-effect strategy, the ineffectiveness of coaching was unexpected.[1]

---

[1] Very few feigners are identified by the SVT strategy.

Rey 15-Item Memory Test (REY–15). The REY–15 is a test that assesses the validity of an individual's self-reported memory deficits (Rey, 1964, as cited in Lezak, 1995; Schretlen, Brandt, Krafft, & van Gorp, 1991). Administration of the test requires that the individual be shown a card that has five rows with three-item sequences (e.g., "1, 2, 3") in each row. The individual is asked to reproduce as many of the 15 items as possible based on his or her memory. Instructions may be straightforward or stress the possible difficulty of the task. Relying on the floor effect, the REY–15 assumes that feigners will fail at simple cognitive task.

Pankratz and Binder (1997) outlined the potential problems in using the REY–15, even as a screen for feigned memory deficits. Different investigators have attempted to use various cut scores for total correct or the use of accurately produced rows. In general, the REY–15 produces modest sensitivity and variable specificity (Resnick, 2005). Despite these limitations, the REY–15 continues to be widely used. In a survey of neuropsychologists specializing in disability cases (Slick, Tan, Strauss, & Hultsch, 2004), the REY–15 remains a popular screen.

Nelson and his colleagues (2003) summarized recent data on the REY–15, which performs poorly with mental retardation and dementia. They noted that its utility estimates could be improved by the addition of a recognition trial (Boone, Salazar, Lu Warner-Chacon, & Razani, 2002); this substantially increased the sensitivity of the REY–15. Regarding its application to offender populations, Heinze (2003) compared performances of suspected malingerers with genuinely disordered defendants. Interestingly, the REY–15 performed adequately as a screen (specificity = .88; sensitivity = .61) with a cut score of 7. When a higher cut score was attempted (e.g., 9), the false-positives increased dramatically as specificity dropped to .61.

The REY–15 continues to be popular in forensic and neuropsychological practice in part due to its simplicity and ease of use. The clinical literature provides an inconsistent picture regarding its usefulness, even as a screen. The variability in cut scores provides a major challenge to forensic practitioners in defending their methods and conclusions in court. Further work is needed on the revised REY–15 that introduced a recognition trial as an additional strategy in the screening for suspected feigning.

Validity Indicator Profile (acceptable). A major advantage of the

VIP is its applicability to feigned cognitive abilities, rather than focusing only on simulated memory deficits. The VIP evaluates suspected performance for both verbal (78 items) and nonverbal (100 items) domains using a forced-choice format.

The development sample consisted of 1048 participants with only 130 completing both the verbal and nonverbal components (Frederick & Crosby, 2000). The clinical sample consisted of 104 individuals that were undergoing neuropsychological evaluation and who had previously been identified as having a brain injury. The nonclinical sample consisted of 944 individuals who were either employees of National Computer Systems, Inc. or were currently enrolled as college students. Information in Table 2 of the Frederick and Crosby (2000, p. 67) indicates that the clinical sample was administered only the nonverbal component of the VIP.

A strength of the VIP is its use of multiple detection strategies including three estimates of response consistency and five estimates of performance curve. As noted by Rogers and Bender (2002), however, the three estimates of response consistency are highly overlapping (M r = .81) and do not provide unique information in the assessment process. With regard to classification, the VIP separates profiles into two distinct categories: valid (also referred to as compliant) and invalid. The invalid profiles are placed into one of three subcategories: (a) careless (i.e., poor effort and high motivation), (b) irrelevant (low effort with high motivation to perform poorly), and (c) malingered (high effort with high motivation to perform poorly).

VIP is purported to be a measure of feigned or grossly exaggerated neuropsychological symptoms and other problematic response styles (Frederick, 1997). However, according to Rogers and Bender (2002), "the measure is best conceptualized as a measure of suboptimal effort" (p. 125). This statement is based on the observation that very few malingerers or simulators were accurately identified by the VIP according to the test manual (i.e., 4% on the nonverbal subtest and 5% on the verbal subtest). In addition, the measure has very high false positive rates for both clinical groups. The VIP misclassified many brain-injured patients as invalid, specifically, 37 percent (verbal) and 26 percent (nonverbal). Most persons with mental retardation failed both subtests.

With regard to appropriate use of the VIP, Frederick (1997) cautioned against its use for individuals with mental retardation or learning disabilities. Not only did the VIP misclassify almost all individuals who had mental retardation (estimated IQ ≤ 75 on the Shipley Institute of Living Scale) but, the author chose to exclude individuals with learning disabilities from the cross-validation sample. Therefore, classification rates are unknown for individuals with learning disabilities.

Further research is needed on the forensic applications of the VIP to diverse offender populations, which are often limited by their education coupled with learning disabilities. The development sample was overwhelmingly European American, who had completed one to three years of college or trade school. In contrast, correctional populations have limited literacy (< grade 6; Haigler, Harlow, O'Connor, & Campbell, 1992) and diverse ethnic representation.

The VIP has significant potential in its use of multiple detection strategies and coverage of verbal and nonverbal domains. Its current applicability to offender populations is circumscribed by it exclusion of learning disabilities and lack of data on offenders with minimal education. In evaluations of offenders with sufficient education and no learning disabilities, the VIP can provide valuable data about their effort on cognitive measures. However, it is critical that problems with effort are not equated with malingering.

SPECIAL APPLICATIONS: MALINGERING IN COMPETENCY CASES

Competence-to-stand trial evaluations are among the most frequently requested pretrial evaluations in the criminal justice system and are estimated between 50,000 to 60,000 cases per year (Bonnie & Grisso, 2000; Skeem, Golding, Cohn, & Berge, 1998). Of interest is that, despite the growing requests for such evaluations, research regarding the malingering of incompetence has gone largely uninvestigated; those studies that do exist, examine the usefulness of specialized screens to evaluate the need for further assessment of malingering.

Gothard, Rogers, and Sewell (1995) were the first investigators to develop a systematic screen for feigned incompetency; they supplemented the Georgia Court Competency Test (GCCT; Johnson & Mullett, 1987) with an 8-item Atypical Presentation Scale (APS). Their initial data looked promising with an overall classification rate of approximately 90 percent. Subsequently, Rogers, Sewell, Grandjean, and Vitacco (2002) tested the APS using a known-groups comparison. The original cut score identified less the 50 percent of potential malingerers; even an optimized cut score was only moderately successful, missing more than 25 percent of probable malingerers. Heinze (2003) produced modestly positive results in her investigation of pretrial defendants (Sensitivity = .58; Specificity = .85). In summary, other malingering screens easily outperform the APS in their validation and clinical effectiveness.

The Miller Forensic Assessment of Symptoms Test (M–FAST; Miller, 2001) was developed as a screen for malingered presentations and tested with criminal forensic populations. The M–FAST is a structured interview that consists of 25 items and can be administered in a relatively brief period of time. The measure was developed using detection strategies (Rogers, 1990a), some of which were adapted from the SIRS (Rogers et al., 1992). Due to the brevity of the instrument, the M–FAST incorporates a very small number of questions for each response style.

The M–FAST was developed using a combination of simulation and known groups designs. Three known-group studies and one simulation study were conducted for the final validation of the measure. When combining all three samples, the total patient sample size was relatively small with 70 forensic inpatients (i.e., incompetent to stand trial) and 16 other patients (i.e., evaluated for disability or mental health services). Miller (2001) found that total M-FAST scores of < 6 indicated the need for further evaluation of malingering. The results of the validation studies suggest that M-FAST functions well as a screen identifying the most suspected malingerers (Negative Predictive Power = .97).

Recently, Jackson, Rogers, and Sewell (2005) tested the effectiveness of the M–FAST to screen criminal defendants that were likely feigning their disorders. Compared to inpatients in competency restoration, the M–FAST total score produced very large effect sizes for those feigning mental disorders. It proved effective at removing defendants with only genuine disorders (i.e., specificity = .90) from further consideration. On the basis of limited research, it appears that the M–FAST is a promising tool that can be used as a screen for malingered responding.

Rogers, Tillbrook, and Sewell (2004) developed a second-generation competency measure, the Evaluation of Competency to Stand Trial–Revised (ECST–R), which included several Atypical (ATP) scales: ATP-Psychotic (ATP–P), ATP-Nonpsychotic (ATP–N), and ATP-Impairment (ATP–I). Because malingering screen often emphasize psychotic symptoms, the ECST–R scales were constructed to cover both psychotic (ATP–P) and nonpsychotic (ATP–N) domains. In addition, the ATP–I addresses the defendant's apparent incapacity to participate in court proceedings based on an array of realistic problems and atypical symptoms. The ATP scales have impressive inter-rater reliabilities ($rs \geq .96$) and produce large effect sizes (Cohen's $ds \geq 1.40$) when comparing probable malingerers to genuine inpatients.

Vitacco, Rogers, Gabel, and Munizza (2006) evaluated the effectiveness of three feigning screens in an inpatient sample of competency referrals: M–FAST, ATP scales, and the Structured Inventory of Malingered Symptomatology (SIMS; Widows & Smith, 2004). They found that each measure was highly effective at retaining potential malingerers with very low false-positive rates (i.e., Negative Predictive Power $\geq .90$). One methodological issue likely to contributing to this success was that probable malingerers tended to be blatant in their efforts to feign (e.g., marked elevations on their SIRS profiles).

An important consideration in determinations of malingering is the primary goal of feigning. It is tempting to assume that defendants who feign during a competency evaluation have the obvious goal of being found incompetent. Cases do occur in which defendants have other motivations, such as personal safety. The ECST–R ATP scales provide additional information about the type of feigning in those cases where malingering has been convincingly established via comprehensive assessments (Rogers & Shuman, 2005).

SUMMARY

In light of *Daubert* and the ethical code governing psychologists, it is imperative that the practicing clinician take the time to research and investigate the appropriateness of tests before using them in an evaluation. As noted previously, the measures presented in this chapter are those that were recommended or deemed acceptable for use in malingering evaluations. As revealed in this chapter, each measure has its strengths and weaknesses and as such, a blanket recommendation for use of any test is unwarranted.

On the basis of information provided in this chapter, it is clear that not one of the instruments is valid for use for all populations. Issues pertaining to age, race, mental status, and intellectual functioning are only a few of the considerations that are critical to the evaluation of malingering. In particular, these issues are of critical importance in the forensic evaluation where the stakes are high and risk of misclassification is great.

REFERENCES

American Psychiatric Association (2000). *Diagnostic and Statistical Manual, Fourth Edition: Text Revision.*

Ashendorf, L., Constantinou, M., & McCaffrey, R. J. (2004). The effect of depression and anxiety on the TOMM in community-dwelling older adults. *Archives of Clinical Neuropsychology, 9*, 125.

Atkins v. Virginia, 536 U.S. 304, 122 S. Ct. 2242 (2002).

Bender, S. D., & Rogers, R. (2004). Detection of cognitive feigning: Development of a multistrategy assessment. *Archives of Clinical Neuropsychology, 19*, 49.

Bianchini, K. J., Mathias, C. W., & Greve, K. W. (2001). Symptom validity testing: A critical review. *The Clinical Neuropsychologist, 15*, 19.

Bonnie, R. J., & Grisso, T. (2000). Adjudicative competency and youthful offenders. In T. Grisso, & R. Schwartz (Eds.). *Youth on trial: A developmental perspective on juvenile justice.* (pp. 73–103). Chicago: University of Chicago Press.

Boone, K. B., Salazar, X., Lu, P., Warner-Chacon, K., & Razani, J. (2002). The Rey–15 item recognition trial: A technique to enhance sensitivity on the Rey–15 item memorization test. *Journal of Clinical and Experimental Neuropsychology, 24*, 561.

Butcher, J. N., Williams, C. L., Graham, J. R., Tellegen, A., & Kaemmer, B. (1989). *MMPI–2: Manual for administration and scoring.* Minneapolis: University of Minnesota Press.

Coe v. Tennessee, 17 S.W.3d 193 (Tenn. 2000).

Downs v. Perstrop Components and ICI Americas, 126 F. Supp. 2d 1090 (E.D. Tenn. 1999).

Frederick, R. I. (1997). *The Validity Indicator Profile.* Minneapolis: National Computer Systems.

Frederick, R. I., & Crosby, R. D. (2000). The development and validation of the validity indicator profile. *Law and Human Behavior, 24*, 59.

General Electric Company v. Joiner, 188 S. Ct. 512 (1997).

Godinez v. Moran, 113 S.Ct. 2680 (1993).

Goldberg, J. O. & H. R. Miller (1986). Performance of psychiatric inpatients and intellectually deficient individuals on a task that assesses the validity of memory complaints. *Journal of Clinical Psychology, 42*, 792.

Gothard, S., Rogers, R., & Sewell, K. W. (1995). Feigning incompetency to stand trial: An investigation of the GCCT. *Law and Human Behavior, 19*, 363.

Green, R. L. (1997). Assessment of malingering and defensiveness by multiscale inventories. In R. Rogers (Ed.) *Clinical assessment of malingering and deception.* (2nd Ed., pp. 169–207). NY: Guilford Press.

Haigler, K. O., Harlow, C., O'Connor, P., & Campbell, A. (1992). *Executive summary of literacy behind prison walls: Profiles of the prison population from the National Adult Literacy Survey*. Washington: U.S. Department of Education.

Heinze, M. C. (2003). Developing sensitivity to distortion: Utility of psychological tests in differentiating malingering and psychopathology in criminal defendants. *Journal of Forensic Psychiatry and Psychology, 14*(1), 151.

Hom, J., & Denney, R. L. (Eds.) (2002). *Detection of response bias in forensic psychology*. Binghampton, NY: Haworth Press.

Hopwood, C. J., Morey, L. C., Rogers, R., & Sewell, K. W. (in press). Malingering on the Personality Assessment Inventory: Identification of specific feigned disorders. *Journal of Personality Assessment*.

Jackson, R. L., Rogers, R., & Sewell, K. W. (2005). Miller Forensic Assessment of Symptoms Test (M–FAST): Forensic applications as a screen for feigned incompetence to stand trial. *Law and Human Behavior, 29*, 199.

Johnson, W. G., & Mullett, N. (1987). Georgia Court Competency Test-R. In M. Hersen & A. S. Bellack (Eds.), *Dictionary of behavioral assessment techniques*. New York: Pergamon Press.

Kovera, M. B., Russano, M. B., & McAuliff, B. D. (2002). Assessment of the commonsense psychology underlying *Daubert*: Legal decision makers' abilities to evaluate expert evidence in hostile work environment cases. *Psychology, Public Policy, and the Law, 8*, 180.

Krauss, S. A., & Sales, B. D. (1999). The problem of "Helpfulness" in applying *Daubert* to expert testimony. *Psychology, Public Policy, and the Law, 5*, 78.

Kumho Tire Co. v. Carmichael, 1526 U.S. 137 (1999).

Lally, S. J. (2003). What tests are acceptable for use in forensic evaluations? A survey of experts. *Professional Psychology: Research and Practice, 34*, 491.

Lane, D. (2003) Base rates. The Connexions Project. http://creativecommons.org/licenses/by/1.0

Lamb, D., Berry, D., Wetter, M., & Baer, R. (1994). Effects of two types of information on malingering of closed-head injury on the MMPI–2: An analogue investigation. *Psychological Assessment, 6*, 8.

Lee, A., Boone, K. B., Lessor, I., Wohol, M., Wilkins, S., &Parks, C. (2000). Performance of older depressed patients on two cognitive malingering tests: False positive rates for the Rey 15-Item Memorization and the Dot Counting Tests. *The Clinical Neuropsychologist, 14*, 303.

Lezak, M. D. (1995). *Neuropsychological Assessment*. (3rd Ed.). New York: Oxford University Press.

Miller, H. A. (2001). *M–FAST: Miller Forensic Assessment of Symptoms Test professional manual*. Odessa, FL: Psychological Assessment Resources, Inc.

Millon, T., Davis, R., & Millon, C. (1997). *The Millon Clinical Multiaxial Inventory-III manual*. (2nd Ed.). Minneapolis: National Computer Systems.

Morey, L. C. (1996). *An Interpretive Guide to the Personality Assessment Inventory*. Odessa, FL: Psychological Assessment Resources.

Morey, L. C. (1991). *The Personality Assessment Inventory: Professional Manual*. Tampa: Psychological Assessment Resources, Inc.

Mossman, D. (2003). *Daubert*, Cognitive malingering, and test accuracy. *Law and Human Behavior, 27*, 229.

Mossman, D. (2000). The meaning of malingering data: Further applications of Bayes' theorem. *Behavioral Sciences and the Law, 18*, 761.

Mossman, D., & Hart, K. J. (1996). Presenting evidence of malingering to the courts: Insights from decision theory. *Behavioral Sciences and the Law, 14*, 271.

Nelson, N. W., Boone, K., Dueck, A., Wagener, L., Lu, P., & Grills, C. (2003). Relationship between eight measures of suspected effort. *The Clinical Neuropsychologist, 17*, 263.

Pankratz, P. & Binder, L. M. (1997). Malingering on intellectual and neuropsychological measures. In Richard Rogers (Ed.) Clinical assessment of malingering and deception. (2nd Ed.) (pp. 223-236). New York, New York: Guilford Press.

Powell, R. P., Gfeller, J. D., Hendricks, B. L., & Sharland, M. (2004). Detecting symptom and test-coached simulators with the Test of Memory Malingering. *Archives of Clinical Neuropsychology, 19,* 693.

Rees, L. M., Tombaugh, T. N., & Boulay, L. (2001). Depression and the Test of Memory Malingering. *Archives of Clinical Neuropsychology, 16,* 501.

Reznek, L. (2005). The Rey 15-item memory test for malingering: A meta-analysis. *Brain Injury, 19,* 539.

Reynolds, C. R. (1998). Common sense, clinicians, and actuarialism. In C. R. Reynolds (Ed.), *Clinical assessment of malingering during head injury litigation.* (pp. 261–286). New York: Plenum.

Rogers, R. (1990a). Development of a new classificatory model of malingering. *Bulletin of the American Academy of Psychiatry and the Law, 18*(3), 323.

Rogers, R. (1990b). Models of feigned mental illness. *Professional Psychology: Research and Practice, 21*(3), 182.

Rogers, R. (1997). *Clinical assessment of malingering and deception.* (2nd Ed.). New York: Guilford Press.

Rogers, R. (2004). Diagnostic, explanatory, and detection models of Munchausen by proxy: Extrapolations from malingering and deception. *Child Abuse and Neglect, 28*(2), 225.

Rogers, R., Bagby, M., & Chakraborty, D. (1993). Feigning schizophrenic disorders on the MMPI–2: Detection of coached simulators. *Journal of Personality Assessment, 60,* 215.

Rogers, R., Bagby, R. M., & Dickens, S. E. (1992). *Structured Interview of Reported Symptoms: Professional Manual.* Odessa: Psychological Assessment Resources, Inc.

Rogers, R., & Bender, S. D. (2003). Evaluation of Malingering and Deception. In A. M. Goldstein, & I. B. Weiner (Eds.) *Handbook of Forensic Psychology.* (Vol. 11, pp. 109–129). NJ: John Wiley & Sons, Inc.

Rogers, R., Jackson, R. L., Sewell, K. W., & Salekin, K. L. (2005). Detection strategies for malingering: A confirmatory factor analysis of the SIRS. *Criminal Justice and Behavior, 32,* 511.

Rogers, R., & Salekin, R. T. (1998). Research report beguiled by Bayes: A re-analysis of Mossman and Hart's estimates of malingering. *Behavioral Sciences and the Law, 16,* 147.

Rogers, R., Salekin, R. T., Sewell, K. W., Goldstein, A. M., & Leonard, K. (1998). A comparison of forensic and nonforensic malingerers: A prototypical analysis of explanatory models. *Law and Human Behavior, 22,* 353.

Rogers, R., Sewell, K. W., Cruise, K. R., Wang, E. W., & Ustad, K. L. (1998). The PAI and feigning: A cautionary note on its use in forensic-correctional settings. *Assessment, 5,* 399.

Rogers, R., Sewell, K. W., & Goldstein, A. M. (1994). Explanatory models of malingering: A prototypical analysis. *Law and Human Behavior, 18*(5), 543.

Rogers, R., Sewell, K. W., Grandjean, N. R., & Vitacco, M. J. (2002). The detection of feigned mental disorders on specific competency measures. *Psychological Assessment, 14,* 177.

Rogers, R., Sewell, K. W., Martin, M. A., & Vitacco, M. J. (2003). Detection of feigned mental disorders: A meta-analysis of the MMPI–2 and malingering. *Assessment, 10,* 160.

Rogers, R., Sewell, K. W., Morey, L. C., & Salekin, K. L. (1996). Detection of feigned mental disorders on the Personality Assessment Inventory: A discriminant analysis. *Journal of Personality Disorders, 67,* 629.

Rogers, R., & Shuman, D. W. (2005). *Fundamentals of forensic practice: Mental health and criminal law.* New York: Springer.

Rogers, R., Tillbrook, C. E., & Sewell, K. W. (2004). *Evaluation of Competency to Stand Trial–Revised (ECST-R) and professional manual.* Odessa, FL: Psychological Assessment Resources, Inc.

Rosenfeld, B., Sands, S. A., & Van Gorp, W. G. (2000). Have we forgotten the base rate problem? Methodological issues in the detection of distortion. *Archives of Clinical Neuropsychology, 15,* 349.

Schretlen, D., Brandt, J., Krafft, L., & van Gorp (1991). Some caveats to using the Rey 15-item Memory Test to detect malingered amnesia. *Psychological Assessment, 3,* 667.

Skeem, J. L., Golding, S. L., Cohn, N. N., & Berge, G. (1998). Logic and reliability of evaluations of competence to stand trial. *Law and Human Behavior, 22,* 519.

Slick, D., Tan, J., Strauss, E., & Hultsch, D. (2004). Detecting malingering: A survey of experts' practices. *Archives of Clinical Neuropsychology, 19,* 465.

Storm, J., & Graham, J. R. (2000). Detection of coached general malingering on the MMPI–2. *Psychological Assessment, 12,* 158.

Taylor, L. A., Kreutzer, J. S., & West, D. D. (2003). Evaluation of malingering cut-scores for the Rey 15-Item Test: A brain injury case study series. *Brain Injury, 17,* 295.

Teichner, G., & Wagner, M. T. (2004). The Test of Memory Malingering (TOMM): Normative data from cognitively intact, cognitively impaired, and elderly patients with dementia. *Archives of Clinical Neuropsychology, 19,* 455.

Tombaugh, T. N. (1996). *Test of Memory Malingering.* New York: Multi Health Systems.

United States v. Gigante, 982 F. Supp. 140 (E.D.N.Y. 1997a).

United States v. Gigante, 996 F. Supp. 194 (E.D.N.Y. 1997b).

United States v. Greer, 158 F.3d 228 (5th Cir. 1998).

Viglione, D. J., Mellin Wright, D., Dizon, N. T., Moynihan, J. E., DePuis, S., & Pizitz, T. D. (2001). Evading detection on the MMPI–2: Does caution produce more realistic patterns of responding? *Assessment, 8,* 237.

Vallabhajosula, B., & van Gorp, W. G. (2001). Post-Daubert admissibility of scientific evidence on malingering of cognitive deficits. *Journal of the American Academy of Psychiatry and the Law, 29,* 207.

Villalba v. Consolidated Freightways Corp., 2000 U.S. Dist. (N.D. Ill., August 10, 2000.

Vitacco, M. J., & Rogers, R. (2005). Assessment of Malingering in Correctional Settings. In C. L. Scott, & J. B. Gerbasi (Eds.), *Handbook of correctional mental health.* (pp. 133–153). Washington, DC: American Psychiatric Publishing.

Vitacco, M. J., Rogers, R., Gabel, J., & Munizza, J. (2006, March). *Evaluating malingering screens: A known groups design of feigning psychopathology with competency to stand trial patients.* Paper presented at the National Conference of the American Psychology-Law Society, St. Pete's Beach, FL.

Wechsler, D. A. (1997). *Wechsler Adult Intelligence Scale–Third Edition.* New York, NY: Psychological Corporation.

Weinborn, M., Orr, T., Wood, S. P., Conover, E., & Feix, J. (2003). A validation of the Test of Memory Malingering in a forensic psychiatric setting. *Journal of Clinical and Experimental Neuropsychology, 25,* 979.

Widows, M. R., & Smith, G. P. (2004). *SIMS: Structured Inventory of Malingered Symptomatology professional manual.* Odessa, FL: Psychological Assessment Resources, Inc.

NAME INDEX

SUBJECT INDEX